FO PHOTOPACK

PHYSICAL FEATURES

Pam Jervis

Ideas pages:

Copiable pages:

Folens Publishers

INTRODUCTION

This photopack provides children and teachers with a range of images which show key landscape features and some of the processes involved in their formation.

Many geographical skills may be developed by studying visual materials. Full use should be made of all the photographs to observe, sketch, identify, describe and analyse physical features.

This resource also includes suggestions for activities, which may lead to group discussion and individual or group research. Several of the activities focus on the interaction between people and the environment, on both a local and a global scale. Others involve work of an experimental or practical nature. At all times health and safety regulations should be strictly adhered to.

Page 3 The Brenta Massif, Dolomites, Italy. Photo © Robert Everts. Tony Stone Worldwide. Page 4 The Daintree River Estuary, Queensland, Australia. Photo © The Image Bank. Page 5 The Caracol Waterfall, Brazil. Photo © Bryan Parsley. Tony Stone Worldwide. Page 6 The Usumacinta River, Guatemala. Photo © David Hiser. Tony Stone Worldwide. Page 7 West Bank, Aswan, Egypt. Photo © Robert Harding Picture Library. Page 8 Kilauea Volcano, Hawaii. Photo © Soames Summerhays. The Science Photo Library. Page 9 Earthquake in Mexico. Photo © Robert Harding Picture Library. Page 10 Algarve, Portugal. Photo © Tony Stone Worldwide. Page 11 Vale of Rheidon, Dyfed, Wales. Photo © Robert Harding Picture Library. Page 12 The Angel Glacier, Jasper National Park, Canada. Photo © Hans Wendler. The Image Bank.

Cover by: In Touch Creative Services Ltd.

Cover photo © David Hiser, Tony Stone Worldwide.

Illustrations by: Jeremy Bays.

Editor: Angela Simms.

First published 1994 by Folens Limited, Dunstable and Dublin.

ISBN 185276601-8

Folens Limited, Apex Business Centre, Albert House, Boscombe Road, Dunstable, LU5 4RL, England.

FOLENS

MOUNTAINS

Photograph 1

Photo © Robert Everts. Tony Stone Worldwide.

The photograph shows the spectacular scenery of the Brenta Massif, which is part of the Dolomite mountain range in northern Italy. These mountains are over 3,000 metres high.

They were formed during the Tertiary period, 65 million years ago, when the continent of Africa moved towards Europe, closing the Tethys Sea. This pushed up a range of young 'fold' mountains – the Alps (see diagram **A**).

Towards the end of the Tertiary period, the climate of Europe cooled dramatically, and a series of ice advances (glacial periods) began. The causes of the Ice Age are not known, but it greatly affected the landscape of many parts of Europe, North America and Asia.

The rugged peaks and steep slopes of the Brenta Massif are a result of erosion by ice. They have been formed by the processes of 'frost-shattering' or 'freeze-thaw' acting upon hard, resistant rock (see page 12). Many mountainous areas are affected in the winter months. However, even in the summer, snow lies in the high mountains.

Starting points

- Ask the children to make a list of words that describe the mountains.
- At what time of year do they think the photographs were taken? Do the weather conditions provide them with any clues?
- The children could find out what type of vegetation covers the mountainsides. They will need to be provided with appropriate reference material.

Activities

- Ask the children to sketch the outline of the mountain peaks. Explain that these have been formed as a result of 'frost-shattering'.
- Demonstrate how freeze-thaw erodes rocks. Obtain a piece of sandstone. Soak it in water, and place it in a plastic bag in a freezer. After a week, take the sandstone out of the freezer and wait for it to defrost. Allow the children to examine it.
- The children could investigate how fold mountains were formed. Use a piece of carpet to represent the sea floor. Ask one child to push from each end. The carpet will crumple into 'mountains'. This shows how plates in the Earth's surface moved against each other, pushing up mountain ranges.

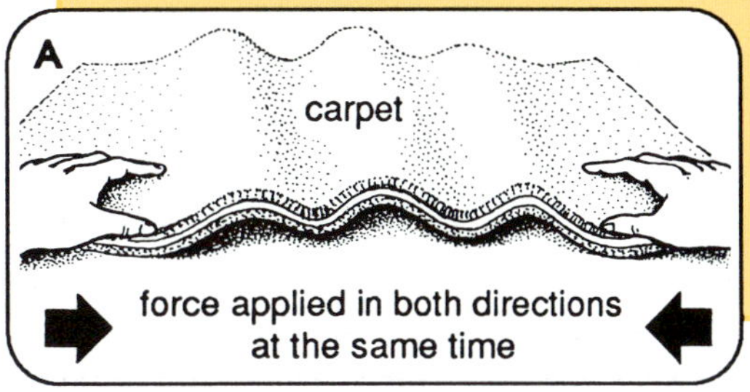

- On a world map, locate and mark the world's highest mountain ranges: the Rockies, Himalayas, Alps, Andes, Urals and Atlas mountains.
- Mountain ranges in different parts of the world have specific vegetation zones. Help the children to research these zones. How do the vegetation zones of the Andes mountains (near the equator) differ from the Alps (shown in **B**)? Why?

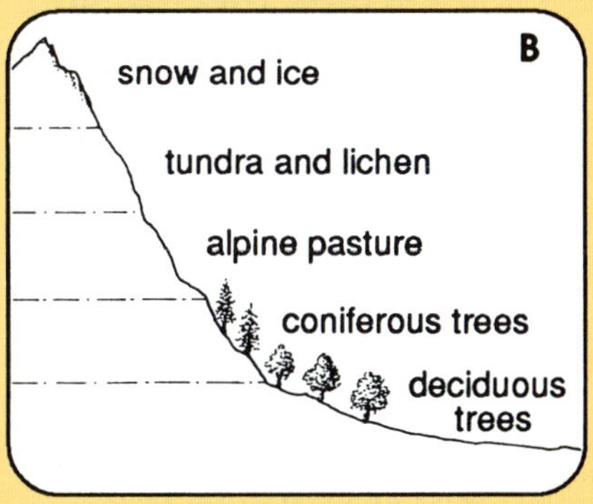

- Alpine farmers practise transhumance. Ask the children to find out what this means. (It is the seasonal migration of livestock to higher grazing land in the summer, and to the foothills in the winter).

BEACHES

Photograph 2

Photo © The Image Bank.

The Daintree Estuary in Queensland, Australia, is a remote coastal area with a sandy beach shoreline. Rivers transport sand and silt to the coast. This material is then moved along the coast by the action of waves and currents – 'longshore drift'. On average, each day, over 10,000 tonnes of material are moved for every kilometre of coastline.

As waves reach the shore, the shallower water impedes their circular motion. The front of the wave steepens, and the crest plunges downwards and forwards, trapping air. This 'explodes', breaking up the water into tiny foam particles.

The water is thrown up on to the beach as the 'swash'. As it moves further across the land its energy decreases and it slows down. Then, gravity draws the water back down the beach as 'backwash'.

In a 'constructive wave', the swash is more effective than the backwash, and material is added to the beach. When waves arrive at close intervals, the swash is stopped by the backwash, and material is removed from the beach. These are 'destructive waves'.

Starting points

- Locate the sand dunes and rivers. What do the children think happens to the speed of a river when it reaches the sea? (It slows down and deposits material.)
- Describe the land area. Do the children think that many people live in this area? How do they know?

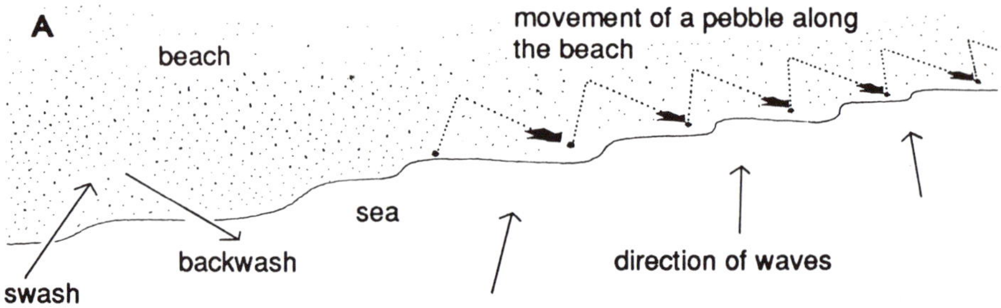

Activities

- Locate the river mouth, on the left of the photograph, and describe what happens when a river loses speed. Draw the children's attention to the areas of sand and silt as evidence of deposition.
- Use a rope to demonstrate the circular movement of waves. Two volunteers should hold the ends of the rope and shake them up and down slowly to form 'ripples'. The ripples show the movement of the waves; the rope is the volume of water – this does not move forwards.
- If possible, organise a class visit to a beach. Experiment to find out whether the waves are 'constructive' or 'destructive'. Place a plastic ball in the sea and ask the children to watch its movement. If it eventually floats out to sea, the waves are destructive.
- Investigate the process of longshore drift (see **A**). Paint some pebbles and ask the children to chart their movement over a few hours. (A few days would be better.)
- Can the children explain how material is moved up and down the beach? Some holiday resorts have to protect their beaches from erosion. Have they seen any evidence of this?
- The children could find out what sand is made from. Collect a sample from a local beach or quarry. Provide groups with magnifying glasses to examine the sand. They should record the colour and size of the crystals. They could then use reference books to identify the crystals.

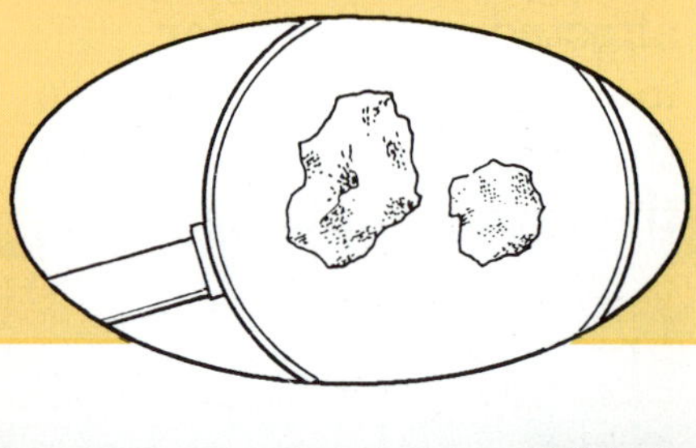

WATERFALLS

Photograph 3

Photo © Bryan Parsley. Tony Stone Worldwide.

The photograph shows the Caracol Waterfall in Brazil, one of several spectacular falls found in the Amazon basin. Most of the world's largest waterfalls are 'cap rock' types. This means that there is a hard, resistant band of rock overlaying a softer stratum.

The waterfall is a result of differential erosion, where the base rock erodes at a faster rate. This means that all waterfalls are ephemeral features in the landscape. They are self-destructive, as the energy they generate leads to recession (backwards erosion) and to their eventual reduction and disappearance.

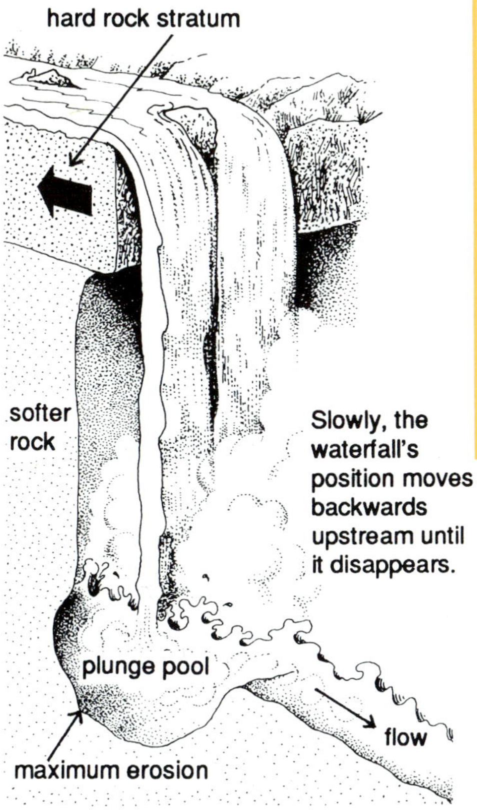

Starting points

- Ask the children to look carefully at the photograph and describe what they can see.
- Locate the bare rock outcrop and ask them to describe it.
- The waterfall is in an equatorial rainforest. Draw the children's attention to the very tall trees, and identify the canopy layer.
- Point to the areas around the waterfall where 'mist' has formed. This is a result of the water falling from a great height, hitting the surface of the pool below.

Activities

- The children could estimate the height of the trees, and from this the height of the waterfall. Suggest they find out the actual height from a suitable reference book.
- Ask the children to examine the photograph. Can they identify the layers of rock?

White hard rock
Dark grey softer rock

What do they think is happening to the dark grey rock? (It is being eroded faster than the hard, resistant white rock.) Point out evidence of this – the cave behind the waterfall where the two rock types meet.

- They could sketch the waterfall. Their sketch should show the two rock types, the cave, the pool formed at the base of the waterfall and the river. Afterwards, they could label these features.
- Locate some of the world's most famous waterfalls (some examples are given in **A**). Mark these on an outline map of the world.
- The children could research and write a report on how waterfalls are useful to people, for example as power sources and tourist attractions.

(A) World's greatest waterfalls – by volume of water

River	Waterfall	Country	Height (feet)	Width (feet)	Flow (cu.ft/sec)
Zaire	Boyoma	Zaire	200	2,400	600,000
Parana	Guaria	Brazil/ Paraguay	347	15,900	470,000
Mekong	Khone	Laos	70	35,000	400,000
Niagara	Niagara	USA/ Canada	160	2,500	212,000

MEANDERS

Photograph 4

Photo © David Hiser. Tony Stone Worldwide.

The photograph shows meanders along the course of the Usumacinta River in Guatemala.

Rivers emerge from a spring called a river source. As they flow downhill across land towards the sea, they often meander. They reach the sea at the river mouth or estuary.

When a river meanders, water in the river channel moves quickly around the outside of the bend and more slowly on the inside. This causes erosion to occur on the outside, where the water is flowing fastest. The river deposits material on the inside bend, forming a beach.

The cross-section of a river channel at a meander will be asymmetrical, with a steep undercut bank on the outside and a gentle 'slip-off slope' on the inside.

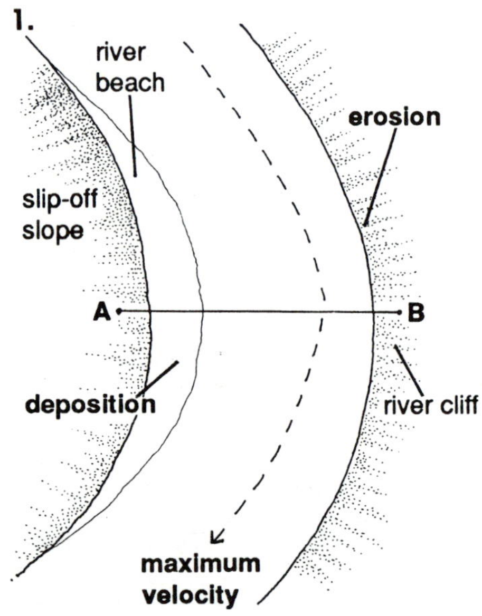

Starting points

- Ask the children to describe the river's course or path.
- What do they think the light/white areas next to the river might be?
- Can they identify the vegetation that covers the land area?
- Do the children think many people live in this area? How can they tell?

Activities

- Demonstrate the following experiment, to show what happens when a river flows across areas of a different gradient. Fill a tray with sand. Slightly tilt it and pour in part of a jug of water. Repeat the experiment, increasing the angle of the tray. (Make sure the sand is damp before starting.)
- All rivers meander. In fact, any liquid flowing over a non-uniform surface is liable to move from side to side. Drop some water on a sloping piece of glass so that the children are able to watch its movement.
- Meanders, once formed, tend to spread along the river channel. The children could investigate this phenomenon. Obtain a skipping rope. Ask for two volunteers to hold it. One child holds their end close to the ground while the other moves their end from side to side, generating meanders along the length of the rope.

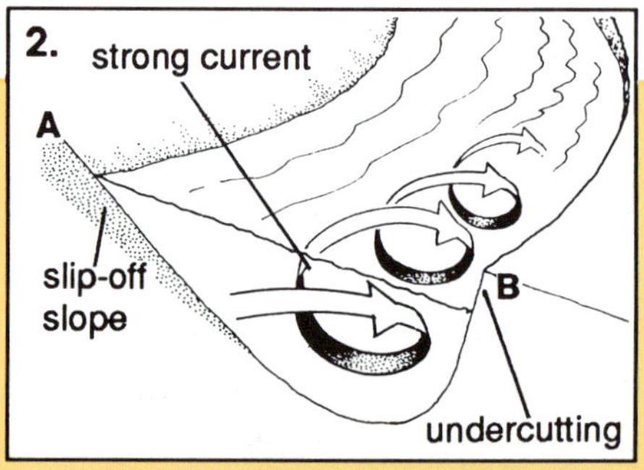

- Why do the children think that sand and silt have built up on the insides of the river bends? (See diagrams **1** and **2**.) What causes the river to drop (deposit) this material? There is no sandy beach on the outside of the bends. What speed do they think the water is flowing at in these areas? (Fast.)
- Show the children why the river deposits material as it slows down. Place some sand in a bottle and fill it with water. Fasten the lid or top tightly, and shake the bottle vigorously. Ask the children to describe what they see. (The sand is suspended in the liquid.) Leave the bottle to stand. What happens to the contents now? (The sand settles at the bottom of the bottle.)

DESERTS

Photograph 5

Photo © Robert Harding Picture Library.

Deserts and semi-deserts cover about one third of the world's land surface. They have low annual rainfall and high evaporation rates. Some deserts are bare sand, others stones or rock. Also, there may be sparse shrub vegetation. Water is only available alongside permanent rivers such as the Nile, or around an oasis where underground water reaches the surface as a spring or well.

When the climate is deficient of moisture and there is an absence of vegetation, the bare rock and soil is exposed to the daily effects of heating and cooling. This causes the breaking down of rock particles. The land surface is exposed to the wind, an effective agent of erosion, transportation and deposition.

The photograph shows the West Bank of the Nile at Aswan, Egypt. For thousands of years the Nile has been called the 'lifeblood' of Egypt. The river's flood plain is a fertile strip of land on either side of the river, which borders on the desert. The photograph shows how deposition has led to the formation of a river cliff.

Starting points

- Ask the children to look carefully at the photograph and describe what they can see.
- Draw their attention to the rich vegetation in the foreground, in contrast to the barren sand in the background. Can the children explain this feature of the landscape?

Activities

- Provide the children with atlases and outline maps of the world. Ask them to locate, mark and label the Sahara, Kalahari, Arabian, Gobi, Attacama and Great Australian deserts.
- Before using the activity sheet on page 13, explain to the children how the shaduf, sakia and Archimedean screw were used to irrigate farmland along the banks of the River Nile.
- Ask them which countries the River Nile flows through. Where does it collect water from? There is little or no rain in Egypt. (See page 13.)
- Look at a world map that shows population densities. Locate the parts of Egypt that are most densely populated. Can the children explain why this is the case?
- Collect photographs of different types of desert landscapes, and ask the children to describe them.

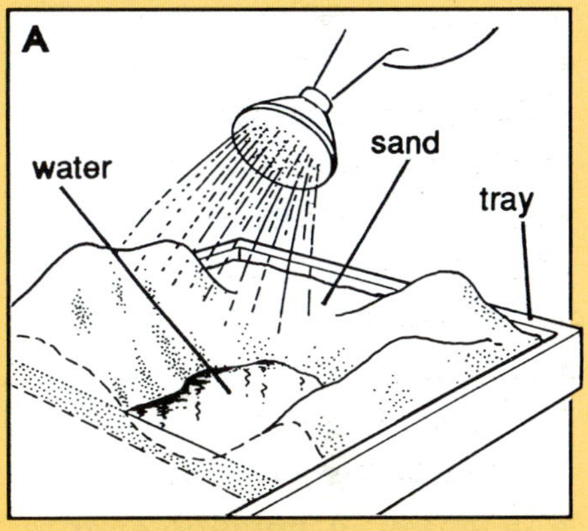

- Make an oasis (as in **A**). Fill a large tray (with sides) with sand, and make a depression in the centre. Add water to the sand using a watering can. Keep adding water until some starts to appear in the hollow. As the sand dries out the water disappears.
- Demonstrate how and why deserts spread so quickly. Pour dry sand on to a flat surface and form it into piles. Encourage the children to watch how the sand grains move and slide easily over each other when they are dry. NB: Do not allow them to blow the sand.

VOLCANOES

Photograph 6

Photo © Soames Summerhays. The Science Photo Library.

The photograph shows an eruption of the Kilauea volcano in Hawaii. Streams of lava can be seen spilling over the sides of the crater. Other rocks and gases are being thrown upwards into the atmosphere.

The Earth's crust is made up of several pieces, called plates. Volcanoes and earthquakes occur along the plate boundaries or margins, where the Earth's crust is weakest. Along these lines of weakness, molten rock called magma seeps upwards from the mantle – a partially molten, plastic layer beneath the Earth's surface. This leads to the formation of a variety of rock types and features.

The best known of these is a volcano. A volcano erupts when pressure builds up within the crust, causing a fracture to form. Gases and molten magma then escape along the fracture.

Lava is molten magma that cools and hardens at the Earth's surface. If it contains much silica, it is viscous and hardens fast. This leads to the formation of a steep-sided volcanic cone (as in **A**). If the lava is basic, it is more fluid and cools much more slowly. This may spread out to form a shield volcano (as in **B**).

Starting points

- Ask the children to look carefully at the photograph. What do they think is happening?
- They could list the colours that appear in the photograph.
- What do they think it would be like to be near to an erupting volcano? What sounds and smells might there be?

A Composite volcano

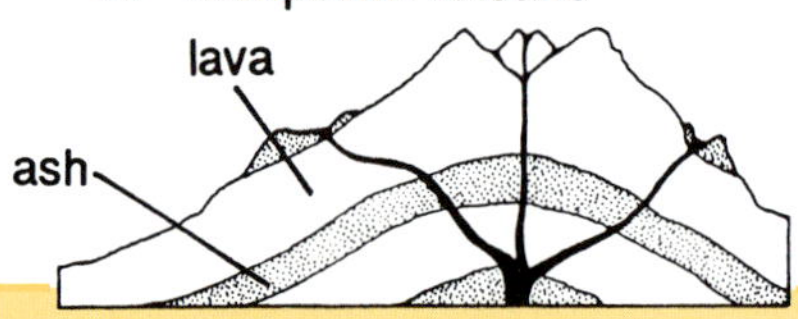

B Basic shield volcano

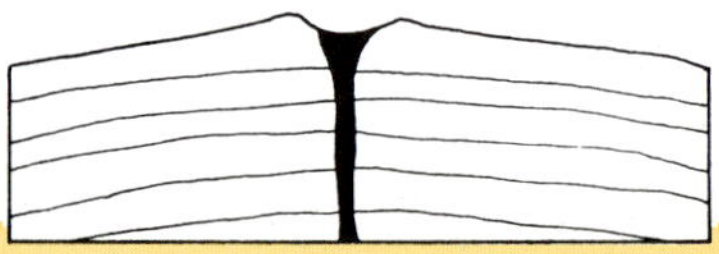

Activities

- Provide the children with atlases and outline maps of the world. They could locate and mark some of the world's volcanoes. Extend the activity by using the Earthquakes and Volcanoes sheet on page 14.
- Demonstrate how volcanoes are formed. The shape of the volcano depends upon how thick (viscous) the lava is. Make some coloured icing. It should be of a thick consistency. Pour it on to an upturned bowl. Ask the children to watch carefully and record their observations. Repeat the experiment using a 'thinner' mixture. Which spreads the furthest? Which forms a steeper slope?
- The children could research the volcanoes in southern Italy – Vesuvius and Etna. Make a collection of brochures for Italian holiday destinations.
- Obtain samples of volcanic rocks: pumice, lava and granite. The children could compare samples of granite and lava. Explain that there are crystals in granite because it cooled down slowly underground. In contrast, lava cooled rapidly on the Earth's surface, and so no crystals are in evidence.
- Children are fascinated by rocks. They could investigate the properties of a variety of volcanic rocks by sketching them, testing for hardness and recording their colour and texture.
- The children could pretend that they are reporters at the scene of a volcanic eruption. Access to a word processing or desktop publishing package will enhance this exercise.

EARTHQUAKES

Photograph 7

Photo © Robert Harding Picture Library.

The photograph shows the after-effects of an earthquake in Mexico, a country which experiences several 'quakes' each year. An earthquake is a vibration or tremor that passes through the Earth's crust. More than 10,000 are recorded each year.

Earthquakes occur along plate boundaries. As the plates move against each other pressure builds up inside the Earth's crust. The most powerful earthquakes are caused by horizontal movements of the Earth's crust, along fault lines such as the San Andreas fault in California. However, many earthquakes occur in the crust beneath the oceans, particularly in the Pacific. These cause a violent displacement of water, which may result in a tidal wave.

Where the first movement occurs, the rock tears apart. This is called the 'focus' of the earthquake. The point on the Earth's surface above it is called the 'epicentre'. From here, 'shock waves' move outwards through the crust and through the Earth's mantle. They are recorded around the world on seismographs, which use the Richter Scale.

Starting points

- ◆ Ask the children to look carefully at the photograph and describe what they can see.
- ◆ What do they think the workers in the photograph are doing?
- ◆ What types of vehicles are shown?
- ◆ Are there any visual clues to indicate in which country the photograph was taken?

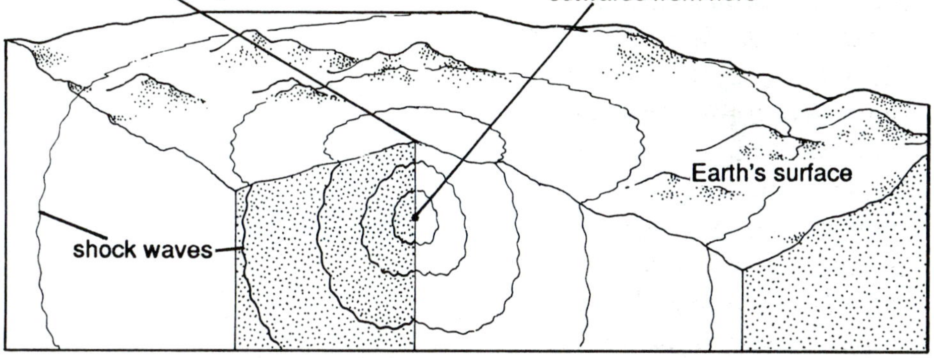

Activities

- Use the information in the introductory section to explain why earthquakes occur. Demonstrate how shock waves pass through the earth. Place some cups and saucers at one end of a table. Hit the other end, so that the children are able to watch them jump and shake.
- Most earthquakes occur near the surface of the earth where the rocks are brittle. Deeper underground the rocks are more plastic and so absorb movement. This could be illustrated using two toffee bars. Warm one of the bars, and place the other in a freezer. What happens when the children try to bend them?
- Earthquakes occur along plate boundaries. Help the children to locate and mark some of the world's worst earthquakes on an outline map of the world (see page 14). Do their sites form a pattern?
- The Richter Scale is a scientific method of measuring the intensity of an earthquake. A sensitive instrument called a seismograph responds to small movements within the Earth's crust. These are recorded and interpreted by scientists. The children could find out more about these instruments and their history.
- Ask the children to write about the dangers of living in an earthquake zone, describing the way in which people's lifestyles and futures may be affected.

COASTLINES

Photograph 8

Photo © Tony Stone Worldwide.

This photograph shows part of the Algarve coastline in Portugal, a popular tourist destination. The striking coastal formations are largely a result of erosion by the sea.

The sea erodes the coastline in four main ways:

- **Hydraulic action**. The force of waves crashing against cliffs causes pressure to build up in fissures in the rock. As these expand, pieces of rock will be loosened and removed by the sea.
- **Abrasion**. Material carried by waves wears away the surface of cliffs, or the sea floor.
- **Attrition**. Material picked up by the sea is worn down into smaller rock particles.
- **Corrosion**. Rock is dissolved by sea water. This process is common where chalk and limestone are the main rock types.

Coastal erosion over a period of time leads to the undercutting of cliffs. This results in the formation of a variety of features, for example caves and blow holes. There may also be a 'wave-cut platform', which marks the area where the cliffs once stood. This will only be visible at low tide.

Starting points

- At what time of year do the children think the photograph was taken? (Summer.) What evidence is there to suggest this? (It is sunny and the sea is calm.)
- The children could write a list of words that describe the rock formations shown.

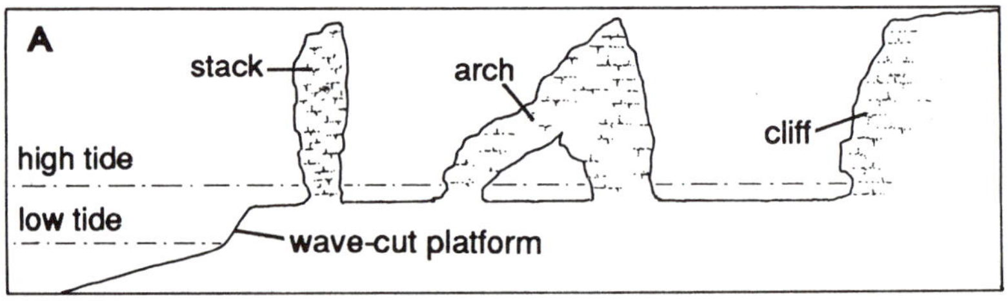

Activities

- Explain that these rock formations have been eroded by the sea. How do the children think this might have happened?
- Obtain samples of different types of rock for the children to examine, for example: granite, sandstone, limestone, chalk. They could try scratching the rocks with a compass point to test their hardness. Which do they think would form the steepest cliffs?
- Ask the children to look carefully at the rocks in the photograph. Do they think these are soft or hard? What evidence is there to suggest this?
- Limestone and chalk may be eroded by hydraulic action, or corrosion. Demonstrate how these rock types are dissolved by dilute hydrochloric acid (see **B**). Explain that most rain and sea water is mildly acidic.
- Ask the children to find out about the location and appearance of famous cliffs, arches and stacks in Britain (see **A**). For example, Flamborough Head, the Needles (Isle of Wight), Durdle Door (Dorset).
- What dangers are there for people who live on cliff tops? Discuss the erosion along the Yorkshire coast, where houses and hotels have fallen into the sea.
- The children could imagine that they are the person in the photograph. They could describe and draw what they might see.

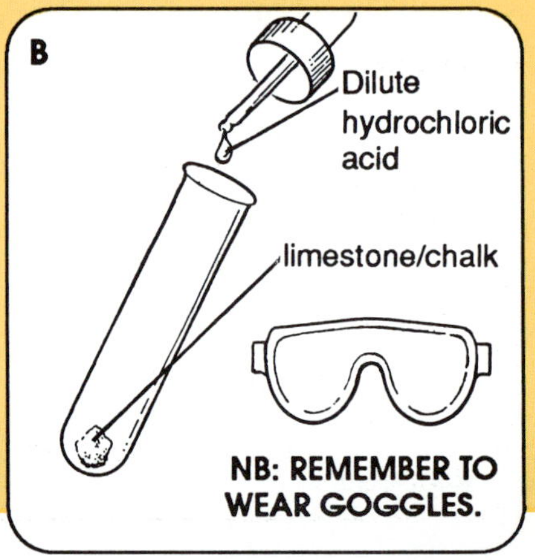

RIVER VALLEY

Photograph 9

Photo © Robert Harding Picture Library.

The photograph shows the Vale of Rheidon in Dyfed, Wales, an excellent example of a river valley in its middle course. Here the river is mainly eroding and transporting material downstream, as it meanders across the valley floor. Some material is being deposited on either side of the river, along the narrow flood plain.

Rivers are able to erode, transport and deposit material. Their ability to do this depends on their energy, which is related to the gradient of the valley floor, the volume of water in the river channel and its velocity.

When a stream has surplus energy, after overcoming the friction of the channel's bed and sides, it will transport eroded material downstream. Deposition occurs when a stream or river has insufficient energy to transport its load.

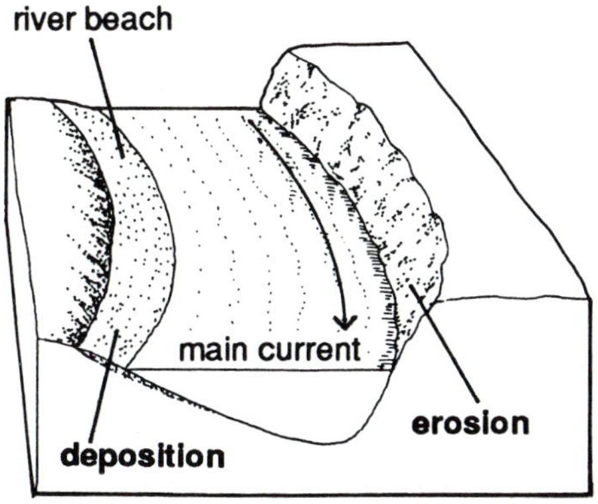

Starting points

- What is the land used for? Can the children find any evidence to support their answer?
- Can they identify the types of vegetation shown in the photograph?
- Ask them to describe the shape of the valley – its sides and the valley floor.

Activities

- Begin by using the activity sheet on page 15. The children could label and add details to the sketch supplied.
- Refer to the introductory section and page 6 to explain how a river transports material. Ask the children why and where rivers deposit material.
- How do they think that rivers affect people living on their banks? How does the material deposited by the river help farmers?
- Encourage the children to find out about the water cycle (as shown in **A**). What happens to the water before it reaches the river?
- The children could make a list of the leisure activities that take place on or in rivers, for example fishing, canoeing and swimming.
- Find out the name of a river in your local area. Obtain a large scale map of the area and show the children its source, course and mouth.
- Provide the children with atlases and outline maps of the world. Ask them to locate and mark some of the world's most important rivers, for example the Amazon, Mississippi and Yangtze rivers.
- Carry out some class research on one of the rivers. How does it affect the people who live near its banks?

A

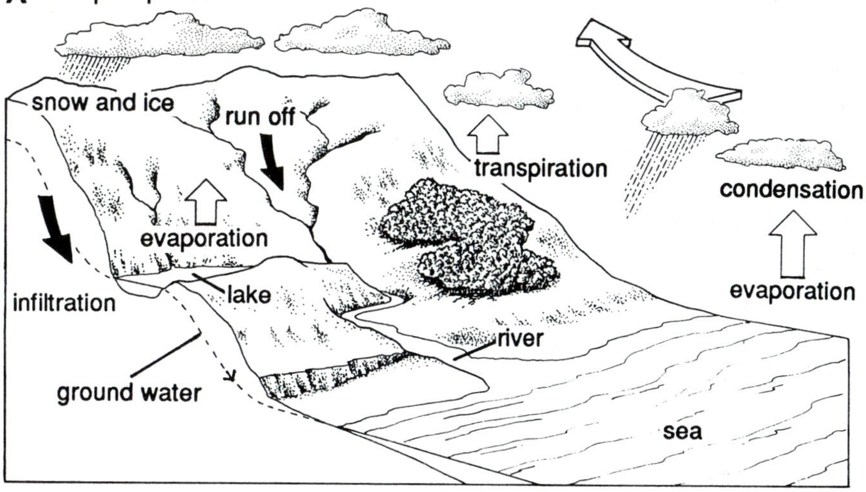

GLACIERS

Photograph 10

Photo © Hans Wendler. The Image Bank.

This photograph shows the Angel Glacier in Jasper National Park, Canada. In high latitudes, or altitudes where precipitation falls as snow, ice builds up which leads to the formation of glaciers.

Glacial erosion can dramatically alter the shape and features of a landscape. There are three main processes involved:

- Water seeps into cracks in the rock. The water expands as it freezes. Eventually, pieces of rock are loosened and break away. This process is called 'freeze-thaw' or 'frost-shattering' (see **A**).
- Ice freezes around loosened rock and, as the glacier moves, it is pulled away. This process is called 'plucking'.
- As the glacier moves downhill, it carries the eroded material. This scrapes along the valley floor and sides. This process is called 'scouring'.

These types of erosion lead to the formation of deep, steep-sided, flat-bottomed valleys, called glacial troughs.

Glaciers also deposit material. When a glacier melts, the ice 'retreats' back up the valley and a 'moraine' (a ridge of material) is left behind.

Starting points

- Ask the children to look carefully at the photograph and describe what they can see.
- They could write a list of words to describe the water in the lake.
- Can they explain what is happening to the ice near the lake?

Activities

- Explain how glaciers are formed. When snow builds up in an area, it is compacted and turns into ice. This process is similar to what happens when a snowball is squeezed very hard.
- Show the children how a glacier moves down the mountain into a valley, using the following experiment. Make a model of a mountain from Plasticine and place it in a tray. Pour a thick mixture of icing sugar and water on to the 'mountain'. Ask the children to watch carefully and record their observations.
- Collect ski holiday brochures. The children could find and label pictures of European glaciers.
- Use an outline map of the world and an atlas to locate and mark areas that are covered by ice all year round. Can the children locate the glacial areas in Europe?

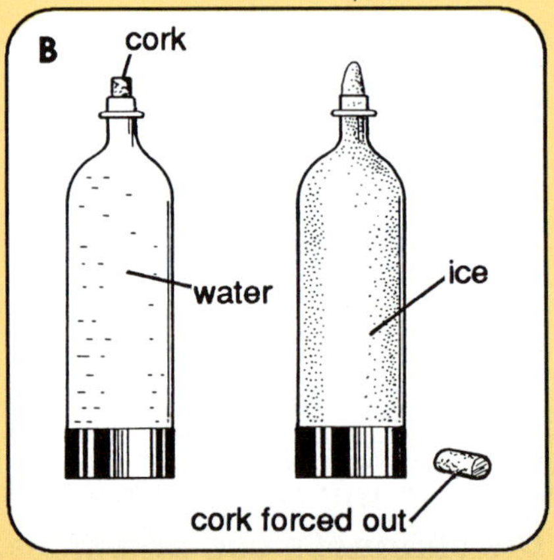

- Demonstrate the power of 'freeze-thaw', an important aspect of glacial erosion (see **B**). Fill a plastic bottle with water. Push a cork into the top and place the bottle in a freezer. Take the bottle out of freezer when the water is completely frozen. What has happened to the cork?
- Ask the children to sketch the glacier in the photograph. They should include and label the crevasses, lake, steep mountainsides and moraine. The activity on page 16 will help the children to identify these features.

THE RIVER NILE

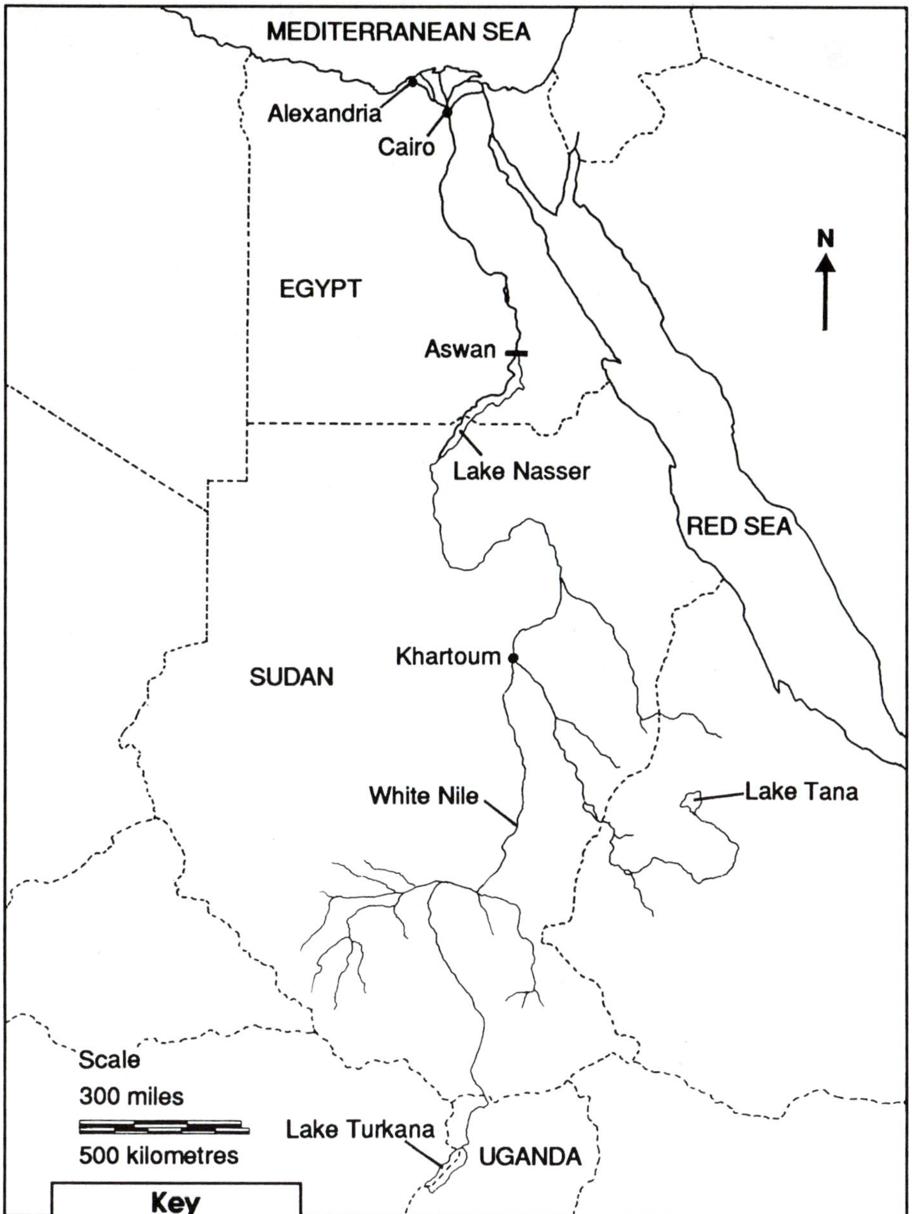

Key

Aswan High Dam

— — Boundary

1. Through which countries does the River Nile pass?
2. Where is the Nile's source?
3. Where is the Nile's mouth?
4. Name one of the Nile's tributaries.
5. Name a place where there is a river confluence.
6. In which direction does the Nile flow?
7. Estimate the length of the Nile.
8. How long is Lake Nasser?
9. Why was the Aswan High Dam built?
10. What problems has it caused?
11. Describe some of the traditional ways in which Egyptian farmers irrigated their farmland.
12. Draw one of these methods. The pictures below will help you.

Traditional Irrigation Methods

Shaduf

Archimedes Screw

Sakia

EARTHQUAKES AND VOLCANOES

Key

The world map shows the locations of some of the world's active volcanoes. Their names are listed in table **A**.

- Find out in which countries these volcanoes are located and complete the chart. You will need to use an atlas.

A

	Volcano	Country
1	Mount St. Helens	
2	Paricutin	
3	Vesuvius	
4	Etna	
5	Mauna Loa	
6	Fuji	

Table **B** lists the dates and sites of some of the world's worst earthquakes.

B

1. 1985 Mexico City, Mexico
2. 1976 Tangshan, China
3. 1970 Yungay, Peru
4. 1923 Tokyo, Japan
5. 1906 San Francisco, U.S.A.

- Choose a symbol and mark these places on the world map. Design a key.

VALE OF RHEIDON

A field sketch of the Vale of Rheidon

- Write the correct letter in each box.

- [ ] Coniferous forest, planted on higher, steep slopes.
- [ ] Rough pasture and grazing land on higher, steeper slopes.
- [ ] Farmland, on flatter valley floor. This is used for pasture and sheep farming.
- [ ] Deciduous trees.
- [ ] Flood plain.
- [ ] River meandering.

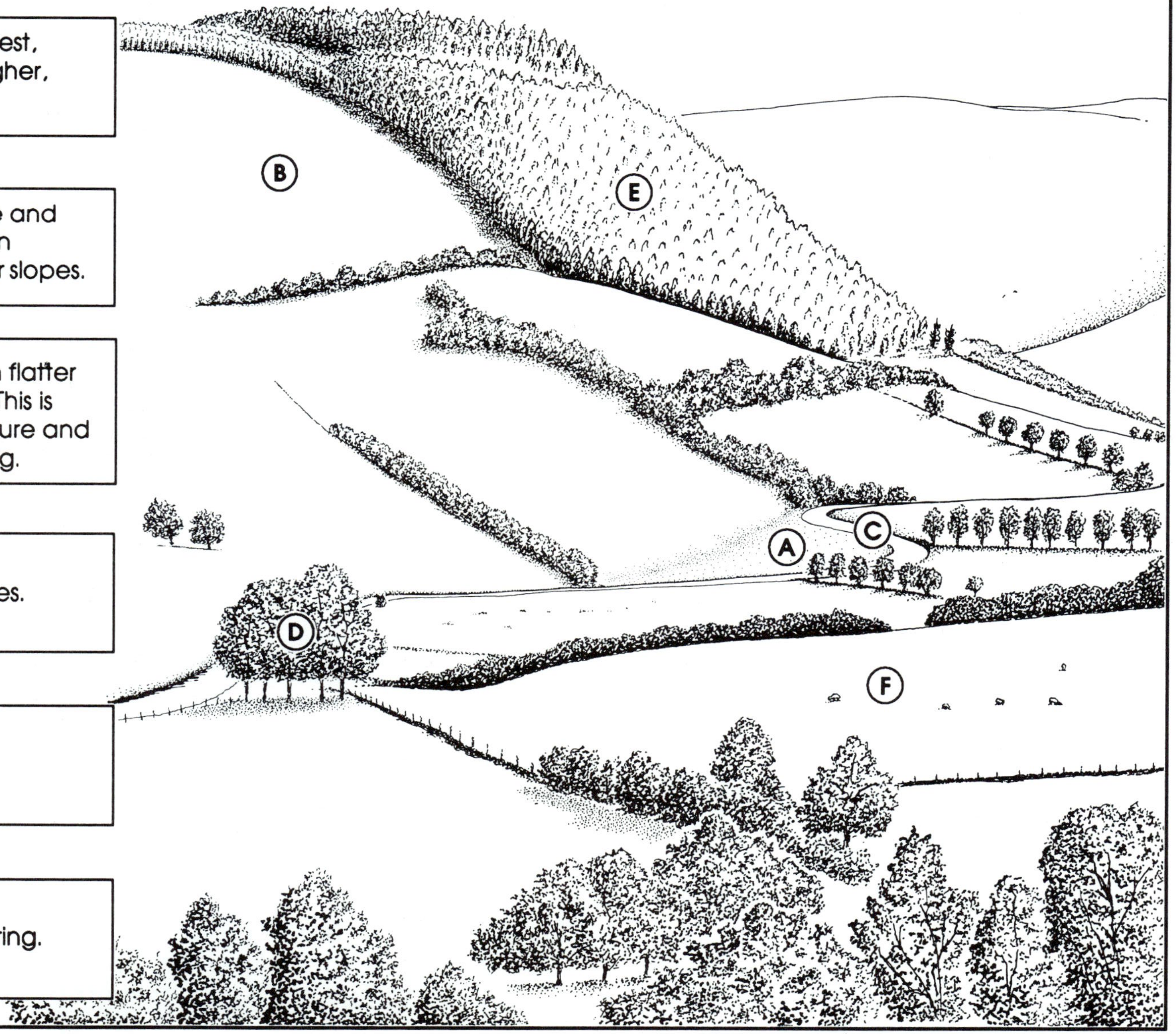

GLACIERS

Look at these pictures of a glaciated valley

- Write the correct letters/numbers in the keys. You may need to carry out some research before you begin.

During the Ice Age

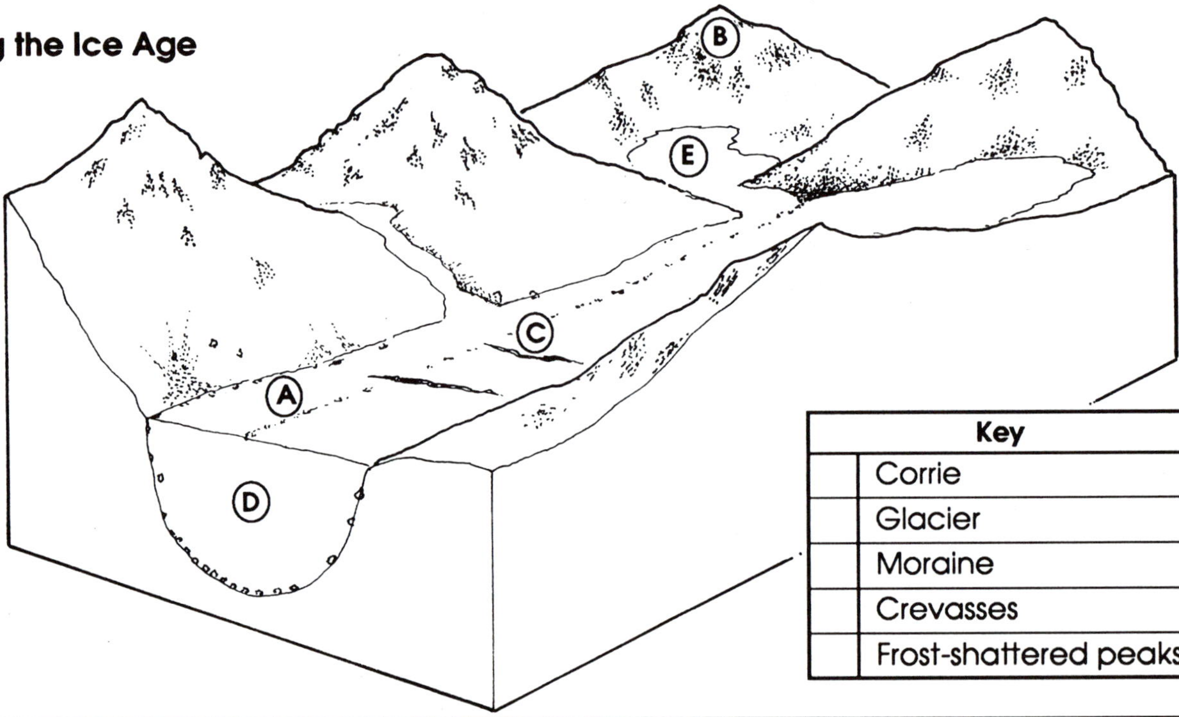

	Key
	Corrie
	Glacier
	Moraine
	Crevasses
	Frost-shattered peaks

After the Ice Age

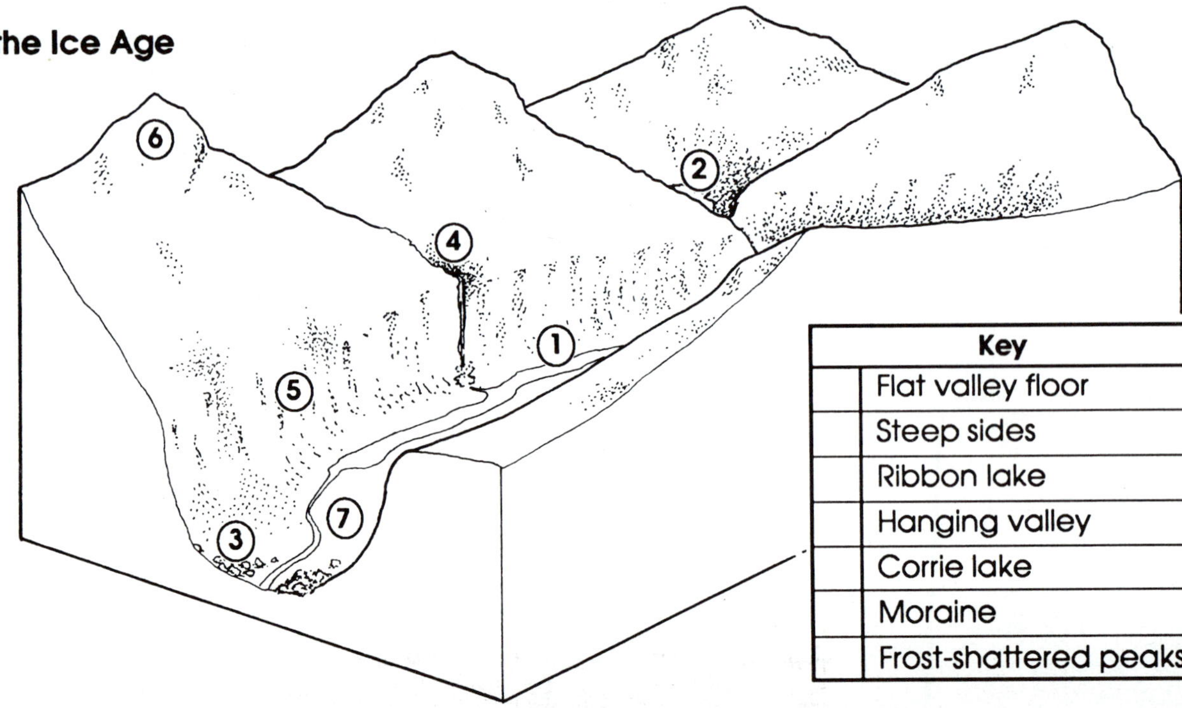

	Key
	Flat valley floor
	Steep sides
	Ribbon lake
	Hanging valley
	Corrie lake
	Moraine
	Frost-shattered peaks

GARDENS, LANDSCAPE, AND VISION IN
THE PALACES OF ISLAMIC SPAIN

D. FAIRCHILD RUGGLES

GARDENS, LANDSCAPE, AND VISION IN THE PALACES OF ISLAMIC SPAIN

THE PENNSYLVANIA STATE UNIVERSITY PRESS
UNIVERSITY PARK, PENNSYLVANIA

MM

Publication of this book has been aided by a grant from
the Millard Meiss Publication Fund of the College Art Association.

LIBRARY OF CONGRESS CATALOGING-IN-PUBLICATION DATA

Ruggles, D. Fairchild.
Gardens, landscape, and vision in the palaces of Islamic Spain /
D. Fairchild Ruggles
p. cm.
Includes bibliographical references (p.) and index.
ISBN 0-271-01851-8
1. Gardens, Islamic—History. 2. Gardens—Spain—History.
3. Landscape architecture—Spain—History. 4. Palaces—Spain—History.
5. Agriculture—Spain—History. I. Title.
SB457.8.R845 2000
712′.0917′671—DC21 98-18914

Printed in the United States of America
Published by The Pennsylvania State University Press,
University Park, PA 16802-1003

It is the policy of The Pennsylvania State University Press to use acid-free paper for the first printing of all clothbound books. Publications on uncoated stock satisfy the minimum requirements of American National Standard for Information Sciences—Permanence of Paper for Printed Library Materials, ANSI Z39.48-1992.

DESIGNED BY LAURY A. EGAN

CONTENTS

LIST OF ILLUSTRATIONS

Color Plates

Black-and-White Illustrations

ACKNOWLEDGMENTS

A book such as this is never the product of one individual; it is a response to earlier scholarship, whether in the form of an embrace, adaptation, or rejection. The innovations of the present book are very much the result of my having had to grapple with the methodology and conclusions of others. That it has made it into print is owing to support from many quarters.

The early stages of the project were achieved with a grant from the American Institute of Maghrebi Studies, a predoctoral fellowship from the Joint Committee for the Near and Middle East of the American Council of Learned Societies and the Social Science Research Council with funds provided by the Ford Foundation and the William and Flora Hewlett Foundation, and an Ittleson Fellowship from the Center for Advanced Study in the Visual Arts at the National Gallery. Research for the book was supported by a liberal J. Paul Getty Postdoctoral Fellowship and a grant for travel to collections from the National Endowment for the Humanities. The last stages of writing and the computer-generated diagrams of sight lines and architectural perspectives were funded by a grant from the Fondation Max van Berchem.

Any lengthy research project depends on the kindness of librarians. Particular thanks are owed to the librarians of the Consejo Superior de Investigaciones Científicas, Thomas McGill and Ted Dalziel of the National Gallery of Art, and the reference librarians of Olin Library at Cornell University. The computer-generated drawings were made with Hary Wilke, CAD wizard and student in the Department of Architecture, Cornell University.

I am deeply grateful to Antonio Vallejo of the Conjunto Arqueológico Provincial de Córdoba, who generously allowed me unlimited access to Madīnat al-Zahrāʾ and explained those parts of the site that have been inadequately published. He also introduced me to some out-of-the-way places of archaeological interest in Cordoba that I would never have found otherwise. I am also indebted to Rebecca Foote, one of few Americans to see al-Rummānīya in Cordoba and with whom I traveled to the Umayyad sites of Syria and Jordan for a couple of bitterly cold weeks in 1992. Margaret Sevcenko was the work's first editor: with a surgeon's skill, she saved those parts of the dissertation that were serviceable. More recently, I am grateful to Senior Editor Philip Winsor (retired) of the Penn State University Press and copy editor Romaine Perin for guiding the book into print.

At Cornell I would like to thank colleagues and former colleagues in the Department of Near Eastern Studies, particularly Leslie Peirce, Ross Brann, and David Powers, for housing me as a visiting scholar in 1994–95 and the fall semester of 1996. I also thank the participants of many symposia and conferences at the Center for Advanced Study in the Visual Arts, the University of Pennsylvania, the Institute for Fine Arts, Cornell, The Medieval Institute (Kalamazoo), the University of British Columbia, and the Aga Khan Program for Islamic Architecture at Harvard and the Massachusetts Institute of Technology, where some of this material was presented; whether in the form of suggestions or rebate, I benefited from the responses. I am appreciative as well of the stu-

dents at Harvard and MIT in my 1993 graduate seminar on Islamic gardens. At various junctures, I have relied on the advice or encouragement of Oleg Grabar, Cecil Lee Striker, and especially Jerrilynn Dodds. Alastair Northedge read and critiqued Chapter 5 and procured the photograph of the Bāb al-ʿAmma. Jonathan Bloom meticulously reviewed the entire manuscript, addressing it both point by point and as an entire argument, and both cheered and kicked me through the final phase of revision. More than eight years ago John Tagg gave me the reading list on "the vision thing," and I have enjoyed our lively discussions on that subject ever since.

Professional colleagues, friends, and travel companions to whom thanks are also owed include my parents, Jeanne and Thomas Ruggles; Tish Ruggles; Ajay and Malini Sinha; Florence Berg; and Cornelia Hughes Dayton. Renata Holod has stood by this project from its infancy when I was working on the idea of hydraulics, society, and space, to its maturation into an exploration of vision and the cultural construction of the gaze. I am grateful for her insights, encouragement, and most of all commitment.

By now, after so much discussion and reading so many drafts, my husband and fellow art historian Oscar Vázquez could have written the book himself. I doubt that I could have finished it without him and cannot begin to express my profound thanks.

A Note on Dates and Translations

The Muslim calendar, which begins with the Hejira (Muḥammad's flight from Mecca to Medina) in 622 C.E., uses a lunar system in which the twelve months (calculated by actual lunar observation) are shorter than those in the solar calendar. Dates in this book are generally supplied in both forms, the Muslim date preceding the common era date (as in 92/711). However, where the common era date does not derive precisely from a Hijri date, as in the case of estimated dates, or when my source of information did not supply the Hijri date, I have not attempted to calculate a Muslim date equivalent to the common era date. Additionally, once a combined Hijri/C.E. date is supplied, only the common era date is provided thereafter.

The translations are my own unless otherwise specifically stated. Because translation is a highly subjective art reflecting the translator's bias, my citations generally list alternative translations for the reader's information. I have generally followed the transliteration system adopted by the *International Journal of Middle Eastern Studies.* Some confusion may ensue when the reader notes variant transliterations such as *Hishām* and *Hišām* or *al-Kushanī* and *Aljoxani* in the titles of non-English works. These are due to the different systems of phonetic transliteration prevailing in each language.

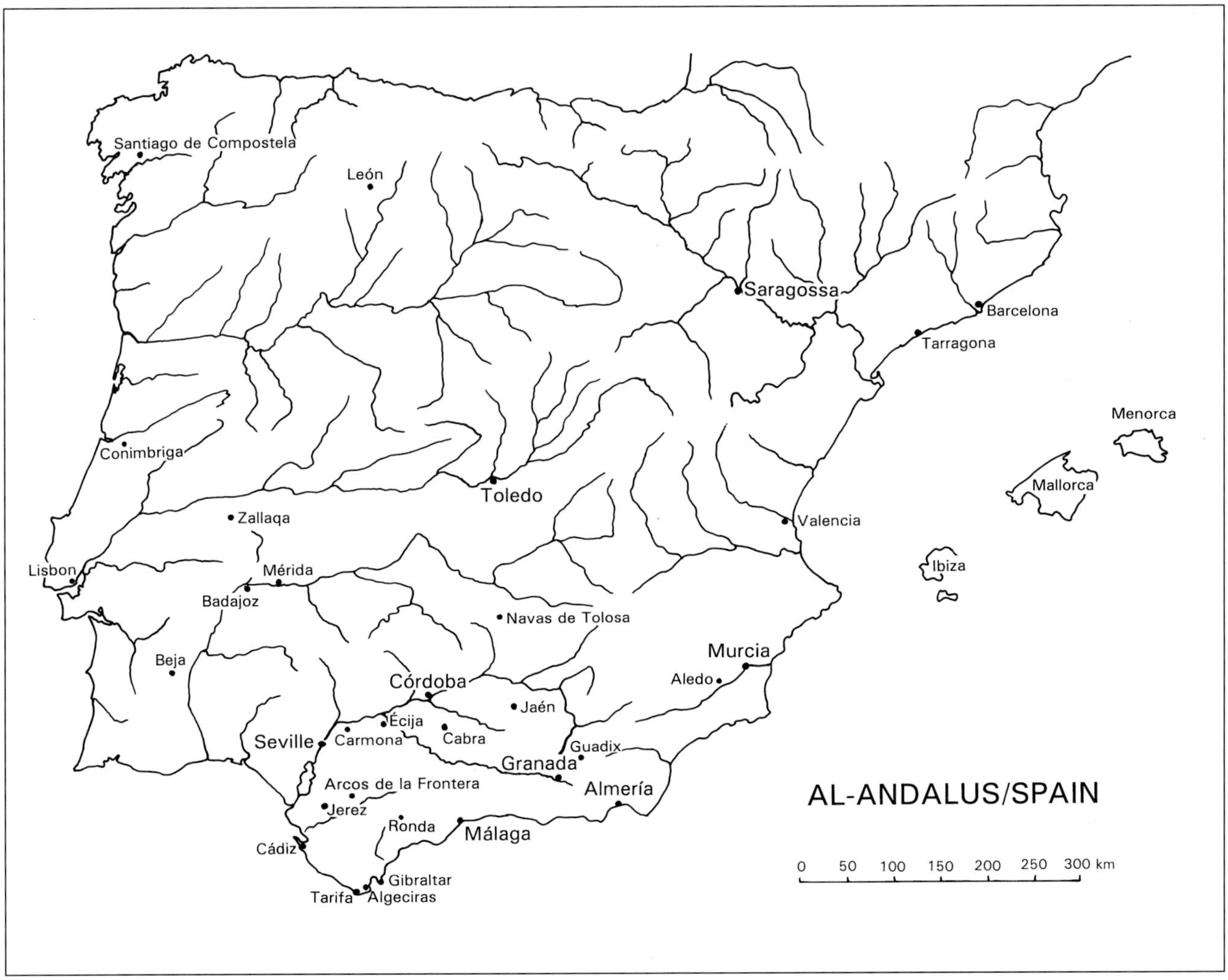
AL-ANDALUS/SPAIN
Santiago de Compostela
León
Saragossa
Barcelona
Tarragona
Menorca
Mallorca
Ibiza
Conimbriga
Toledo
Valencia
Zallaqa
Lisbon
Mérida
Badajoz
Navas de Tolosa
Murcia
Aledo
Beja
Córdoba
Jaén
Écija
Seville
Carmona
Cabra
Guadix
Granada
Almería
Arcos de la Frontera
Jerez
Ronda
Málaga
Cádiz
Gibraltar
Tarifa
Algeciras
0 50 100 150 200 250 300 km

INTRODUCTION

Is there such a thing as an Islamic garden? The gardens of the Islamic Mediterranean appear to share forms and meanings such as a Roman legacy and a sense of the ideal place described in the Qur'ān and represented in mosaics, frescos, stuccos, and ivories as a garden. In the absence of in-depth studies, however, these apparent similarities have often led to inflexible and universalizing statements, such as the claim that "the Islamic garden" is an expression of the human longing for paradise. In the Qur'ān paradise is described as verdant, shady, and with four flowing rivers. However, the varied organization of earthly gardens in different places at different times—sometimes quadripartite with four streams and sometimes not, with trees or without, with pavilions either centrally placed, overlooking the garden from one end, or absent altogether—challenges this notion of earthly gardens reflecting the heavenly paradise: the supposed ubiquitous religious value was clearly not given the same weight everywhere. I prefer to explain the typological difference between one garden and another in more secular terms, interpreting the "classic" quadripartite, cross-axial form of the garden as a reflection of the agricultural landscape, and garden symbolism (at least until the eleventh century) as environmental, economic, and political rather than explicitly paradisiac.

The Iberian Peninsula from eighth-century Cordoba to fifteenth-century Granada was famed for its verdant landscapes and many handsome gardens, which medieval authors likened to necklaces, ropes of pearls, and garlands encircling the cities. This landscape was formed during the period of Umayyad rule (eighth through tenth centuries), as a result of the expansion of agriculture and changes in its practice as well as cultural and political reorganization according to eastern models. In this book I argue that during the first 150 years of Islamic al-Andalus, a language of landscape developed for palace gardens that encoded a system of values in a set of visually organized objects, comprising its pavilions, walks, fountains, pools, trees, and flowers. The intended viewer was primarily the caliph and secondarily his court. Once implemented at the magnificent palace-city Madīnat al-Zahrā', the idea of a palatine environment with ample gardens adorned with exotic flowers and theatrical waterworks was repeated and developed until its culmination at the Alhambra. Moreover, the system of looking at the gardens from architecturally fixed points that became symbolic representations of the ruler's authority and power was also repeated, although its meaning changed with the changing political and economic context. Although all of the great garden-palaces of Islamic Spain are included here, entire chapters are devoted to Madīnat al-Zahrā' and the Alhambra because the former, though in ruins, marks the formative phase of garden design and the latter, though its gardens were not particularly innovative, survives in excellent condition and offers the most complete picture of what a medieval Islamic garden-palace was like.

In addition to addressing questions of aesthetic systems and visual reception, the study merges architectural with environmental history. A garden is not distinct from the building that it surrounds, or that surrounds it, and therefore any study of early gardens necessarily demands an

investigation into the typology of the early Islamic palace. Similarly, the garden is composed of plants, soil, and water, requiring that garden studies consider agricultural and hydraulic histories as well. The integration of these fields, with their particular methodological approaches, distinguishes this study of Islamic landscape from previous studies in Islamic garden history.

Readers who are interested principally in the architecture of gardens may choose to skip Part 1 and begin reading at Chapter 3. However, as I explain in Chapters 1 and 2, garden form and meaning are the progeny of human society and the cultivated landscape and cannot be understood solely as the product of religion or a continuous architectural typology. Chapter 1 answers the question of what kind of landscape the Muslims inherited from the Romans and Visigoths, how they altered it, and perhaps most important of all, what they thought of it. Chapter 2 explores the textual record of the agriculture practiced in that landscape which was the context for palace gardens. Chapters 3 and 4 focus on al-Andalus and describe the palaces built in Cordoba up to and including Madīnat al-Zahrāʾ. Chapter 5 looks more closely at al-Andalus's relationship with its main competitors in the east and the political and ideological changes that gave rise to the innovations evident at Madīnat al-Zahrāʾ. By looking at the palaces built after Madīnat al-Zahrāʾ, Chapter 6 demonstrates that palace's importance as an architectural prototype in Cordoba. Chapters 7 and 8 treat palaces of the eleventh through fifteenth centuries, culminating with the Alhambra, where for the first time inscriptions were added to the already extant formula of the cross-axial courtyard garden and the mirador with panoramic landscape views. Chapter 9 concludes the book with a discussion of theatrical illusion in the garden, iconography, and the theme of paradise.

Although picture books abound, there are surprisingly few scholarly treatments of pre-sixteenth-century Islamic gardens. In Spain, the social and spiritual meaning of gardens was interpreted by Georges Marçais[1] and, more recently, James Dickie.[2] Leopoldo Torres Balbás studied garden typology, and was the first to propose a chronology of the cross-axial garden in western Islam.[3] Without these fundamental studies, the present book could not have been written. However, the earlier studies were hindered by the lack of garden excavations and particularly by the paucity of information on what is without doubt the most important garden site in Spain and North Africa: Madīnat al-Zahrāʾ.

Buried under a thick mantle of soil and vegetation for almost a thousand years, only a small area of Madīnat al-Zahrāʾ has been excavated, and no serious attempt has yet been made to examine the soil layers of the garden beds or to use techniques such as seed flotation and pollen analysis to determine what plants were cultivated and where. Of the archaeological reports, which have appeared sporadically, few have merged archaeological data with the available textual, topographical, and agricultural sources.[4] In fact, the palace has never been the subject of a complete monograph, for although the former excavator Félix Hernándex Giménez had planned a detailed study, it was never completed. Instead his notes on the site were published posthumously without visual documentation and with the lacunae, inconsistencies, and spareness of the unfinished manuscript.[5]

Lacking information on Madīnat al-Zahrāʾ, garden scholars have relied on the comparatively well-published, physically intact, and visually stunning Alhambra and created a reverse chronology of Hispano-Islamic garden history based on slim evidence from it and a few other known and partially excavated sites. But the Alhambra is at the end of the trajectory of garden-making in Islamic Spain, and to rely on it too heavily for information about the early period is problematic.

Moreover, the Alhambra was built when the fortunes of Islam on the Iberian Peninsula were in decline—Cordoba, Toledo, and Seville already having fallen into Christian hands—which must have altered the meaning of the symbolism of power in the garden and its attendant architecture. Madīnat al-Zahrā᾽ on the other hand, stands at the beginning of the trajectory: it is the earliest surviving monumental example from the group of gardens made for the Umayyad rulers in which the growing taste for extravagant gardens can be traced.

Furthermore, garden historians have been slow to use the wealth of information on agricultural history that agronomists and historians of science have provided for Islamic Spain. Farming manuals, botanical treatises, and agricultural calendars from the medieval period offer a detailed picture of the state of the cultivated landscape in the tenth through fourteenth centuries.[6] Although such sources rarely describe actual gardens and never the royal palace gardens that are the subject of this book, as a group they tell of a landscape undergoing dramatic transformations and, equally as important, allow a glimpse of how those changes were perceived by a variety of persons at the time. It was Andrew Watson's research on the transmission of specific plant varieties to Spain that originally made me notice the close relationship between agriculture and gardening and to think about the ramifications of a few important botanical changes for an entire landscape and economy.

In addition to site excavations and surveys, which reveal specific facts about a particular place, and agricultural literature that describes the entire landscape, invaluable information is available in the historical chronicles and geographies. Al-Maqqarī and Ibn ʿIdhārī are the principal historians of Islamic Spain, and they drew freely upon earlier writers.[7] Despite the fact that al-Maqqarī wrote at the beginning of the seventeenth century, he often cited an earlier source containing eyewitness testimony such as in his felicitously detailed account of the construction of Madīnat al-Zahrā᾽, discussed here in Chapter 4. Among the chroniclers of individual dynasties, ʿĪsā᾽ Ibn Aḥmad al-Rāzī, Ibn Ḥayyān, and one anonymous writer are largely responsible for what is known of the Umayyads;[8] many later dynasties had their own historians.[9] In the fifteenth and sixteenth centuries, Granada was visited by European travelers Jerónimo Münzer, Antoine de Lalaing, and Andres Navagero, who with an outsider's eye described buildings and parts of the city that have since been destroyed.[10] These combined primary sources provide the material for modern histories of Islamic Spain, such as those of Conde (now outdated), the fundamental works of Dozy and Lévi-Provençal, and more recent treatments by Rachel Arié, David Wasserstein, Gabriel Martínez-Gros, and others (see Bibliography).

Because gardens and palaces figure prominently in the courtly poetry—the *risāla* and the *muwashshaḥa* for which Spain became famous—that body of literature often describes flowers and colors of which not a trace remains for the archaeologist. In the case of Granada, the verses of Ibn Gabirol in the eleventh century depict gardens that were closely related to those of the thirteenth- and fourteenth-century Alhambra.[11] Although it would be naive to accept them as literal descriptions of any actual garden, they give a sense of the metaphorical "readings" of Andalusian gardens. An important early study of Andalusian poetry is that of Adolf Friedrich von Schack;[12] the pioneering modern study of eleventh-century Andalusian poetry was written by Henri Pérès;[13] and a useful recent treatment of poetry and prose pertaining to Andalusian architecture is that of María Jesús Rubiera.[14]

Architectural inscriptions are particularly valuable primary texts because they are contempo-

rary and have a privileged physical relationship to the building that they adorn. Unfortunately, however, the only palace for which an extensive program of poetic epigraphy exists is the Alhambra, although there were other palaces in Nasrid Granada and possibly earlier that once were similarly inscribed.

Finally, a source that should not be discounted, though its contribution is limited, is the visual representation of gardens. The only known medieval paintings of a Hispano-Islamic garden are in the Vatican Library's *Bayāḍ wa Riyāḍ* manuscript (see Chapter 8).[15] Although the dating and attribution are circumstantial, these images of streamside gardens in which birds sing and lovers strum musical instruments offer an extraordinary picture of how some gardens of the fourteenth century, or earlier, may have been planted. Moreover, in the vibrant garden environment are depicted features such as flying walkways and trellises, whose presence in early gardens is otherwise attested to only in textual descriptions and archaeological excavations. Additional representations of thick leafy foliage such as those found on stucco wall carvings, marble plaques, ivory boxes, and textiles are very stylized yet suggest a palatine world in which courtly ceremony and the arts were set in garden contexts.[16]

Although the present book was first conceived as a study of the typology and meaning of early Andalusian palace gardens, my way of thinking about gardens and landscape has changed considerably. Instead of seeing gardens as organized containers of ornamental plants—that is, as a material collection of things—I now see each garden as a set of visual relationships that includes the architecture and the landscape both within and around it. The emphasis on vision has led to an exploration of the ever-expanding literature on that subject, much of which was written in the context of gender studies, cinematography, and photography, or as an effort to deconstruct the practice of art history.[17] I have worked on the question of vision continuously for the past five years, and feedback from other scholars in the field of art history has directed me toward a new understanding of visuality, the subjectivity of the viewer, and the close relationship of representations and power.

While I have brought to light some previously ignored textual passages and discovered several new facts, the book does not revolve around the introduction of these. The archaeology of the Alhambra and the Castillejo of Murcia, although still incomplete, is sufficient to allow historians such as myself to speculate about the broader and interrelated themes of architectural elevation and the iconography of sovereignty. The book's purpose, then, is interpretive and synthetic, proposing a new way of looking at landscape that is influenced by current studies on visuality and the theory that an object does not merely exist but must be "read" by someone for whom the act of reading or viewing is socially constructed. Hence, ultimately my primary focus is not on the exact contours and cultivars of a particular garden but on how its occupants might have viewed it; not on the material stuff of gardens and architecture but on the space within and around it where perception occurred. In a sense, the book presents two studies and two approaches to landscape that, while interdependent, can be read separately. For this reason the book is divided into three parts, the first dealing with the garden's formation as a microcosm of the cultivated landscape, and the second and third dealing with the reading of the garden and its optic order.

PART ONE

LANDSCAPE

1

HISTORY AND LANDSCAPE

A fertile country, rich and abounding in fruit.
—Ibn Khurradādhbih

Islam arrived on the Iberian Peninsula in 92/711. Rowing across the Straits of Gibraltar from Morocco, the Muslim-led army of Arabs and Berbers stepped onto the shore of a landscape that had been shaped by Romans and then by Visigoths. During the ensuing centuries (which number almost eight if one chooses the fall of Granada in 1492 as a convenient end point), that landscape was dramatically altered as water was pumped into the fields via wells, aqueducts, and huge creaking wheels, and formerly barren areas were tilled and cultivated. Gardens, already a widespread aspect of the Roman economy and culture, became a signal element of Islamic culture in Spain, and indeed throughout much of the Islamic world.

The explanation for these gardens, and the great pains taken to build the hydraulic infrastructure necessary to make them prosper, has long been attributed by historians to the human desire to experience on earth the paradise that the Qurʾān describes as a verdant and shady garden with four flowing streams. That thesis is attractively simple, and all the more so in that if one chooses the Qurʾān as the sole generator of cultural meaning, one cannot contest or repudiate the conclusions. However, cultural practices evolve in response not only to religious ideals and mandates, but also to geoclimatic realities, historical precedents, and a myriad of other factors. The why and wherefore of gardens are not always as simple or obvious as "paradise on earth."

Romans to Muslims: A Chronology of Events

Under Roman rule the peninsula was divided into three large provinces, of which Baetica, with its capital at Cordoba, occupied the lower half of the peninsula, a territory roughly corresponding to the Islamic kingdom of al-Andalus. The Romans introduced a system of land use and hydraulic exploitation that left an indelible mark on the society and landscape, some of which can still be seen: Tarragona's theater; the town of Italica outside of Seville; Ronda's and Segovia's magnificent aqueducts; the villas of Conimbriga (Portugal) and Pisões (near Beja, Portugal); and Merida's bridge, theater, amphitheater, roads, and temples; not to mention the mosaics, sculptural fragments, walls, and roads found in every city and town of Roman foundation.

After a long period of prosperity for the peninsula as a Roman colony, trade began to decline and the economy to stagnate in the fourth century. The economic decline left Spain vulnerable to attack, and in the fifth century a succession of Barbarian tribes from the north—the Suevi, Alani,

Vandals, and Visigoths—invaded it. The most long lasting of these invaders were the Visigoths, who settled in Castile in northern Spain, making their capital at Toledo, which remained the most important Iberian city until the arrival of the Muslims. In the middle of the sixth century, Byzantine colonies were established along the southeastern coast and islands and even in Cordoba from 554–71, but only negligible traces of them remain.

Under the Visigoths the vestiges of Roman civilization were maintained, probably because the indigenous population was only slightly disrupted by the change in administration. A relatively small number of Visigoths—estimated at between one hundred thousand and four hundred thousand—governed eight or nine million Roman-Iberians by the middle of the sixth century.[1] Roman cities, waterworks, roads, aqueducts, and bridges were taken over by the centralized Visigothic administrative system, and the Roman bimetallic coinage system was continued.[2] Roman irrigation techniques continued to be practiced. Roman agricultural treatises were read, and cereals, grapes, and olives formed the staple crops.[3] Large agricultural estates were created through the combined means of forcible seizure, new ways of allocating land, and marriage alliances between landed families.[4]

After a cultural efflorescence in the mid-seventh century, the Visigothic kingdom fell into decline. The progressive ruralization of the Iberian Peninsula that had begun at the end of the Roman period continued under the Visigoths. As the cities declined, so did industry, trade, and the circulation of money. To escape taxation the wealthy moved from the cities to their country estates, and as the cities decayed, merchants and artisans likewise fled. When those in rural areas suffered economic distress, they were forced to sell their property to wealthy lords, and to become, in practice if not by law, serfs. One of the most deleterious effects of this seignorial system was the separation between the landowners to whom taxes were paid and the actual cultivators, so that the profits from agricultural production ceased to be reinvested in agriculture. The mostly Visigothic upper class paid few or no taxes, while the mostly Hispano-Roman laborers paid exorbitant amounts. Eventually, to escape the narrow confines of peasant life and the hardships of excessive taxation, the laborers began to migrate from the countryside to new towns, causing the agricultural system to suffer still further.

When the Muslim army arrived, the Visigothic kingdom was in shambles, due to economic deterioration exacerbated by several decades of plague and famine (in the famine of 707–9 half the population of Spain was reputed to have died).[5] Politically, as well, the Visigothic hold was shaken by the seemingly endless struggle for succession to the throne and by the severe oppression of the formerly prosperous Jewish population.

The invading army was led by the Berber general Ṭāriq ibn Ziyād. His troops were ferried from Morocco, governed by Mūsā ibn Nuṣayr, to the southern tip of Iberia, which they called al-Andalus (derived from the Visigothic *landahlauts,* meaning "allotted territory"),[6] from where Ṭāriq's lieutenant, Mughith, marched to Cordoba and Ṭāriq marched to the Visigothic capital of Toledo, taking it easily. A larger army arrived with Mūsā soon after, completing the conquest.[7] The Arabic chroniclers cast the events in the light of a conquest by superior Muslim forces, while the Visigothic chroniclers lamented the "burning of beautiful cities,"[8] but the invasion of 711 may be more accurately described as a shift in alliances at a time of deep political and economic crisis, the Iberian

people collaborating with, rather than resisting, the Muslims and Berbers who arrived "more as settlers than conquerors."[9] The Arabic historians' emphasis on the fantastic and heroic dimensions of the conquest may even have led them to invent the character of Ṭāriq and others to explain place-names for which the etymology was unknown or forgotten.[10]

For the next forty years, al-Andalus remained a minor province ruled by governors appointed by the Umayyad caliphs of Damascus. Although incursions were made into southern France during this period, Islamic rule was not stable enough to support such territorial breadth. Al-Andalus became an independent kingdom in 136/755 when the twenty-five-year-old Umayyad prince ʿAbd al-Raḥmān I (r. 138/756–172/788) arrived. He had fled the Abbasid coup in 132/750, in which the leading members of the Umayyad family in Syria and Iraq had been assassinated, and made his way through North Africa to the Iberian Peninsula, where he established the Hispano-Umayyad dynasty. After one successful attempt to topple the new emir in 146/763, the Abbasids did not meddle further in the affairs of al-Andalus, which, being on the western fringe of the Islamic landscape, was not of serious significance to them.[11]

In the eighth, ninth, and tenth centuries the Umayyads of Spain enjoyed long reigns. The Umayyad emirs generally lived to their natural ends and oversaw long-range programs for the consolidation of political power, no mean feat on the Iberian Peninsula, where the lack of navigable river arteries impeded communication and high mountains harbored rebels (such as Ibn Ḥafṣūn in the mountains above Granada in the ninth century). As the kingdom was stabilized, agriculture emerged from its slow decline and brought economic prosperity. By the ninth century, under ʿAbd al-Raḥmān II, Cordoba was recognized as a minor cultural center, as evidenced by the slow stream of visiting poets, artists, and scholars to the court. In the tenth century under ʿAbd al-Raḥmān III (r. 300/912–350/961), Cordoba could set its sights on rivaling Baghdad as a world capital. Interesting, skilled, educated people flocked to ʿAbd al-Raḥmān III's court from Europe and the East seeking patronage; foreign kings sought alliances with him; and geographers praised the kingdom's prosperous landscape of farms and garden-palaces. Cordoba and al-Andalus were, so to speak, finally on the world map.

Landscape and Culture

Immediately after the Islamic invasion, the preexisting property lines were honored, which meant that the Roman-Visigothic system of large latifundia with wealthy landlords and rent-paying laborers lingered. The continuity in landownership is exemplified by the Visigothic count Teodomiro, who was allowed to retain his extensive land holdings in the region of Murcia and Alicante in southeastern Spain, and whose daughter brought two large farm estates as dowry when she married an Arab.[12]

Gradually, however, the Visigothic system gave way to contractual agreements between free parties. The reasons for this are not entirely clear, but probably the Muslim system of distributing abandoned lands to soldiers as payment served to put small parcels of property into many hands. These were then developed to their maximum potential as a response to the demand caused by the

brisk trade in agricultural goods. Evidence suggests that similar trends toward free proprietorship of small farms occurred in areas of the Christian-ruled north in the same period. For example, in the ninth and tenth centuries Leon and Castile were peopled by cultivators who owned small properties, individually and collectively, whereas in Galicia and northern Portugal serfs predominated.[13] Possibly the greater number of small landowners in the frontier zones is a reflection of the freedoms made possible by social disruptions.

In al-Andalus, the worker (*ʿāmir*) paid rent to the owner (*munāṣif*) in the form of a percentage of the harvest.[14] Since both parties stood to gain from a bumper crop, there were incentives to improve the land and methods of cultivation. Often the landlord would contribute the capital necessary to improve the physical facilities or to do the planting. The owner would undertake to clear the land (*mawāt*) before renting it out and might share the cost of seed, might contribute to the cost of buying draft animals, or—most capital intensive of all—might build the irrigation installations such as wells, canals, and waterwheels that would be used and maintained by the farmer-tenant.[15] The system was regulated by an inspector, who determined the percentage to be paid to the landlord (in either cash or produce) on the basis of average annual yield (*al-mutawassiṭ fī-l-iṣāba*) well before the harvest was collected.[16] Contracts typically covered one- or two-year periods beginning with the initial sowing. Clearly such an orderly system could only work where political stability and climatic regularity prevailed.[17]

Andalusian harvests yielded six grains for each grain sown.[18] The profit margin in this 1:6 ratio, even taking into account the capital outlay for draft animals and seed, was far greater than the 1:3 ratio of medieval France, where from one year to the next and from one region to the next the ratio of sowing to reaping could vary from a meager 1:1.7 to as high as 1:4. The studies of Georges Duby indicate that from one region of France to another and from one year to the next, yields could vary drastically, and that despite hard labor, the people often suffered hunger. European agriculture in the tenth century produced lower yields due to the unpredictable weather, lack of irrigation systems, poor use of manure for fertilization, extensive practice of fallowing (and hence low output per total acreage), and even the survival of slash-and-burn farming in which land was cultivated until its fertility was exhausted.[19] In contrast, such inefficient practices appear rare in Andalus.

The Iberian Peninsula was fertile and well suited to irrigation-based agriculture. It is watered by five great rivers: to the north are the Ebro and Douro Rivers; the Tajus River flows past Toledo in the center of the peninsula; south of this is the Guadiana River; and the southernmost is the Guadalquivir River, which connects Cordoba and Seville, as well as Granada via its tributary the Genil River, with the south coast and nearby access to the Mediterranean. Multiple ranges of mountains and hills create a series of isolated miniclimates with good alluvial soil. The richest of these is the broad valley of the Guadalquivir where in Seville the temperature on a January day averages 59 degrees F (41 degrees at night) and rises to 96 degrees F on a typical July day. Rainfall is fairly predictable, averaging 3.7 inches in November, the wettest month, and 0.1 inches in July, the driest;[20] in the summer, seasonal streams fed by melting snows and water deposits compensate for the lack of precipitation, and many of these streams were diverted to supply irrigation systems.

The Umayyad rulers of al-Andalus from the outset enjoyed long reigns that allowed them to realize long-term improvements in economy and administration, such as the installation or repair

of irrigation systems, the construction and regulation of urban markets, and the promotion of efficient farming practices. Agriculture, and particularly arboriculture and viniculture, requires such year-to-year stability: one military rampage can wipe out acres of valuable orchards that will require as much as ten to twelve years to grow back. Although the medieval historian Ibn ʿIdhārī relates many such disasters in the Islamic period, the warfare usually occurred on the frontiers of the kingdom or in rebellious zones at a distance from the seat of government.[21]

The chronicler Ibn Ḥayyān relates a terrible story of ʿAbd al-Raḥmān III's campaign against the fortress of Muez in the year 308/920–21 and his defense of the Viguera fort, in the course of which he destroyed all nearby Christian fortifications, laid waste the fields, and set a fire that burned a huge area measuring a ten-day march by ten-day march.[22] Elsewhere Ibn Ḥayyān says that the farms outside Seville had been deserted due to the war.[23] The most vivid of all is his account of ʿAbd al-Raḥmān III's army, which, prevented from taking booty in Pamplona, instead demolished the fortress of Alava and laid waste the village and land around it. One hamlet after another was destroyed while soldiers with axes chopped down the vineyards and the trees laden with fruit. On either side of the road crops burned and their ashes, blown by the wind and floating onto the warring throng, "were better perfume than amber and more aromatic than powdered musk."[24]

In the tenth century, the Umayyad kingdom of al-Andalus began to reap the benefits of agricultural improvements in fertilization, available cultivars, and hydraulic engineering that had begun in the late eighth century and accelerated through the ninth. Since the economy of the medieval world was based almost entirely on agriculture and the trade of its products, these improvements had a profound effect on the economy. Production in al-Andalus increased in quantity and quality, resulting in surpluses, flourishing markets, and capital investment in the countryside where farms were located, which in turn contributed to greater yields. This prosperity affected the way in which landscape was used and perceived. Because land generated wealth, elements of landscape began to be used symbolically to express that value. The vehicle of this landscape imagery came to be found in that microcosm of landscape, the garden; the relationship of the garden to landscape was analogous to that of a painting and its visual subject.

While to some extent both medieval Christianity and Islam were preoccupied with the relationship of humankind to God and of the transitory world of the body to the eternal world of heaven, both societies had a strong secular dimension. Although most scholars assume that the Qurʾānic theme of paradise—described as a "garden watered by four streams"—is the only explanation for garden-making and landscape transformation in Islam, it is critical to recognize the extent to which other environmental, economic, and political factors played a role. In some general sense the meaning of all gardens may derive from a ubiquitous concept of the cosmos and paradise, but the specific symbolism of Islamic gardens in the eighth through tenth centuries referred to human society and the physical environment in which the achievements and aspirations of people were played out.

The garden does more than merely reflect the relationship between humankind and the natural environment. As the intermediary between the two, it provides the means by which humans organize the natural world and make it comprehensible. It is also an arena for the expression of attitudes toward the role of the human being on earth: brash conqueror, protector and steward of vital resources (contemporary discourse on ecology argues that for the past century this role has

been neglected while the conqueror role has dominated), placator of unpredictable and frighteningly powerful natural forces, or even victim of ecological disasters (another aspect of current discourse on the environment). The garden changes its form as a result of changes in human perception, and perception changes according to who is doing the looking and the meaning that is read into the object being viewed. However, it is not only the viewer who causes variance in the reading of landscape. The environment itself also changes, often as a result of human interaction with it, although such interaction does not necessarily occur with the intention of causing environmental transformation.

That the land has history is easy to demonstrate. For example, in Syria and Jordan there are Umayyad ruins with olive presses, housing for a sizable population, the remnants of walled enclosures, and vestiges of irrigation systems attesting to the former presence of large estates devoted to olive culture in a terrain that is now arid desert. Such ruins testify that the Syria-Jordan landscape has changed from one made artificially fertile through the introduction of water, to one that is drier and less productive today.[25] In this case, changes in the physical landscape were discovered through archaeological means. In other instances, changes in the physical environment are recorded in the memory of its people. Spanish folklore tells of a landscape so dense with vegetation that a squirrel could travel all the way from the Straits of Gibraltar to the English Channel by hopping from bough to bough and never touching the ground, an image in stark contrast to the sparsely wooded terrain of central and southern Spain today. According to this scenario, bountiful nature (inhabited by woodland creatures rather than human beings) was in a "pure" state in the days before it was affected by civilization and agriculture. English folklore similarly depicts an island of richly forested lands in the days before agriculture and animal husbandry stripped it of its trees. The story rests on fact—the clearing of the landscape is well documented in both England and Spain—but in the course of being remembered generation after generation, it has become conventionalized into legend. This aspect of remembrance is important because it is through memory that images are formed of what the landscape should be, and what the landscape would be were it not for human interference in it.

The second of the above examples, that of England, directs us toward another aspect of landscape: its layers of cultural meaning. The cultural meaning of the physical landscape has been largely unacknowledged within studies of landscape painting and description. However, few are the lands that are untouched by human activity, and fewer still are those that, once seen by human eyes, are not mentally reorganized so as to impose order upon them, if only through the making of an association between the newly glimpsed land and the more familiar and known landscape. In this sense, landscape is *always* a constructed object.

A landscape may be a subject of representation, and it may be a medium for representation. Or, as is the case with gardens and landscape architecture, a landscape may be both a subject and a medium. The symbolism and form of gardens have often been regarded as parallel to either painted or written representations of gardens, yet the garden poses its own methodological considerations, foremost of which is the fact that the language of the garden is the landscape itself. It is not translated into descriptive media. Rather, the garden is a constructed microcosm of the landscape and is thus both landscape and an image or model of landscape. Therefore, any changes in the physical

land must be examined for their affect on the garden, since an elemental change in vocabulary is implied. The change in vocabulary also affects the construction and organization of the garden, and these in turn must affect our interpretation of the garden's social meaning.

Three of the most important dimensions of the social meaning of the constructed landscape and gardens are claiming, legitimizing, and inhabiting. The claiming, or appropriation, of a landscape occurs when land is conquered, as was the southern half of the Iberian Peninsula when the Arab-Berber army invaded. Although the Islamic conquest was more of a transition and restructuring of power than a bloody takeover, medieval historians cast it in terms of forceful appropriation, to emphasize the fact of the claiming of the land by the new arrivals and to designate them as rulers over the recently acquired territory.

After the invaders staked claim to al-Andalus, the legitimization of ownership was necessary in order to prove that the new owner-rulers were placed there by divine intention. The most compelling sign of this invoked by Arabic historians and geographers was the degree to which al-Andalus flourished under Islam. The fertility of the land was interpreted as a sign of divine approbation, the reward bestowed by God for successful human enterprise. According to the Arabic historical writings, prosperity was restored to the Iberian Peninsula under Islam. Ruins of Roman structures such as Cordoba's bridge spanning the Guadalquivir River or such as the city walls, which were in such disrepair that they were easily scaled by the Muslim invaders, were interpreted as tangible evidence of the older civilization's deterioration. When the bridge and walls were rebuilt by the Muslim rulers and grand new buildings erected, they were not so much restoring Cordoba to its former glory as imposing themselves as bringers of a wholly new order. For this reason, Arabic historians and geographers stated that the bridges, walls, and gates of Cordoba were Islamic, when in fact archaeological scrutiny reveals that their foundations are Roman.

The third important aspect of cultural meaning is the inhabitation of the land. Settlement was viewed as a social good, and the worth of a landscape was measured by its degree of or potential for settlement. The inhabited landscape was valued because it was endowed with the benefits of civilization in the form of religion, law, and physical amenities. One area receiving praise from medieval Arabic geographers was the Guadalquivir River plain's almost continuously inhabited and cultivated stretch of land from Cordoba to Seville. Although it was lauded for the beauty of its gardens and trees, the productive and economic aspect of the vegetation was more highly valued. In contrast, the uninhabited landscape that was not within the realm of human stewardship (whether Muslim or Christian) was devoid of value. Wilderness was not romanticized, but was feared and abhorred. Thus, the distinction made in Arabic texts between *ʿāmir* (cultivated) and *ghāmir* (uncultivated) areas of the peninsula indicates the relative worth of two kinds of landscape.[26] Indeed, even in the thirteenth century Ibn Saʿīd could praise the landscape of al-Andalus by asserting that a traveler would find the land thickly settled with villages, farms, and orchards and would not encounter any uncultivated area.[27] In the Andalusian consciousness, uninhabited, uncultivated terrain was without any value, for it served neither the Muslims nor the Christian kingdoms of the north. It lacked economic value because it yielded nothing, and lacked cultural value because it did not mediate between humankind and the natural environment.

On another level, the inhabitation of Iberia was equated with the spread of Islam worldwide.

The expansion of Islam denoted the reintroduction of civilization to the impoverished society of Iberia and the conviction that the Islamic rulers were intended by God's will to supplant earlier Christian ones just as the message of Muḥammad replaced earlier messages.[28] With these questions of socially shared beliefs in religion, civilization, and truth, geographical space and territory became arenas for the expression of ideological convictions.

With the exception of negligible, long-term, climatic changes, alterations in the physical environment are largely due to human activity.[29] Water is introduced to or drained from an area of land; trees and shrubbery are removed from a hillside, causing erosion of the topsoil; and animals are put to graze on a field, cropping the grass and preventing trees from growing. The modern period has regarded such changes cynically, as being damaging to the integrity of the environment and its human occupants, and indeed many attempts to change environment, such as the application of pesticides or the liberal spread of nitrogen fertilizers on agricultural lands, have produced mixed blessings. However, this was not the case in the medieval period, when almost all human use of the environment was seen as beneficial to both the landscape and society. Thus, the medieval perception of undomesticated nature (fearsome) and the landscape (remunerative through human endeavor) is quite different from views of nature and the landscape held after the beginning of the industrial revolution.

Furthermore, in Umayyad al-Andalus the city was not a blight but a center of culture and enlightenment, and the countryside was closely associated with the city. Unlike Roman villas and English country manors placed at such a distance from the city as to be removed from its sphere of influence, Andalusian villas were located on the margins of the city in a mediating position between city and countryside. The principal investment in the countryside, its landscape, and its economic productions came from the urban centers. City and country were not functional opposites. More accurately, land was on a conceptual spectrum, at one end of which was uninhabited wilderness devoid of human interaction, and at the other end, the city teeming with people and social interactions. The opposition was between space that had value and space that lacked value because, uninhabited, it was unimaginable. Nature was only appreciated for the quality and quantity of human interaction with it. For this reason, it is to the interaction of human society with the physical environment that we must look for an understanding of changes in landscape perception.

Cordoba as Center

A fundamental change in the relationship between people and the environment in the early and medieval periods of Muslim rule was due to territorial expansion. The seventh and eighth centuries saw the tremendous and rapid spread of the religion of Islam and with it Islamic law, definition of community and citizenship, political and economic systems—in sum, a shared set of social values—from the Arabian Peninsula through Jordan and Syria and northward, eastward as far as the Indus Valley, and across northern Africa to Morocco and the Iberian Peninsula.[30] The first point of political center in the Islamic world was Damascus under the Umayyads, followed subsequently by Baghdad under the Abbasids. But in Spain from 756 onward, territorial expansion was organized

around a new central point: Cordoba. Minor rebellions in marginal Andalusian provinces were quelled and brought under the control of the central administration, and excursions were made to the northern frontier to repel the threatening armies of Aragon, Asturias, Leon, and Galicia and to wrest additional territory from their control. However, the frontier loomed far larger as a mental construct than as an actual geophysical barrier, since the boundaries were always in flux. Governors of border provinces frequently switched allegiance or made pacts with the enemy in order to save their own necks. Thus, the frontier was maintained as a result of constant pressure from both sides and was pushed back by means of a delicate balance of political negotiations reinforced by military force.

Al-Andalus had a well-developed fortification network on its frontiers and in the interior, for the most part dating to the tenth century.[31] The south coast, even today, is dotted with guard towers and fortresses built to forestall an attack from the sea by the Abbasids (a serious threat for only a brief period), North African tribes, and Vikings. But because Cordoba was at the center of an expanding circle of territory, the chance of an invasion (such as the unexpected Viking raid of Seville in 230/844) was slim and defensive architecture was minimal. However, internal revolts could and did take place, such as during the civil-war years of 1010–13 when a defensive ditch was built around Cordoba, according to Ibn Ghālib. It was constructed at a distance from the city, encircling the medina and all its suburbs, including Shaqunda on the opposite bank of the river, and extensive farm and pasture lands—a total area of five thousand hectares.[32] Although the city's urban center, the medina, was enclosed by tall, thick walls, suburbs and farmland sprawled around it, unprotected by defensive walls, and as the population grew, other attractive suburbs graced by trees and gardens sprang up. The frontiers of al-Andalus were too far away to have immediate impact on the lives of Cordoba's farmers, merchants, and city dwellers.

At least until the end of the tenth century, land around Cordoba was plentiful. But not all land was valued equally. Whereas theoretically land was abundant in al-Andalus, in actual fact the most important agricultural lands ringed the cities, the most valuable being closest to the urban center and the less valuable located in wider rings at a greater distance from the center (Fig. 1). The farthest ring was usually taken up by animal pasturage because it required the greatest amount of land and the least amount of labor and capital investment, and because the animals could be herded to the city on the hoof. In contrast, in the inner rings of farmland where the demand for land was high and the supply limited, the most labor-intensive crops were grown, such as vegetables and flowers used for the perfume industry. These lands were close to the populations consuming what they yielded, minimizing the cost of transporting the goods to market and the workers to the fields. Proximity to the city put the surrounding ring of farmland advantageously close to agrarian and architectural investments from the urban center. For example, the ring closest to the medina of Cordoba was the mostly densely built and cultivated until ʿAbd al-Raḥmān III founded Madīnat al-Zahrāʾ in the outer ring, thereby creating a new secondary center.[33]

In addition to the economies of scale in transportation, there is a third aspect of the relationship of the countryside to the city, which is less easy to recognize. This is the fact that as cities grow, the increase in population density puts pressure on the land to yield more food. Recent demographic studies have challenged the older Malthusian model of limits to growth that postulated that the

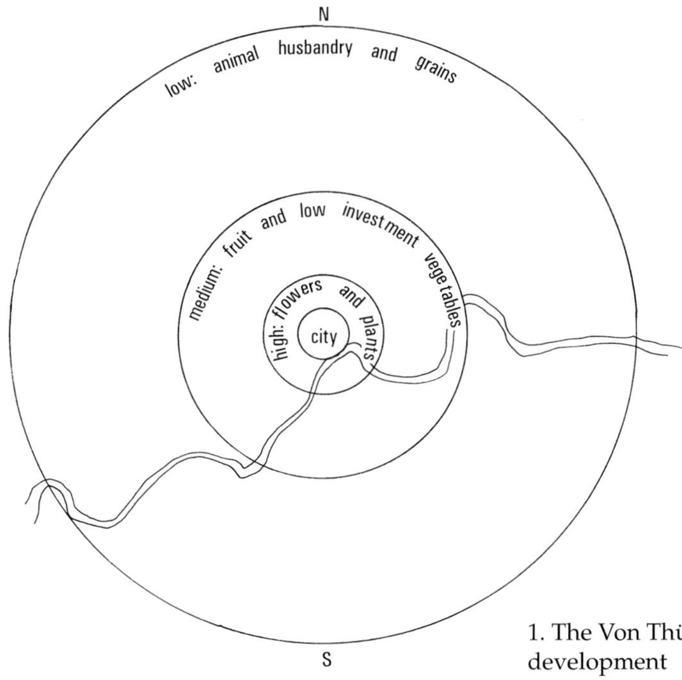

1. The Von Thünen model of agricultural development

environment has finite production capacities, imposing limits on the size of a population that can be sustained by a given portion of land. According to Malthusian theory, the population cannot expand until the introduction of an innovation, such as a more efficient plough or a disease-resistant plant varietal, allows increased agricultural output.[34] However, research by Ester Boserup suggests that the inverse may be true. That is, instead of demographic growth happening as a result of agricultural innovation, demographic growth may be its *catalyst*.[35] Clearly neither the Malthusian nor the Boserup model can be said to be unilaterally operative in all cases; however, in Umayyad Cordoba, the repeated instances of agricultural improvements during two and a half centuries indicates that it was unrelenting pressure that led to agricultural transformation (i.e., Boserup's model) rather than one or two dramatic innovations that allowed expansion of population size. A larger population size means less land per person, forcing each acre to yield more food through the intensification of labor or technological investment. As the population size increases, which Cordoba's did between the eighth and tenth centuries due to immigration, low mortality, and elevated birthrate,[36] the higher demand for agricultural products gives farmers the economic incentive to install expensive irrigation systems, to experiment with short-season interim crops, and to replace fallowing with the rotation of complementary crops.

Population growth in Cordoba undoubtedly placed demands on the agricultural economy of the city and its surrounding farmlands and promoted innovation in agricultural techniques, but it was clearly not the sole engine driving agricultural change. One of the most persuasive catalysts for change was economic, not technological. The single most effective technical device—irrigation—

was already known and had been in use since Roman times; it was the systematic social acceptance and implementation of known techniques, rather than innovation, that was the key factor in improving Andalusian agriculture.[37] Irrigation in combination with new plant types imported from abroad allowed the exploitation of seasonal, climatic, and geographic zones previously deemed marginal.[38] Significant factors contributing to agricultural transformation were the natural endowments of the Iberian landscape, the transformation of raw materials into tradable goods, Andalusia's excellent location vis-à-vis trade with Europe, the east, and northern Africa, the accumulation of wealth as a result of trade, the increased security as a result of military strength, the importation of eastern knowledge and models of administration, and finally, as stated above, the new cultivation of previously nonarable land areas.

Impressions of Landscape

Some historians have supposed that the Arabs chose to conquer places with climates and landscapes similar to their own,[39] but this is certainly not true of the Iberian Peninsula, for the Maghrebi army was more Berber than Arab in composition and, while southern Spain may resemble northern and central Morocco with its mountainous terrain and winter rains followed by a long sunny dry season, neither is particularly like Egypt, Syria, or the Arabian peninsula. But they did like to *re-create* familiar landscapes and were willing to exert a great deal of effort in making the necessary changes to do so.[40] Although the pre-Islamic landscape can be imagined, we do not know how it impressed the new arrivals when they first crossed the Straits of Gibraltar. We only know that many chroniclers of the tenth century and later described the kingdom of al-Andalus as verdant, fertile, productive, and beautiful.[41] The earliest of them, Ibn Khurradādhbih (205/820 or 211/825–300/911), called it "a fertile country, rich and abounding in fruit," and others used similar phrases.[42] Ibn al-Faqīh al-Hamadhānī (d. after 290/903), added that Murcia, Jaen, and Faḥṣ al-Ballūṭ were known for their silver and mercury mines and that Cordoba had a mild climate, producing few date palms but plenty of olives, cotton, and flax; but he also remarked that the town of al-Baht was in deserted countryside (*fī baʿḍ mafāwizihi*).[43] Ibn Ḥawqal, a Fatimid sympathizer, visited al-Andalus (in 947–51) during the reign of ʿAbd al-Raḥmān III. While he did not like the Andalusians, he found their cities to be prosperous and their well-irrigated agricultural lands fertile.[44] Al-Muqaddasī, also writing in the tenth century, repeated hearsay praise for Jaen, whose twelve springs and productive fruit orchards provisioned much of al-Andalus.[45] Aḥmad al-Rāzī (d. 344/955), a particularly valuable source because he drew on earlier ones, wrote that al-Andalus was blessed with a healthy climate, good air, ample forests, and broad valleys producing delicious fruit. Cordoba, he said, was surrounded by handsome forests, and the plain on the opposite side of the river had a great many fine trees.[46] In the late twelfth century at a poets' competition to compare the beauties of al-Andalus to those of the Maghreb, al-Shaqundī recalled the Guadalquivir Valley with its well-tended parks (*manāzih*), gardens (*basātīn*), vineyards (*kurūm*), and groves of trees (*anshām*).[47] Although al-Shaqundī's verses belong to a separate and far more sophisticated genre than geography,

his eagerness to represent al-Andalus's natural beauty offers much the same sort of picture. The geographical sources and belles lettres are based on a common reading of al-Andalus, and they reveal a great deal about the ideal and the real landscape.

In summary, the Iberian Peninsula was a naturally fertile landscape well suited to irrigation-based agriculture. It flourished under Muslim rulers, who provided a stable political environment conducive to agriculture and carried out deliberate programs of reform. The model of a landscape forced to become more productive is important to our understanding of the meaning and aesthetics of landscape because it profoundly altered the relationship between the human being and the land, changing the way in which landscape was used and perceived. Other factors, such as influences from Abbasid Iraq, Byzantium, the Maghreb, and Fatimid Ifriqiya, also shaped the attitude toward landscape. However, these, combined with the potentially strong influence of a single very effective patron, such as the caliph or prime minister, could only be implanted into an already receptive host environment.

Chroniclers and geographers were quick to recognize the merits of the Andalusian landscape, and their descriptions indicate how landscape was "read" in the medieval period. Productivity was the measure of beauty: it was understood that through the introduction of Islam and the order imposed by the Umayyads, al-Andalus was transformed from dereliction to verdant prosperity. The landscape of al-Andalus came to look different and to be valued differently in both the economic and cultural sense.

2

BOTANY AND THE AGRICULTURAL REVOLUTION

Agriculture is the base of civilization; on it depends life and all its benefits.
—Ibn ʿAbdūn

The ninth century was a period of prosperity and internationalism in al-Andalus, and nowhere were these circumstances enjoyed more than in Cordoba. With surplus wealth the urban merchant class invested in the countryside surrounding Cordoba, buying land and creating suburban estates that were irrigated by means of private wells, waterwheels along the river, and the seasonal streams that ran from the low range of mountains north of the city. Historians and geographers of the following century remarked that these estates were places with gardens and orchards for recreational enjoyment as well as for agricultural production. New applications of agricultural methods made areas fertile that had hitherto been deemed inhospitable, and even arid zones were made temperate thanks to the mitigating ability of irrigation. The landscape looked different—verdant, settled, and ordered with walls, rows of trees, and roads—because it *was* different. It had experienced a revolution in agriculture.

The medieval Arabic historians represent al-Andalus as a landscape changed through human endeavor and divine sanction. The degree of human investment is evident in the many descriptions of gardens and plant collecting, and it is recorded in the copious literature on plants written in al-Andalus beginning in the tenth century. That investment was represented in the most transformed landscape of all, the formal garden. The textual documentation and the visual representation of the changing landscape were of profound interest to the rulers who succeeded the Umayyads in the eleventh century. Although there are no gardens remaining from that time, descriptions in geographies and histories tell us of their existence and appearance. Additionally the agricultural manuals are a valuable source of information.

The agricultural continuity from the Umayyads to their successors is somewhat surprising in light of the major political and social changes. Al-Andalus changed dramatically in the eleventh century from having a centralized government ruled by a distinguished Arab dynasty to becoming a decentralized net of city-states in which Arab and Berber leaders vied for power.

Taifa Politics

ʿAbd al-Raḥmān III's son al-Ḥakam left at his death a ten-year-old heir, Hishām II (r. 366/976–399/1009 and 400/1010–403/1013). Because the child-prince was too young to rule, the vizier Ibn Abi ʿĀmir, called al-Manṣūr (r. 371/981–392/1002), was appointed as his regent. Al-Manṣūr quickly seized power, incarcerating the prince in the Madīnat al-Zahrāʾ palace at a distance from the city, and proceeded to rule as king in fact, if not in name. The Amirids held firm power for seven years after al-Manṣūr's demise, until 1009 when civil war (*fitna,* literally "disruption")[1] erupted in Cordoba, spreading quickly to the rest of al-Andalus. One contributor to the unrest was the army. Expanding upon a precedent set in the ninth century, al-Manṣūr had altered the demographic and ethnic stability of the peninsula by recruiting large numbers of Berber soldiers from North Africa to form an elite mercenary army. These Berbers did not belong to the older Cordoban community, were loyal to the Amirids rather than the Umayyads, and were deeply resented by the old guard. The tensions extended well beyond the Berber-Arab divide, for there was also a rift between old and new Muslims (of both Berber and Arab lineage). Although the Amirids had been the real powers in Cordoba since the death of al-Ḥakam, violent protests were voiced when one of al-Manṣūr's sons persuaded Hishām to designate him as heir. The public anger grew into open rebellion, which lasted for two years, during which Berbers and Arabs, with intervention by the Christian kings of the north and European slaves (the *ṣaqāliba*), fought for control of Spain.[2]

Although the Umayyad line did not immediately disappear, none of the legitimate successors to Hishām (whose death is shrouded in mystery) lasted more than three years during the period 399/1009–422/1031. Instead, power shifted to the hands of regional authorities. Eventually, in place of the provincial governments administered by a strong central ruler in Cordoba, small independent entities sprang up, called taifa kingdoms (*mulūk al-ṭawāʾif*). Many of the new taifa rulers were the governors who were already in place during the caliphate or were leading members of aristocratic families, so that, despite the lack of a political center in the eleventh century, the local configurations followed the same administrative divisions as had existed during the caliphate.[3] Of the taifa splintering of al-Andalus, the last Zirid king of Granada, ʿAbd Allāh, wrote: "Every leader revolted in his own city, and fortified himself in his castle, after first taking thought for himself, and enrolling soldiers, and storing up money; and they contended with each other for the world, and each of them was covetous of the rest."[4]

Rivals for political power and cultural supremacy, the taifa kings converted their capital cities into miniature Cordobas, attracting to their courts the artists, poets, and scientists who had fled Cordoba's turmoil. Thus the brilliant cultural activity that had flourished under Umayyad and Amirid patrons was redistributed to the various taifa courts. Al-Shaqundī, in his thirteenth-century debate, said that the taifa kings stimulated the arts and sciences by spending huge amounts of money on them: "The market for the sciences was brisk and they competed in giving recompense for prose and poetry. And there was no greater glory for them but that it should be said that the learned so-and-so lived in such-and-such a kingdom and that some poet was in the court of such-and-such a king." And he continued: "The poets balanced themselves between taifa kings like breezes in gardens, and plundered their treasuries like a military sack."[5]

Likewise, competition among the taifa kings gave scientific enterprise an urgency that proved beneficial to the state of agronomy. Agronomists and botanists, formerly patronized by al-Ḥakam and al-Manṣūr, left for Granada, Toledo, and Seville, where they created experimental gardens and wrote manuals on how best to practice agriculture.

Botanical Gardens

As early as the eighth century, exotic plants were deliberately acquired and transplanted into Andalusian soil. Ruṣāfa, the country palace estate of ʿAbd al-Raḥmān I, was well stocked by its builder with valuable plants. The thirteenth-century historian Ibn Saʿīd wrote that Ruṣāfa had beautiful irrigated gardens and that ʿAbd al-Raḥmān had sent a messenger to foreign parts to obtain special plants, so that "al-Ruṣāfa became famous for the excellence of its plant varieties."[6]

Rulers were instrumental in importing and naturalizing exotic plants such as the superior pomegranate procured from Syria by ʿAbd al-Raḥmān I. A tenth-century historian related that the emir had sent one of his men to Syria to escort his sister to Spain. She refused to go, claiming that she was too old to make the trip, and instead sent generous gifts that included some excellent pomegranates.[7] The fruit was inedible by the time it reached al-Andalus; nonetheless, ʿAbd al-Raḥmān distributed the spoiled pomegranates among his followers. One of them, Safar b. ʿAbd Allāh, planted his and thus introduced a new variety of fruit to al-Andalus, which was thenceforth known by his name: al-Safarī.[8] Al-Maqqarī, gathering his information from earlier sources, wrote:

> The king handed over to Safar a part of these pomegranates and the latter was so impressed with their beauty that he wanted to do an experiment [*khabara*] with them. He took them to a small hamlet [*qariya*] in the district of Rayy [near Malaga] where he worked with the seeds, planting, nourishing, and then transplanting them until there grew a tree that gave fruit and matured. He gathered the fruit, still astonished at its beauty, and took it immediately to ʿAbd al-Raḥmān, who was able to verify that it was identical to the pomegranates from Ruṣāfa [in Syria]. The emir asked him how he had done it, and he told him the procedure he had used. The emir admired his discovery, appreciated his efforts, thanked him for the work he had done, and recompensed him generously. He then planted the pomegranate in Ruṣāfa and in his other gardens. That pomegranate species eventually spread and the people planted groves of them."[9]

This is the first reference to the deliberate and controlled acclimatization of an exotic species, and perhaps even to a botanical garden.[10] Because the evidence is supplied by a tenth-century source two hundred years after the events in question, the story may possibly be a concoction reflecting the powerful agronomic interests of the later period. But in my view, such exchanges in which the flora of one landscape was encouraged to adapt and survive in a new environment precisely mirrors the process of human cultural adaptation. The story may have been preserved because it was a metaphor for this adaptation, but this does not discount its validity as evidence of an early interest in botany and practical agronomy.

The agricultural writer Abū al-Khayr (probably eleventh century) mentioned that in 225/840 the poet Yaḥyā al-Jazāl smuggled inside a stack of books the seeds of a new variety of fig, called al-Dunaqāl, from Byzantium into Cordoba, where they bore fruit.[11] The stories of the Safarī pomegranate and the Dunaqāl fig demonstrate that plant species did not merely arrive by chance in al-Andalus; they were sought after, procured, and cultivated with great care in experimental gardens until they were naturalized and could grow and be propagated in al-Andalus.[12]

Botanical gardens were also planted in medieval European monastic communities, as the well-known plan of St. Gall indicates.[13] Commissioned as an ideal scheme for a monastery between 816–36, it depicts a vegetable garden with eighteen beds containing onions, leeks, celery, radishes, chard, parsnips, among other vegetables, as well as a small medicinal herb garden containing lilies, roses, climbing beans, pepperwort, costmary, Greek hay, rosemary, mint, sage, rue, iris, pennyroyal, watercress, cumin, lovage, and fennel. Elsewhere on the grounds there was a fruit orchard with a cemetery in its midst.[14] There are only a few non-native plants or trees indicated on the plan and it is difficult to assess the degree to which foreign plants were sought and cultivated. The earliest European gardens intended expressly for scientific study and the domestication of foreign varietals were much later: the botanical gardens at Padua (planned in 1542, built in 1545), Pisa (1544), Bologna (1547), and Zurich (1560).[15]

Most of the new plants introduced to al-Andalus before 1492 came from the East, notably India and China. In the westward migration that followed the Islamic conquests, plants were carried by the immigrants either in the form of seeds and cuttings or inadvertently in the form of dried herbs and foodstuffs, and these were introduced into new environments where some of them took root and flourished. The extent to which foreign seeds, fruit pits, grain kernels, or cuttings could survive in new surroundings depended on the climate, soil, and water. In some cases, the new and old climate were identical or were so closely matched as to require only small adjustments. An example of this is the incremental diffusion of a species from one area into adjoining areas previously deemed marginally arable but made more hospitable by the digging of wells to augment the water supply. Sugarcane, for instance, requires a moist environment. Although in tropical climates the plant is harvested in the fall after the summer rains, in al-Andalus, where the rainy season is during the winter months, it was harvested in the spring.[16] The "agents of transmission"[17] were traveling scholars, pilgrims making the *ḥajj* to Mecca, and merchants traveling along trade routes buying grains, dried fruits, and herbs in one place and selling them in another. The markets of Cordoba, for example, were famous for the wide variety of foods sold in them, both domestically grown and imported from abroad.[18] Although these examples of diffusion can be deduced from patterns of human behavior, only the instances of caliphal plant collecting are caught in history's net.

In addition to the Safarī pomegranate and the Dunaqāl fig, other cases of royal botanical collecting are known. Ibn Wāfid created a botanical garden (or an experimental one) in Toledo for the taifa ruler al-Maʿmūn in the eleventh century,[19] and in 1171 the Almohad caliph Abū Yaʾqūb Yūsuf I ordered fruit brought from Granada and Guadix to Seville to be planted in the gardens of his palace al-Buḥayra. These were varieties of the pear called *kumithrī* by botanists, those of other trees called *ʿabqar* and *al-azra,* as well as apples.[20] In the late twelfth century, the physician and botanist Muḥammad b. ʿAlī Ibn Faraḥ, known as al-Shafrān, made a botanical garden for the Almohad sultan Muḥammad al-Nāṣir in Guadix.[21]

Calendars and Botanical Treatises

Of the surviving Andalusian agricultural literature, the oldest is the so-called *Calendar of Cordoba* (*Kitāb al-anwā'*), dedicated to al-Ḥakam II and written between 357/967 and 366/976 by ʿArīb ibn Saʿd (d. 370/980) and a Christian bishop named Rabīʿ bin Zayd, known as Recemundo.[22] The *Calendar* merged a Mozarabic liturgical calendar with an astrological almanac giving a month-to-month set of directives for farmers: tilling in January; plowing from March through May so that the earth was opened up to allow the rain and air to penetrate the soil; and sowing at the end of May to retain the moisture and nutritive benefits of the soil. The Latin names of the months were used because the Latin solar calendar was more suitable for agriculture than was the shorter Muslim lunar calendar, in which the months fell on different dates each year. The agricultural labors were collated with seasonal religious festivals (including Christian holidays) and astronomical cycles. In an eleventh-century agricultural manual by Ibn Wāfid, the calendar was solely a schedule of agricultural labors.[23] The liturgical Christian calendar—an unusual inclusion in any case—was presumably discarded because Ibn Wāfid's book was intended for a Muslim patron, and yet a Muslim calendar of religious holidays was not substituted.[24] Ibn Wāfid restricted his information to when to perform each activity and how to perform it.

The recording of seasonal agricultural activity had, of course, classical precedents and appeared equally in Islamic and Christian spheres.[25] In European illustrated calendars made just before 830, the months were depicted as abstract personifications, but in the Carolingian period, which so profoundly influenced the rest of medieval Europe, the months were illustrated with the seasonal activities of plowing, slaughtering, and harvesting.[26] It has been suggested that the catalyst for the change in the manner and subject of representation was agricultural change itself in Europe, the most important of which was the introduction of triennial crop rotation in the late eighth century.[27] As in al-Andalus, the importance of fundamental changes in practice was perceived by the populace (or at least its leaders) and expressed in the visual and written literature.

Although the *Calendar of Cordoba* is the oldest agricultural treatise in al-Andalus, there is evidence for earlier texts that have not survived. The most important of these was a beautifully illustrated Greek copy of Dioscorides' *De Materia Medica,* a treatise on medical practice and plants with pharmaceutical properties written about 78 C.E., sent as a diplomatic gift by the Byzantine emperor Constantine VII Porphyrogenitus to ʿAbd al-Raḥmān III in 337/948.[28] Unlike Pliny's *Natural History* which was a folkloric compendium, Dioscorides made his own direct observations so that his work bears the Hellenistic legacy of science based on data rather than cosmic philosophy.[29] Galen's *De simplicium medicamentorum temperamentis et facultatibus* (c. 129–200 C.E.), translated into Arabic in the ninth century for the Caliph al-Mutawakkil of Baghdad, was equally well known, and Dioscorides and Galen together provided the foundations for medieval pharmacology, botany, and medicine. But in Spain, Dioscorides had the greater impact because of the luxuriousness of the Byzantine gift copy and because it contained pictures of plants.

Due to the difficulty of correlating Greek plant names with Arabic equivalents, they were usually transliterated rather than translated, and because of the ensuing confusion in nomenclature, the resulting edition was impractical.[30] Constantine warned ʿAbd al-Raḥmān III that his edition would be of little use without an expert to read it, but according to the biographer Ibn Abī Uṣaybiʿa:

"There was no Hispano-Christian at that time in Cordoba who knew how to read ancient Greek. For this reason, the book of Dioscorides remained in ʿAbd al-Raḥmān III al-Nāṣir's library in its original Greek. Of this work, therefore, only Stephan's translation, imported from Baghdad, could be found in the hands of the public."[31] ʿAbd al-Raḥmān then asked Constantine for a translator, who arrived in 340/951–52 in the person of a monk named Nicholas. Ibn Abī Uṣaybiʿa makes it clear that Stephan's rudimentary ninth-century translation was used in Cordoba and that Nicholas was occupied solely in making a gloss of the Greek plant names for use in the Iberian context. Nicholas glossed the Greek words into Latin; then the caliph's Jewish physician, Ḥasdāy ibn Shaprūṭ, translated the Latin into Arabic. The improved translation that emerged was based on the earlier work of Stephan.[32]

The correspondence accompanying the gift edition of the manuscript and its subsequent preservation in Ibn Abī Uṣaybiʿa's biographical dictionary shows the importance attached to the utility of the Dioscorides manuscript. With its handsome illustrations, the Byzantine gift was not simply a beautiful objet d'art but a treasure of information. Although the manuscript no longer exists, presumably its illustrations depicted the plants described in the Greek text, providing an invaluable key to identifying the plants of the clumsy nomenclature in the older Arabic version.

Nicholas's work for ʿAbd al-Raḥmān III was by no means the first instance of scientific botanical study in Cordoba. Ibn Abī Uṣaybiʿa tells us that Yūnus ibn Aḥmad al-Ḥarrānī came from the east bringing his skills as a physician to Cordoba circa 800 in the reign of Muḥammad.[33] The physician Yaḥyā ibn Isḥāq, a convert to Islam in the time of ʿAbd al-Raḥmān III, wrote a book summarizing Greek medical knowledge.[34] As physicians these men were also necessarily pharmacological botanists. But the Dioscorides manuscript was more significant than any of their works because it was the basis for a new scientific paradigm in which the natural flora of al-Andalus became the subject of close analytical study that combined the information in the ancient texts with direct observations of native plants.

This interest in botany was fostered by caliphal patronage. Al-Ḥakam II, even more than his father ʿAbd al-Raḥmān III, drew scholars to his court, until an entire school of botanists had been established in Cordoba. Their leader was Ibn Juljul who, as physician to al-Ḥakam, continued the work of glossing and adapting the Dioscorides manuscript.[35] Ibn Juljul not only provided Arabic versions of foreign plant names, he also added his own considerable knowledge of Iberian botany to the text, and thus began the tradition of writing treatises that were adaptations, commentaries, and expansions of Dioscorides.

Ibn Juljul wrote *An Explanation of the Names of Simple Drugs in the Book of Dioscorides* (*Tafsīr asmāʾ al-adwīya al-mufradāt min kitāb dīyusqūrīdis*) in 372/982 and *Generations of Physicians and Scholars* (*Ṭabaqāt al-aṭibbāʾ wa-l-ḥukamāʾ*) in 377/987.[36] Other important botanical writers and teachers[37] were Muḥammad ibn al-Ḥusayn ibn al-Kattānī, who was al-Manṣūr's physician;[38] Ḥāmid ibn Samajūn (d. 1001), who wrote pharmacological works and also served al-Manṣūr;[39] Abū'l-Qāsim Khalaf b. al-ʿAbbās al-Zahrāwī, also known as Abulcasis (d. 1009–10), who wrote an important medical text and served as court physician to al-Ḥakam II and al-Manṣūr;[40] Abū ʿAlī al-Ḥusayn b. ʿAbd Allāh, also known as Ibn Ṣina or Avicenna (980–1036), who wrote the *Canon of Medicine* (*Kitāb al-qānūn fī-l-ṭibbi*) with a section on simple drugs;[41] Abū ʿUbayd Allāh b. ʿAbd al-Azīz al-Bakrī

(d. 1094) of Huelva and Cordoba, who wrote a botanical work in addition to several geographical works;[42] and Aḥmad al-Ghāfiqī (probably first half of the twelfth century) from the Cordoba region, whose book on simple drugs was without doubt the most comprehensive of the treatises and was the basis of the pharmaceutical *Collection of Terms* (*al-Jāmīʿ li-mufradā*) of al-Idrīsī (d. 560/1166) and Ibn al-Bayṭār (d. 646/1248).[43] Sometime soon after the *Calendar of Cordoba,* Ibn ʿĀṣim (d. 403/1013) wrote a calendar that mentioned earlier agricultural and calendrical works.[44]

Because Dioscorides was accepted as the legitimate basis for all further botanical study, botanical expertise among Andalusians was confirmed by a thorough knowledge of Dioscorides. From the study of botany through texts and observation it is but a short step to the creating of botanical collections and from there to naturalizing exotic species and experimenting with techniques of grafting and cross-fertilization, in short to the science of agronomy. By the eleventh century, the breadth of literature had expanded from plant identification to plant cultivation, which was recorded in the agricultural manuals.

Agricultural Manuals

Like calendars and botanical treatises, the agricultural manual (*kitāb al-filāḥa*) also had classical precedents. Andalusian agronomists frequently cited Lucius Junius Columella, born in Cadiz on Spain's south coast in the first century C.E. Columella had read the Latin agricultural work of his compatriot Marcus Terencius Varron (Barūn to Arabic writers) while at the same time gaining first-hand expertise managing his father's property. Thus he prefigured later Andalusian agronomists who carried the written word in one hand and a trowel in the other. From more recent traditions came works such as the Byzantine *Geoponika,* a collection of agricultural notes composed for the Emperor Constantine Porphyrogenitus in the mid-tenth century.[45] Although Persia produced many botanical treatises, there are few agricultural manuals from the early period.[46] The earliest known Arabic agronomic text is Ibn Waḥshīya's *al-Filāḥat al-nabaṭīya,* written in 291/904 C.E. by an Iraqi.[47] It was purported to be a much older text, no doubt as a means of giving it antique pedigree, but in reality it was a medieval recapitulation of older geoponic writings on agricultural practice.[48] The *Nabaṭīya* reached al-Andalus in the tenth century and provided the basis for all subsequent agricultural manuals in much the same way as Dioscorides served botanical research.[49]

Citations in later agricultural manuals indicate that an agricultural manual was written by the Cordoban ʿArīb Ibn Saʿd (300/912–c. 370/980), one of the authors of the *Calendar of Cordoba.*[50] Neither the text of that work nor its title is known today, which is all the more unfortunate, since it was probably the earliest Andalusian agricultural manual. The second earliest was the *Abridged Book of Agriculture* (*Mukhtaṣar kitāb al-filāḥa*), which is believed to have been written in Cordoba by Abulcasis and dated sometime between 975 and his death in 404/1013–14.[51] These texts were written by Cordobans and thus we can see the roots of Andalusian agronomy in that city. Also dated to the tenth century is the *Book on Order of the Times of Planting and Cultivation* (*Kitāb fī tartīb awqāt al-ghirāsa wa-l-maghrūsāt*), possibly by Ibn Jawās (about whom almost nothing is known).[52]

The agricultural manuals vary in their contents but typically included chapters on soil and

water classification, animal husbandry, horticulture, viniculture, arboriculture, and sometimes food preservation. The interest in soil classification reflected the desire to improve the land: for example, dry sandy soil could be improved with organic additives to retain more moisture and thus support more delicate plants. The amelioration of the soil was part of a wide-based attempt to make previously unarable land fit for cultivation and thus to expand the land area available for farming, as well as to intensify cultivation on existing lands and to increase yields. The drive to improve the land and increase agricultural production was the result of the agricultural revolution that crested in the tenth century, and it is thereafter linked to the changed political climate in Spain in the eleventh century.

Ibn Wāfid (b. 389/998–99 or 398/1008, d. 467/1075), who spent his adult life in Toledo, is said to have studied medicine under Abulcasis, though he could not have been more than fifteen when his teacher died, so the apprenticeship would have been brief.[53] In addition to producing a synthesis of Dioscorides and Galen,[54] he wrote the *Collection* (*Majmūʿa*), which inspired Gabriel Alonso de Herrera's *Agricultura general,* written in the early sixteenth century. Ibn Wāfid was director of the garden of the taifa king al-Maʾmūn in Toledo, and his biographer commented that "he had complete mastery in agriculture and was knowledgeable in its procedures."[55]

His manual is divided into eighty-seven chapters followed by an agricultural calendar. The chapters deal with soil types; water and how to detect its presence in the soil; the most astrologically propitious seasons for building farmhouses; fertilizers; seed selection; things that damage grain (such as hailstorms); when to sow wheat and barley; when to reap; the threshing barn; granaries and bakeries; how to select sites for vineyards; choosing vine shoots to plant and how to plant them; olive oil preparation; and the soil preparation for and sowing of lettuce, cabbage, chard, turnips, radishes, onions, leeks, garlic, celery, basil, cucumbers, melons, and sugarcane. More than fifty chapters of the original text are missing, but there then follows a set of specific instructions on when to plant, prune, and harvest each type of plant and tree. It ends with a section on beekeeping, pigeon keeping, and pesticides such as myrtle and cumin. Ibn Wāfid rarely refers to other authors and does not mention practical agricultural experience of his own, although the details of the manual reveal prodigious knowledge. Compared with later agricultural manuals, his treatise seems weighted more toward botanical information than toward agriculture, reflecting his training in the Dioscoridian school of botany.

Abū al-Khayr of Seville wrote his manual in the second half of the eleventh century.[56] Like Ibn Wāfid, he discusses soil preparation, fertilizers, sowing and harvesting, and olive, flax, cotton, and palm culture.[57] He explains crop rotation and the double cropping in winter and spring of flax and wheat or barley, and he says that the terrain of a field should not decline toward the north lest it be deprived of sunlight. Abū al-Khayr is very specific in his instructions. For example, for olive propagation he recommends the following:

> From the tree's main branch one should cut a sucker that is 10–12 palms in length. Then dig a hole 5 palms deep and 3 palms in circumference in the place where the tree is to grow. Put the shoot in the hole and fill it with earth, first spreading pebbles around the base of the shoot [for drainage], and then creating a slight depression in the earth around

> it to collect water. These plantings should be spread 20 cubits apart, minimum, to allow for maximum tree growth later.[58]

He describes other forms of propagation and emphasizes his familiarity with these techniques, commenting, "We have had the experience of doing this ourselves."[59]

Ibn Baṣṣāl wrote the *Diwān al-filāḥa* and an abridged version of the same called *Concision and Clarity* (*al-Qaṣd wa-l-bayān*), the contents of which survive in part because of Ibn al-ʿAwwām's summarization of them.[60] Ibn Baṣṣāl was well traveled in the Mediterranean and had occasion to learn about agriculture from his observations in Syria and Egypt. He succeeded Ibn Wāfid in Toledo, then fled after the Christian conquest of the city in 478/1085, going to the court of al-Muʿtamid, the taifa ruler of Seville. There he was the teacher of an anonymous botanist (who may have been Ibn ʿAbdūn the *ḥisba* writer) who later wrote a pharmacological treatise for physicians (*ʿUmdat al-ṭabīb fī maʿrifāt al-nabāt li-kull labīb*) (after 542/1147). Ibn Baṣṣāl's manual catalogues with assiduous attention to detail and variety all the known ways of cultivating and controlling soil, water, and growing conditions in order to produce the best plants. He makes no reference to other authors and the book lacks the chapter on animal husbandry and veterinary medicine found in other manuals.[61] Ibn Baṣṣāl (whose name is derived from a rare adjectival form meaning "he who tends bulbs")[62] is described in the biographical dictionaries of his time as a skilled botanist and gardener: "[Toledo has] wild pomegranate trees that are unlike anything else, the wild pomegranate approaching the state of the domestic pomegranate. Toledo is very famous for its techniques of cultivation and grafting. Ibn Baṣṣāl, the leader of agronomy there, said 'I saw a tree in that city which had a different variety of fruit.'"[63] The same source describes an unusual fig tree in the palace garden, half the fruit of which was green and the other half white.[64] No doubt it was a case of grafting multiple limbs onto a single rootstock, as is commonly practiced today with roses and ornamental trees.

Ibn Baṣṣāl's text lists four types of water (rain, spring, river, and well) and ten types of soil (soft and light, mountainous, sandy, black and well manured, white, etc.) and the plants that prosper in each.[65] The third chapter covers seven types of fertilizer (horse, mule, sheep, pigeon, and human manure as well as garbage and ashes from bathhouse furnaces). The fourth chapter discusses soil preparation and the method and tools used in leveling the earth so that water will flow evenly through the garden plots. In the same chapter he refers to the three types of land: first, land that has never been ploughed—*būr*—which he says is the worst because it is as if it were asleep or paralyzed; then land that has been worked (*maʿmūr;* which can mean both "cultivated" and "inhabited") but still has last year's stubble; and finally land that has already been ploughed (*qalīb*). He comments, "Of course, this is all well known except to the stupidest laborer."[66] Writing in the late eleventh century, he sees the landscape not as sharply divided between that which is habitable and that which is not, as Ibn Ḥawqal had more than a hundred years earlier, but rather as a three-tiered system of land, all of which was potentially usable. By the eleventh century the distinction of land in al-Andalus was not between inhabited (*ʿāmir*) and uninhabited or desolate (*ghāmir*), but between land that had already been worked at least once (*maʿmūr*), and land that had not yet been ploughed but soon would be (*būr*). Equally significant is the description of land that was "asleep," implying that the farmer could rouse it with the plough.

In the fifth chapter Ibn Baṣṣāl refers to an illustration accompanying the instructions for planting palm trees.[67] Although there was no image in either the Arabic text or the fifteenth-century Castilian translation,[68] this reference to one indicates that illustrations were developed to support written instructions in these manuals. Their existence is hardly surprising, given that botanical manuals such as Dioscorides and Ibn Bayṭar's *Book of Simples* had them.

Ibn Baṣṣāl describes how to plant vines and trees (nut, olive, and fruit as well as ash, elm, and cypress) stating precisely how deep the hole should be, how far apart each young shoot, and the dimensions of each garden bed. He discusses the cultivation of vegetables, melons, citron, capers, legumes, cotton, sesame, saffron, poppy, henna, spices and herbs, and flowering and aromatic plants such as the rose, gillyflower, violet, lily of the valley, chrysanthemum, narcissus, basil, marjoram, marshmallow, camomile, and wormwood (absinthe). He closes with a section on the preservation of fruits.

This list of flowers and plants combined with the dimensions of garden beds and plant spacing ought to provide information sufficient to reconstruct a typical Andalusian garden of the eleventh century, but unfortunately there are few clues to how the plants would have been arranged. Most of the plants he lists also had commercial value as dye, perfume, and spice, and their cultivation for the market would have been quite different from their arrangement in a formal garden. Poetry from the period confirms that the same plants and flowers appeared in pleasure gardens and that they had symbolic meanings, but in the absence of visual representations of such gardens and of data from botanical archaeology, it is almost impossible to reconstruct the placement of the plants within the garden or to learn in what quantity they occurred.

Ibn Ḥajjāj of Seville is said to have written, among other works, *al-Muqniʿ* (466/1073); no copy survives but because it was the principal source for Ibn al-ʿAwwām, large portions have been reconstructed.[69] Ibn Ḥajjāj experimented with olive propagation in the area known as the Aljarafe outside of Seville and mentions seeing fig trees mixed with viticulture in the Guadalquivir Valley.[70] In addition to possessing practical expertise, Ibn Ḥajjāj was well acquainted with the classical sources on agriculture, as well as with the work of contemporaries such as Abū al-Khayr.

An anonymous agricultural manual exists (Ms. 4764 [Blochet], folios 47a–64a, Paris) which has been attributed to the late tenth or early eleventh century on the basis of the originality of its material.[71] Abū ʿAbd Allāh Muḥammad ibn Mālik al-Murrī, called al-Ṭighnarī, flourished in the twelfth century and served the taifa prince of Granada before moving to the court of the Almoravid governor Abū-l-Ṭāhir Tamīm b. Yūsuf Ibn Tāshufīn (r. 501/1107–512/1118) to whom he dedicated his opus, *Zahrat al-bustān wa-nuzhat al-adhhān* (The flower of the garden and the pleasure of the intellect).[72] The fact that al-Ṭighnarī worked in Granada meant that he knew an agricultural system different from that Toledo or of Seville, which were considerably farther north and far less mountainous. However, he observed agricultural practice in other regions as well and met Ibn Baṣṣāl in Seville in 494/1100–1.[73] The agricultural work of Ibn Abū-l-Jawād (or Jawwād) was cited by other agronomes as a *risāla* (literally "letter"), which indicates that it was only a short and relatively minor summary of agricultural information from other sources.[74]

Ibn al-ʿAwwām (fl. twelfth–thirteenth centuries in Seville) is not known to have made any sig-

nificant contributions to Andalusian agronomy, but he made a huge compendium of earlier agricultural writings called the *Kitāb al-filāḥa* that includes works known only through his mention of them. Although he did have direct practical experience in cultivation, the derivative nature of his work is typical of later agricultural writings and points to the end of experimental botanical and agronomic research.

Ibn Luyūn (681/1282–750/1349) wrote his *Kitāb ibdāʾ al-malāḥa wa-inhāʾ al-rajāḥa fī uṣūl sināʿat al-filāḥa* (Book on the principles of beauty and the purpose of learning which treats the fundamentals of the art and agriculture) in Almeria in 749/1248.[75] His manual is in verse, rhymed with the particularly easy and common *rajaz* meter to facilitate memorization. Although the contents were unoriginal, Ibn al-ʿAwwām's and Ibn Luyūn's are the only treatises to have been preserved in their entirety. Like his predecessors, Ibn Luyūn discusses soil types and distinguishes between *ʿāmir* (cultivated) and *ghāmir* (uncultivated) land, which he writes is unproductive although it can be made to produce.[76] Regarding leveling the earth, Ibn Luyūn notes that the soil in a garden bed (*ḥawḍ*) should be sloped in such a way that water will distribute itself evenly. He describes a rudimentary but efficient device for doing this that consists of a cord stretched between two stakes spaced fifteen units apart, with a weighted plumbline (*mīzān*) measuring one unit in length dropped from the farthest end of the cord. He writes that bedding plants should be organized in rows with lengths of string to mark each one, and that the beds should be rectangular following a 1:3 ratio, reaching no more than twelve cubits in length and less if water is scarce.[77]

Among his instructions for fertilizing, irrigating (including information on an underground conduit or *qanāt*), plowing, propagation of plants, and the cultivation of a wide variety of plants and trees, Ibn Luyūn notes regional differences in agricultural practice. The labors of the months, for example, should be done according to the country's own customs, and elsewhere he cautions that trees found in the wild must be domesticated gradually. He classifies seeds according to the season in which they grow best, and his remarks that some (coriander, spinach, radish, and cabbage) can be grown the year round testifies to the fact that by the late twelfth century Andalusian farmers had pushed the physical landscape to yield continuously with very little fallowing.

The verses are rather prosaic and amateurish, for Ibn Luyūn was neither a good poet nor a skilled agronomist. He derived his information from Ibn Baṣṣāl, al-Ṭighnarī, Ibn Abū-l-Jawād, and Aristotle, among others, and from the regional farmers themselves.[78] However, his text served a useful purpose in compiling for Almeria agricultural information from other parts of al-Andalus. Indeed, he emphasized the practical utility of his manual, writing, "You should try this" and "Try it and you will see."[79]

Today Ibn Luyūn is best known for his instructions on the placement and design of the manor house within a garden:

> With regard to houses set amidst gardens an elevated site is to be recommended, both for reasons of vigilance and of layout;
>
> And let them have a southern aspect, with the entrance at one side, and on an upper level the cistern and well,

Or instead of a well have a watercourse where the water runs underneath the shade.

And if the house have two doors, greater will be the security it enjoys and easier the repose of its occupant.

Then next to the reservoir plant shrubs whose leaves do not fall and which [therefore] rejoice the sight;

And, somewhat further off, arrange flowers of different kinds, and, further off still, evergreen trees,

And around the perimeter climbing vines, and in the centre of the whole enclosure a sufficiency of vines;

And under climbing vines let there be paths which surround the garden to serve as margin.

And amongst the fruit trees include the [common] grapevine similar to a slim woman, or wood-producing trees;

Afterward arrange the virgin soil for planting whatever you wish should prosper.

In the background let there be trees like the fig or any other which does no harm;

And plant any fruit tree which grows big in a confining basin so that its mature growth

May serve as a protection against the north wind without preventing the sun from reaching [the plants].

In the center of the garden let there be a pavilion in which to sit, and with vistas on all sides,

But of such a form that no one approaching could overhear the conversation within and whereunto none could approach undetected.

Clinging to it let there be [rambler] roses and myrtle, likewise all manner of plants with which a garden is adorned.

And this last should be longer than it is wide in order that the beholder's gaze may expand in its contemplation.[80]

Ibn Luyūn's description is an elaboration on similar instructions on house siting offered by Ibn Wāfid:

> The best place in the farm for building houses is the highest place because of the fact that they will neither be flooded nor totally dry and the run-off will help provide water to the rest of the farm and its gardens and fields. And it is preferable that the houses be built on a riverbank and their doors and windows open eastward. This is because the east winds are more salubrious than the winds from the west, and also because the heat of the sun removes the ill effects of bad air. The houses should be tall and broad with wide doorways so that they are well ventilated. In this way their inhabitants will be most healthy.[81]

Ibn Luyūn and Ibn Wāfid's advice on where to place houses, pavilions, wells, and large trees provides valuable information for garden history. However, because their descriptions were not based on a known site—it may have been an imagined ideal[82]—they are of limited usefulness. Was Ibn Luyūn referring to an ordinary farmhouse or to a more pretentious manor house? Was he de-

scribing a farm of his own time and place, or was he repeating a formula from previous authors? Just as the botanical observations in the Dioscorides commentaries allow one to only partially reconstruct the flora of medieval al-Andalus without offering a clear image of what the landscape looked like, so too the information in any single agricultural manual does not allow the reconstruction of the *structure* of the garden, but only a list of its individual components with recommendations for cultivation.

The manuals, calendars, and botanical treatises are remarkably similar. They all state the great variety of methods available for doing the same thing and then describe the procedures in detail, as if each were important to the science of agriculture. But how important were these texts in furthering agriculture in al-Andalus? What was the purpose of describing in detail all the known ways of accomplishing the same end? It is hard to imagine ordinary farmers, already schooled in the oral tradition, leaving their plows to consult these texts. Even assuming that farmers could read (in which case their literacy would probably not extend beyond the recognition of Qurʾān verses learned in school as children), the tremendous expense of manuscripts put them out of reach of most people. On the other hand, the information in the manuals is unquestionably intended for practical application. The function of the texts is all the more puzzling in a culture where learning was generally transmitted orally and when one considers the profusion of texts, most of them covering the same information.

The explanation lies both in the state of agriculture and book technology in al-Andalus during the tenth through twelfth centuries. Stories about the acquisition and dissemination of new plant cultivars such as the Safarī pomegranate demonstrate that innovations were adopted quickly. The dissemination of actual practices had economic rewards; it does not take long for a new plant variety or a new method of grafting to become widespread provided there is a recognizable economic advantage in adopting the innovation. Possibly the science of agronomy changed more rapidly than could be passed on orally in one or two generations of teachers and students, and there was a need for a written record to capture that knowledge and facilitate its transmission. To provide a state-of-the-question summary of agricultural science, authors extracted older works before adding their own comments accumulated daily as a result of direct experimentation and scientific observation. For this reason, the manuals should be regarded as technical workbooks of cumulative authorship and not as signature works of any single author.[83]

During this period, the book industry began to grow. Paper was introduced to al-Andalus at least as early as the tenth century, as evidenced by descriptions of the materials of papermaking from about 900.[84] Al-Maqdīsī stated that al-Andalus produced excellent paper in the second half of the tenth century,[85] and this undoubtedly was a significant factor in allowing al-Ḥakam to amass his great library, the catalogue of which was said to be 880 pages long.[86] By the eleventh century, paper was produced widely in al-Andalus and Andalusian artisans had achieved a reputation abroad for their skill in paper- and bookmaking.[87] Paper, made of flax or hemp, offered an alternative medium for preserving information that was manufactured more quickly, inexpensively, and hence in greater quantities than parchment. As a result, simultaneously as there arose a perceived need for recording the rapidly increasing additions to scientific knowledge, the physical means of doing so was on hand. The constant updating of botanical data and techniques of cultivation in the

form of revised editions of Dioscorides or multiple versions of agricultural how-to manuals thus coincided with a change in technology that facilitated book production.

Nevertheless, these science books were not cheap, nor was their information and terminology readily comprehensible to ordinary readers. Who read the manuals? Certainly not the small-scale farmer who could neither afford them nor read the complex and technical explanations. Were they intended to record for an elite class the methods already practiced by the agriculturalists? In other words, were they an intellectualization of practical applications? When Abū al-Khayr commented that in Sicily farmers plowed the field ten times before planting the cotton, he was referring to a system already in place.[88] But when Ibn Ghālib noted that the advice of Ibn Baṣṣāl was followed by the farmers,[89] and Ibn Luyūn urged his reader to try the method of planting that he suggests, they were directing their words to someone engaged in making decisions about how land was to be cultivated. One deduces from this that the described techniques were not well known and that the purpose of the manuals was to encourage wider use of them.[90]

Another explanation is that manuals did not compete with or replace oral transmission of knowledge but coexisted as one aspect of it. Perhaps the agricultural manuals were mnemonic strategies in the sense of that studied by Mary Carruthers in medieval European culture:[91] the book was not a replacement for the oral transmission of memory/knowledge but a visual (i.e., written) sign system for the text that existed both in oral and written form. Certainly, Ibn Luyūn's rhymed manual suggests that written and oral texts were consonant. Clearly an investigation into the nature of Islamic oral and written culture, like Carruthers's study, would be useful, but lies outside the scope of the present book.

Most of the manuals were written for royal patrons and appear to have been disseminated to landowners and aristocratic gentlemen farmers who could then exhort the tenants and workers toward better and more profitable modes of cultivation. The fact that al-Manṣūr read agronomic literature personally, including a new work on plowing and soil aeration written by one of his governors,[92] indicates that these texts addressed an audience of rulers and decision makers. Rulers often took a specific interest in agricultural techniques, probably with the idea of boosting productivity. For example, when a farmer presented four enormous melons to al-Muʿtamid (461/1069–484/1091), the taifa king of Seville expressed surprise and admiration and began to interrogate the farmer. The man explained that the melons did not normally grow so large but could be made to do so by pruning away all but ten branches of the vine and supporting the fruit on wooden supports.[93] This is precisely the kind of agricultural practice described in the manuals and one can well imagine, from this anecdote of a ruler's encounter with a farmer, that he would wish to preserve the information in written form. The information on agriculture came both from prior treatises and directly from the field, whether through the experimentation of scientists or the daily experience of farmers, but the inscription of that knowledge on paper was effected for an educated, wealthy, and socially empowered audience.

Although the school of botanical-treatise writers was formed in the mid-tenth century, the agronomic manuals were, for the most part, written in the late tenth century and thereafter. The eleventh century was the most intense period for collecting data and translating and copying agronomic texts,[94] but the agricultural revolution itself began more than a hundred years earlier. The manuals

could not therefore have caused the revolution; rather, starting with Abulcasis in Cordoba, they catalogued the vast quantity of information acquired during that time and preserved it in books that must have enjoyed a fairly wide circulation, judging from the number of copies, commentaries, and even later Castilian and Catalan translations that were made.

Patronage

Cordoba, as the capital of the kingdom, was the center of scientific scholarship and source of agrarian investment. But when the caliphate collapsed in the early eleventh century, patronage did not collapse with it. Although the caliphate's demise changed the political climate and patronage of scholarship and science in al-Andalus, the chain of scholarly transmission was unbroken. If anything, the fissuring and regrouping that followed strengthened scholarly activity by causing the resettlement of scientists in cities such as Toledo and Seville and by stimulating the creation of new centers of learning and of scientific investigation. The quantity of works produced in the eleventh century reflects the political multiplicity of the taifa courts as well as small regional differences in botany and agriculture.

Although agricultural development occurred at the level of the individual farmer, invoking a series of small decisions (whether to dig a well for irrigation, to plant both a summer and winter crop, to experiment with a new kind of fig), caliphal patronage was a tremendously important part of the engine driving agrarian transformation and the resultant economic boom in the tenth century. The caliph supported research such as the translation of texts from the east[95] and the formation of botanical-study collections, and he was the eager recipient of novel plant species obtained in the East by travelers. Whereas ordinary farmers adhered to traditional methods, altering the system only when there was a demonstrated advantage to doing so, the caliph was expected to set the example, rather than follow it, and thus he encouraged the cultivation of exotic species, enjoyed for their rarity, beauty, or exquisite taste. Species imported by him eventually were planted by an entire spectrum of naturalists, botanists, and agriculturalists. Given the impact of the caliph's role in agricultural development, it is hardly surprising that the most profound changes in Cordoba's economy and landscape occurred during the longest caliphal reign, that of ʿAbd al-Raḥmān III.

Rulers collected plants and botanical information for a variety of reasons. Culinary taste was one of the motives.[96] Many of the fruits and herbs produced in the gardens that were first used for medicinal purposes soon appeared in the royal banquets, where they were featured as delicacies. At the same time, the emulation of eastern refinement led to a growing demand for exotic foods: one can easily imagine the sensory impact of the banana and of sugarcane, when tasted for the first time. From palace banquets an interest in such foods spread to the aristocracy, government leaders, scholars, and traveling dignitaries and filtered downward through the social strata, creating a new demand. At some point local cultivation replaced importation, which stimulated the expansion of the range of foods produced.[97]

Offering strange and marvelous dishes at a banquet was only one reason for cultivating botanical rarities. Collecting was part of a king's role: as he should be a great warrior and a scholar, so

should he be a connoisseur and collector of fine things. In addition to collecting objects, a king was supposed to gather brilliant men and beautiful and accomplished women to his court. To attract the most celebrated scholars, the caliphs of al-Andalus promoted learning of all types, scientific as well as literary, for there was no line drawn between science and belles lettres. The emphasis on science, which grew from an undisciplined interest in the eighth and ninth centuries to a full-fledged school of scientific research in the tenth, complemented the passion for collecting rare species of fruit and flowers. Augmented by scientific study, the Andalusian love of gardens and of nature, for which evidence exists as early as the reign of ʿAbd al-Raḥmān I, quickly acquired a new dimension. The new improved species and the caliph-induced public enthusiasm for gardens and improved agricultural production transformed the countryside of Cordoba into a more literally and economically fruitful landscape.

Having beautiful and extensive gardens was an important aspect of territorial proprietorship, particularly for the caliph, whose stewardship of the landscape as a whole was acted out in his creation of gardens. Agriculture, as Ibn ʿAbdūn said (quoted at the beginning of this chapter), was the economic foundation of al-Andalus. It produced food for consumption, raw materials such as fibers for clothing, leather, dyes, wood for manufacturing and building, foodstuffs, and manufactured goods for trade. Ibn ʿAbdūn stated the case well in his twelfth-century *ḥisba* manual for Seville's town management. He gave advice on the storage of grain, the maintenance of pure supplies of potable water, and the regulation of market prices and minimum standards of quality:

> The ruler must order that a greater effort be invested in the cultivation of the soil. It ought to be protected, and the cultivators ought to be treated benevolently and taken care of while they work the fields. The ruler must order his viziers and the important people in his capital to undertake agricultural endeavors of their own. This will better profit both him and them; their fortunes will increase, and the people [as a whole] will gain because of their greater ability to provision themselves and to prevent hunger. The country will prosper, life there will be more pleasant, and its defense will be more efficient and reliable. For agriculture is the base of civilization; on it depends life and all its benefits. On account of grain one sees the loss of lives and fortunes, and cities and men change masters. When one ceases to produce grain, fortunes are altered and the entire organization of society slumps.[98]

Similar sentiments were voiced by the author of the *Irshād al-zirāʿa,* an agricultural handbook written in 1515 in Herat, who wrote that "the good order of the world and the perpetuation of the human race" depended on agriculture.[99]

In addition to support for agronomic study, there is at least one example of a caliphal directive regarding investment in agriculture in al-Andalus. When one of al-Ḥakam's generals subdued the rebel fortress of Jabal al-Karam in the south, he received a letter from the caliph explaining that the troops would be stuck there for the winter but that money would be sent to Ceuta, where it would be available if needed. The general was admonished to concentrate on the business of ensuring that his soldiers would have enough food: "If you could manage that the majority of people working in the countryside would employ teams of oxen in working the land, kept somewhat apart from the

rebels, without inflicting harm or upsetting the local inhabitants, it would be one of the things most in keeping with the *amīr al-muʾminīn*'s projects, whose intention is none other than to obtain the prosperity of those lands and the safe-keeping of the people."[100]

Ibn ʿAbdūn stressed the role of the ruler in maintaining the pace of agricultural development, and the disaster that could await him if he did not: the undoing of the agricultural system had proved the undoing of kings. The system needed leadership, but the leader also needed the system. Social stability was necessary for agriculture to flourish, for in war agriculture came to a standstill. It takes forty years for an olive tree to reach full maturity, producing fifty kilos of olives in alternate years (a smaller tree will produce ten kilos).[101] Hence every farmer planting olive trees does so as an investment for the next generation, and destroying or damaging such a tree has serious consequences for both the present and future generation. Thus, not only was the ruler important as the primary patron of agricultural investment, the stability of his rule was necessary to the unfolding of the agricultural revolution.

An Agricultural Revolution

Andrew Watson, who is credited with the first articulation of the theory of an agricultural revolution in medieval Islam, has also been roundly criticized on the grounds that many of the innovations he claims for the eighth through eleventh centuries in Islam were already known to the Byzantines and Sasanians.[102] His detractors point out that the most important innovation affecting the Hispano-Islamic landscape—irrigation—was not the result of a sweeping revolution but of slow, steady expansion in landscape infrastructure accompanied by changes in the social system regulating it.[103] The idea of an agricultural revolution, however, was not invented by Watson.

In the sixteenth century, Philip II's secretary Francisco Idiaquez had recognized the skill of the descendents of the Muslims (Moriscos) in improving the Iberian landscape: "There was no corner or plot of land that should not have been turned over to the Moriscos because they alone were sufficient to bring about fertility and abundance in all the land [and] because they knew how to cultivate it so well."[104]

In 1876 the historian Antonio García Maceira pointed to the differences between Roman and Islamic methods of cultivation: "Spanish agriculture was, thus, in the time of the Roman and Goths, timid and traditional. It filled the soil with products that grew there almost spontaneously, but did not take pains to improve them and increase their numbers with new imports from other zones and regions, bringing in this way, with new richness and new practices and usages, new methods and advantages and surer means of advancement."[105] But, he continued, the Arabs caused a "revolution" by implementing the knowledge that they acquired through observation during their peregrinations, and the result was extensive agricultural settlement.[106] Leaving aside the question concerning the mythical aspects of the image of the peripathetic Arab, and the commentator's understanding of the mechanics of change in Hispano-Islamic society, it is clear that he perceived an agricultural landscape profoundly altered by the Muslims.

A current theory suggests that Islamic society did not introduce agricultural changes but

merely restored the prosperity that had been lost after the collapse of the late Roman Empire.[107] This perspective is gained from archaeological research, rather than from a comparative reading of texts, and runs counter to the picture presented by the medieval Arabic historians. But those same historians also claimed that Islamic society entirely rebuilt rather than merely repaired the architectural landscape of Spain, a view that archaeological investigation has disproved. This perception of sweeping transformation and the claim of agency is significant because, while it may deceive with respect to its image of a complete overhauling of agricultural practice, it does honestly signal dramatic acceleration. Although many of the so-called innovations in Andalusian agrarian practice were known to the Romans, these were applied to the Andalusian landscape in a thorough and systematic manner that was new. The system of crop rotation, fertilization, transplanting, grafting, and irrigation were implanted so rapidly and thoroughly because the legal code governing landholding and tenancy provided an incentive to improve farming practices and because the upward spiral of economic growth rewarded investment. Indeed, the Andalusian revolution in agriculture was not so much a matter of new techniques as of new social institutions to regulate and maintain them.[108]

Under Islamic rule, the Iberian landscape changed profoundly. The changes began in the late eighth century under ʿAbd al-Raḥmān I, who took a keen interest in garden-making and the acquisition of foreign plant species, and they reached a critical point in the early tenth century, just before the reign of ʿAbd al-Raḥmān III. The evidence is confirmed by the image of the constructed landscape proffered by the medieval Andalusian authors themselves in the calendars, botanical treatises, and agricultural manuals.

The economy of agricultural production was a self-perpetuating cycle of profits accrued from trade, invested in agrarian reforms that produced abundant crops and special plants for the export trade, in turn yielding more profits. The profits were reinvested in the land, which yielded greater profits and drove the engine of economic growth. Catalysts such as the arrival of the Dioscorides treatise and caliphal patronage led to the conceptualization of landscape as a resource to be exploited and molded by human will. The confidence in the human ability to master the environment is everywhere apparent in the agricultural literature. It is apparent in the transformation of the natural landscape itself, and it is discernible in the role of nature in the architectural landscape of farms, mansions, palaces, and gardens.

Color Plate 1. The self-contained small garden at Madīnat al-Zahrā' was planned on an intimate scale with a deep water tank and paved paths and coursing channels of water dividing the garden into halves.

Color Plate 2. The Salon Rico at Madīnat al-Zahrā' was a large reception hall with ornately carved stone walls, two rows of white columns bearing brightly colored red and white arches, and a blind niche at the rear of the hall that was called a "mihrab" by contemporary writers.

Color Plate 3. A thick buttress wall supported the man-made esplanade of the upper garden at Madīnat al-Zahrā'. The mirador on its west side had a dramatic view of the lower garden, laid out in a mirror image of the upper garden, and the river valley in the distance.

Color Plate 4. The twelfth-century garden in the Seville Alcazar (in the present-day Casas de Contratación) is divided into deep quadrants that were planted with aromatic plants and flowers. The water channels that coursed along the paved walkways irrigated the garden and appealed to the senses.

Color Plate 5. Although the planting and layout of the garden in the central courtyard of the Aljaferia are modern, the polylobed arcade and pool at the northern end have been accurately restored, giving a sense of the refinement and delicacy of its original decoration.

Color Plate 6. This courtyard is one of the only parts that remains from the eleventh-century Alcazaba of Malaga. The triple-arched portico at the south end of the courtyard opens toward a chamber that leads to a mirador with ornamental arches.

Color Plate 7. The Court of the Lions at the Alhambra is divided cross-axially by paved walkways inlaid with water channels. These rivulets flow from small basins in the pavilions and chambers on the ends and sides of the courtyard toward the central fountain of twelve spewing lions. The tranquillity of the symmetrical composition is enlivened by the water's movement and gentle spray.

Color Plate 8. The water stairway in the Generalife descends through a grove of trees to the Patio de la Sultana. The water that flows in the scalloped channels in the handrails sends up a cool spray that is a welcome refreshment during the hot, dry summer months.

Color Plate 9. The Torre del Mihrab is a small, elegantly decorated prayer hall used by residents of the Partal Palace. Upon entering, the worshipper faces a mihrab niche of carved stucco, but to either side are windows, one pair giving onto the garden, the other pair opening toward a magnificent landscape panorama.

Color Plate 10. A painting in the *Bayāḍ wa Riyāḍ* manuscript represents a garden with trees, plants, and trellised vines. While a hare leaps up the steps, waterfowl swim in a watertank adorned with decorative fountainheads. (Vatican)

Color Plate 11. The Lindaraja Mirador is elevated above a garden and, before the garden walls were raised by the Hapsburg King Charles V, looked over that carefully nurtured garden space toward the distant landscape that lay beyond and below the palace walls.

Color Plate 12. Granada's defensive walls were visible from the north pavilion in the Generalife's Acequía Court. Although most of the views from the Alhambra and Generalife stretched far into the distance, as if to suggest an extensive territory, the Nasrid domains were considerably diminished by this point in Andalusian history.

PART TWO

GARDENS AND ARCHITECTURE

3

PALACES AND ESTATES OF CORDOBA, 711-936

The recreation grounds and celebrated places of Cordoba were like "the scattering of a string of pearls."
—Ibn Saʿīd

An individual garden belongs to a large ecological, topographical, architectural, and historical context, and to understand the significance of any one garden we must look at the entire landscape in the broadest sense. Similarly, to understand innovations such as the planting of extensive and botanically diverse gardens in royal palace estates, it is instructive to look at all the estates built outside of Cordoba during the emirate and before. Their mediating position between the city and country followed the practice of the Romans and the Umayyads of Syria; but the great amount of land cultivated and the new types of plants grown demanded a large-scale investment in waterworks, which allowed denser settlement around the city, which in turn impelled patrons to go farther and farther from the city in search of pleasant, open areas for founding recreation estates.

Several decades ago Karl Wittfogel posited a model of a highly centralized system of irrigation administration based on the notion that the enormous planning and investment required to construct an extensive irrigation system could be accomplished only by a powerful, centralized authority controlling both the source of the water and the labor force needed to build and maintain the canals transporting it.[1] Wittfogel's "hydraulic hypothesis," which purported to explain the rise of early tyrannies, then prompted numerous studies demonstrating the viability of a diametrically opposite, consensus-based model.[2] The value of Wittfogel's model was its insistence that culture was dependent on ecological and technological adaptation. But while Wittfogel regarded the allocation of limited environment resources—primarily water—as the single most important factor determining the organization of human society, other studies have shown that, to the contrary, it is a complex assortment of social factors that shapes the way in which a group of people adapt to an environment. For example, population growth rather than centralized planning may spontaneously propel a society toward investment in irrigation systems and agricultural intensification and innovation in order to make the same amount of land support an increased number of people.[3]

Thomas Glick argued that the essential issue is not who controls the water, but who benefits from the agricultural surpluses that are produced by it. He wrote that Cordoba's prosperity was

due not to the directive of an omnipotent king and a centralized bureaucracy but rather to a chain of events that began with the initial Islamic conquest, which stimulated the Andalusian economy, caused money to circulate, and nourished an urban merchant class, who bought land and made capital investments in the countryside in the form of wells, waterwheels, and canals for irrigation.[4]

By the tenth century the Andalusian landscape was punctuated by developed urban centers, and none was larger than the capital, Cordoba. Cordoba had merchant classes enriched by commerce and by the inflation from the increasing amounts of metal coinage in circulation. Looking for a place to spend their accumulation of excess wealth, they turned to the land around them, buying properties that would yield an annual return on their investment in the form of rent or a marketable crop, and yet that would also provide them with country residences in which to enjoy moments of leisure. Just as the economic excess of the city was taken into the surrounding countryside to be invested in agricultural estates, so the countryside brought its agricultural excess back to the city to be sold in its markets. This pattern of urban investment in the agricultural landscape, which served to bind the city and country socially and economically, is an essential factor in the process of urban expansion that occurred in the Muslim world, and particularly in al-Andalus in the seventh through eleventh centuries.[5]

Emerging from the tradition of farming, gardening, and bucolic pleasures was the constellation of villas built around Cordoba in the eighth, ninth, and tenth centuries. One such estate is variously called a *munya* (pl. *munan*), *qaṣr* (pl. *quṣūr*), and even *muntazah* (pl. *muntazahāt*) in the Arabic histories. While these are easily distinguished from the walled city (*madīna*), it is not always possible to differentiate between a *munya* and a *qaṣr,* or a *munya* and a *muntazah.*

In the Arabic texts, the term *munya* generally refers to a country house that is surrounded by gardens that are agriculturally productive and revenue producing as well as recreational, and that provides a seasonal or temporary residence for the owner.[6] A geographer in the late tenth century who asked, "What is a *munya?*" received the reply, "A garden [*bustān*]."[7] When individual estates are referred to, the word *munya* is always used except in the case of estates containing multiple dwellings where the terms *qaṣr* and *munya* may both be applied to the same site. While *qaṣr* means "palace" or "enclosure," it can also refer to any delimited architectural space, defining that space or building in terms of its restricted physical dimensions.[8] For this reason, a *qaṣr* may contain within its own enclosure smaller enclosures and buildings and may attain the size of a small city, as at the Alhambra or at the Alcazar of Almeria.[9] *Muntazah* means "recreation ground" or "park" and can refer to an uninhabited area of countryside where one can stroll and enjoy nature.[10] It describes not the physical character of the space (as does the word *qaṣr*), but rather, the way that space is perceived and experienced. It is a generic term for any place or *munya* where there are grounds for promenading in fields, through woods, and along streams. For example, Ibn Saʿīd and al-Nuwayrī refer to the *munyas* of Cordoba as "*muntazahāt.*"[11] Other terms such as *dār* (pl. *dūr*), *balāṭ* (pl. *abliṭa*), and *manzil* are less frequently used to describe the residences built outside of Cordoba.

Of the thirty or more estates mentioned by Ibn Bashkuwāl, Ibn Saʿīd, Ibn Ḥayyān, al-Rāzī, al-Ḥimyarī, and others, at least ten can be dated to the first part of ʿAbd al-Raḥmān III's reign, before the building of Madīnat al-Zahrāʾ. At least eleven more were built during the reigns of ʿAbd al-Raḥmān III and al-Ḥakam II, while Madīnat al-Zahrāʾ was under construction. The remainder ap-

pear to have been built either during or after the rule of the ʿAmirid viziers (976–c. 1010); and for a few the date of construction cannot be determined from the sources.

The newer quarters outside Cordoba's walls were looted in 1009–10; today the ruins of those *munyas* lie buried beneath the fields, patios, and walls of modern developments. Although archaeological remains have been excavated here and there, few if any can be matched with actual sites. Complicating the matter further is the fact that the few site identifications proposed in the early part of this century, on the basis of stylistic analysis with dated sites, have since been disproved. Although precise identifications and chronology are impossible, a great deal can be learned from examining the *munyas* as a group.

As agricultural estates, the *munyas* fit into our model of concentric rings of agricultural zones (Fig. 1 on page 12) according to which the most important and most expensive agricultural enterprises occupy the inner rings surrounding the city. The estates were labor intensive with respect to the emphasis on ornamental plants such as roses and violets (which require irrigation), and capital intensive with respect to the enormous expenditures on architecture. It is hardly surprising, therefore, that most of the estates were built in the innermost ring. That tradition was not broken until the late ninth century when the emir ʿAbd Allāh founded his al-Naʿūra estate at a considerable distance from the city. The building of Madīnat al-Zahrāʾ beyond even the outermost of Cordoba's agricultural rings continued that departure, although in a limited sense Madīnat al-Zahrāʾ also became an entirely new center with its own agricultural periphery.

Information on Cordoba's *munyas* comes from three sources. The first is the references to individual sites found in Arabic chronicles, biographies, histories, and poetry.[12] The second is the physical remains in the zone surrounding the walled medina; the area on the western side, in particular, has yielded deposits of ashlar blocks and, more rarely, precious fragments of stucco and marble. The third source is the topography and hydraulic development of the landscape of the Guadalquivir Valley.

Roman and Visigothic Palaces

The Cordoban taste for country estates may owe something to the Roman legacy of villas built along the fertile plains of the Guadalquivir River valley (and others). In the province of Cordoba the remains of sixteen Roman villas have been surveyed and excavated; there were even more such villas near Seville where the Roman cities of Itálica and Carmona were situated. In the outskirts of the city of Seville alone, medieval Cordobans and travelers to Cordoba might have seen 194 villas, or whatever was left of them.[13] At least two had peristyle gardens and water pools, one at the site known as the Fuente de las Piedras in Cabra (Cordoba Province) and the other known as El Santiscal in Arcos de la Frontera (in Cadix Province but along a well-traveled road between Seville and the coast).

What impression did such estates, probably already half ruined in the eighth century, make on the newly arrived Muslims? Medieval Arabic historians and geographers were interested in Roman, Byzantine, and Visigothic history, as is evident from Ibn ʿIdhārī's chapter on the history of the

conquest of al-Andalus.[14] They occasionally noted Roman architectural remains, such as Merida's bridge, palace, and temples, and Idrīsī mentioned Toledo's "curious" aqueduct, although he did not identify it as Roman.[15] But in general, such references to Roman and Visigothic architecture are the exception rather than the rule, suggesting that the Roman and Visigothic layers underlying the Islamic cultural and architectural landscape were not foremost in that society's consciousness.[16]

There are, nonetheless, instances of the reuse of Roman and Visigothic architectural elements and sculptures in a variety of Islamic buildings in Spain: stone capitals in the Mosque of Bibi Mardum in Toledo, a Roman sarcophagus at Madīnat al-Zahrā᾿, and stone slabs carved with Visigothic ornamentation at the Alcazaba of Merida. Two columns were found at a site along the road to Castillo de la Albaida, two kilometers northwest of Cordoba, both pertaining to an Islamic palace but the capital of one of them of Visigothic manufacture.[17] The presence of spolia in Islamic buildings, in addition to being a sensible reuse of valuable materials, connoted the subsuming of the older civilization through its material remains into the new Islamic society. But this connotative level of meaning did not extend to the way in which these building elements were used. While Hispano-Islamic architecture owed a great debt to the Visigoths, the debt was entirely at the morphological level. Forms such as the horseshoe arches of the Cordoba Mosque were extracted from the Visigothic typological context, where they had been employed individually to mark the opening of apsidal niches and portals; they were then used in the entirely different context of the hypostyle mosque, deployed en masse for the effect of infinite continuity and spatial homogeneity. Thus Visigothic forms were used but were thoroughly Islamicized in the process.[18]

The other architectural traditions consciously evoked by Andalusian builders were Syrian. These references complicate the question of the Roman legacy of Hispano-Islamic architecture because Syria too had been settled and built upon by the Romans. The Roman architectural sublayer is in fact so ubiquitous in the Mediterranean that it is difficult to distinguish between instances where a Hispano-Islamic form was derived from Roman Syria (where the Umayyad capital city of Damascus was located), and where such a form was inspired by regional Iberian prototypes.[19] Indeed, the eclecticism of Islamic art is well documented; the art is a lively admixture of Roman, Byzantine, Sasanian, and Visigothic techniques, forms, and motifs in which the sources are rarely acknowledged. However, on the ideological level, when Islamic historians and geographers praised an Andalusian city by likening it to any other city, the reference was always to the east, and usually to Damascus or Baghdad. When a palace was similarly praised, and perhaps compared with the palace of some ancient ruler, it was likened to one of the famous palaces of Solomon or another figure incorporated within the Islamic tradition.[20] The Hispano-Umayyad interest in history was not directed toward the ancient Roman monuments and kings of the Iberian Peninsula, but to the fabulous, often mythical historical figures and places of the Islamic heartlands that, like al-Andalus, were former Roman provinces. Thus it is difficult to assess whether Andalusian builders mined the vocabulary of Roman or of Syrian decorative motifs and architectural typology in al-Andalus.

The first palace inhabited by the invading Muslims was the Alcazar of Cordoba (Fig. 2). It, or at least some palace on the same site, had been there at least as early as the Visigothic period. In the twelfth century Ibn Bashkuwāl described it as an agglomeration of structures built by the Byzantines, Romans, Visigoths, "and bygone peoples impossible to describe."[21] It may have been the

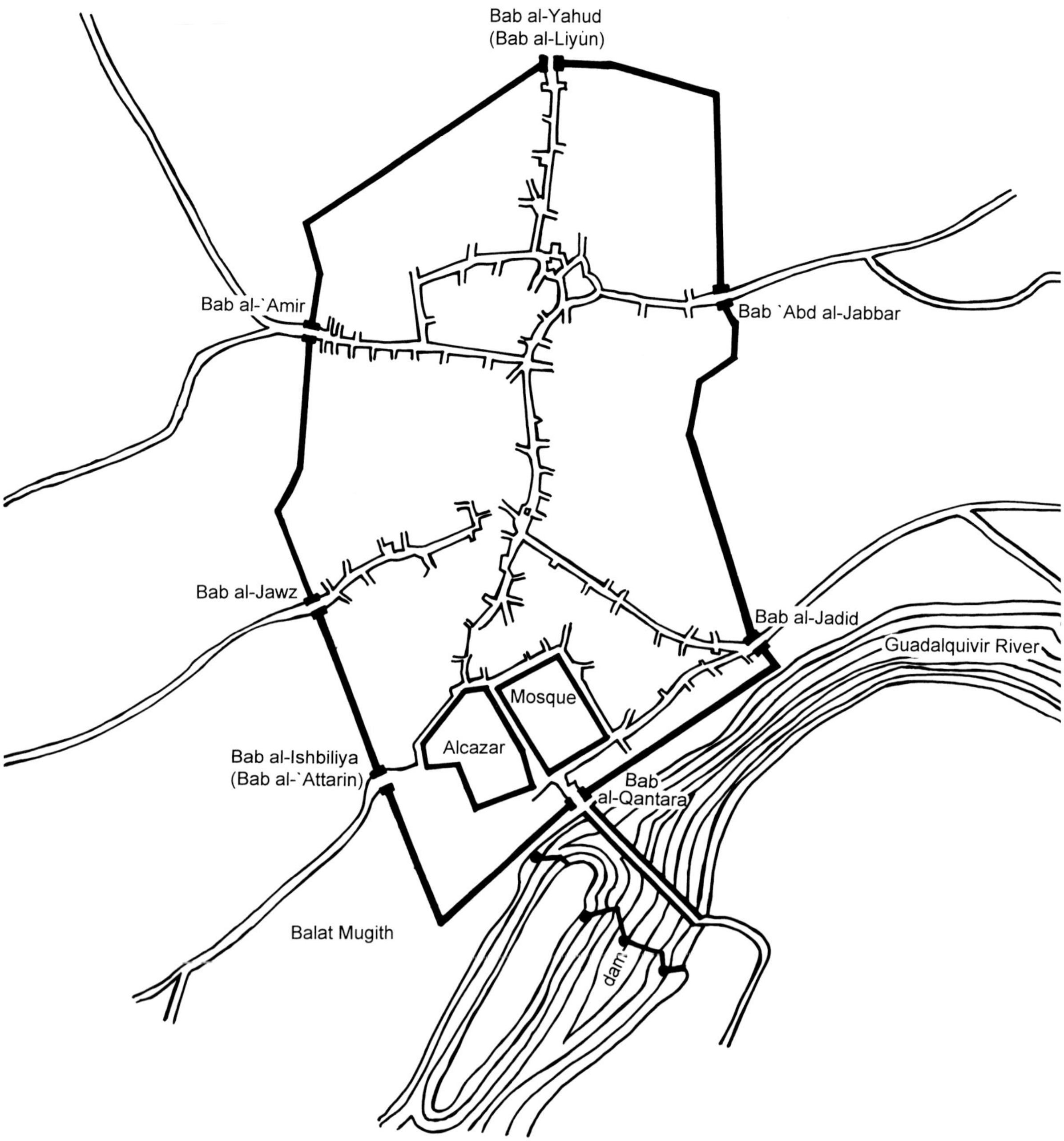

2. Plan of Cordoba showing the location of the Alcazar and the Balāṭ Mughīth.

palace of the last Visigothic king, Roderic, described by early authors. According to the foundation myth, one day when the Visigothic king was hunting in the woods where Cordoba was eventually to be founded, a hawk that he was pursuing descended into a thicket. When the thicket was cleared to release the bird, a magnificent stone building was revealed, which the king immediately perceived to be the work of a great ancient ruler. He ordered the building restored and made it his

temporary residence, thus inducing his subjects to settle there and to create the city that became Cordoba.[22] According to the anonymous eleventh-century *Akhbār majmūʿa,* when Mughīth, who was leader of an Arab-Berber battalion, attacked and conquered the city in 93/711, he chose as his residence the "balāṭ qurṭuba" (palace of Cordoba). From there he sent word of his victory to the governor of Morocco, Ṭāriq ibn Ziyād, who served under the authority of Mūsā ibn Nuṣayr, the governor of the entire Maghreb and Ifriqiya.[23] When Mūsā arrived in Cordoba, however, he appropriated the palace, forcing Mughīth to move to a house near the Algeciras Gate.[24] Thus the texts describe two residences, one of which was presumably the pre-Islamic building that became the Alcazar, or *qaṣr,* of the Muslims. Admittedly, even the earliest account of the palace was written 250 years after the events described. What is important here is not the detail but the assertion by later authors that the Muslim governor appropriated the Visigothic palace.

The Balāṭ Mughīth, to which Mughīth moved, was a magnificent house on the southwest side of Cordoba, outside the city walls and near the great bridge. Ibn Ḥayyān said that Mughīth built it following a trip to Damascus.[25] However, the author of the *Akhbār Majmūʿa* gave a slightly different account, according to which Mūsā forced Mughīth to move to the house by the Algeciras Gate, explaining that the house had been the property of the deposed Visigothic king, and that it acquired the name of the Balāṭ Mughīth only after passing into Mughīth's hands. This more plausible account explains the palace's privileged position just outside the walls of the medina almost adjacent to the Alcazar.[26] The anonymous account also gave it the name al-Yuṣṣāna and claimed that it was an excellent palace with olive and fruit trees and abundant water, probably drawn directly from the river.[27]

Although the palace was not called a *munya,* it was a forerunner of later garden estates and deserves to be included among them. Like a *munya,* it was built outside the old Roman city walls, and as with the *munyas*, the description of its gardens was given priority over its architecture. When the city grew beyond the perimeter of the medina walls in the tenth century, the Balāṭ Mughīth became the center of a populous suburb, but in the period of the Visigoths and the first Arab governors, the extramural landscape of Cordoba was still relatively undeveloped. The Balāṭ Mughīth is important evidence that the Cordoban taste for country residences built amid gardens and orchards predated the arrival of the Arabs and Berbers.

Both the Balāṭ Mughīth and the Alcazar were Visigothic palaces appropriated by the Muslims. If the Visigothic gubernatorial palace had been demolished to make way for a new alcazar, the Andalusian historians surely would have taken the opportunity (as on so many other occasions) to praise the new Islamic palace; the fact that they did not do so leads to the conclusion that the older building served continuously as the Islamic governor's palace. The first gubernatorial palace in Islamic Cordoba was of Visigothic origin and it was on a Visigothic foundation that newer structures were added in the following centuries.

The Alcazar stood inside the walls of Cordoba at the southwest corner of the medina, adjacent to the congregational mosque. Until Madīnat al-Zahrāʾ supplanted it, the Alcazar was the seat of government, containing the emiral palace, various reception halls, and administrative offices. It was a place both of business and recreation, adorned by graceful halls and gardens with basins and pools, and it was there that the Umayyads first experimented with garden-making on Iberian soil,

later transplanting to *munyas* outside the city walls what they had learned. The confining walls of the Alcazar and the medina did not permit endless construction of spacious halls with central courtyard gardens, which was the basic unit of the Mediterranean Islamic palace. To preserve the architecture-garden equation, builders of wholly new palaces sought new sites in the uncluttered countryside beyond the city walls. In this undeveloped landscape the equation relaxed; more emphasis was placed on gardens, which became larger and more numerous, even to the point of including entire orchards.

The Islamic Alcazar was a conglomeration of several palaces contained within one walled enclosure; it occupied a far greater area than the "new" Alcazar, which stands on a part of the old site today. In the eleventh century al-ʿUdhrī wrote that it measured eleven hundred cubits in circumference, occupying approximately one-sixth of the medina, which may be accepted as reasonably accurate if the gardens to the southwest of the complex were included.[28] Its principal facade was on the south side facing the river and overlooking a great paved esplanade called al-Hassā.[29]

The Alcazar could be entered either on the south side through its main gate, called the Bāb al-Sudda, which overlooked the river and led straight into the administrative quarters, or through the Bāb al-Jinān (Gate of the Gardens).[30] It could also be entered on the east side either through the Bāb al-Jāmiʿ (Gate of the Congregational Mosque) or through the Bāb al-ʿAdl (Gate of Justice), situated above the passageway that connected the palace with the congregational mosque.[31] On the north side were the Bāb al-Ḥadīd (Iron Gate), Bāb al-Wādī (Gate of the Stream) and a postern gate called the Bāb al-Qariya (Gate to the Village or Orchard), linked to a gate of the same name in the medina.[32]

The allocation of administrative and residential spaces within the Alcazar is not well known.[33] A separate garden zone was irrigated by water brought from the mountains of Cordoba in abundant amounts, and circulated through the palace by means of lead pipes or lead-lined channels. The pipes entered the Alcazar precinct on the north side, ran through each and every courtyard and emerged to fill fountains, large tanks, and lovely ornamental basins outside.[34] Ibn Khaldūn wrote that the emirs Muḥammad I, ʿAbd al-Raḥmān II, and ʿAbd Allāh were avid builders, erecting palaces of perfection and grandeur in the Alcazar, among them al-Bahw (the Spacious), al-Kāmil (the Perfect), al-Munīf (the Eminent), and the Majlis al-Zāhir (Hall of Splendor).[35] Next to the latter ʿAbd al-Raḥmān III built the Dār al-Rawḍa (Garden Palace), although it may have stood outside the walls of the Alcazar.

More is known about al-Kāmil than about the other palaces because it is there that the councillors of the government debated who should succeed ʿAbd al-Raḥmān II (d. 238/852). When the successor was chosen, a messenger was sent with the announcement through the Bāb al-Jinān on the south facade of the Alcazar to where the emir's sons were housed outside the Alcazar. This tells us that al-Kāmil was built prior to 852 and that it stood within the Alcazar's enclosure walls, probably in the southern part of the palace complex.[36]

The chronology and architectural form of the various palaces within the Alcazar, their locations within the complex, and their relationship to one another are all obscure. Ascertaining the precise location of each palace is complicated by the fact that until ʿAbd al-Raḥman III moved the court and administration to Madīnat al-Zahrā', each ruler redecorated and added to the Alcazar. An account of the breaking of the Ramadan fast in the summer of 364/975 shows the degree of crowding in the

old palatial complex.[37] In the ceremony, al-Ḥakam held an audience in the west hall of the Dār al-Rawḍa while his son and designated heir, Hishām, received guests in the Majlis al-Zāhir. Viziers waited in the Dār al-Kāmil before entering the halls, the Qurayshi and Umayyad families waited in the Bayt al-Wizāra, and the *mawlas* (dependents) waited in the main hall of a building known as the Balāṭ al-Rīḥ, while the judiciary waited in its gallery. For lack of space, apparently, audiences were held in small groups in the Alcazar.

The Alcazar was inhabited and remodeled from the eighth through the tenth century. However, when ʿAbd al-Raḥmān I had first arrived from Syria to become emir in 756, the Alcazar was unimproved from its state forty-five years earlier, when Mūsā and his lieutenant Mughīth lived there. The antiquated palace that served adequately for the Umayyad's appointed governors was either not impressive enough for the grandson of the last Umayyad caliph of Damascus or not suitable to his Syrian taste. He therefore built himself a new palace, Munyat al-Ruṣāfa, outside of Cordoba, naming it and modeling it after his grandfather's estate near Raqqa in Syria where the prince had lived as a child.[38]

The Ruṣāfa Palace

The Munyat al-Ruṣāfa was the first palace in Cordoba to be built new by the Muslims, and it dates to the reign of ʿAbd al-Raḥmān I (138/756–172/788).[39] Variously called a *qaṣr* and a *munya* by the chroniclers, Ruṣāfa was located three kilometers northwest of Cordoba on the edge of a stream running down from the mountains. The area is still known today as Arruzafa and was excavated by Rafael Castejón before a tourist hotel was built there.[40]

Although the excavations did not reveal the presence of gardens, pools, or water channels, the Arabic sources describe Ruṣāfa as a beautiful palace with an ample garden stocked with rare and wonderful plants and handsome trees brought from afar. Perhaps some of the plants were intended to remind the patron of other places, such as ʿAbd al-Raḥmān I's native Syria. Various Arabic historians quote a poignant poem that ʿAbd al-Raḥmān reportedly composed in Ruṣāfa when he was homesick for the days and places of his youth:

> A palm tree stands in the middle of Ruṣāfa, born in the West, far from the land of palms.
> I said to it: "How like me you are, far away and in exile, in long separation from family
> and friends.
> You have sprung from soil in which you are a stranger; and I, like you, am far from home.
> May dawn's clouds water you, streaming from the heavens in a grateful downpour."[41]

In the Syrian Ruṣāfa, as in its Andalusian echo, gardens played a prominent role. There, south of the walled Byzantine city, a team of German excavators recently found the remains of a palatial complex of stone that included, slightly to the southwest, a large irregular enclosure with a raised square stone pavilion in a quadripartite garden irrigated by a winding stream (Fig. 3).[42] They identified the complex as the palace of the Umayyad caliph Hishām (105/724–125/743), making its garden the earliest dated and excavated cross-axial example in the Islamic world.[43] The fact that Ibn

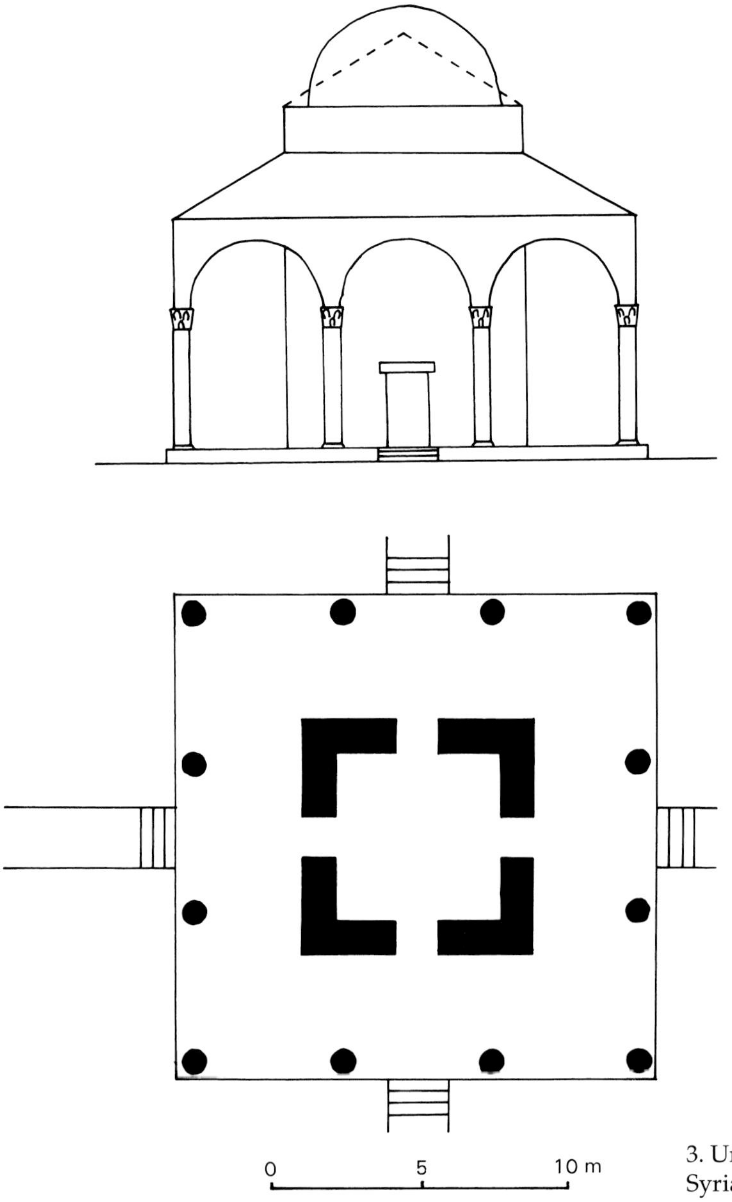

3. Umayyad garden in Ruṣāfa, Syria (after T. Ulbert)

Saʿīd explicitly stated that the Ruṣāfa of Cordoba was named and modeled after the Syrian Ruṣāfa, and this after a lengthy description of its gardens, suggests that this first Hispano-Islamic estate owed its emphasis on gardens in part to Syrian precedents.[44]

The Syrian Ruṣāfa was cross-axially planned with a centrally placed pavilion; perhaps, if the Cordoban Ruṣāfa was similarly laid out, it was the direct link in the transmission of these design principles from Syria to Spain. The Arab elite in al-Andalus were from Syria (or were the children of Syrian émigrés) and would have been familiar with these garden ideas. This manner of transmission is perfectly plausible, but it is not provable, simply because there is no archaeological evi-

dence for the presence of a cross-axial plan at the Cordoban Ruṣāfa. In the absence of archaeological excavations, there is no information about the plan of any garden in Cordoba before Madīnat al-Zahrā', founded in the tenth century. However, the discoveries in Syria are conclusive in one respect; they point to Arab, rather than Persian (as previously supposed), precedents for the quadripartite layout that eventually become ubiquitous in royal Islamic gardens.

The Cordoban Ruṣāfa had three significant features: it had gardens, it was located away from the city, and it complemented the Alcazar as a royal residence. Ibn Saʿīd remarked that Ruṣāfa was built as a site for recreation, but that ʿAbd al-Raḥmān I loved it so much, he abandoned the urban Alcazar to live in Ruṣāfa for most of the rest of his life.[45] Ruṣāfa became his primary residence, where he conducted governmental business,[46] the first instance of a Muslim ruler in Spain transferring a large portion of the government from the Alcazar to a new palace at a distance from the city. The precedent for such a shift came from Umayyad practice in Syria, where rulers moved easily between the countryside and the city. So long as Cordoba was the capital of al-Andalus, the Umayyad princes continued to return seasonally to the Alcazar but to live as much as possible in Ruṣāfa, which was inhabited and expanded at least until the middle of the ninth century, and the newer palace estates. The Alcazar's central location in the medina and next to the congregational mosque was advantageous, but its buildings did not suit the Umayyad architectural ambitions, and so all the Umayyad rulers built or acquired large estates outside the crowded medina. Ruṣāfa was the first of these *munya*s and became a prototype for Hispano-Umayyad exurban palace construction.

One of Ruṣāfa's architectural features that appeared in subsequent palace estates was its emphasis on nature. That Ibn Saʿīd praised the gardens of Ruṣāfa more than its buildings suggests that they were more spectacular and innovative than was the architecture; indeed, most of his account is devoted to the story of how ʿAbd al-Raḥmān sent his agents abroad to procure exotic plants and trees.[47] The priority of gardens is one of the features of al-Ruṣāfa that appeared in all subsequent Hispano-Umayyad palaces, and with it, a dependence on an artificially augmented supply of water to support the extensive cultivation of domestic and exotic plants. In some instances, the fountains and pools of a *munya* are described in detail; in others the presence of water is merely implied by the mention of verdant vegetation; but in all cases, palace and *munya* gardens depended on irrigation fed by water from wells or aqueducts.

The *munya* builders of Cordoba followed the precedent set by ʿAbd al-Raḥmān I at Ruṣāfa, building away from city noise and congestion and away from the limitations imposed by an already crowded medina. But, just as ʿAbd al-Raḥmān could not withdraw too far from the capital and the old Alcazar, where government offices that did not require his direct supervision continued to function, so later *munya* builders had to stay within reach of the city's markets and central services. Ruṣāfa and subsequent *munya*s were all situated near the city but not in or next to it. Although urban progeny, *munya*s were preferred over urban residences because, removed from the noise and congestion of the city, suburban life was more conducive to the enjoyment of art and literature, essential aspects of the leisurely life of the aristocracy.

Ruṣāfa and its aqueduct stimulated new development and attracted people to the area north of Cordoba. By the ninth century Ruṣāfa was a prosperous neighborhood of villas and at the end of

the century was endowed with a mosque by an Umayyad princess;[48] in the mid-tenth century it elicited praise from the normally disparaging Ibn Ḥawqal.[49] Although with the passing of time, new royal estates were built on the west and east sides of the city, supplanting Ruṣāfa, the palace of ʿAbd al-Raḥmān I was not entirely abandoned. As the number of diplomatic visits from abroad increased, Ruṣāfa and other royal estates were used to house important guests: in 351/946 an envoy from an anti-Fatimid leader in Tunisia stayed there, and during the reign of al-Ḥakam II, the defeated Ordoño IV of León was housed in Ruṣāfa as a special sign of hospitality and the honor befitting his rank.[50] Ruṣāfa continued to serve until it was burned in 401/1010.[51]

Emiral and Caliphal Estates

Ruṣāfa marked the northern limit of the expansion of Cordoba. Also on the north side was the Faḥṣ al-Surādiq (Fig. 4), built sometime before 306/971.[52] Although the Faḥṣ itself was used primarily for military assemblies and parades, Ibn Saʿīd called it a *muntazah* (recreation ground).[53] Given the military aspect of the site, it is unlikely that the Faḥṣ al-Surādiq included gardens or constituted a residential estate.[54]

South of Cordoba, the Munyat ʿAjab was built in the early ninth century on the bank of the Guadalquivir opposite the mosque (Fig. 4). It was founded by (or possibly named for) ʿAjab, the wife of al-Ḥakam I, as a *waqf* (charitable endowment), the agricultural produce of which was assigned to the nearby leper colony.[55] A suburb of abundant gardens and a large cemetery, called the cemetery of the Arrabal, grew up around the Munyat ʿAjab, but traces of it have been obliterated by the shift of the Guadalquivir's course toward the southwest.[56] That the southern zone did not subsequently develop as much as the rest of Cordoba's outskirts was not due to the proximity of the leper colony, but because the area to the southeast, known as al-Rabaḍ (literally "the suburb") was razed by al-Ḥakam I after its inhabitants revolted in 202/818 and he forbade them to rebuild.[57] As a result, while Cordoba expanded to the north, west, and east, its new suburbs often forming around centers such as *munyas*, no such centers were established in inauspicious al-Rabaḍ. Whereas we have already seen the importance of royal patronage in stimulating agronomy, science, and agriculture, al-Rabaḍ is an example of antipatronage and demonstrates in a negative capacity the influence of the emir.

On the opposite bank was the Munyat al-Naṣr, situated where the river twisted around al-Rabaḍ, southeast of the medina (Fig. 4).[58] Dating to the reign of ʿAbd al-Raḥmān II (822–52), it was built by and named for the emir's favorite eunuch-slave, Naṣr. Although the estate was cultivated and inhabited in the reign of ʿAbd al-Raḥmān II, it must have been substantially rebuilt in the reign of his grandson ʿAbd Allāh (r. 888–912) because al-Ḥimyarī attributed it to him. He described this *munya,* known also as the Arḥāʾ al-Ḥinnāʾ, or "henna mills," as a spacious city (*madīna*) with remarkable constructions within an olive grove called al-Rakīn along the river in its southeast corner. The space between the river and al-Rakīn was frequented by drinkers and promenaders who enjoyed the cool breezes off the river. Al-Ḥimyarī wrote that a poet sighed, when absent from Cordoba:

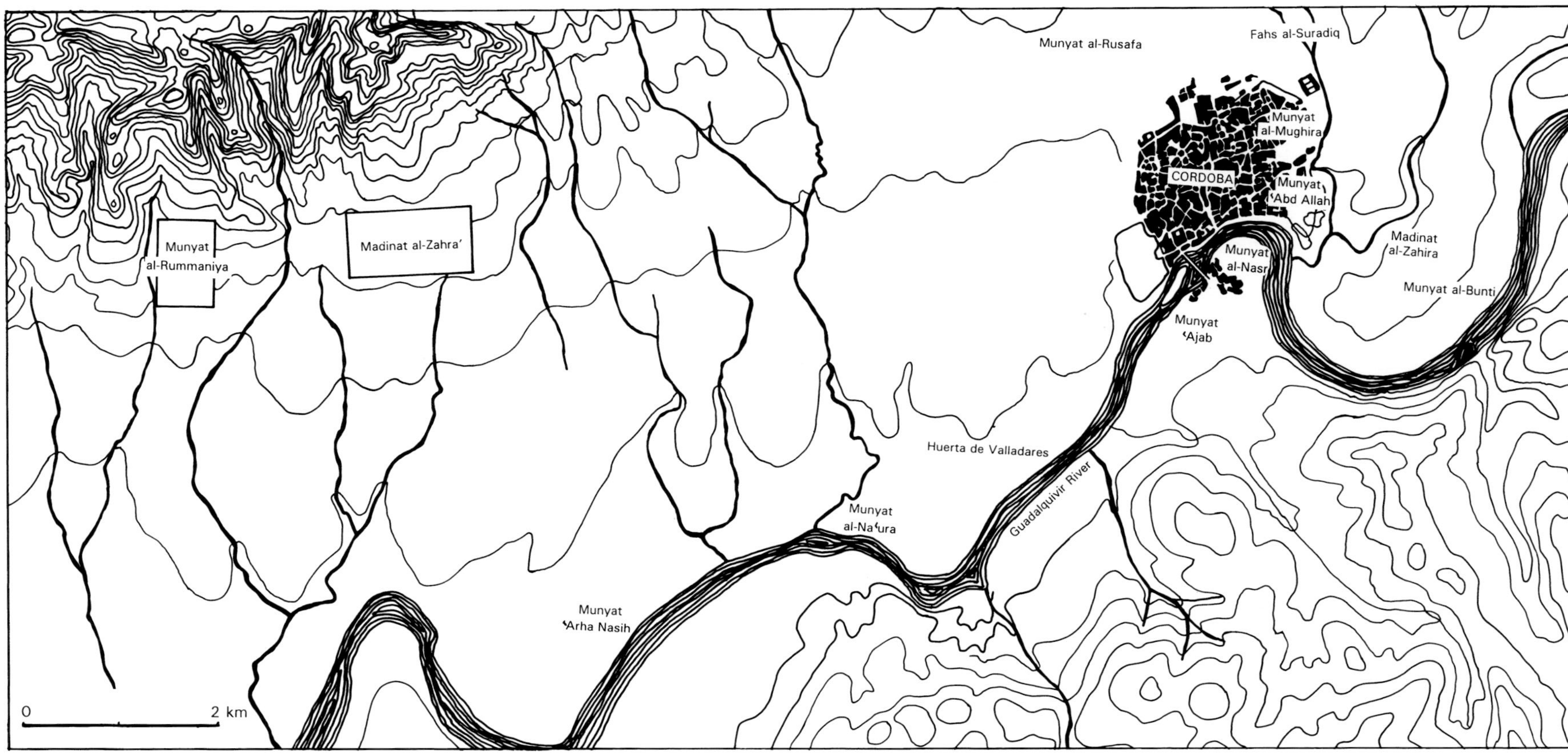

4. Plan of Cordoba and surrounding estates, 711–936

"Give my regards to Rakīn," and he said to it: "since you are absent, I cannot find repose in the breeze's shade.
May rain enhance your shade and the coolness of your water, morning and evening, when the cruel hot wind blows."[59]

Another poem indicates that the *munya*'s buildings, surrounded by gardens, were visible from Cordoba.[60] After the death of the slave, it appears to have served as the residence for the celebrated courtier and singer Ziryāb,[61] and then in time it passed to the emir ʿAbd Allāh and his heirs, who used it as a guest house for important visitors such as the Byzantine ambassador in 338/949 and the embassy from Barcelona in the summer of 971.[62]

ʿAbd al-Raḥmān II built many palaces and *munya*s in addition to the Munyat al-Naṣr.[63] He was reputedly the first emir to bring fresh drinking water to Cordoba, introducing it first into his palaces and from there, letting the excess collect in a large tank from which the public could help themselves.[64] The medieval historians, instead of chastising the pleasure-loving ʿAbd al-Raḥmān II for his enormous expenditures and for removing himself from contact with the people of Cordoba, praised his architectural patronage as a pious act. Clearly, in their eyes, emiral beneficence that served him also benefited Islam and his people.

On the east side of Cordoba was the Munyat al-Buntī, or Alpontiello. The only reference to it is in Ibn Ḥayyān, who relates that in 300/913 ʿAbd al-Raḥmān III went hunting at Alpontiello accompanied by a distinguished cortege.[65] This may provide the identification for the archaeological remains found on the east side of Cordoba in the area of al-Rambla and Balīsh. Although it cannot be proved conclusively, the *munya* probably does not date any later than the reign of ʿAbd al-Raḥmān II (r. 206/822–238/852), because thereafter ʿAbd Allāh is not known to have built any *munya*s besides the one bearing his name; since ʿAbd al-Raḥmān III was only twenty-two years of age when he became emir in 300/912, and al-Buntī already existed by 913, it is unlikely that he was the estate's patron. The documentation for his reign is ample and even an early building project would not have eluded the historical record. The Munyat al-Buntī was probably built by someone other than an emir, or if by an emir, either ʿAbd al-Raḥmān II or his son, Muḥammad I, the former being more likely, since he was known for building palaces and recreation estates.

An additional Cordoban palace, not necessarily the residence of an emir, was described by the poet ʿAbbās ibn Firnas in the time of ʿAbd al-Raḥmān II. He described it as having arches like full moons supported on columns, palm trees extending their fronds to show off their clusters of fruit.[66] Muḥammad I (r. 852–86) built or made substantial additions to an estate named the Munyat al-Kantish to the west of Cordoba, planting it with fruit trees and endowing it with lovely pavilions. It was situated on the riverbank some distance along the Cordoba-Seville road in the old Roman quarter of Quintus, hence the Arabic corruption "Kantish."[67]

ʿAbd Allāh's Estates

ʿAbd Allāh's name is associated with three estates. The Munyat ʿAbd Allāh belonged to the suburbs on east side of Cordoba, possibly located in what later became the garden of San Pablo or the garden

of San Augustín (Fig. 4).[68] His two favorites were the Munyat al-Naṣr and the Munyat al-Naʿūra. Although the Munyat al-Naṣr had been built at least thirty-five years before he acquired it, ʿAbd Allāh placed his architectural stamp on its buildings. According to Ibn Ḥayyān, "He took great care with this *munya* and did not hold back from any expense in its embellishment. He improved the construction, introduced new ornamentation in the buildings, and increased the flow of water to the cisterns."[69] The Munyat al-Naʿūra stood on the banks of the river west of Cordoba next to the suburban esplanade (*faḥṣ*) of al-Muṣāra (Fig. 4). Ibn Ḥayyān wrote: "He bought it in the days of his father, the emir Muḥammad. He planted it and made it into a handsome orchard, amply laid out, since his wish was to make his estate pleasant and delightful. To this end he enlarged it and planted it with trees and plants, and he was prudent in his expenditures. At the same time he had the deed to the land which included the grounds and their surroundings, acquired from Khalīl al-Bayṭār in the year 253 [867]."[70]

The Estates of ʿAbd al-Raḥmān III

ʿAbd Allāh's grandson, ʿAbd al-Raḥmān III al-Nāṣir, was the greatest and most innovative of the Umayyad builders. He can be associated with three estates: Ibn Shuhayd's villa, the Dār al-Rawḍa, and the Munyat al-Naʿūra; as well as with the great palace city of Madīnat al-Zahrāʾ (Fig. 4).

Ibn Shuhayd's villa was a large estate with extensive forests and was probably located at some distance from the city, whose suburbs had become built up by the time of ʿAbd al-Raḥmān III's reign. The fact that it is called a *qariya* (village, hamlet, or villa) rather than a *munya* indicates that it was not within the immediate suburbs of Cordoba. Ibn Khaldūn recounted that in 327/939 the poet gave ʿAbd al-Raḥmān "a villa [*qariya*] yielding many thousands of *mudd* of grain and with stone buildings. In one year it provided a profit of eighty-thousand dinars and twenty-thousand of the most handsome trees of the most durable and straight wood, valued at fifty-thousand dinars."[71] Ibn al-Faraḍī related that Ibn Shuhayd bought the estate in its completed form with buildings, waterworks, cultivated fields, orchards, and thick forests. Ibn Shuhayd himself wrote that the yield of the estate's forests was "so abundant that when his [ʿAbd al-Raḥmān III's] servant Ibn Khalīl wanted upwards of three hundred and twenty thousand trees, and could only procure about two thousand every year, I undertook to furnish him the remainder out of this estate."[72]

Although the numerical assessments conflict, the universal emphasis on yield in these accounts indicates that lumber was in great demand. At precisely this time, architects, carpenters, and masons were building Madīnat al-Zahrāʾ, the largest construction in tenth-century al-Andalus, and Ibn Shuhayd's villa undoubtedly provided vast quantities of wood necessary for door panels, screens, furnishings, roofs, temporary scaffolding, and the permanent bracing in walls.[73] Although the fact that it was not mentioned in al-Maqqarī's extraordinarily detailed account of Madīnat al-Zahrāʾ's construction may appear to argue against this, the silence of the sources with respect to the origin of the wood only confirms that it was obtained locally and thus unworthy of comment.

The estate passed into ʿAbd al-Raḥmān's hands during the early years of Madīnat al-Zahrāʾ's construction, and the reason for the lavish gift was manifestly political. The same year, ʿAbd al-

Raḥmān doubled Ibn Shuhayd's income and bestowed upon him the title of *dhū al-wizāratayn* (double vizier), making him the highest-ranking official in al-Andalus.[74] If the gift of the villa was an attempt to curry favor with the caliph, it achieved the desired results.

The second of the estates associated with ʿAbd al-Raḥmān is the Dār al-Rawḍa (House of the Garden). On the western side of Cordoba there was a suburb called the Rabaḍ al-Rawḍa, presumably associated with this palace.[75] Ibn Khaldūn wrote:

> In the Alcazar was the Majlis al-Zāhir, al-Bahw, al-Kāmil, and al-Munīf, and on the side of al-Zāhir he [ʿAbd al-Raḥmān III] built his great palace, which he called Dār al-Rawḍa. He brought water to the palaces and from all the quarters of the earth he summoned master architects and artisans who came to him from Baghdad and Constantinople, and he set about building the recreation estates. After that, he busied himself with the Munyat al-Naʿūra outside the palaces.[76]

The distinction that Ibn Khaldūn makes between the other halls and the *dār* points to the difference between mere segments of buildings and a larger residence.[77] However, he does not give a precise location for the Dār al-Rawḍa and indeed, writing as a latter-day historian rather than as a contemporary observer, may not have known. The eyewitness al-Rāzī was no clearer. He recounted that al-Ḥakam received guests at the breaking of the Ramadan fast in 364/975 in the west hall of the Dār al-Rawḍa, while Crown Prince Hishām received in the Majlis al-Zāhir of the Alcazar, but he did not indicate whether the Dār al-Rawḍa was part of the Alcazar or distinct from it.[78]

The secondary sources are equally confusing. Lévi-Provençal wrote that the Dār al-Rawḍa was built within the walls of the Alcazar but elsewhere that the Dār al-Rawḍa was in a western suburb adjacent to the Marwanid cemetery in the interior of the Alcazar.[79] In the first statement, Lévi-Provençal claimed that the Alcazar was already so built up that older buildings must have been demolished to clear space for the new Dār al-Rawḍa, but neither Ibn Khaldūn nor al-Maqqarī suggest anything of the sort. Perhaps the confusion lies not in the texts themselves, but in our understanding of the layout and confines of the Alcazar.

The Alcazar was certainly too crowded to allow the insertion of a large structure such as the Dār al-Rawḍa without the removal of other structures. But since no demolitions are recorded, it is quite possible that the palace was not built within the Alcazar but rather was appended onto the side, as Ibn Khaldūn literally put it—"ilā jānib al-zāhir" (to the side of al-Zāhir)—either in the space between the Alcazar and the gardens on the southwest side or in the gardens themselves. A diagram following one made by Lévi-Provençal shows how such an extension would have been possible (Fig. 5). Although walls in medieval Islamic cities were generally fixed and not removed even when the population expanded beyond their perimeters, that part of the city wall dividing the Alcazar from the its gardens and orchards was already pierced by gates, and since it was incorporated into the body of the Alcazar it might well have been removed to allow the expansion of the palace, as the diagram suggests. Equally possible is that the wall remained physically intact but ceased to act as a barrier, so that the Dār al-Rawḍa, although built outside the walls in the strict sense of the word, could by means of doors still have been considered part of the Alcazar.

The Dār al-Rawḍa marked the first step in ʿAbd al-Raḥmān's architectural campaign moving

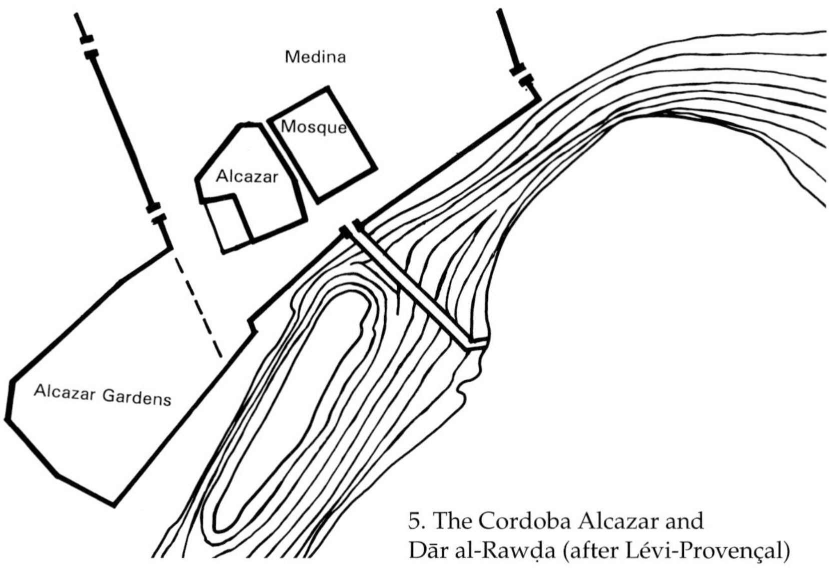

5. The Cordoba Alcazar and Dār al-Rawḍa (after Lévi-Provençal)

west from the Alcazar to the Munyat al-Naʿūra and to Madīnat al-Zahrāʾ. The Dār al-Rawḍa was too much a part of the city to be a true *munya,* but it stood in a garden zone with piped water and initiated a new type of palace in which the rusticity of a *munya* was blended with the urbanity of a palace.

Until moving to Madīnat al-Zahrāʾ, ʿAbd al-Raḥmān III made the Munyat al-Naʿūra ("noria," or waterwheel) his chief residence. He launched military campaigns from there and conducted business in the palace, including the execution of war captives.[80] The estate was enormous, having some thirty buildings and an open area in front for large gatherings.[81] Indeed, the fact that al-Rāzī called it *qaṣr* as well as *munya* is an indication of its size and importance.[82] The best eastern architects and masons were brought to build and decorate the palace, and thus when exquisitely carved fragments of stone decoration were found by Rafael Castejón in the site called Alcaide in 1957, he naturally believed that he had discovered the site of Munyat al-Naʿūra.[83]

One of the engineering wonders of al-Naʿūra mentioned by all the medieval Arabic authors was its water system, consisting of pools, canals, an impressive aqueduct, and a waterwheel:

> At the beginning of this year [329/940], al-Nāsir finished the construction of the extraordinary man-made aqueduct that brought fresh water from the mountains to the Qaṣr al-Naʿūra on the west side of Cordoba. Water flowed through fabricated channels on a fantastic arrangement of connecting arches, emptying into a large pool at the edge of which was a lion enormous in size, unique in design, and fearful in appearance. . . . It was plated with gold and its eyes were two brilliantly sparkling jewels. Water entered through the rear of the lion and was spewed into the pool. It was dazzling to behold in its splendor and magnificence and its copious outpouring, and the palace's entire range of gardens were irrigated by its juices which flowed over the grounds and surrounding area.[84]

Although Madīnat al-Zahrāʾ eventually eclipsed the Munyat al-Naʿūra, ʿAbd al-Raḥmān III never lost interest in it. In 326/937–38, a year after work was begun on al-Zahrāʾ, he ordered that the road running along the river between al-Naʿūra and the Alcazar of Cordoba be paved to make it passable during the muddy winter months, which shows that the traffic between the two was heavy enough to warrant such an expense, despite the drain on resources caused by the constructions at Madīnat al-Zahrāʾ.[85] Four years later he built another paved road to unite Munyat al-Naʿūra with Madīnat al-Zahrāʾ; it was finished in one month "to the great benefit of his new residence called al-Zahrāʾ."[86]

A large estate such as al-Naʿūra, heavily capitalized with investments such as the irrigation system and agricultural improvements, was one of the profitable enterprises that supported the caliph's ambitious architectural objectives elsewhere, and the economic vitality of such an enterprise was unchallenged when the patron's whims led him to seek new expressions of identity and power. Although the Munyat al-Naʿūra lost its symbolic role as the seat of political power and was eclipsed by the brilliance of its successor, it was never abandoned.

Years later, al-Ḥakam visited the *munya* occasionally on his trips between Madīnat al-Zahrāʾ and the Alcazar, where he spent the colder months. In the last year of his life, after suffering what was probably a stroke at Madīnat al-Zahrāʾ, he was advised by physicians to return to the Alcazar. On the slow and painful journey, he passed the night at Munyat Arḥāʾ Nāṣiḥ and the next day proceeded to the Munyat al-Naʿūra, where he and his retinue paused for midday prayer. He was met there by an escort who left with him through the *munya*'s Bāb al-Manṣaba.[87] Doubtless by this time, the character of the Munyat al-Naʿūra had changed from what it had been a century earlier, when it belonged to ʿAbd Allāh. Cordoba had expanded both in population and in area, thanks to the fashionable trend toward building *munya*s and manor houses in the zone outside of the city's western wall. ʿAbd al-Raḥmān's reward of four hundred dirhems to those building near Madīnat al-Zahrāʾ also helped settle the area;[88] by the end of al-Ḥakam's reign, the city's western suburbs were almost as densely populated as the medina itself.[89] Like Ruṣāfa and other large estates, the Munyat al-Naʿūra by the tenth century had attracted settlement around its perimeter, and as the city expanded, its outskirts changed from rustic to suburban. Eventually, greater Corboda must have abutted al-Naʿūra so that, like the Alcazar a century and a half earlier, the estate was hemmed in by buildings and held captive by the very restrictions its builder had wished to evade. This steady urban encroachment, which began before the founding of Madīnat al-Zahrāʾ, may have been a factor in ʿAbd al-Raḥmān III's decision to build the new capital so far from Cordoba.

The contradictory desire for an inhabited yet bucolic landscape figured continuously in Cordoba's pattern of growth. Royal and aristocratic builders sought gardens, pools, and graceful pavilions in an abundance of the kind of space that was lacking in Cordoba's dense medina. Yet, for them to enjoy the refined pleasures of country life, enhancements such as walls, roads, and waterworks—in short, the accoutrements of the urban life they were ostensibly trying to escape—were needed. If economic prosperity can be said to have allowed the development of the surrounding landscape, the accompanying demographic expansion compelled it, so that, looking back from the thirteenth century, the historian Ibn Saʿīd admiringly likened the constructed and inhabited estates encircling Cordoba to pearls (quoted at the beginning of this chapter).[90] The fortunate result of these factors

was the investment in estates that yielded bountiful returns. Equally important, the owners of the *munya*s, who had one foot in the city, took pride in the productivity and beauty of their country retreats. The enjoyment of nature and landscape became an established part of the cultural life of Cordoba: emirs such as ʿAbd al-Raḥmān I composed odes to palm trees and poets sang of the beauty of their palace gardens.

Of all the *munya*s built before Madīnat al-Zahrāʾ, the Dār al-Rawḍa and the Munyat al-Naʿūra are the most revealing because they show aspects of ʿAbd al-Raḥmān III's taste and style of architectural patronage that later appear more markedly. Although in the al-Rawḍa and al-Naʿūra palaces ʿAbd al-Raḥmān experimented with complex architecture on a large scale, it was not until he founded Madīnat al-Zahrāʾ that he could experiment with an untouched site that provided unlimited space in an undeveloped area at a considerable distance from the city.

All of his palaces consumed a spectacular amount of water. For the Dār al-Rawḍa, water was piped into the Alcazar, and for the Munyat al-Naʿūra it was carried by aqueduct from a mountain range north of Cordoba. Al-Naʿūra's water was brought into one of the halls of the palace and, in a wonderful piece of architectural theater, poured out of a fantastic lion fountain into a large collecting pool, and then irrigated the estate's gardens before its overflow was dumped into the river. The role of water in giving life to the gardens surrounding the halls of the Munyat al-Naʿūra was celebrated through these displays of abundance.

The installation of a hydraulic system solely for the support of a palace and its gardens has a long history in Islamic foundation stories, and in the Cordoban context, begins with the Muslim appropriation of the Alcazar and the founding of al-Ruṣāfa. Through decorative fountains and pools, water was shown to be the symbolic giver of life to the surrounding vegetation, and by extrapolation, the prince who built the aqueduct that brought the water was understood to be the provider of that life-giving substance. Large amounts of water were needed to support gardens and orchards in that dry area, especially where tender varietals and plants imported from moist climates were grown. The abundant waterworks of the Dār al-Rawḍa, Munyat al-Naʿūra, and Madīnat al-Zahrāʾ are an indication of how large their gardens were and suggest that many varieties of plants were grown in them. The investment in expensive water systems, although hardly a new direction in estate building, was a prominent feature of ʿAbd al-Raḥmān's patronage and can be attributed to his interest in botany and his taste for extensive gardens. This taste is evident in the descriptions of the various gardens that he made and it is visually apparent in those gardens that survive at Madīnat al-Zahrāʾ.

4

MADĪNAT AL-ZAHRĀʾ

Madīnat al-Zahrāʾ is among the wonders of the world.
—Ibn Khalliqān

Of all the handsome palace estates that encircled Cordoba from the eighth to the early tenth century, Madīnat al-Zahrāʾ is the sole survivor. This is fortunate for our study of buildings conceived in relation to a landscape of gardens, orchards, and nature because the conception and construction of Madīnat al-Zahrāʾ represent a formative moment in garden and architectural history and were the result of the blending of Mediterranean (Roman) and eastern (Persian) traditions. Even in its own day, the dazzling royal palace-city was recognized as an extraordinary creation, as Ibn Khalliqān's praise, cited above, attests.[1] Moreover, it is one of the few royal palace-cities anywhere in the early Islamic domains that was not buried under subsequent urban development. Although at the time of its rediscovery in the nineteenth century it was a ruin without a single standing structure, it is known today from the detailed descriptions offered in histories written by Ibn Ḥayyān, Ibn ʿIdhārī, and al-Maqqarī and from archaeological excavations carried out from 1910 to the present.

Félix Hernández Giménez, a former director of the site's excavations, is the only person to have attempted to summarize the archaeological findings and describe its urban plan and buildings thoroughly, but his study was never finished. It appeared posthumously with neither plans nor photographs and was riddled with gaps and inconsistencies that rendered it difficult if not impossible to use.[2] This, combined with the lack of regular excavation reports, has hindered the production of secondary analytic studies of the site, despite the palace's importance to Spain and to the built environment of Islam.

Madīnat al-Zahrāʾ was a self-sufficient city, conceived on a monumental and urban scale with its own mosques, baths, markets, and urban administration. Although it stood well apart from the swathe of green estates outside of Cordoba, it was never fully disassociated from the capital. The fact that it was called both *madīna* (city) and *qaṣr* (palace) in the Arabic texts indicates its dual identity and is an important key to understanding its urban and at the same time bucolic character. When construction began on Madīnat al-Zahrāʾ in 325/936, Cordoba was surrounded by suburban estates. Madīnat al-Zahrāʾ was built much farther away than the farthest of these and in many respects seemed to constitute the center of an entirely new province (*iqlīm*).[3] It had its own city manager (*ṣāḥib al-madīnat*), police chief (*ṣāḥib al-shurṭa*), judge (*qāḍī*), and congregational mosque, all of which duplicated civil, commercial, and religious functions already in place in Cordoba and allowed autonomous administration. Indeed, in the mid-tenth century al-Rāzī referred to both Cordoba and Madīnat al-Zahrāʾ as capital cities (*al-ḥaḍaratayn qurṭuba wa-l-zahrāʾ*).[4] However, Madīnat al-Zahrāʾ was not simply a newer, fiat version of Cordoba. It did not supercede the older city; nor

was it, like the fifteen other provincial capitals, secondary to Cordoba. Rather, it was a new type of urban center in which aesthetic innovations serving the apparatus of sovereignty outweighed the agricultural convenience of proximity to the central marketplace.

ʿAbd al-Raḥmān and the Caliphate

The impetus for the innovations at Madīnat al-Zahrāʾ was due to a significant political change in al-Andalus and, indeed, in the Islamic world. Although legitimate caliphs in principle, the Hispano-Umayyads were not in a position to address the issue of religious leadership during the eighth and ninth centuries, for they were too busy defending the northern frontier against the Asturians and Franks and maintaining their position of authority in the face of internal challenges. The situation changed in 300/912, however, when ʿAbd al-Raḥmān III, at the age of twenty-one years, inherited the throne from his grandfather, ʿAbd Allāh. The young emir intensified his grandfather's campaign of political consolidation, quelling internal rebellions and demanding allegiance from provincial governors, and of military and diplomatic expansion, conquering territories along the northern frontier and forging strategic alliances with Christian and North African kingdoms alike. It was a period of military strength and economic prosperity in which al-Andalus enjoyed the first glimmers of international importance. In 316/929, with a solid economic and political domestic foundation to support him and bolstered by treaties and diplomatic ties with Byzantium, Christian Spain, and North Africa, ʿAbd al-Raḥmān III declared himself caliph—*amīr al-muʾminīn*—taking the name of al-Nāṣir (the Victorious).

ʿAbd al-Raḥmān's adoption of caliphal titulature was a public affirmation of transformations that had already occurred in al-Andalus. Although it did not change the actual political balance of power (the gesture was all but ignored in eastern Islamic lands)[5] it was an ideological statement calculated to provoke recognition of al-Andalus's coming of age. On one level, it was a message aimed at al-Andalus and its tributaries confirming the political and religious unity that the Islamic kingdom had recently begun to enjoy. The longtime rebel and apostate Ibn Ḥafṣūn had finally been suppressed; successful military campaigns waged against the northern Christian kingdoms resulted in territorial gains; coastal Maghrebi outposts such as Ceuta and Melilla had been secured, thereby improving al-Andalus's naval advantage; and finally the explosive rate of conversion to Islam during the tenth century no doubt instilled in the emir a sense of divine approbation.[6] ʿAbd al-Raḥmān's power in the political and religious sphere far exceeded that of his Andalusian grandfathers: the moment had arrived to exert his rightful authority.

On another level, the message was aimed at the Abbasids and Fatimids. Old rivals, the Abbasid caliphs had declined considerably since their abrupt seizure of power almost two hundred years earlier. They had overspent their treasury on wanton architectural displays, their tight hold on the empire had been broken by marginal ethnic groups and regions achieving independence, and by the second quarter of the tenth century the caliphate was completely dominated by the Shiʾite Buyid princes. The most significant Mediterranean challenge to Abbasid hegemony was made by the Fa-

timids of Tunisia. In 297/910 the Fatimid leader ʿUbayd Allāh declared himself caliph, adopting the name of al-Mahdī (the Rightful Guide), and took the city of Raqqada from the Abbasid-appointed Aghlabid governors.[7] The Fatimids were the first independent Shiʾite dynasty and their political ties with Berber rulers in the Maghreb gave strength to Shiʾism along the North African coast. The Umayyads wished to prevent the introduction of a Shiʾite presence in al-Andalus, which the Fatimids were secretly encouraging.[8]

The Fatimids were not the only challengers to Abbasid Sunni authority, but they were the most successful. The religious authority of the Abbasids as caliphs was thus deeply undermined by the early tenth century and once the bold step had been taken so near al-Andalus, there was little to stop the Cordoban emir from posing a more legitimate Sunni counterclaim.[9] Moreover, whereas the Abbasids were a remote enemy, the Fatimid headquarters in Tunisia constituted a far more serious threat, poised strategically at a point midway along the southern shore of the Mediterranean. They attacked Fez in 309/921; and until the end of the century Berber chiefs switched allegiances back and forth between the Fatimids and Umayyads, and from Shiʾism to Sunnism as the balance of power shifted in North Africa.

If by the tenth century al-Andalus had "arrived," it was partly the result of having expanded its horizons beginning in the ninth century. The reign of ʿAbd al-Raḥmān II (r. 206/822–238/852) was a critical period of transition between the early decades of struggle for survival and the period of consolidation that followed. At this time, administration was reshaped and refined in order to cope with the expanding trade networks, burgeoning domestic economy, and rapid urbanization in the peninsula. The old Umayyad way of governing was simply not sophisticated enough to handle these profound structural and cultural changes while simultaneously under pressure to defend the country from internal revolts among the Mozarabs and external aggression from the quarter of the Franks, Basques, Asturians, and even the Normans.[10] ʿAbd al-Raḥmān II began to change the state administration from a simpler consensus-based model to the more complex and hierarchical model of the Abbasids.

ʿAbd al-Raḥmān II's reign was the catalyst for many of the innovations attributed to ʿAbd al-Raḥmān III. For example, the first alliances between the Hispano-Umayyads with the Byzantines against the Franks and the Abbasids were forged by ʿAbd al-Raḥmān II, thereby opening western Mediterranean trade to both Andalusian and Byzantine vessels.[11] Mediterranean shipping routes became an important factor of economic prosperity because in order to profit from its prodigious agricultural productivity, al-Andalus had to be able to exchange goods with foreign markets. High-quality fruit, olives, herbs, grain, textiles, and minerals were exported to northern Africa via the Guadalquivir River and to the Mediterranean from the seaport of Almeria in exchange for luxury goods and money. By the end of the eighth century, the Andalusian economy was based on a widely recognized monetary system of dinars and dirhems. The fact that its wealth was convertible into abstract coinage gave al-Andalus an advantage over its Christian neighbors and permitted greater fluidity of commercial interchange as well as the accumulation of excess capital by merchants and others.

The new system of centralized administration that ʿAbd al-Raḥmān III implemented after he

had secured the submission of the provincial governors of al-Andalus simply advanced the Abbasid-style system of hierarchical bureaucracy that had already been introduced under ʿAbd al-Raḥmān II.[12] Offices were organized according to rank and responsibility and supervised by the *ḥājib,* the Andalusian equivalent of the Abbasid office of vizier, later superceded by the rank of *dhū-l-wizāratayn* (double vizier), also adopted from the Abbasid east.[13] Economic stability was imposed through state monopolies and controlled markets. Cultural influences from the east were also introduced at this time. Although Abbasid artistic and literary conventions were more marked in the courts of ʿAbd al-Raḥmān III and al-Ḥakam II at Madīnat al-Zahrāʾ, the first celebrated purveyors of eastern culture in al-Andalus arrived in the ninth century.

Perhaps the most important of these was the musician Ziryāb, who arrived in Cordoba in 207/822 traveling from Baghdad by way of the Aghlabid court of Ziyādat Allāh I in Qairawan.[14] An accomplished singer and composer, he brought musical techniques and improved musical instruments from Baghdad as well as introduced to the Andalusian court the fashions and hairstyles of the Abbasid capital and the art of elegant dining. The importance of his innovations is not in the actual items but in the new expectation of fashionability, because with the arrival of this fascinating and beautifully plumed musician, Cordobans for the first time recognized their provinciality and started to compare themselves with the elite inhabitants of the great capital cities, most notably Baghdad.

To vie with the Abbasid and Fatimid caliphs, ʿAbd al-Raḥmān required a brilliant court where arts, literature, and science could flourish under his generous patronage. The appropriate setting for such cultural gatherings was a magnificent palace of ceremonial gates, reception halls, pavilions, and gardens. Madīnat al-Zahrāʾ—built to provide such a space—was the direct result of his appropriation of caliphal status, and was modeled upon the spectacular palaces of his rivals, most particularly Samarra, the Abbasid caliphal city.

The Founding of Madīnat al-Zahrāʾ

Madīnat al-Zahrāʾ figures prominently in the historical and geographical descriptions of al-Andalus and Cordoba.[15] Its founding was a major event in the eyes of contemporary chroniclers, for it was undoubtedly the largest construction complex they had ever seen. It had a special meaning for later historians as well, who saw it as a symbol of the downfall of the Umayyad caliphate in al-Andalus and subsequent loss of the peninsula to the Christians.[16] The city was begun on 1 Muharram 325 (November 19, 936) according to Ibn Ḥayyān, who got his information from Madīnat al-Zahrā's chief architect via the *faqīh* Ibn Daḥūn.[17] Various historians stated that it was built at the southern foot of the Jabal al-ʿArūs, "between the mountain and the plain," approximately four miles west of Cordoba.[18] (It is, in actuality, ten kilometers from Cordoba). Ibn Ḥayyān, in a notice dated 942, wrote that an alcazar was built on the site known as Qurqurīṭ below Cordoba (presumably meaning downstream along the Guadalquivir and west of the city) where in the third quarter of the ninth century Muḥammad I had enjoyed a *munya.* Al-ʿUdhrī specifically attributed Madīnat al-Zahrāʾ to this place, but other sources emphasized the novelty of the terraced landscape and gran-

deur of the enterprise, describing it as an entirely new foundation rather than as an extension or renovation.[19] It is logical to assume that some farms and simple country residences preexisted in that area in the fertile land along the river—indeed, as discussed in the previous chapter, we know that the emir Muḥammad had built the Munya al-Kantish along the riverbank west of Cordoba—but the unprecedented scale and architectural drama of Madīnat al-Zahrāʾ and its hillside location completely eclipsed them. The descriptions emphasize the palace-city's prominent landscape feature—the mountain— and the fact that it was built at a considerable distance from the city. Although Madīnat al-Zahrāʾ was not much farther away than the Munyat ʿArḥāʾ Nāṣih as the crow flies, the riverbank was built up along its northern side for a distance of several kilometers west of Cordoba and carried steady traffic along its unpaved roads. In contrast, the area around al-Zahrāʾ was more remote, consisting of isolated farms and few paths.

The story of Madīnat al-Zahrāʾs foundation was couched in terms of pious charity. Supposedly, one of al-Nāṣir's concubines died and left a legacy for the purpose of ransoming Muslim prisoners in the land of the Franks. When none could be found, the caliph gave thanks to God and then proceeded to use the money to build a city, named after another of his concubines, al-Zahrāʾ, for whom he felt a great attachment.[20] This story, which appears in only one history, is probably apocryphal. It is doubtful that the woman al-Zahrāʾ existed, and even if she did, it is unlikely that the new capital of al-Andalus would have been named for her. The tale is a variation on a topos and is comparable to the story of the Persian palace built for Shirīn by her lover King Parvīz between Baghdad and Hadhan.[21]

This foundation story was accompanied by an anecdote that was equally spurious but contained a kernel of profound metaphoric truth about the relationship between architecture and landscape, or humankind and nature.

> [Madīnat al-Zahrāʾ] was built at the foot of the Jabal al-ʿArūs. . . . But when the concubine al-Zahrāʾ sat in one of the palace's halls and contemplated the whiteness and radiance of the city on the slopes of that [dark] mountain, she said: "O my lord, do you not see the beauty of that lovely girl in the embrace of that dark Ethiopian?" So, he ordered that the mountain be leveled. [Dissuaded by his staff], he then ordered that the dark trees be chopped down and replaced by fig and almond trees. And there was no prettier sight, especially when they were in bloom.[22]

In this tale, the "natural" landscape of dark ilexes (holm oaks) was transformed through human intervention—and one man's supreme volition—to an aesthetically preferable, manufactured landscape of flowering trees. The caliph is characterized as an all-powerful steward, able to level the landscape and to control nature, but with admirable results.

One of the most profound changes wrought at the site was the introduction of water from the hills above via an aqueduct that traversed the uneven terrain by means of bridges and tunnels (Fig. 6). The water entered al-Zahrāʾ at the center of the north side, dropped three meters into a basin measuring roughly 1.5 by 1.5 meters, and passed into a closed, stone-vaulted reservoir from where it ran to the rest of the complex via channels, pipes, and underground sewers.[23] Surplus flowed from the palace to the plains below, irrigating farms and estates. Although praised as an

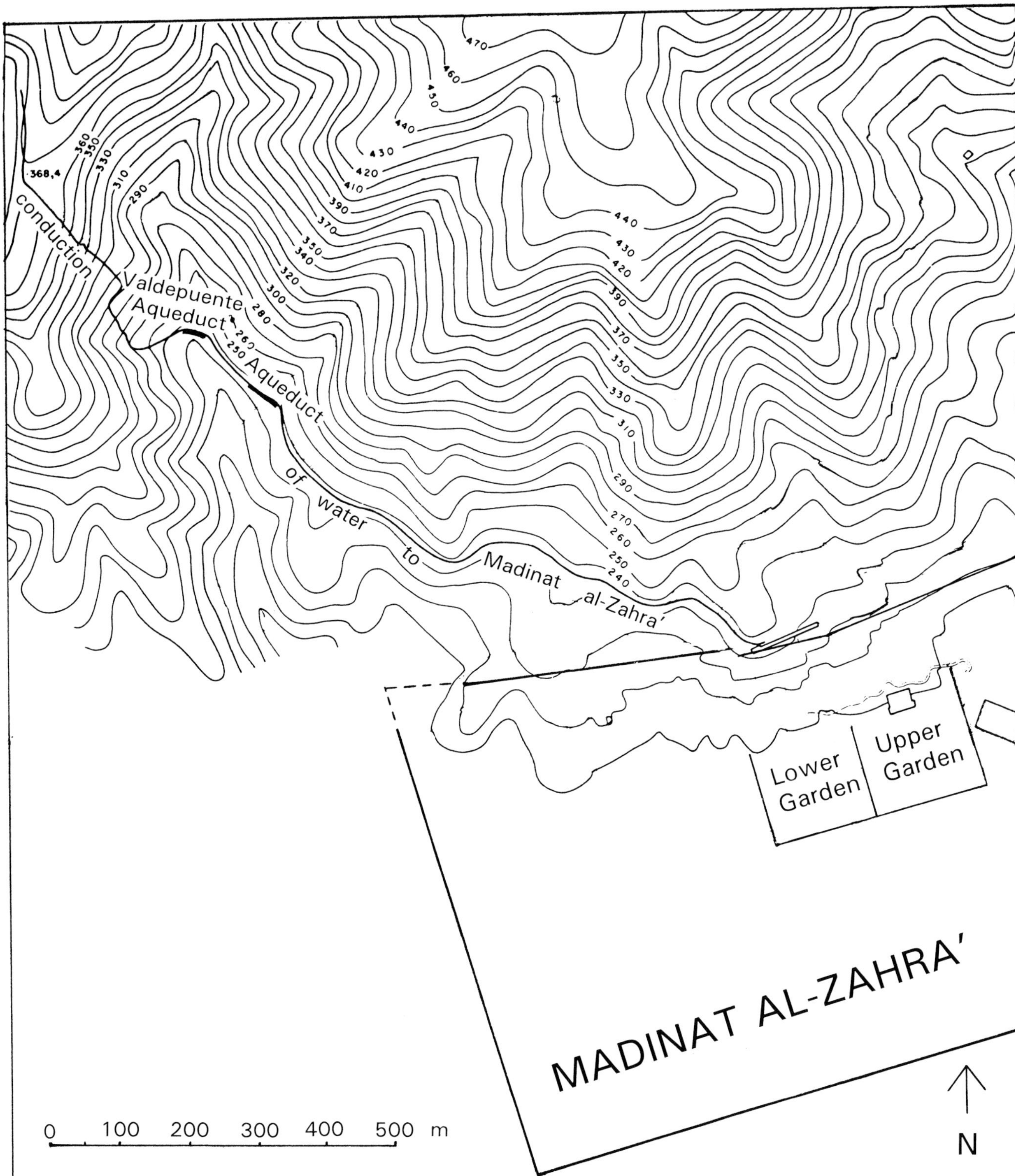

6. The conduction of water to Madīnat al-Zahrā'

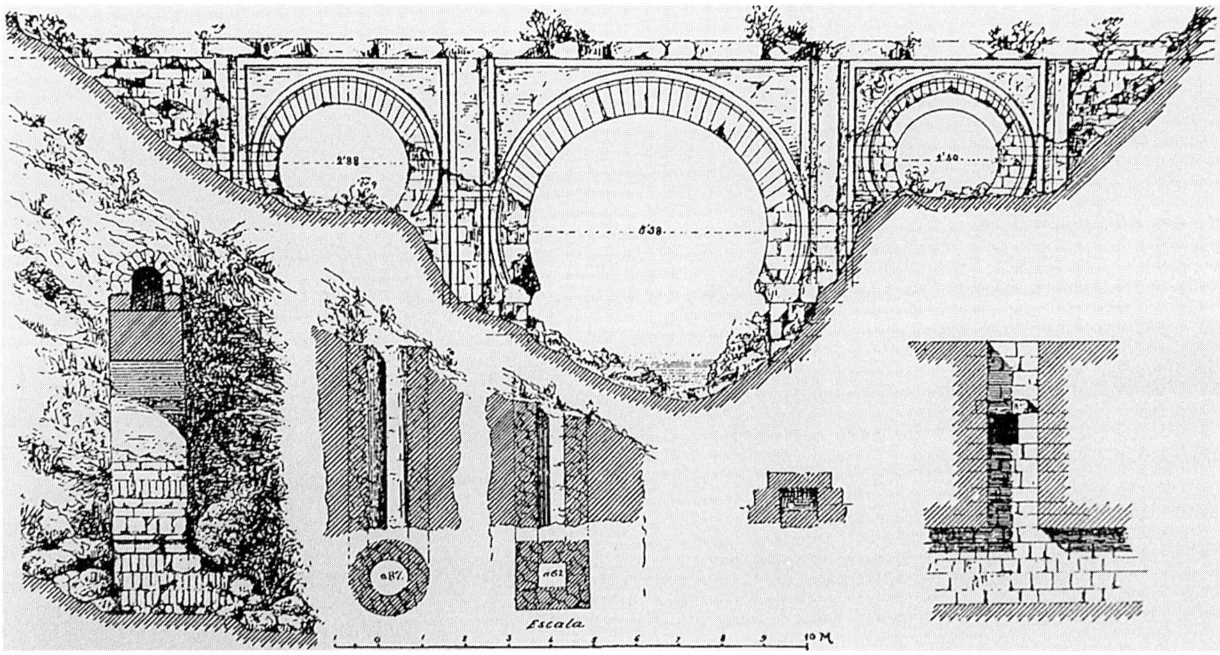

7. The Valdepuentes Aqueduct above Madīnat al-Zahrāʾ (R. Velázquez Bosco)

entirely new construction by contemporary chroniclers, modern archaeological excavations reveal that long portions of the aqueduct between al-Zahrāʾ and the plains below were Roman fabric.[24] In Roman times, this aqueduct served the villas and farms (the remains of many of which have been discovered) on the rich alluvial soil between the mountains and the river.[25] As in the case of Cordoba's city walls and bridges, the Umayyads did not hesitate to renovate Roman remains and in so doing, to claim them as their own.

This aqueduct was independent of the aqueduct supplying Cordoba because the latter ran at too low an altitude to serve Madīnat al-Zahrāʾ. The aqueduct stood intact until the sixteenth century, when it was dismantled by the monks of San Jerónimo to build their monastery uphill from the site; but vestiges of it can still be seen today in the hills above the palace-city (Fig. 7). Ambrosio Morales, who saw the water system before it was taken apart, wrote that it was enormous:

> The whole aqueduct was so high that a man could almost walk upright . . . and it was three feet wide. The walls are of handsome masonry and the arch of the vault is of an extremely durable mortar. . . . The water comes from the Sierra and where the aqueduct encounters great mountains, they made it tunnel beneath and through them so that its course flows continuously. . . . When the aqueduct has to cross valleys, they make handsome bridges which give name to the valleys so that they are called the Valleys of the Bridges.[26]

The construction of the palace-city lasted forty years and was supervised by ʿAbd al-Raḥmān III and his heir al-Ḥakam.[27] ʿAbd al-Raḥmān, although an active military leader in his youth, suf-

fered a terrible defeat in the campaign of Alhandega in 327/938, and from then on ceased to lead his army personally and instead "dedicated himself to the pleasures and constructions in which he reached a point which his forebears had never reached nor his descendants thereafter."[28] He became so absorbed in the construction site that he even skipped Friday prayer in the congregational mosque of Cordoba for three weeks in succession, provoking the judge (*qāḍī*) to chastise him publicly.[29]

The historical accounts are quite specific about the persons and materials employed for the massive project. As a result, we know that the chief architect (*al-ʿarīf al-muhandis*) was Maslama b. ʿAbd Allāh and the chief mason (*ʿarīf al-bannāʾīn*) was ʿAbd Allāh ben Yūnus, who, accompanied by Ḥasan ibn Muḥammad and ʿAlī ben Jaʿfar al-Iskandarānī, brought marble from Ifriqiya to Madīnat al-Zahrāʾ.[30] The names of stone carvers appear in inscriptions on the capitals and bases found on the site and on others reused elsewhere in later constructions (Figs. 8 and 9), and while these names are Muslim, the style in which they worked was clearly an excellent adaptation of Byzantine practices.[31] Inscriptions on wall plaques and pilasters of the Salon Rico give the name of Shunayf al-Fataḥ several times as the director of works as well as naming various stone carvers.[32]

A few things can be said about even the anonymous workers at Madīnat al-Zahrāʾ. Aside from the skilled artisans brought from Baghdad and Constantinople to work on the Munyat al-Naʿūra who stayed on to work at Madīnat al-Zahrāʾ, al-Nuwayrī mentions twelve thousand Christian workers (*ṣanāʾiʿī*) used as forced labor.[33] Doubtless this figure is an exaggeration, since al-Maqqarī says that ten thousand paid laborers and slaves worked there daily. Paid laborers earned a wage of between one and a half and three dirhems.[34] Al-Maqqarī says that one thousand workers were employed to build the mosque, which was completed in a record time of forty-eight days; of these half were skilled artisans.[35]

One thousand five hundred beasts of burden, mostly mules, were used each day, four hundred of which were owned by the caliph and the others hired from their owners for a monthly fee.[36] A huge amount of construction material was consumed: this included six thousand blocks daily of dressed stone, not including tiles and paving slabs;[37] 1,100 loads of lime and plaster every three days;[38] and 4,300 large and small columns being used altogether. Most of these columns were new: 1,013 were from Ifriqiya, 140 were sent by the Byzantine emperor as a gift, 19 came from the kingdom of the Franks, and the remainder came from Rome, Tarragona, Almeria, Malaga, and elsewhere in al-Andalus. The white marble was from Almeria, the streaked from Malaga, pink from Cabra, and blue-gray from Peñatejada.[39] Fifteen thousand wooden door panels plated with iron or polished bronze were also installed.[40]

The cost of some of the materials has been recorded. Each column cost eight *sijilmasi* dinars, and the caliph paid ʿAbd Allāh b. Yūnus ten dinars for each piece of marble brought from Carthage and Tunis, although al-Maqqarī says that reliable historians correct this figure to three dinars for small pieces.[41] The total estimates of the cost of building the palace-city vary, but the sources agree that one-third of the kindgom's revenues were devoted to its construction and upkeep.[42]

The architectural remains are too minimal and fragmentary to allow an archaeological assessment of these figures. Perhaps the emphasis on foreign materials is a topos meant to center the city amid a panoply of prized materials from the north (the Franks), east (Byzantium and Carthage),

8. Madīnat al-Zahrāʾ capital with inscription encircling the top (Meadows Foundation Fund, Meadows Museum, Southern Methodist University, Dallas)

9. A column base at Madīnat al-Zahrāʾ

and south (the African coast). However, judging from Byzantine examples in which heavy pieces of marble were shipped from quarries near Constantinople to Ravenna in the fifth and sixth centuries and to Venice in the thirteenth, it is perfectly plausible that Madīnat al-Zahrāʾ imported massive chunks of stone from abroad.[43] The inconsistency of the figures recorded by al-Maqqarī, Ibn Ghālib, and others—who were not eyewitnesses—casts doubt on their numerical accuracy; however, the fact that the source of these later historians was, first, ʿIsāʾ Ibn Aḥmad al-Rāzī, who was the son of a prominent geographer and historian and served as al-Ḥakam II's official chronicler; second, Ibn Faraḍī, who was born and died in Cordoba 351/962–403/1013; and third, Ibn Ḥayyān, who lived in Cordoba from 377/987–88 to 469/1076 and obtained his information from ʿAbd al-Raḥmān's architect Maslama bin ʿAbd Allāh, via Ibn Daḥūn (or Daḥīn), indicates that the figures were originally compiled by a contemporary observer.[44] Furthermore, the extraordinary detail here in relating such mundane facts as the amounts of lime and numbers of mules appears in no other description of Andalusian construction, suggesting that in this case the narrators were consulting an accounts book.

The sources draw attention to ʿAbd al-Raḥmān's active involvement: he ordered materials, commissioned artisans, and oversaw everything. The emphasis on the king as builder is unusual: the accounts of earlier palaces described them as finished structures. Even palace estates such as Ruṣāfa that were built by fiat are described only briefly with but passing mention of the materials and agents of construction. The specificity of detail in the accounts of Madīnat al-Zahrāʾ and the particular stress laid upon ʿAbd al-Raḥmān's participation serve to emphasize the innovation of its design. An unusually complex foundation intended to express dynastic authority and personal power, its construction required constant vigilance.

Historical Descriptions of the Buildings

The life of Madīnat al-Zahrāʾ is given in two different biographies. One was written by the historians and observers who described those parts of the city to which they gained access, ignoring areas that were unseen, such as the caliph's quarters, or unworthy, such as the bakeries and workshops, or simply too obvious to warrant description, such as the main gate to the city. The other biography is written by the archaeologists who since the beginning of this century have unearthed walls, column bases, steps, pavements, and garden quadrants with the objective of visualizing the relationship of these disparate parts. These two versions of the palace-city coincide but rarely mirror each other exactly, and for this reason they will be dealt with separately.

Madīnat al-Zahrāʾ measures 1,518 by 745 meters and was built on sloping ground in three great terraces (Fig. 10).[45] Al-Idrīsī and al-Ḥimyarī give almost identical descriptions: "It is a city with [three] stepped constructions; one precinct [*madīna*] on top of another so that the ground floor of the upper level is on level with the roofs of the level below. Each one of its parts is separately walled. On the upper level are the palaces, beautiful beyond description. On the middle level are the gardens and orchards; and on the lower level are the houses and the congregational mosque."[46] Al-Nuwayrī says that the topmost level is "next to the mountain" and that on the level below the miradors (*manāẓir*) and palaces (*quṣūr*) are gardens with a variety of trees.[47]

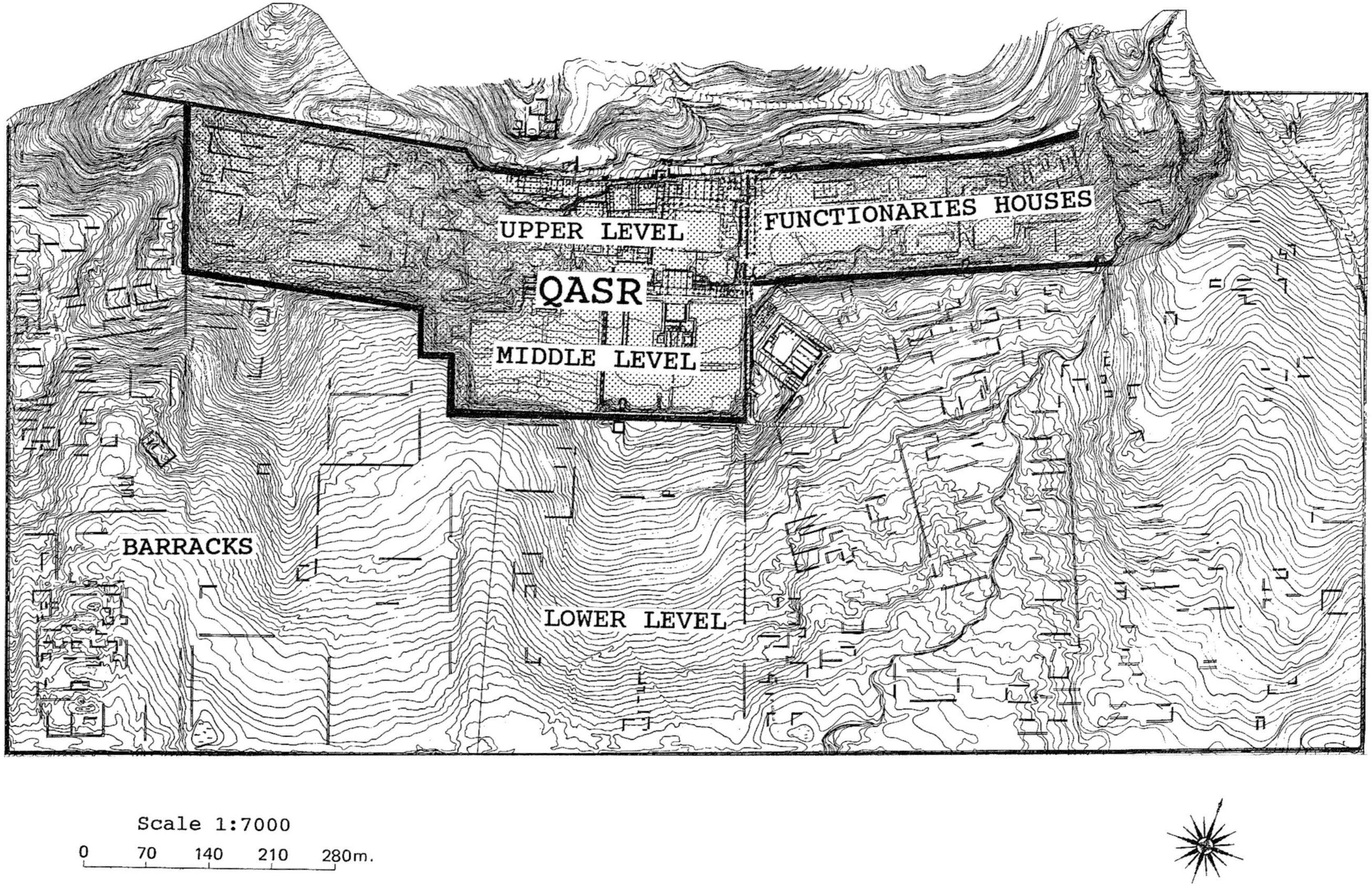

10. Plan of Madīnat al-Zahrā' (after S. López-Cuervo)

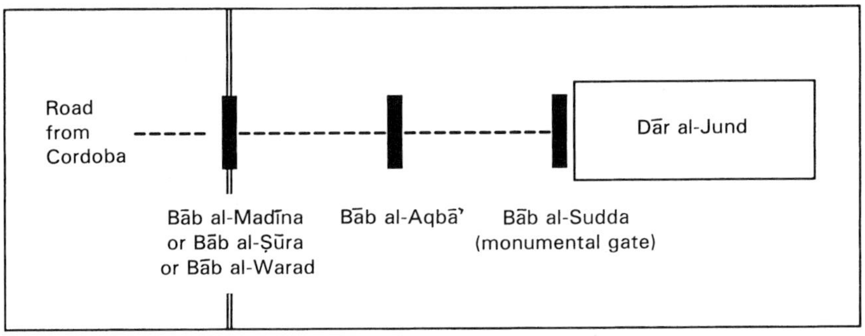

11. Schematic diagram of gates to Madīnat al-Zahrā'

Four gates are mentioned in accounts of ceremonies held at al-Zahrā' (Fig. 11). Nothing is known about the Bāb al-Jinnān (Gate of the Gardens) except that it was next to the Bayt al-Aʿmāl (Workers' House). The main gate to the city, in the southern wall, was variously called the Bāb al-Madīna (Gate of the City), Bāb al-Warad (Gate of Arrival or Roses), or the Bāb al-Ṣūra (Gate of the Statue); the latter because a statue of a female figure stood over the portal. Although contemporary sources said that the figure represented the beloved concubine al-Zahrā', there was a similar statue over Cordoba's Roman gate that most certainly was not a Muslim image.[48] More likely, it was a Venus reused from one of many Roman villas or gates along the Guadalquivir Valley.[49] The confusion between the concubine and the goddess is perfectly logical in Arabic, since the astrological name for Venus is al-Zahrā', and indeed, one wonders if it was the presence of this unusual statue that engendered the romantic theory that the palace-city was named for a slave. When the Almohad Caliph Yaʿqūb al-Manṣūr visited the ruins in 586/1190, he ordered that the statue be removed and taken away.[50]

Next was the Bāb al-Aqbā' (Gate of the Vault of Dome), which led from the lower level to the elite zone, or *qaṣr,* consisting of both the upper and middle levels. If we accept as literal the statement that the Bāb al-Aqbā' was the "first of the *qaṣr*" then it becomes clear that the part of the city called the Qaṣr comprised both the top level of palaces and the middle gardened level.[51] Last, the Bāb al-Sudda was located at the entrance to the Dār al-Jund, or military and equestrian headquarters, which in turn functioned as a protective intermediate zone between the lower levels of the city and the upper level of reception halls and residences of the elite. The Bāb al-Sudda is the only gate that has been excavated and restored (Fig. 12). All three of these gates were sufficiently large that a visitor could enter on horseback, dismounting in the Dār al-Jund's courtyard or in front of its reception hall, but few were allowed the privilege.[52] Ordinary riders dismounted upon entering the city at Bāb al-Madīna, or if they were being admitted to the Qaṣr, at the Bāb al-Sudda.

Given the vagueness of the descriptions of all but the most unusual edifices, it is difficult to judge where the various buildings and offices were. We know that the lowest level held the ordinary houses and the mosque, and that al-Zahrā' as a whole contained four hundred houses for the caliph, his retinue, and his followers,[53] but houses for ordinary people, servants, gardeners, soldiers, and shopkeepers are hardly mentioned. Eyewitnesses described Madīnat al-Zahrā' as having 125 build-

12. The monumental Bab al-Sudda at Madīnat al-Zahrā᾿

ings in addition to storage houses for butter and oil, a prison, and gardens (*riyāḍāt*). Slaves, middle-ranking functionaries, and most of the soldiers lived outside the Qaṣr on the western side, while the nobility and high functionaries had houses on the east side.[54] None of these dwellings have been excavated, but if the historical descriptions are correct, the traces of the skewed structure visible in aerial photographs probably belong to the mosque that served this population of servants and soldiers, as distinct from the larger congregational mosque east of the middle level.

The sources mention ateliers (*dār al-ṣanaʿāt*), a prison (*al-duwayra*), and a zoo. These were presumably located on the lowest level, or the middle level east and west of the Qaṣr. The *ṣāḥib* of textile making and *ṭirāz* lived in a house east of the Qaṣr.[55] The mint (*dār al-sikka*) was off to one side.[56] The supervisor of horses lived in the center of the palace near the Dār al-Jund where the stables were located.[57]

The zoo was large and had a moat (*siyāj*). In addition to the aviary protected by netting (*sibaq*),[58] exotic animals were kept there, such as the lions that had been housed in the ravine under the bridge in front of the Cordoba Alcazar before the zoo was built.[59] Some of these animals arrived as diplomatic gifts from North African allies. For example on one occasion, ʿAbd al-Raḥmān was presented with 20 chargers, 23 camels, 10 Sudanese marmot sheep, 2 gazelles, and 8 ostriches; on another he received castrated dromedaries in extravagant trappings, 20 pregnant camels, 18 Maghrebi chargers and various other horses, and one lion.[60] The palace's enormous fishponds, probably located on the lower level, constituted a food source for al-Zahrā's inhabitants; the fish consumed twelve thousand loaves of bread daily as well as a large number of black beans.[61]

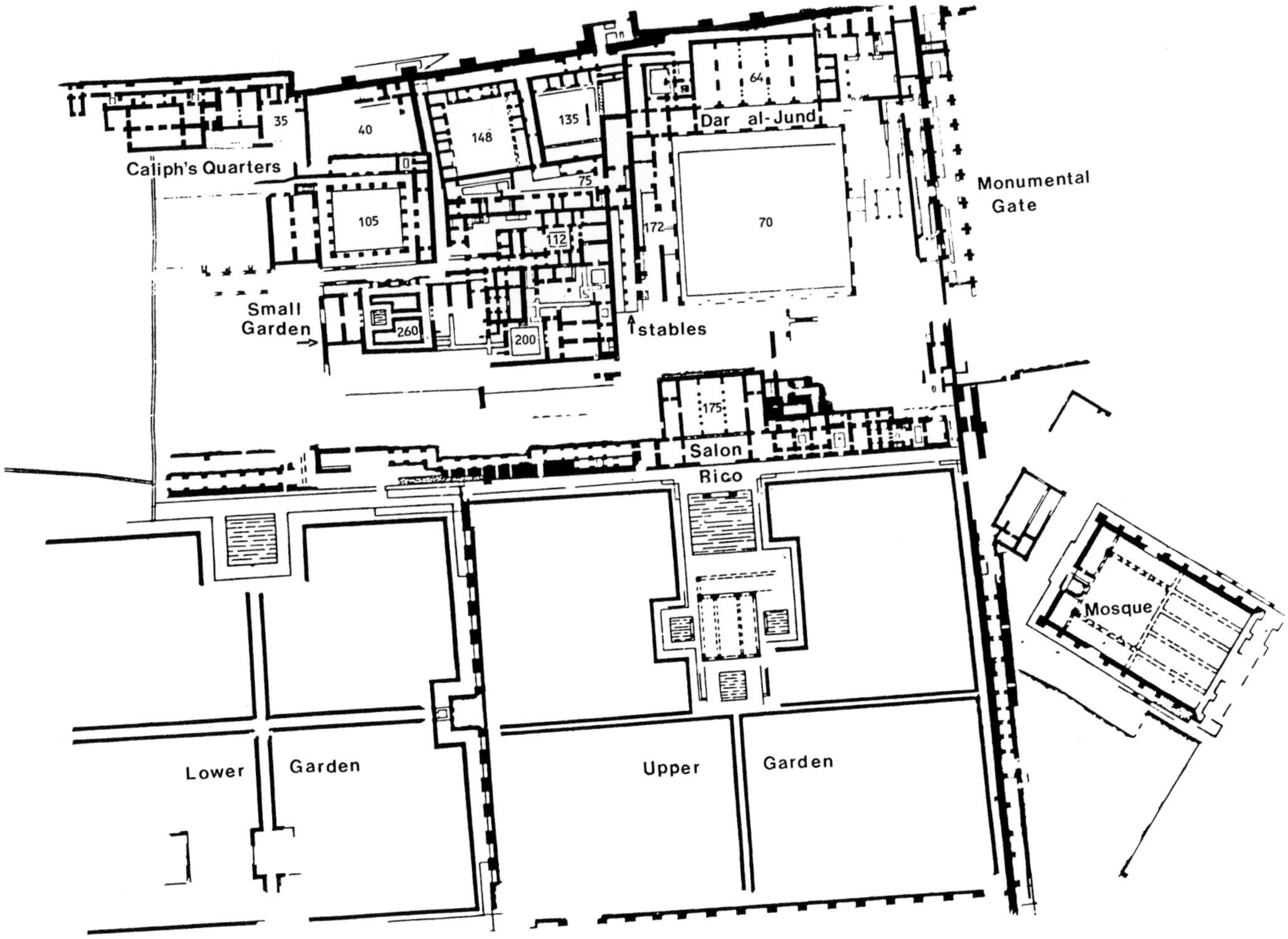

13. Plan of middle and upper (*qaṣr*) zone of Madīnat al-Zahrā' (after Conjunto Arqueológico Madinat al-Zahra')

The middle level consisted of gardens and orchards, irrigated and cultivated with many rare species of fruit trees (Fig. 13).[62] In one garden a large pool had channels with flowing water and steps leading down into it where one could sit.[63] On the third and highest level were the reception halls and notable buildings. The names of these are very confusing because the sources refer to the same structures by different names, and archaeologists have compounded the confusion by providing fanciful names of their own or by applying, sometimes incorrectly, medieval names to the excavated structures.[64] Here we will use the serviceable numbering system established by Hernández Giménez and the early excavators in combination with the medieval nomenclature where it is secure.

The most puzzling structure mentioned in the medieval histories is the Saṭḥ al-Mumarrad, which was either an esplanade or an open corridor along which were located the most luxurious of the official reception halls: the Majlis al-Gharbī (West Hall), the Majlis al-Sharqī (East Hall) and the Majlis al-Dhahab (Hall of Gold). In the swearing-in ceremony at the time of al-Ḥakam's ascension

to the rank of caliph, he sat on the throne (*sarīr al-mulk*) in the central nave on the south side of the Saṭḥ al-Mumarrad (possibly the pavilion in the upper garden), while his guests were arranged in the two halls al-Sharqī and al-Gharbī. After taking the oath of allegiance to the new caliph, each person was seated either to the left or right of the throne and lined up according to rank: the elite slave corps (*akābiru al-fityān*) in white tunics with girded swords, then the *fityān al-wusāfa* in coats of mail and unsheathed swords aligned along the Saṭḥ and its rooms (*fuṣlān*), then the lancemen, eunuchs, and so on, all the way into the Dār al-Jund, through the Bāb al-Sudda and the Bāb al-Aqbā᾽ to the Bāb al-Madīna, or city gate.[65] On other occasions al-Ḥakam sat on his throne in the Majlis al-Sharqī in the Saṭḥ, or on the throne in the Majlis al-Gharbī.[66] In a reception for King Ordoño, the sources mention a throne in the Majlis al-Sharqī, where al-Ḥakam received his visitors, and another empty throne in the Majlis al-Gharbī. Clearly each of the reception halls had a throne.

Al-Maqqarī says that the Saṭḥ al-Mumarrad gave onto the gardens (*al-mushriq ʿalā al-rawḍa*) and was adorned with the Majlis al-Dhahab (Hall of Gold) and a pavilion (*qubba*) that had gardens, large pools, and sculpted water basins with extraordinary figures.[67] The names are confusing but this Majlis al-Dhahab, or golden hall, may be the fabulous golden caliphal palace (*qaṣr al-khilāfa*), and the aforementioned pavilion may be the same building as the *qubayba* that was situated just slightly above the *ṣarḥ al-mumarrad* (the word *ṣarḥ*, or "lofty edifice," being a scribe's logical but erroneous substitution for *saṭḥ*, or "terrace").[68] Possibly this *majlis/qubayba/qaṣr* is the building known today as the Salon Rico (Fig. 13, no. 175), for the description of a richly decorated hall overlooking gardens fits the Salon Rico. On the other hand, the *qubba/qubayba* could also be the garden pavilion directly opposite the Salon Rico.

The caliphal palace (*qaṣr al-khilāfa*) overlooked gardens and had a magnificent hall with a gold and silver roof and walls of thick, colored marble, and in the middle of which hung a magnificent pearl that had been a gift to ʿAbd al-Raḥmān from Leo, emperor of Constantinople. The hall had eight doors on each side formed by marble columns that supported interlacing arches of ebony and gold, inlaid with gold, gems, and mosaic. In the center of the hall was a large tank of mercury.[69] Al-Maqqarī claimed that it was a dazzling sight: "As the sun entered through these doors and its rays played off the roof and walls of the hall, it sparkled with light, confounding all vision. When al-Nāṣir wished to impress visitors, he would signal to one of his slaves to cause the mercury [in the tank] to vibrate, whereupon in the chamber there would appear a flash like that of lightning bolts that would fill their hearts with fear."[70]

The idea of a pool of quicksilver was not original to ʿAbd al-Raḥmān al-Nāṣir but copied from the palace of the governor of Egypt, Khumārawayh Ibn Ṭūlūn (r. 884–96) in al-Qaṭa᾽iʿ. There Ibn Ṭūlūn planted gardens in the courtyards and installed in the palace's Golden Chamber a square tank of mercury measuring fifty cubits on each side, on the gently undulating surface of which the insomniac governor slept on a leather mattress.[71]

According to a story that turns up in most of the histories, when ʿAbd al-Raḥmān's richly ornamented pavilion was finished, he was pleased and asked his advisors if it was not truly remarkable. All agreed that no other king had ever accomplished anything like it, except the *qāḍī* Mundhir b. Saʿīd, who severely criticized his impious profligacy. Shamed, ʿAbd al-Raḥmān repented and ordered the gold ceiling removed and replaced with an ordinary one of wood.[72]

The Dār al-Mulk is mentioned often in the texts and appears to be an elite residence where the caliph, his heir, brothers, and distinguished guests lodged. Al-Maqqarī wrote that al-Ḥakam's brothers were housed there, and that at al-Ḥakam's ascension ceremony after ʿAbd al-Raḥmān's death, the guests "were housed according to their station in the portal chambers (*fuṣlān*) of the Dār al-Mulk."[73] In 361/972, the Dār al-Mulk was renovated and refurnished, and a door opened west of the *faṣīl al-fityān* (annex of the slaves who were his personal bodyguard) to facilitate the caliph's comings and goings.[74] Prince Hishām's lessons were also conducted in the Dār al-Mulk's east hall, where al-Ḥakam occasionally came to observe them.[75]

Al-Nuwayrī relates a story about a pavilion built outside the walls of Madīnat al-Zahrāʾ by al-Ḥakam, according to which one of the caliph's officers illegally seized land from a woman living nearby for the caliph to build a mirador (*manẓara*). The caliph, ignorant of the wrongdoing, spent a large sum to build an extraordinary mirador. But when the women took her case to court, the judge ruled against the caliph. Realizing the transgression, he immediately made restitution for the property and gave her both the wonderful pavilion and the gardens that he had built on it.[76] The story is doubtful, but some sort of mirador was indeed built near Madīnat al-Zahrāʾ as evidenced by traces of such a structure on a hillock above the city's northern enclosure wall that can be detected in aerial photographs (indicated on Fig. 10).

The Buildings Excavated

The descriptions of Madīnat al-Zahrāʾs structures are maddeningly inexact with respect to location and visual appearance, but the archaeological excavations are equally flawed as a source of information. Only 10 percent of the vast palace-city has been unearthed and that area, comprising the upper and part of the middle levels, stood on terraces that suffered greatly from erosion. Furthermore, although archaeologists have been able to reconstruct faithfully a number of buildings that were spatially central to the palace-city, they tell us little about the specific role or even the identity of most of them. However, there are a few exceptional cases where the texts and excavations join to help us recognize and understand a major building. The great congregational mosque, excavated by Pavón Maldonado in the 1960s, is one of the few buildings that can be securely identified with the building mentioned in the medieval histories (Fig. 14).

The mosque was completed in 329/941, built in forty-eight days by a team of one thousand workers (*nasama*) of which three hundred were masons (*bannāʾ*) and two hundred were carpenters (*najjār*); five hundred were ordinary laborers (*ujarāʾ*) and the rest were skilled artisans (*ṣānāʾiʿ*).[77] The mosque was placed below the middle terrace on its own platform, making it readily accessible to the ordinary inhabitants who lived on the lowest level as well as to the privileged, who reached it by a bridge extending to the roof of the mosque from the garden above (Fig. 15).

Also securely identified among Madīnat al-Zahrāʾs buildings is the Dār al-Jund (Fig. 13, no. 64), the military headquarters of the palace-city. It and various adjoining structures—the Dār Jaʿfar (Fig. 13, no. 200), the stables, and the monumental east gate—were excavated beginning in the 1950s, and restored in 1975–82 by site director Rafael Manzano Martos. The Dār al-Jund was a hall

14. The foundations of the mosque at Madīnat al-Zahrā᾿

15. The space between the upper garden and mosque formerly bridged by the *sābāṭ*

16. Dār al-Jund

of five naves, the central nave wider than the others, running perpendicular to a hall fronting the esplanade. The five naves opened to this hall through a wall pierced by double and triple arches supported by columns (Fig. 16). Although the plan of the Dār al-Jund resembles the Salon Rico (see Fig. 13), its facade was considerably plainer, lacking columns and presumably arcades. The hall's interior had little surface decoration but instead relied for effect on columnar arcades with white stone capitals and a voussoir pattern of alternating red and white stucco. Because of its austerity and the cheaper decorative techniques of the hall, the excavators concluded that it was a utilitarian building, not used for formal receptions.[78]

The Dār al-Jund's unpaved esplanade (Fig. 13, no. 70), although planted as a garden after its excavation in 1974, originally served as a corral for equestrian activities. The bedrock is close to the surface and extensive irrigation was absent, making the planting of gardens unlikely.[79] East of the courtyard was the monumental gate, the Bāb al-Sudda (Fig. 12), which measures more than sixty meters in length and consisted of great rectangular pillars supporting horseshoe arches of alternating red and white voussoirs. Above the central arch, which is slightly higher than the rest, was an aedicula from which the caliph could review the troops or watch exercises in horsemanship in the open area on the other side of the gate. Pedestrian and equestrian traffic alike passed through this center arch to enter a flagstoned passageway that rose at a gentle incline and led via a deflected path to the courtyard of the Dār al-Jund. The Dār al-Jund and this monumental gate served as a

checkpoint through which visitors passed en route to the Salon Rico. If they were permitted to ride horseback through the city, they would dismount at the Dār al-Jund, leaving their horses in its stables and walking from there to the reception halls and waiting chambers.

On the east side of the Dār al-Jund's reception hall was a residence that probably belonged to one of the high-ranking officers of the army. On the west side were stables with a sloping floor for easy cleaning, and housing and a bath for the staff. Farther to the west was a conglomerate of residential and service rooms including a residence (Fig. 13, no. 112) known as the Dār Jaʿfar after the *ḥājib* Jaʿfar ibn ʿAbd al-Raḥmān.[80] After Jaʿfar's death, al-Ḥakam's favorite *fata* Fāʾiq, overseer of textile production and *ṭirāz,* was instructed to move from his former quarters on the east side of al-Zahrāʾ to the more central Dār Jaʿfar. It was considered a sign of great favor to be housed so near the caliph's own quarters.[81] The Dār al-Jaʿfar consists of a cluster of small rooms and courts that evidently served a purely residential purpose with no ceremonial character, although they did have the benefit of direct access to the bath that was shared with the more sumptuous small garden (Fig. 13, no. 260). The rooms face west in order to fit into the irregular, leftover space allotted to them.

Above and to the north, the Dār al-Ḥājib consisted of two sets of self-contained domestic quarters (Fig. 13, nos. 148, 135). Of the two structures, the west block (no. 148) was the more formal (Fig. 17). South of this building it is a drop of seven meters down to the bodyguard quarters grouped around a narrow courtyard. There were no rooms along the south side of no. 148, allowing the

17. Residential Quarters #148

possibility that it opened outward to the south horizon for a view and that a ramp or stairs provided access to the level seven meters below.[82]

Located below the Dār al-Ḥājib and above Jaʿfar's House was a small area of leftover space that probably formed the guards' quarters (Fig. 13, nos. 75, 73, 53). This area was an important intermediary zone between the Dār al-Ḥājib, the Dār al-Jund, and the smaller dense group of service and residential rooms below (Fig. 13, nos. 112, 200), functioning as the transition zone between the public reception areas to the east and the administrative areas to the west. Here there are vestiges of a stairway leading to the upper level.[83]

West of the Dār al-Ḥājib were two residential units (Fig. 13, nos. 40, 35). Courtyard no. 40 and its rooms border the caliphal quarters along no. 40's west side. Room no. 35 had a pool with a sunken center and a latrine in the corner. Because this dwelling was near to the caliphal residence, it is logical to assume that it housed someone in close contact with the caliph, possibly the chief of the guards (*sāhib al-shurta*) or another high-ranking officer.[84]

At a sixteen-meter drop below room no. 40 and north of the small garden (no. 260) there was a plain, square structure (no. 105) with a great, central, paved courtyard surrounded by a trabeated portico (Fig. 18).[85] The building was two storied with a gallery on the upper floor off of which were small chambers for living and storage.[86] In the northwest corner a tunnel led to an unexcavated area to the west, and a stairway climbed a natural protrusion of rock that may have led to the caliphal quarters or to the upper floor.[87] The plan resembles a caravansery and indeed it may have served as a hostelry for royal guests or high-ranking staff.

Above and to the west of no. 105 was an area that, although in poor condition resulting from the collapse of its southern side, has yielded such rich decoration that it has been tentatively identified as the caliph's quarters, or Dār al-Mulk. Two capitals inscribed with al-Ḥakam's name were found in this area, indicating that it was built by that caliph.[88] Because of its location off to one side, some historians have speculated that it was where al-Ḥakam's young son was incarcerated by the regent and all-powerful *ḥājib* al-Manṣūr.[89] A well-guarded passageway ran between the residence and the city wall behind it, but this could have served equally to protect or imprison the caliph.

The small elegant residence (Fig. 13, no. 260) dubbed the "Prince's Garden" by the excavators is rectangular in plan, measuring roughly twenty meters long by nineteen meters wide, and is contained at its east and west ends by halls stretching almost the entire width of the garden (Fig. 19 and Color Plate 1). A wall (now crumbled) curtailed the south side, and on the north side, a double flight of steps leads to the buildings and circulatory road of the level above (Fig. 20). A paved walkway bordered by water channels forms a longitudinal axis that divides the garden into slightly unequal halves, and an axially aligned square pool occupies the space in front of the western hall (Fig. 21). Water ran into this verdant enclosure via sunken channels and continued its course downhill toward the large gardens of the middle level. In the northeast corner of the garden a narrow corridor leads to the bath complex that was shared with the Dār Jaʿfar. This garden residence may have been original to the founding of the city or a later addition by al-Ḥakam II. Its occupant is unknown but, judging from the luxury and beauty of the surroundings, he or she was very privileged: perhaps the heir apparent or, in later years, Prince Hishām's powerful mother, Ṣubḥ.

18. Room #105 (the "khan")

Approximately nine meters below the Dār al-Jund and its courtyard was the reception hall that has been named the Salon Rico or Hall of ʿAbd al-Raḥmān III (Figs. 22 and 23).[90] It had three naves on column arcades, the center nave slightly wider than the lateral naves, and on either side lateral bays running parallel to the naves. A transverse hall ran perpendicular to the three naves; it opened on the south side toward the garden through an arcade of five identical arches on six columns (Fig. 24). The Salon Rico had a trabeated ceiling and a pine roof that was restored in the twentieth century as a system of parallel gables following the example of the Mosque of Cordoba. Behind the hall, between the building itself and the high wall of earth resulting from the change in the terrace levels, was a second wall that served to protect the hall from the runoff of ground water from the upper level.[91] The hall's interior was dim, natural light penetrating only through the southern facade's arched openings (Fig. 25). In the summer, when the sun's arc is high, rays of direct sunlight barely cross the threshold of the hall, and the lofty interior is relatively cool. In the winter, when the sun passes at a lower, more southerly arc, light penetrates in the middle of the day, warming and brightening the interior for several hours. This heat, augmented by braziers, was preserved at night by closing the massive doors of the facade.

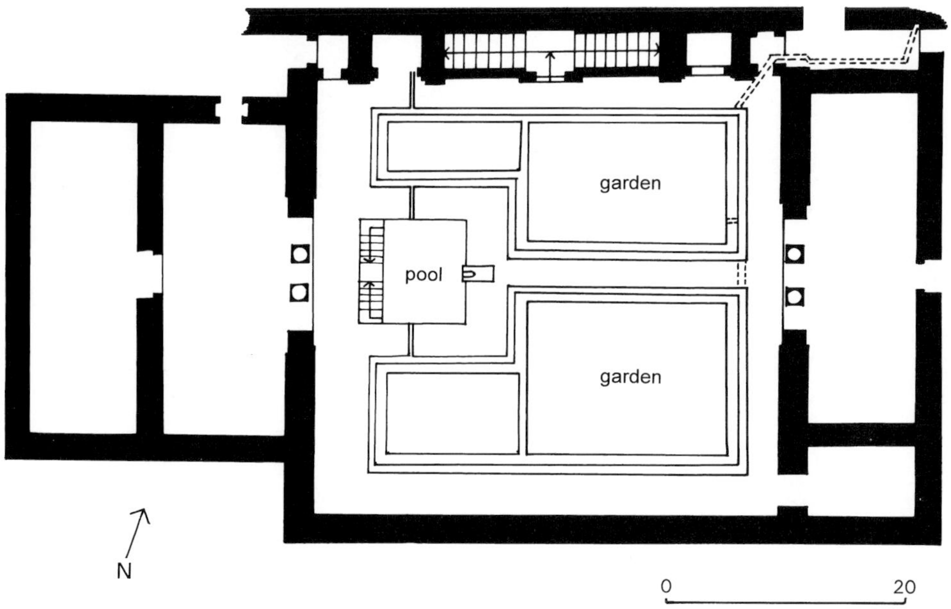

19. Plan of the Small Garden

20. The Small Garden's north wall with steps leading to the khan

21. The Small Garden's west hall and water tank

The two rows of columns were of blue-gray and of red marble, forming a bichromatic system as seen later in al-Ḥakam's extension to the Mosque of Cordoba. The blue columns were engaged, with Corinthian capitals, and the red columns were freestanding, with composite capitals.[92] Most of these were carted away as spolia in later centuries, but six capitals, three pilasters, and one base were excavated in the Salon Rico.[93] These and others found on the site and still others that been attributed to Madīnat al-Zahrāʾ on the basis of style and their inscriptions are deeply drilled in the Byzantine manner (Fig. 8). This expensive and virtuoso technique was either executed by highly skilled artisans from Constantinople, some of whom had come to work on ʿAbd al-Raḥmān's additions to the Alcazar a few decades earlier, or equally likely, it was the work of Muslims who studied with those same Byzantine masters.

The floor was paved with white marble and the walls were revetted with a white marble dado that reached a height of between fifty-eight and seventy-five centimeters.[94] Running around the top of the dado was a red stucco band above which was a decorative frieze in which were set slightly projecting decorative panels of stone approximately 4 centimeters thick (Fig. 26). Although these fell when the Salon Rico was destroyed with the rest of the palace-city in the eleventh century, they have been painstakingly collected and in many cases reassembled by the archaeologists of the

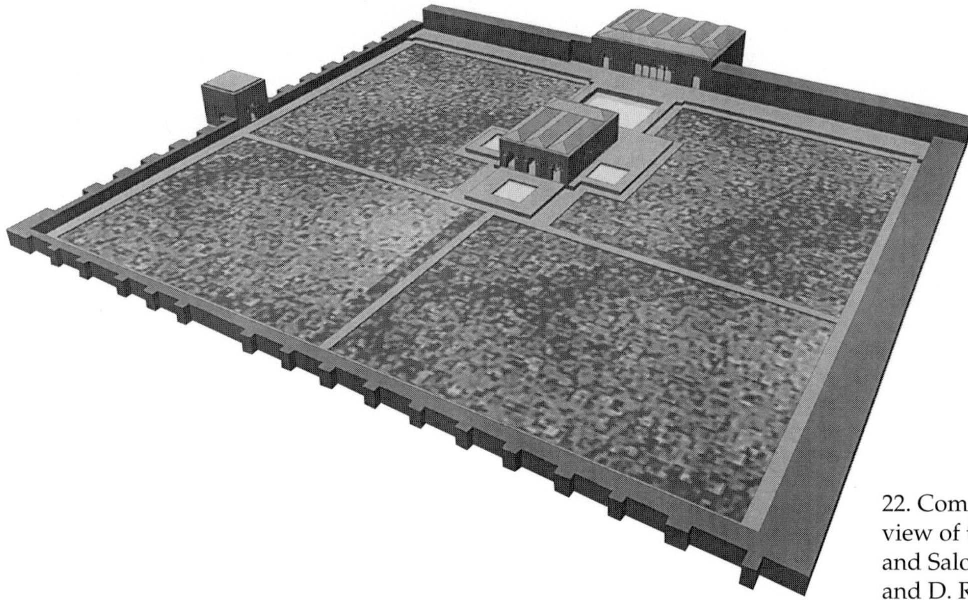

22. Computer-generated view of the upper garden and Salon Rico (H. Wilke and D. Ruggles)

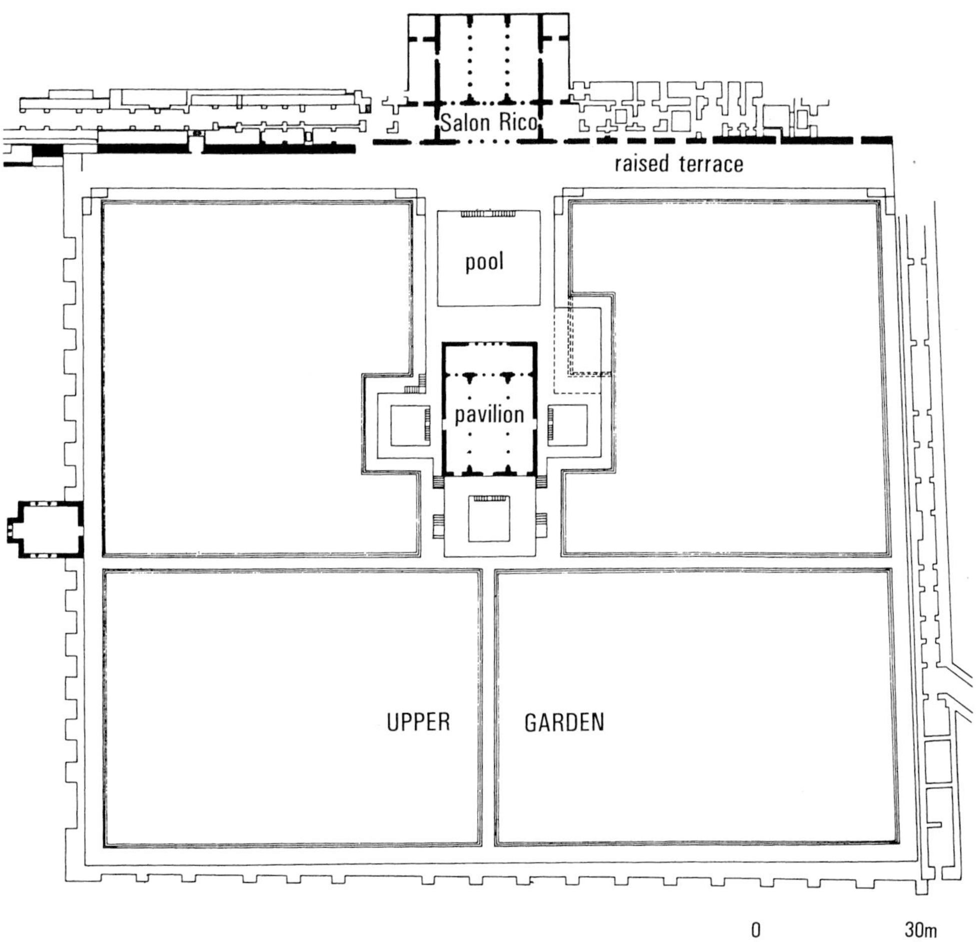

23. Plan of the upper garden at Madīnat al-Zahrā' (after A. Jiménez Martín)

24. The Salon Rico

Conjunto Arqueológico (Fig. 27). The lively vegetal designs of the panels here and elsewhere in the Salon Rico have both Roman and Abbasid precedents but were adapted to a new, specifically Andalusian, decorative repertoire.[95] The horseshoe arches borne on the twin arcades of seven columns had alternating red and white voussoirs (Color Plate 2) in conformance with the royal style established in the Cordoba Mosque as early as the eighth century (Fig. 28), except that here the polychromy was realized in stucco and the white voussoirs were carved with vegetal motifs not unlike those of the wall panels. At the rear of the central nave a blind niche or simulated door continued the alternating red-and-white motif of the nave arcades.

Several fragmentary inscriptions were found in the rubble. On one of the side walls where a doorway leads to the side chamber, a central tablet with a Kufic inscription lists the architects. A capital, column base, and plaque name ʿAbd al-Raḥmān al-Nāṣir as the hall's patron with the various dates 342/953–54, 343/954–55, and 345/956–57.[96] But ʿAbd al-Raḥmān was giving audiences in "the hall overlooking the gardens" in 338/949 and holding official audiences elsewhere in Madīnat al-Zahrāʾ even as early as 333/944.[97] The epigraphy suggests that the Salon Rico was built two decades after the palace was founded, and archaeology reveals that older structures were demolished to make room for the new hall. This may explain, in part, the confusion in names and the description of the layout of the ceremonial halls that occurs in the histories.[98]

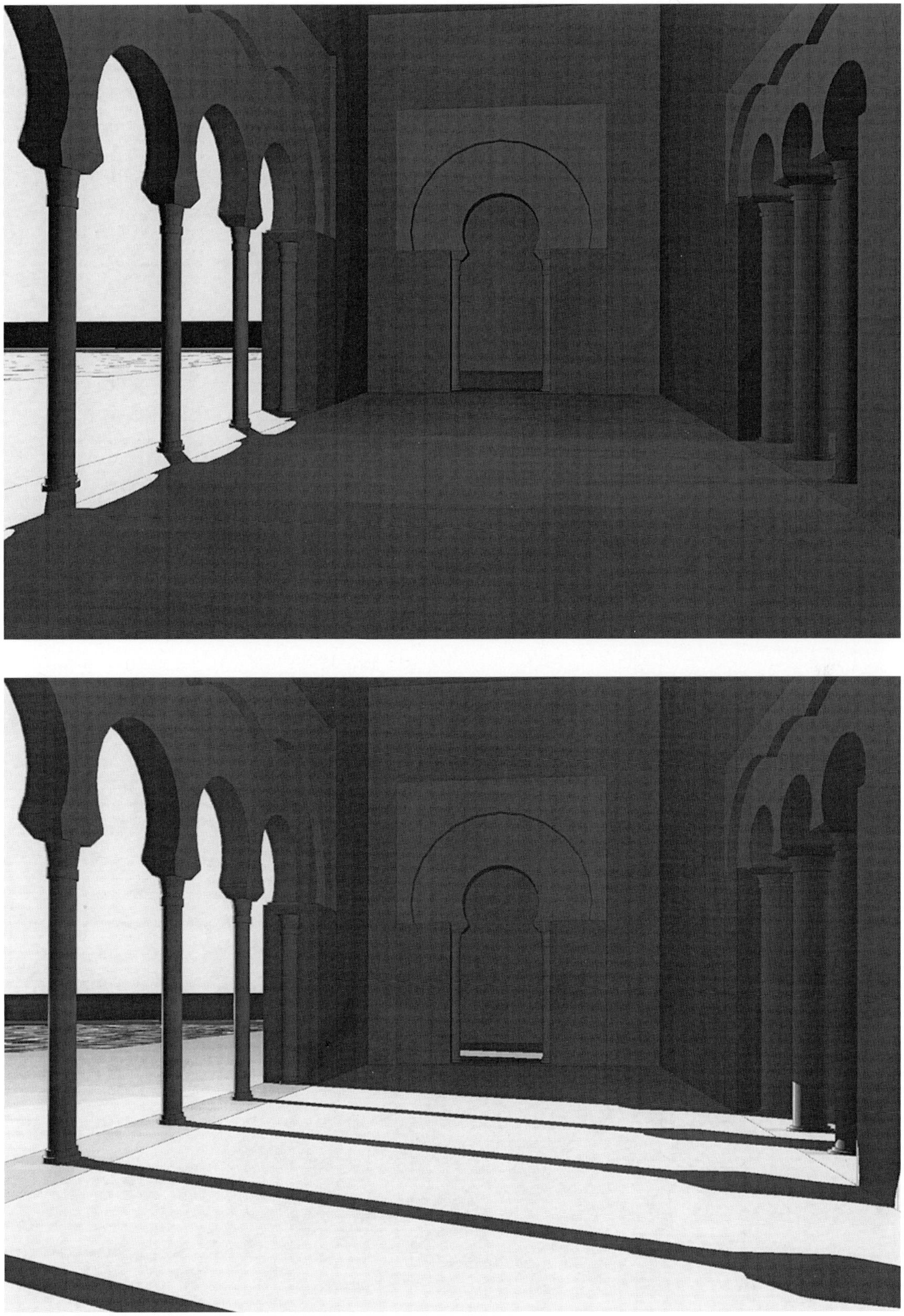

25. Top: the Salon Rico at noon in the summer solstice. Bottom: the Salon Rico at noon in the winter solstice (H. Wilke and D. Ruggles)

26. Decorative stone panel fragments from the Salon Rico (R. Velázquez Bosco)

27. Stucco fragments on the ground prior to being catalogued and reassembled

28. Red and white arches in the Mosque of Cordoba

Adjoining the Salon Rico on its east side was a small, richly decorated bath complex with antechambers, a latrine, and a small open courtyard (Fig. 29). Epigraphic fragments date the baths to 350/961–62.[99] The courtyard was paved and supplied with running water, and in its center was a freestanding, ten-faceted water basin, half the facets of which are carved with palmette designs. The bath communicated with the Salon Rico by means of the walkway that ran along the edge of the garden and evidently served the caliph, courtiers, and literati who gathered there.

The Salon Rico and its auxiliary buildings opened onto an extensive walled upper garden (163 by 144 meters as measured from the exterior of the thick containing walls) that was crossed by paved walkways (Fig. 30).[100] Two parallel walkways ran along the front of the Salon Rico, the lower one eighty-five centimeters below the upper, connected by ramps fitted into the corners of the garden quarters. The lower walkways divided the garden into four quadrants and were bordered by channels for irrigation (Fig. 31). The north arm was taken up by a large rectangular pool measuring nineteen meters on each side and a pavilion surrounded by smaller tanks. The pavilion faced the Salon Rico and, like it, was composed of three naves fronted by a longitudinal hall.

Access to the terrace containing the Salon Rico and the upper garden was restricted to four points (Fig. 32). In the northwest corner the upper garden communicated with the lower garden via

29. Bath courtyard

30. View of the upper garden and the foundations of the pavilion opposite the Salon Rico

31. Water channels and corner ramps in the upper garden

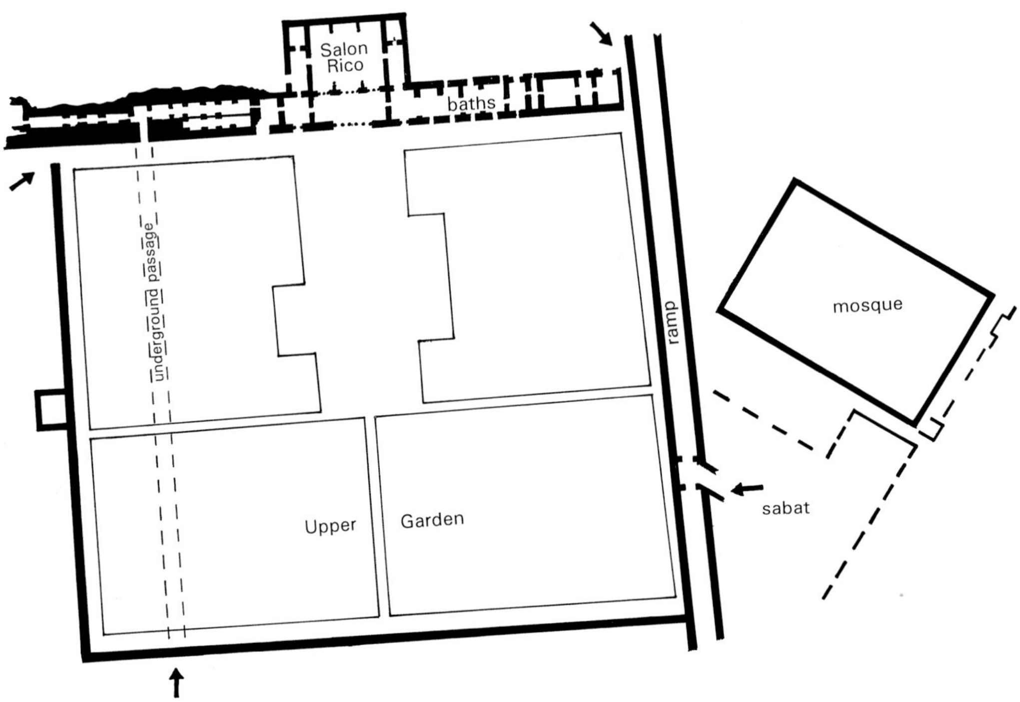

32. Access to the upper garden

33. Underground corridor running below the upper garden

a sloping ramp and an extremely narrow and winding set of stairs that were presumably used for service (but the archaeological authenticity of these stairs is questionable, since they belong to a part of the buttress wall that was almost entirely rebuilt in the process of shoring up the upper garden).[101] A subterranean passageway ran from the Salon Rico's west corridor under the upper garden to the lower south terrace (Fig. 33). This passage was later blocked, presumably by al-Manṣūr as part of his modifications to Madīnat al-Zahrāʾ when he incarcerated Hishām.[102] A staircase east of the Salon Rico gave access to the terrace above and the Dār al-Jund.[103] On the east side a bridge united the upper garden with the mosque.

The bridge (*sābāṭ*) was an urban device imported into this palace setting; in Cordoba such a passageway connected the Alcazar to the congregational mosque, passing over the busy street that ran between the two buildings. The Cordoba passageway had been installed by ʿAbd al-Raḥmān III's grandfather and mentor, ʿAbd Allāh, to protect himself from assassination and to facilitate his movement between palace and mosque, and it was duplicated at Madīnat al-Zahrāʾ for presumably the same purposes. It also shows that the close relationship between mosque and governor's palace (*dār al-imāra*) that developed in Syria under the Umayyad caliph al-Walīd was still maintained in al-Andalus more than two hundred years later.

In summary, the sources with their generous accounts of the founding and construction of Madīnat al-Zahrāʾ do not always correlate with the excavated site. For example, while the historians named six pavilions and reception halls, only three (including the Dār al-Jund) have been archaeologically revealed. Doubtless the collapse of the terrace below the caliphal quarters destroyed some halls, and rebuilding during the reigns of ʿAbd al-Raḥmān III and al-Ḥakam II means that the site had various phases, the chronology of which is undetermined. Despite the excavation of important areas of the palatial quarter, one must use caution in matching tenth-century descriptions with the site as it exists today. Because it has been incompletely excavated, one cannot assume that the halls described in the medieval written sources are, by fortunate coincidence, identical with those that have been unearthed and restored. Matters are further complicated by the fact that while we know how halls such as Madīnat al-Zahrāʾs Majlis al-Sharqī were used in palace ceremonies, the medieval histories do not tell us how these halls might have been used at other times and by whom.

5

MADĪNAT AL-ZAHRĀʾ, SAMARRA, AND THE VIEW

And one-third of the city [was] gardens overlooked by miradors and palaces.
—Al-Nuwayrī

Madīnat al-Zahrāʾ sprang from the Cordoban tradition of building *munya*s and recreation estates in the agricultural zone surrounding the city, yet it was an architectural type new to al-Andalus. Like earlier estates, the palace Madīnat al-Zahrāʾ was built well apart from Cordoba in a green and well-watered landscape, but unlike the others, Madīnat al-Zahrāʾ was not a *munya.* It was larger, more architecturally complex, and functionally more diverse and self-sufficient than its precursors, and as a result it was less dependent on Cordoba's urban center. In size it surpassed the Munyat al-Naʿūra, the largest of the *munya* estates; it was, in fact, an altogether new type of palace, born of the typological union of the agricultural *munya* that took shape within the regional context of Cordoba, and the sophisticated palace architecture that had developed in the east in the preceding century.

Until the middle of the tenth century, the favored locations for estates were the west and south sides of the city, on the flat ground of the Guadalquivir Valley along the river. The Balāṭ Mughīth, Munyat ʿAjab, Munyat al-Naṣr, Munyat al-Naʿūra, and Dār al-Rawḍa were all built on or near the banks of the Guadalquivir in a landscape of natural beauty, or one made beautiful through irrigation and the planting of graceful trees. In describing the *munya*s, Arabic authors placed more emphasis on the beauty and salubriousness of their locations and vegetation than on the actual architecture of the buildings. Water systems consisting of aqueducts, norias, channels, pools, and fountains figure in such detail in the texts that today it is easier to map the hydraulic landscape of caliphal Cordoba than it is to reconstruct one of its palaces. Relatively simple and self-contained, and depending upon the immediate environment of pleasant greenery and cooling waters for aesthetic effects, the *munya*s were distinguished more for the lovely environments created within and around them than for the architectural design of their buildings.

The delight in nature and agricultural estates seems to have been a Roman legacy inherited by the early Umayyads and transmitted from Syria to the already thoroughly Romanized Iberian Peninsula. The pavilion in the garden of Hishām's palace at Ruṣāfa in Syria was elevated above the surrounding garden (watered by a nearby stream) on a plinth, with three steps on each side from which extended walkways raised above ground level.[1] That it was designed for an elevated view of

the garden with vistas on all four sides is evident from the apertures in the pavilion's walls and surrounding arcade and from the axial walkways (discussed in Chapter 3). From this Syrian palace, or others like it, ʿAbd al-Raḥmān I and his followers brought the idea of country estates endowed with cross-axial gardens, fountains, and graceful pavilions to al-Andalus; a century and a half later the quadripartite plan appeared at Madīnat al-Zahrāʾ, the earliest surviving Andalusian palace with extant gardens.

Perhaps the distance separating al-Andalus from the center of Islam, which had the unfortunate effect of keeping the kingdom isolated for two centuries, had the positive result of allowing autonomous architectural development in the west, much as the poets of Cordoba, although steeped in the literature of the east, developed—according to their own accounts—a more humanistic content, experimenting with new poetic forms (such as *muwashshaḥāt*), romantic love poetry, and sensitive responses to nature's beauty.[2] But that isolation, which began to dissolve in the ninth century, had vanished by the tenth. ʿAbd al-Raḥmān III al-Nāṣir introduced new elements, inviting foreign artists, scholars, and literati to his court, with a profound impact on the arts of al-Andalus. These visitors from the eastern Mediterranean—Constantinople and Baghdad in particular—brought with them new ideas about art, architecture, and palace ceremonial that immediately fused with the Umayyad *munya* tradition. The fruit of this union was Madīnat al-Zahrāʾ, where the new eastern concept of palatial magnificence and complexity using rich materials for highly theatrical effects was realized in a verdant Umayyad landscape of gardens and orchards.

ʿAbd al-Raḥmān III emulated his Abbasid and, to a lesser extent, Fatimid enemies and Byzantine allies. The extraordinary splendor and luxury of Madīnat al-Zahrāʾ rivaled not only the Abbasid palaces of Samarra and Raqqa but other Mediterranean competitors such as the late ninth-century Tulunid palace at al-Qaṭāʾīʿ (Egypt) which, in turn, took Baghdad as its model. Indeed, the impact of Abbasid architectural innovations were felt across the Islamic world, from Central Asia (and the palace of Lashkar-i Bāzār) to northern Africa. The courtyards of this Tulunid palace were planted with myrtles, palms, fruit trees, roses, and saffron, and received exotic plants from as far away as Khurasan that were then grafted onto native stock to create hardy new plants.[3] One hall had a mercury pool, mentioned in the previous chapter. These gigantic palaces, in which water courses ran through courtyards and trees were gilded,[4] belonged to a new paradigm of exorbitant consumption and opulence that differed markedly from the stately but comparatively simple Umayyad complexes of Syria and emiral al-Andalus. Madīnat al-Zahrāʾ was the first Andalusian palace to take its place within this paradigm. According to al-Maqqarī: "When al-Nāṣir built the palace of al-Zahrāʾ, which was the utmost of splendor and magnificence, everyone agreed that nothing of its kind had ever before been built in Islam. Those who entered it from faraway places and of different social ranks—an arriving king, a visiting ambassador, a successful merchant, all of them intelligent and perceptive—judged that they had never seen or heard of anything like it, nor imagined the existence of such a thing."[5]

Lévi-Provençal believed that ʿAbd al-Raḥmān took the Byzantine empire as his model.[6] Al-Andalus united with Byzantium in the tenth century against the Fatimids and the Abbasids, with instances of the Byzantines lending fighting ships to aid the Umayyads and other instances of the Umayyads aiding the Byzantine navy.[7] However, while the political alliances were strong, and

while the Byzantines made diplomatic gifts of books, works of art, and the services of artists and scholars, the Byzantine political and cultural might was used primarily to enhance al-Andalus's position vis-à-vis competing Muslim powers, particularly the immediate threat of the newly risen Fatimids, who ruled Tunisia with Sicily and northern Morocco as tributaries. Ultimately the goal of ʿAbd al-Raḥmān was not simply to make his kingdom more like Byzantium but to learn from Byzantine artists and scholars in order to compete better in the Mediterranean arena, with Baghdad standing as the model of cultural achievement. That city, not Constantinople, was the standard against which all Islamic kingdoms measured themselves, and it was stock praise to call a city the rival of Baghdad.[8] For example, for Ibn Ghālib, the people of al-Andalus were like those of Baghdad with respect to their elegance, cleanliness, intelligence, the sensitivity of their characters, and so forth.[9] Al-Maqqarī cited Ibn Saʿīd's comment that al-Rāzī's history of Cordoba paralleled Ibn Abī Ṭāhir's history of Baghdad,[10] and he noted that when Ibn Shuhayd was the first functionary to be named double vizier (*dhū al-wizāratayn*) of Cordoba, it was in imitation of Saʾīd Ibn Mukhlid, vizier to the Abbasids at Baghdad.[11] Historians compared Cordoba's size, population, and importance to that of Baghdad, and they compared the Guadalquivir River to the Tigris or the Nile. Even when the comment was negative, as when Ibn Ḥawqal remarked that Cordoba was barely half the size of Baghdad, the Abbasids were still the standard of comparison.[12]

The Abbasid Palaces

That Madīnat al-Zahrāʾ was profoundly influenced by Abbasid palace typology is evident from a comparison with two Samarran palaces: the Jawsaq al-Khāqānī, more appropriately called the Dār al-Khilāfa (caliph's residence), built about 836, and Balkuwārā, built 849–59 (both excavated by Ernst Herzfeld in the early part of this century).[13] These palaces resembled cities, deep within which the caliph and his throne room were located, reached only by a long route via gates, courtyards, gardens, antechambers, and reception halls. In Baghdad, the Abbasid caliphs had begun the process of distancing themselves from the general populace in the eighth century for security reasons. Al-Manṣūr built himself a huge round city consisting of concentric defense walls that enclosed rings of residential quarters and in the heart of which were the palace and administrative quarters (Fig. 34). As the caliph removed himself architecturally and ceremonially from ordinary interaction with his people, he became a more mysterious and remote figure.[14] But eventually Baghdad became too confining, and frictions arose between the residents and the troops stationed there; the markets had already been moved outside the walls and various suburban pleasure palaces built in the environs. In 221/836 al-Muʿtaṣim sought an entirely new residence in Samarra, where he constructed monumental palaces for himself and his sons with extensive courtyards and multiple walls with limited points of ingress that satisfied the complementary desires for safety and extravagantly luxurious ceremonial spaces.

Madīnat al-Zahrāʾ reveals a similar concern for multiple enclosure walls containing a variety of residences, administrative quarters, and stages for display. Like the Abbasids of Samarra, ʿAbd al-Raḥmān withdrew from the capital city, bringing with him those attendants, administrative of-

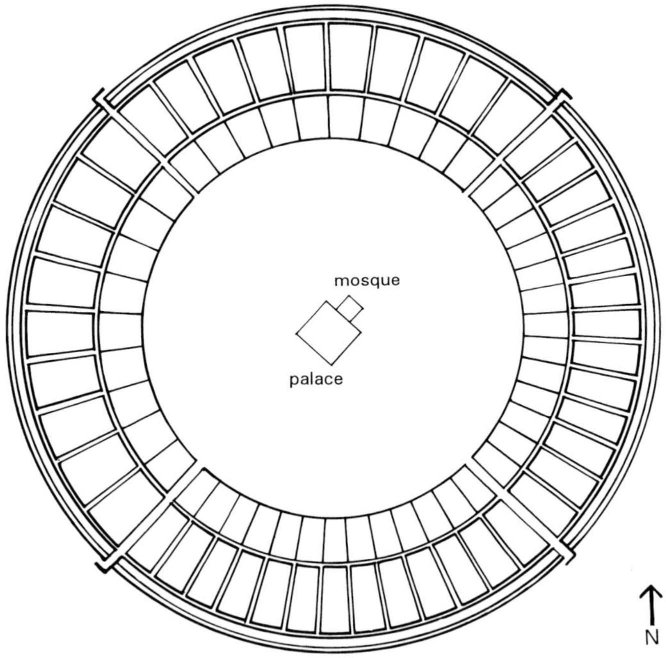

34. Plan of the round city of Baghdad (after K. A. C. Creswell)

ficials, merchants, and craft workers deemed necessary for his new role as caliph, the title of which he had adopted six years earlier, in 929.[15] In proclaiming himself caliph, he raised his rank from prince of a small kingdom on the fringe of the Islamic world, to one of theoretically international stature, contraposing his claim to that of the Abbasids and the Fatimid pretenders.

The question of the Umayyad claim to the caliphate had lain dormant for almost two centuries. On the one hand, the Umayyads adamantly rejected the Abbasids as usurpers and, within a year of their arrival in al-Andalus, had ordered that the *khuṭba* (Friday sermon) be pronounced in the name of the current Umayyad emir.[16] But on the other hand, they were in no position to incite the ire of the Abbasids, faced with the latter's superior military strength. In any case, the Hispano-Umayyad caliphate was not accepted outside the western Mediterranean since, as Mas'ūdī wrote in 332/944, they did not rule over the sacred places of Arabia.[17] Thus, 'Abd al-Raḥmān III's claim to international stature was more of a reality in the eyes of the Umayyads and their Maghrebi allies than in Abbasid eyes; in short the Umayyads were far more preoccupied with the Abbasids than vice versa. They were at once alarmed and fascinated by the Abbasids; yet while they sought to forestall a possible military invasion, they welcomed an invasion of another sort.

The Abbasidization of the administrative structure of al-Andalus had begun as early as the ninth century and was soon followed by cultural and artistic emulation as well, until by the tenth century, the ruler of Cordoba had more in common with his Abbasid rival than with his Syrian ancestors.[18] The Abbasids had redefined the cultural and political role of the caliph and set new standards of cosmopolitan sophistication in their magnificent palaces, surrounded by poets, musicians, scholars, and artists. The descriptions of ceremonies at the court of Madīnat al-Zahrā' indicate

that Abbasid ceremonial was matched by Hispano-Umayyad pomp in which visitors to the caliphal palace, escorted through halls and courtyards of the palace, were both confused by its complexity and astounded by its magnificence. In a celebration of the return from the Maghreb of the military commander Ghālib accompanied by the Banū Idrīs, the inhabitants of the court were positioned hierarchically in the Majlis al-Sharqī and its terrace and adjoining halls, the royal brothers, viziers, and supervisors arrayed in magnificent raiments like the "pearls of a necklace." When everyone was in place, the visitors were ushered into the palace through two lines of infantry and archers, pausing first at the Dār al-Jund, then proceeding to the House of Viziers, the high terrace, and the hall where the caliph awaited them "in a most solemn, brilliant, majestic, and impressive manner."[19] The studied pageantry of this event resembled the reception of the Byzantine embassy in the court of the Abbasid caliph al-Muqtadir at Baghdad in 305/917, where the visitors passed through courtyards and corridors in the palace, which was filled with followers and troops. They were taken to the Court of the Horses and passed by the Park of Wild Beasts. They proceeded next to the New Palace, which was an enclosure between gardens with a central pool surrounded by four hundred palm trees dressed from top to bottom in painted cloths hung with golden rings. Then they went to the Tree Court, a palace called Paradise, and on and on until they were finally brought before al-Muqtadir in the palace called the Crown (*tāj*), which gave onto the Tigris River.[20]

Madīnat al-Zahrā᾽ was comparable to the Samarran palaces in size, and was approximately one hundred times bigger than the largest Umayyad palace (Fig. 35). The highly complex subdivision of spaces and the separation of public reception areas from personal living quarters in the plan of Madīnat al-Zahrā᾽ reflects an Abbasid-like sophistication. Samarra's Dār al-Khilāfa contained a monumental entrance, several gardens and esplanades with pavilions, a central reception complex consisting of multiple halls arranged around a domed throne room, residential zones including a women's quarter and military barracks, great and little *serdābs* (subterranean chambers), a treasury, a mosque (not shown on Creswell's plan), and at the eastern end of the palace a polo ground, hunting preserve, race track, and zoological gardens. Madīnat al-Zahrā᾽ had a monumental gate, several gardens and esplanades, a central reception complex, residential quarters for the caliph, his heir, advisors, and generals, a mint, barracks, at least two mosques, an aviary, a fishpond, and a zoo. Clearly Madīnat al-Zahrā᾽ had more in common with the Dār al-Khilāfa than with any Cordoban antecedent. The Munyat al-Naʿūra was the largest of the forerunners with its thirty-odd residential and service buildings, and yet it could not compare to Madīnat al-Zahrā᾽ in size, opulence, or functional diversity. Madīnat al-Zahrā᾽ was a city unto itself, and its scale and magnificence was a new architectural phenomenon in the kingdom of al-Andalus.

One aspect of architectural splendor that stemmed from the Abbasids was the inclusion of large gardens within the walls of the caliphal palace. The love of nature, and even the cross-axial garden plan, was an Umayyad legacy, as we have seen, but the Abbasids espoused a grandiosity in which space and the control of vision within it served the state ideology. Underlying both the Umayyad and Abbasid architectures was a debt to an older conceptualization of domestic nature that was non-Islamic (i.e., Roman and Sasanian, and even these shared some common roots). The Umayyad predilection for living away from the city in estates surrounded by nature was overlaid in tenth-century Cordoba with Abbasid formal elements, scale, and grandiosity. The transmission

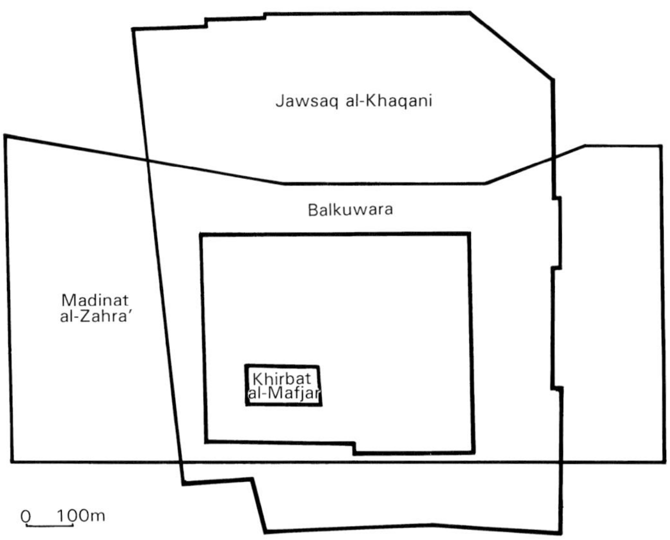

35. Comparison of the size of Madīnat al-Zahrā' with Umayyad and Abbasid palaces

of architectural motives and ideas from Samarra to Cordoba occurred when scholars and poets traveled between the courts: for example, when Ziryāb arrived at the court of ʿAbd al-Raḥmān II in the ninth century, he was an important purveyor of eastern music, manners, and sartorial fashion.[21] Abbasid poetry was also brought by artists such as the gifted singer Qamar, a female slave from Baghdad serving in the retinue of Ibrāhāim ibn Ḥajjāj, the governor of Seville.[22] Additionally, foreign artisans such as architects and mosaicists from Byzantium and Syria found work in al-Andalus. Ziryāb and many others traveled to al-Andalus via North African centers, such as the Aghlabid, Tulunid, or Fatimid courts, so that it is hard to judge when eastern notions of royal splendor came directly from the Abbasid center and when they came via these important Mediterranean intermediaries.[23] The Aghlabids, in particular, governed in the name of the Abbasids and were important purveyors of Abbasid ideas in the central Mediterranean until they were conquered in 196/909.

Fiat Cities and Foundation Myths

Baghdad, Samarra, Madīnat al-Zahrā', and the ninth-century Aghlabid cities of Raqqada and ʿAbbāsīya (near Kairouan) were large-scale foundations built at the behest of powerful rulers with tremendous financial resources. They were suburban developments built as escapes from teeming, bustling capital cities. In the case of Samarra and Madīnat al-Zahrā', the patron experimented by building palaces in other suburban locales before commencing with the palace-city. Just as the Abbasid caliph al-Muʿtaṣim (r. 218–27/833–42) gave land grants to his followers to encourage settlement. ʿAbd al-Raḥmān III made grants to his followers to settle in the vicinity of al-Zahrā'.[24] The creation of an entirely new city served two purposes: centrality and identity.

First, the sovereign could design the new city with himself as the centerpiece. Baghdad, Raqqa (Syria, 772), and Ṣabra-Manṣūrīya (near Kairouan) were all cities stamped with sovereign identity, with radial axes leading from city gates outward to the rest of the world.[25] At the imperial capital Baghdad, the ruler used this device to mark his position—signified by the royal palace in where he sat under a double dome—at the intersection of the axes, symbolically the center of the universe.[26] While Samarra's palaces and Madīnat al-Zahrāʾ were not round, each nonetheless enveloped its royal inhabitant in a frame that separated him from his people and provided him with a throne room or reception hall from which he dominated the rest of the palace. Madīnat al-Zahrāʾ, Balkuwārā, and the Dār al-Khilāfa were monumental complexes that were like palaces in terms of the ground plan and the security measures to protect the royal inhabitants, yet resembled cities with respect to their size and complexity.

Second, by building anew, the king bypassed the established power base and long-standing associations of the older city, which had sprung to life decades or centuries ago and already had an existence independent of whichever king inhabited it. Furthermore, building upon a site where nothing had existed previously was a symbolic act with charitable resonance. He introduced civilization into emptiness in a manner that recalls the distinction between *ʿāmir* and *ghāmir* lands (see Chapter 1) and cast him as omnipotent benefactor. Whether or not the site was actually as desolate originally as the chroniclers would have us believe is irrelevant. The patron retained the identity of central authority, controller, and ruler while he inhabited the palace, and the palace existed thereafter as a tangible testimonial to him. It was not enough to occupy an already built palace; each ruler had to build anew in order to set in motion the cycle of collecting artisans and materials, choosing the site, bestowing the surrounding parcels of land, making himself the supreme actor and central point of the expanding territory. In the words of the Abbasid caliph al-Mutawakkil: "Now I know that I am indeed a king, for I have built myself a city and live in it."[27]

It is surely for this reason that ʿAbd al-Raḥmān was dissatisfied with his additions to the Munyat al-Naʾūra. Despite the improvements, the original identification of it as ʿAbd Allāh's *munya* stuck, so that it never acquired the prestige desired for a caliph. To give architectural expression to his new title, he had to found a new palace estate, larger and more splendid than any of the *munya*s and in an area that was not imbued with the identity of a previous patron. Creating Madīnat al-Zahrāʾ was the architectural equivalent of giving himself caliphal titulature.

In the palaces of Baghdad, Samarra, and al-Zahrāʾ, size, magnificence, and pomp were stressed.[28] However, despite the great wealth displayed within the palaces, none of it was immediately visible from the exterior. Entry was reserved for a select group of individuals; that the rest could only imagine the opulence within the palace walls added to the mystery enshrouding the palace and increased the perception of the distance separating the king from his people.[29] Most Cordobans saw Madīnat al-Zahrāʾ only from a distance. Access to the city, which was entirely walled, was controlled through a few well-guarded portals, and of those who were allowed entrance, only the aristocracy, selected scholars and poets, and visiting ambassadors were received in the halls of the middle and upper levels of the Qaṣr. Indeed, Madīnat al-Zahrāʾ was largely used for entertaining international visitors and for major festivals. For public audiences and the dispensing of justice to the local populace, ʿAbd al-Raḥmān and his son al-Ḥakam received not at Madīnat al-Zahrāʾ but at Cordoba; and there they also returned regularly to greet the public on holidays and

review military parades from a chamber above one of the portals of the Alcazar. Because Madīnat al-Zahrāʾs splendor was unlike anything else in Cordoba at the time (even the Cordoba Mosque's glittering mosaic mihrab and dome over the bay in front of the mihrab were not added until after 350/961), the palace was the object of fascination and wonder. The profusion of gold tile work, ebony doors, and marble basins and the spectacular entertainments held in Madīnat al-Zahrāʾs halls were copiously described by historical chroniclers and became legendary. The new style of architecture, rich in ornament and costly materials, seems to have generated historical documentation equally rich in detail.

The fact that fiat foundations were built quickly and on a large scale was a sign of the sovereign's omnipotence, for only he could garner such a prodigious workforce. The summoning of skilled experts in building demonstrated, symbolically, that his authority reached to the four corners of the world. In his foundation of Baghdad, for example, the Abbasid caliph al-Manṣūr "issued a written demand abroad that they should send him all those who knew anything about construction, and there arrived one hundred thousand various artisans and laborers;" and at Samarra, too, the caliph al-Muʿtaṣim summoned specialized artisans and materials.[30] In like manner, ʿAbd al-Raḥmān sought the best artists and materials from the Islamic and Christian worlds to decorate his palaces, beginning with Dār al-Rawḍa and the Munyat al-Naʾūra and culminating with Madīnat al-Zahrāʾ. The theme of vast numbers of imported laborers served to emphasize the extensive political influence of the Abbasid and Umayyad kings and to demonstrate their power since, by means of a mere summons, workers from near and far scurried to do their bidding.

Another device enhancing royal prestige in architecture was the foundation myth that conveyed the notion of pious deeds and the ineluctability of fate. Accordingly, while al-Muʿtaṣim and ʿAbd al-Raḥmān were portrayed as great founders who had only to issue the command in order for their words to be immediately carried out, they were also portrayed as instruments of God's will. Madīnat al-Zahrāʾ was supposedly built with a concubine's bequest only after all Muslim prisoners of war had been rescued from Christian hands.[31] While the story conflicts with more reliable statements that the palace construction consumed one-third of the annual state revenues, it provided a convenient and quasi-beneficent post facto justification for the exorbitant expenditures, so that ʿAbd al-Raḥmān's self-aggrandisement acquired a veneer of good works: his first priority was the repatriation of his soldiers, and only when that obligation was met did he turn to palace building. Several decades later, when the site for a second palace-city, Madīnat al-Zāhira, was chosen, it, too, was justified by a foundation story. After divinatory calculations had identified the locality near Cordoba as the place for the new palace city, an elderly woman said to the caliph's man, "Long ago we heard that a city would be built here and that its king would settle near this well. How hard the Amīr al-Muʾminīn has tried in his inquiries about it; yet that which God decrees is inevitable!"[32]

The prophecy resembles one associated with Samarra according to which the caliph al-Muʿtaṣim did not select the site at random but learned that it was predestined to be a palace-city. He was told: "'In our ancient books this place is named Samarra. It is the city of Sem, son of Noah. According to these books, it will be rebuilt in future centuries by the care of an illustrious king, crowned with success and victories. . . .' To which he replied, 'By God, it is I who will build it; I will reign over it and my descendants will, too.'"[33] In light of the propensity among Arabic geographers and historians for likening Cordoba to Baghdad, the parallel was surely deliberate. In these foun-

dation accounts the king is represented as the pious instrument of God's will. Moreover, a teleology is constructed in which the rule of the king and the foundation of the palace-city that will be the seat of his authority and power is preordained, divinely appointed.

The foundation *topoi* that endowed the geographical site with meaning, and the founder with pious intent, were part of the myth-making apparatus deployed by these rulers. ʿAbd al-Raḥmān III was the first of the Spanish Umayyads to arrogate caliphal authority, and for his palace, Madīnat al-Zahrāʾ, he chose a model that could express the ideas of earthly omnipotence and divine ordination. His adoption of the Abbasid model of the royal seat, including its fiat-foundation and construction *topoi,* is therefore not surprising.

Abbasid Gardens and Views

The windows, terraces, and elevated portals of Abbasid palaces were designed with the idea of presenting views and framing the act of vision. In contradistinction, at the Umayyad country palaces such as Qaṣr al-Ḥayr West (dated by inscription to 109/727), Khirbat al-Mafjar (c. 739–43), and Khirbat al-Minya (c. 712–15) nothing was discovered by the archaeologists to suggest that there were windows, except for narrow slits for defense, or places such as balconies, terraces, and elevated portals dedicated to pleasurable views. The plans of these complexes—rectangular enclosures with central courtyards—are inner directed, and even the throne rooms looked inward to the courtyard rather than onto the exterior landscape. The only place where there is evidence to suggest that the topography was architecturally exploited to enhance ceremonial is the Umayyad caliphal residence Muwaqqar (Jordan), the cistern of which was dated by inscription to 104/722–23. This palace was built on an artificial platform on a rise in the landscape, where the city's outer horizon seems to meet the countryside beyond.[34]

In contrast, at Madīnat al-Zahrāʾ and many of the Abbasid palaces the rustic location and huge size of the palace-cities allowed the incorporation of considerable areas of landscape and different kinds of gardens within the walls of the palace and even in close proximity to the formal reception chambers, which were often elevated. Moreover, the gardens were planned to aesthetic advantage. Instead of being mere groves of fruit trees, the gardens were laid out symmetrically with paved walkways, pavilions, fountains, and pools. The greatest emphasis on visual organization and ornamentation was focused at the throne room in the center, reached by passing through gardened courtyards. This palace block was in turn surrounded by a median zone of gardens that were less charged with ceremonial purpose and thus, perhaps, less artistically arranged. This in turn was surrounded by an extramural zone of fine houses with gardens that ultimately dissolved into an area of ordinary agricultural cultivation, beyond which were uncultivated lands stretching toward the horizon and denoting the boundaries of civilized space.

Vistas and the experience of walking through the Abbasid palace gardens were not left to chance but guided by means of the careful placement of built structures either set within or overlooking the cultivated enclosure. The drama of these views was unprecedented in the Umayyad period: like palatial grandeur and opulence, they were an Abbasid device associated with the apparatus of sovereignty that was adopted by ʿAbd al-Raḥmān when he became caliph.

The emphasis on belvederes and viewing points was already evident in the round city of Baghdad, where the caliph could simultaneously display himself and watch the traffic in and out of his city from a domed viewing station (*majlis*) over each of the city walls' four portals. These portals looked immediately at the reviewing ground, mosques, stables, and various state offices, but beyond these, from the Khurasan Gate, which was reputed to be his favorite, he could also see the palaces and gardens that graced the riverbank on that side of the city.[35]

At Samarra, the keen interest in vision appeared in the Musharrahāt Palace, which had the elevated Burj al-Qā'im, built by al-Mutawakkil (r. 232–247/847–61), and it was evident in al-Mutawakkil's man-made mound, the Tall al-ʿAlīq, with its nine-room kiosk from where he could watch the training of his horses.[36] At the Dār al-Khilāfa, the monumental entrance on the west side of the palace offered an elevated view of gardens, the Tigris River, and the landscape beyond (Fig. 36).[37] The long axis around which the palace is organized began from this great portal, identified as the

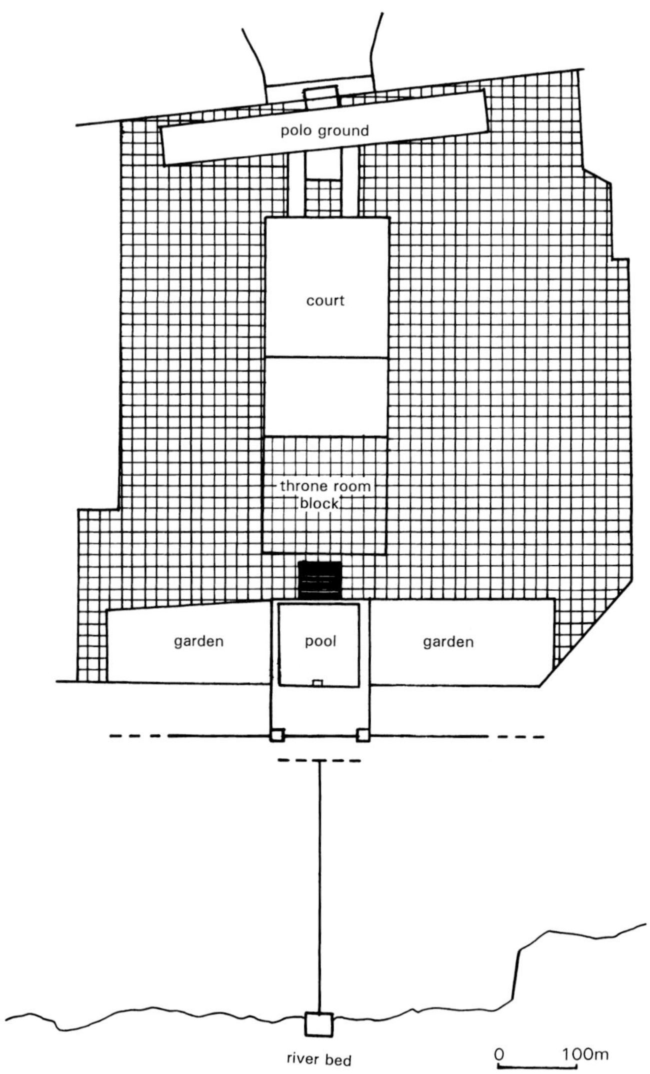

36. Schematic plan of the Dār al-Khilāfa

Bāb al-ʿĀmma, which led eastward into the palace proper through chambers and courtyards until reaching the square, domed throne room standing in the center of four iwans arranged in cruciform plan. From there, the axis extended through three more courtyards until reaching the enormous, almost rectangular, enclosed polo ground running north to south.

On the palace's western facade, the great portal consists of three iwans opening westward toward an extensive garden zone (Fig. 37). Due to sloping ground, the foundations are raised steeply on this side, giving an extended prospect of the palace gardens and the landscape beyond, as shown in the sketch made by Henri Viollet shortly before 1913 (Fig. 38). According to the Arabic texts, this was the formal gate into the palace; processions terminated at this point and executions were carried out here.[38] Old photographs showing remains of masonry at the second story suggest that there was a reception hall over the portal with a view to the gardens and beyond, and this is how Herzfeld's drawing reconstructed the portal.[39] An enormous flight of steps descended gently from the terrace, which projected in front of the portal to the gardens seventeen meters below. The gardens flanked a large square water tank (115 or 130 m). From this tank a pair of walls extended the central axis in the direction of the Tigris River, which marked the boundary of the garden.[40] Between the tank and the Tigris to the west was a large raised pavilion (or platform) with views toward the palace's Bāb al-ʿĀmma as well as toward the river and its opposite bank. Above, the portal and its terrace afforded a view onto the gardens, where nature was presented on an intimate scale, and a panorama of the river and countryside. The terrace and portal where ceremonial processions arrived was functionally important as the formal point of transition between the exterior and interior of the palace; this was paralleled by a second visual function as a viewing platform, or mirador, with the gardens as the mediating element through which the rest of the landscape was seen.

Prospects were also created at the other end of the Dār al-Khilāfa. On the far side of the long polo ground extending across most of the palace's eastern facade, a two-story pavilion (which Northedge calls a spectator's lodge)[41] looked in one direction onto the polo ground and in the other direction onto a hunting park and racetrack. Although in this instance attention was surely paid more to the sports than to the landscape, the pavilion was designed to provide two entirely different elevated points of view.

Eight kilometers to the south, the Balkuwārā Palace also abuts the river on its southwest side (for simplicity we shall call this south) (Fig. 39).[42] There were two major entrances to this complex: one on the riverside, where important visitors might arrive by boat, and the other at the north end. From the north portal, one passed through two large rectangular courts divided into halves (or possibly quarters, although this is speculative) by paved walkways and with a walkway running continuously around the perimeters. One then entered a smaller third court, rectangular and bipartite (or possibly quadripartite) in plan and with a rectangular pool or fountain placed at the intersection of the two axes.[43] The central axis then led to a square central throne room surrounded by four iwans in cruciform arrangement. Continuing southward along the same axis, one passed through a three-iwan portal whose triple-arched facade was richly decorated in mosaic, mother-of-pearl, and gold.[44] The portal faced a garden surrounded by a pilastered enclosure wall except on its south edge where it bordered the river, deeply cut (15 m in Herzfeld's time) into its bed. In the garden's center stood a rectangular water basin. To either side of the garden there were pavilions richly decorated with gilded frescoes.[45]

37. Bāb al-ʿĀmma (photo courtesy of Paul Fox, Samarra Archaeological Survey)

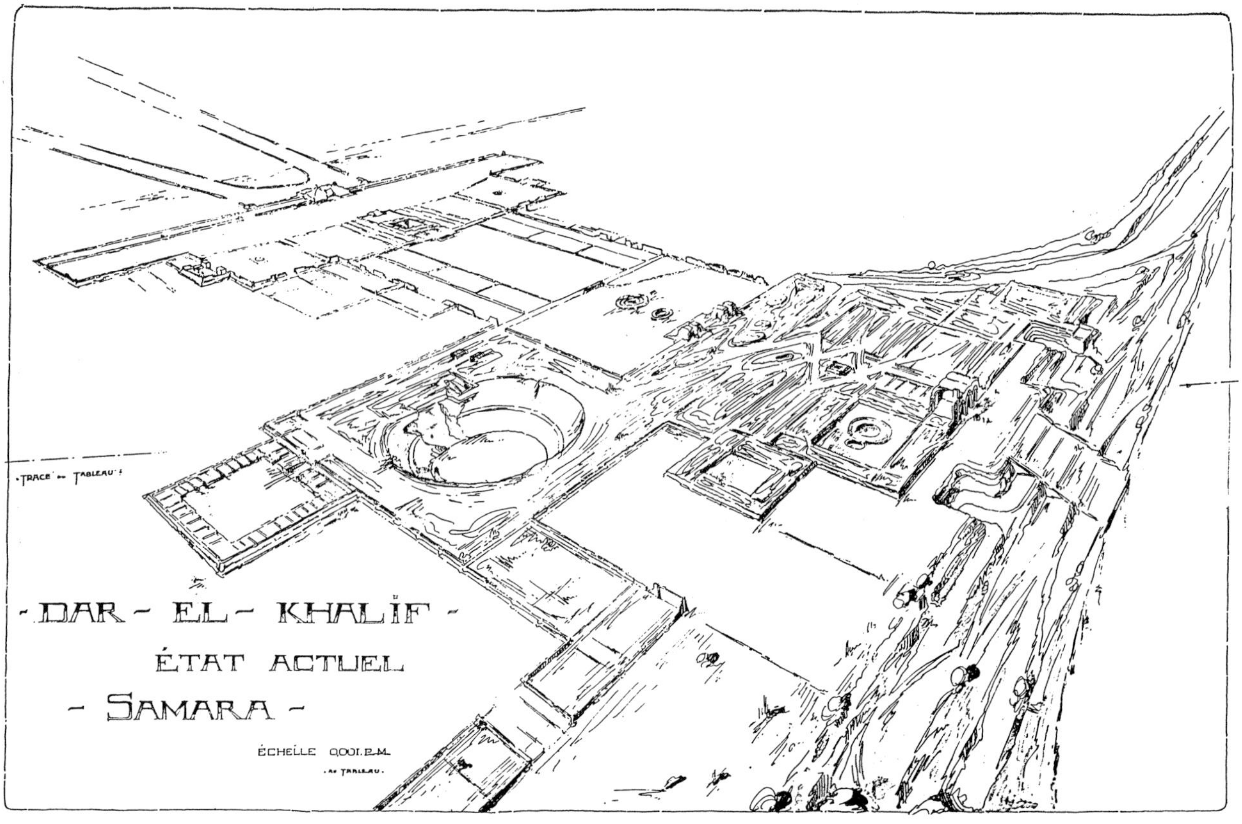

38. The Bāb al-ʿĀmma and its view (H. Viollet)

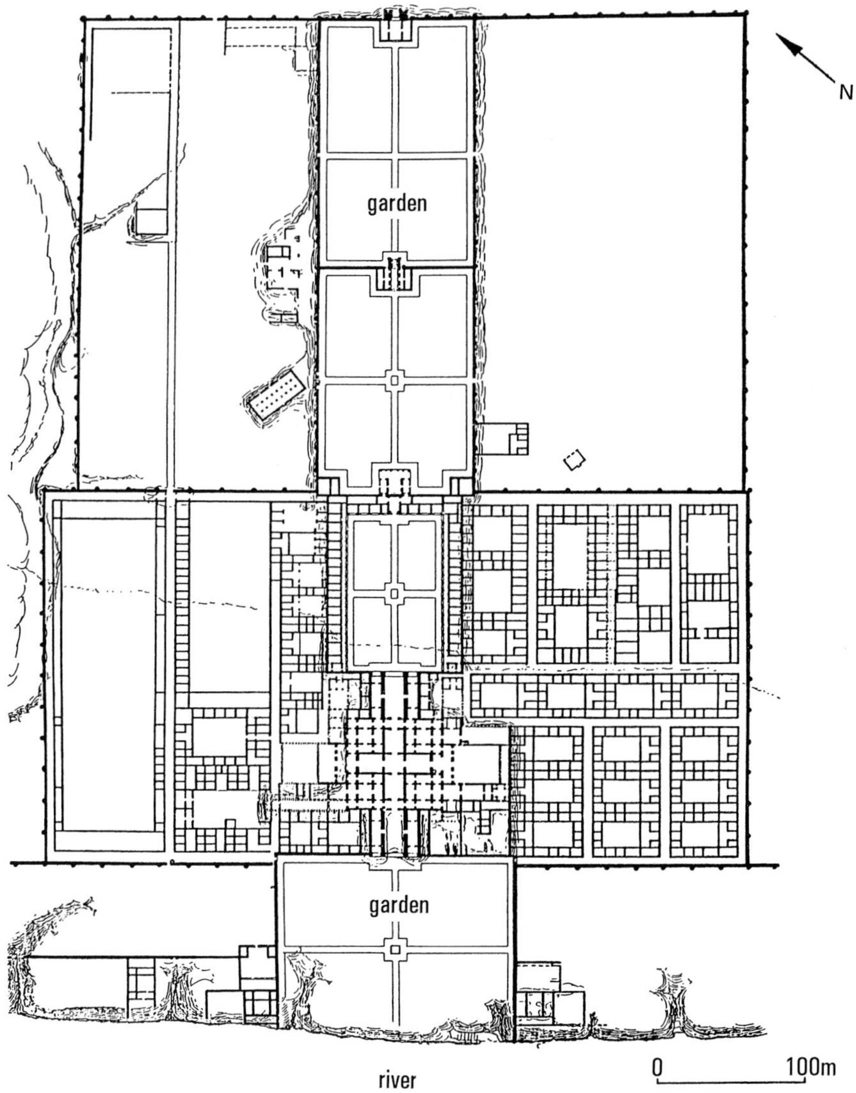

39. Plan of the Balkuwārā Palace, Samarra (after K. A. C. Creswell and E. Herzfeld)

Herzfeld's plan indicated that the iwans stood slightly higher than the garden but the exact difference in levels was not stated. The iwans were probably raised by no more than a few steps. The south side of the garden was fifteen meters above the river and opened toward it so that from the vantage point of the iwans there was a view across the gardens to the river beyond. Although less dramatic than the Bāb al-ʿĀmma, here too the iwans functioned as a three-part mirador offering views with two focal lengths: the garden and, beyond it, the landscape on the opposite side of the river.

Inside Balkuwārā an altogether different kind of view was possible along the major axes. Herzfeld noted that the rectangular central block of the palace was slightly elevated and that the floor level rose from court to court with the central throne room at the highest level. He wrote:

> The palace is so placed that one standing in the central room sees towards the north-west the mighty line of halls, the three Courts of Honour with their gateways and the streets of the outer quadrangle; to the south-west the halls, the garden, the river, and the limitless undulating plain of the Jazīra; in the transverse axis appears . . . the valley of the river and, two and a half leagues away, the Qaṣr al-ʿĀshiq and the Qubbat as-Sulaibīya. . . . The slight differences in level are employed and increased so that the whole middle strip is somewhat higher than the side strips, and in it again there is a rise from court to court. The level of the Throne Room surpasses all other parts of the palace; its floor-level is about the same as the level of the flat roofs of the lateral strips.[46]

Of course, Herzfeld was speaking of a ruined building where standing walls did not impede the view. But his observation that the throne room's floor was on level with the flat roofs of more distant buildings suggests the possibility that even in the ninth century the royal occupant of this raised hall could survey the landscape byeond the palace walls. The throne room and the iwans giving onto the riverside garden, which were raised to provide spectacular views, reflect the Abbasid understanding of the power implied by far-reaching visual perception. It is significant that these manipulations were, for the most part, achieved within a garden context, for as we shall see at Madīnat al-Zahrā', vision and gardens were key elements in an extended system of representation and metaphor.

A third palace excavated at Samarra is that situated above the so-called Palace of Ḥuwaiṣilāt, believed to be the Qaṣr al-Jiss mentioned by Ibn Serapion.[47] When the Ḥuwaiṣilāt Palace was excavated in 1936 and 1937 by the Department of Antiquities of the Government of Iraq, the upper palace was partially excavated and a sketchy cross-section and floorplan were drawn (Fig. 40).[48] The site was in poor condition but the vestiges of fine stucco ornament suggested a royal occupant. The upper palace was situated between the Tigris River and the banks of the Iṣḥaqī Canal, and was built

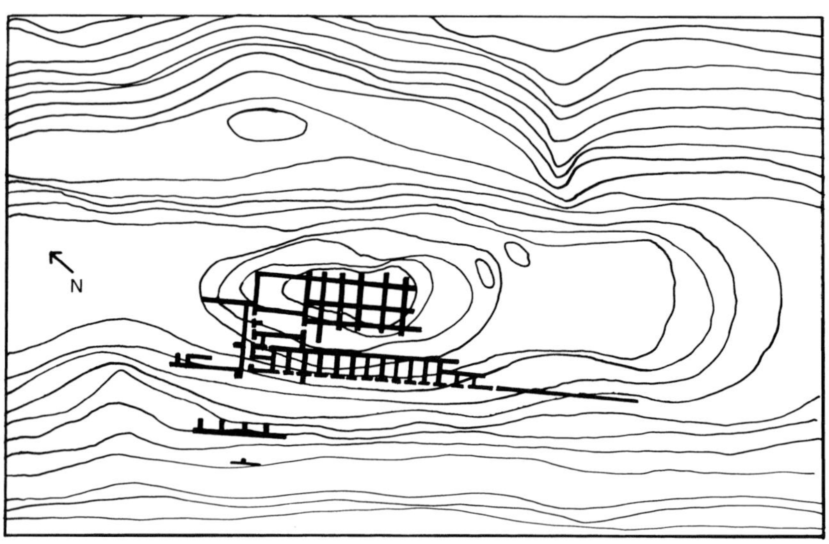

40. Plan of Ḥuwaiṣilāt (after the Iraq Department of Antiquities)

on a hill in a series of terraces disposed on each slope, with smaller chambers facing the canal and the larger chambers facing the river. The architecture was arranged to exploit the visual possibilities of varying topographical levels, as at the other palaces.

Some other Samarran palaces such as the Qaṣr al-ʿĀshiq also had views, but that the preponderance did not have them suggests that the vista was not an absolutely necessary part of royal architectural equipment. However, the argument here is not that the view became the most essential aspect of sovereign apparatus among the Abbasids. Indeed, one cannot pinpoint any single architectural device as signaling caliphal sovereignty (the reading of the caliph's name in the Friday sermon [*khuṭba*] was oral and performative rather than architectural). Rather, the view was one of many such devices, which included domes, niches, and thrones, that was adopted by later dynasts in al-Andalus, as well as at Lashkar-i Bāzār in Afghanistan and the Qalʿa Banī Ḥammād in Algeria, who were leaders in a culturally linked Islamic world and had been profoundly impressed by Abbasid architectural innovations.

Madīnat al-Zahrāʾs Gardens

Commanding a central position on the middle level of Madīnat al-Zahrāʾ, the reception hall known as the Salon Rico opened from a slightly elevated position onto the quadripartite upper garden (see Fig. 22). Across a tank of water stood the pavilion, giving the effect of a slightly smaller mirror image of the Salon Rico. Although, aside from evidence to suggest rows of columns on its interior, the superstructure of the pavilion is unknown, the disposition of the water basins around it suggests that it had windows or doors opening onto the gardens and basins on all four sides, giving the illusion that the pavilion was afloat in a tank of water. The device of pavilions appearing like islands and the introduction of water and nature into architectural settings owed a great deal to imperial Roman villas.[49] Excavations of the remains of the Hispano-Roman villa El Santiscal, for example, turned up a rectangular peristyle court with a garden and a large pool (Fig. 41); and at the Domus Augustana in Rome there were at least four constructed islands or pavilions in large pools of water

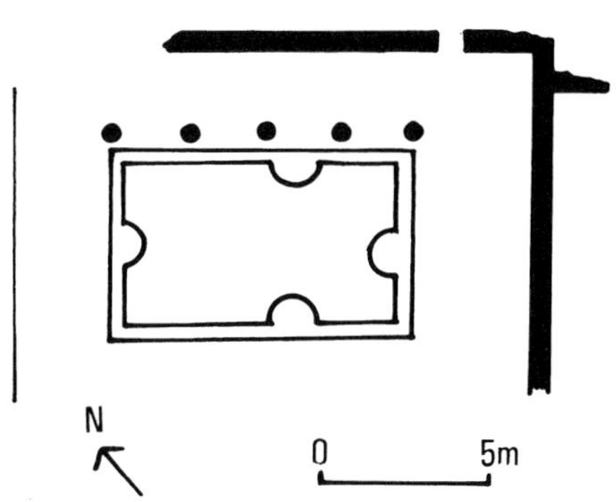

41. Plan of El Santiscal villa (after J.-G. Gorges)

in open courtyards.[50] At Madīnat al-Zahrā' and in later, more fully developed water structures, the pavilion and pools stood amid greenery, the water serving as a horizontal surface across which the viewer had an unimpeded view of the surrounding garden. Madīnat al-Zahrā''s garden pavilion was an early experiment in Islam with the floating-pavilion idea and the close association of water and architecture, and it inspired a tradition that can still be seen in surviving Mediterranean gardens and palaces, such as the Agdal basins in Almohad Marrakesh and the Norman Ziza and Cuba Palaces in Palermo.

The Arabic texts describing Madīnat al-Zahrā' emphasized the views and corroborated the existence of miradors in the gardens. Al-Nuwayrī's description of Madīnat al-Zahrā''s terraces, quoted at the beginning of this chapter, referred to miradors overlooking gardens (*basātīn taḥt manāẓirihi*).[51] The Arabic for "mirador" is *manẓar/manāẓir,* which is derived from *naẓara* (to perceive, see, gaze). The Arabic word *manẓar* is thus defined by the act of vision, exactly as is the Spanish word *mirador* (a place for looking), deriving from *mirar,* "to look," which English has co-opted.[52] Al-Rāzī described the same relationship of an elevated hall overlooking gardens, stating that al-Ḥakam sat "on the throne in the mihrab of the eastern hall overlooking the gardens" (*ʿalā al-sarīr fī miḥrāb al-majlis al-sharqī al-munīf ʿalā al-riyāḍ*);[53] the phraseology *nāfa ʿalā* meaning "to be high above [something]."

In the upper garden's walled enclosure there were several fixed points for viewing nature. The first was the Salon Rico, which formed a boxlike space, blind on three sides but opening southward through a frame of five horseshoe arches on columns to direct the view to the pavilion, pool, and gardens (Figs. 42 and 43). The pavilion opposite the Salon Rico offered four equally calculated views. Three of these were of gardens and water, and the fourth of the Salon Rico itself and the large pool, which, from the vantage point of the pavilion, would have reflected the image of the Salon Rico illuminated by the southern rays of sunlight (Fig. 44).

Hernández Giménez believed that one of the buttresses bracing the west wall of the upper garden's terrace contained a mirador in its tower that looked across the lower garden, twelve meters below, toward the landscape beyond the walls of the palace city (Fig. 45 and Color Plate 3).[54] Hernández Giménez admitted that the hypothetical mirador was suggested to him by the Alhambra's many towers and miradors with their views of the hilly landscape of Granada.[55] Since neither the buttresses nor the walls survive intact at the level of the upper garden, archaeological evidence can neither prove nor disprove his mirador theory. One of the buttresses was significantly larger than the others, but this does not necessarily mean that it housed a mirador. However, the logic of the layout of the gardens argues in its favor. The lower garden repeats the quadripartite layout of the upper one, and although this fact is obvious on the plan, it is not perceptible at ground level *except* at the proposed tower mirador, for only at that point, after having walked along the east-west axis of the upper garden, can one look over the buttress wall to see the axis continue in the replica laid out below. The only place to perceive the mirroring effect is at the mirador where the two gardens are joined in the human eye (Fig. 46).

Additionally, a ramp from the northwest corner of the upper garden to the northern side of the lower garden may have offered a view onto the gardens below and across the "natural" landscape

42. View from the Salon Rico

43. Computer-generated reconstruction of the Salon Rico's view of the pavilion (H. Wilke and D. Ruggles)

44. Computer-generated reconstruction of the pavilion's view of the Salon Rico (H. Wilke and D. Ruggles)

of the plains beyond (Fig. 47).[56] The ramp arrived at a paved terrace running across the north side of the lower garden, which gave an elevated perspective onto a large rectangular pool and the garden (Fig. 48). Although the south wall of the lower garden has not been excavated, it could not possibly have been high enough to curtail the views from either the ramp or the terrace. As in earlier Abbasid models, the architecture exploited changes in elevation to promote views onto the flowers, pools, and pavilions of the enclosed garden as well as across the garden to the landscape of the plains beyond.

The vistas sweeping across both garden and landscape at Madīnat al-Zahrā's upper and lower gardens belie the traditional notion of an Islamic garden as an enclosed, private space. The Small Garden (Fig. 13, no. 260), however, does accord with this traditional type. North of the lower garden and at a considerably higher elevation, the Small Garden's elegant, intimate space is bisected by a long axis to which the cross-axial plan is subordinated (see Figs. 19 and 21 and Color Plate 1). The Small Garden's plan is a slightly irregular rectangle that measures approximately twenty meters long by nineteen meters wide, and is contained at its east and west ends by two halls stretching almost the entire width of the garden. Each of these halls faces the garden through an aperture of three arches supported on engaged pilasters and columns. Like the Salon Rico's upper garden, an axially aligned square pool occupies the space in front of one of the halls. Although a transverse

45. The view from the buttress wall

46. A computer-generated reconstruction of the upper garden's east-west axis and the mirador (H. Wilke and D. Ruggles)

47. The lower garden's north side with ramp

48. View from the lower garden's ramp

axis is achieved by the thin strip of pavement that crosses the slightly sunken zones of vegetation in front of the pool, in so small a space the organizing power of a true cross-axial plan is unnecessary, and the garden "reads" as a bipartite composition. It is visually as well as physically contained by its enclosure walls and any opportunity for a view from it to the lower gardens was blocked by the south wall.

The Small Garden was handsomely decorated, yet its modest proportions precluded the staging of receptions and elaborate ceremonies. It was, rather, a private space probably used only by the caliph, the heir al-Ḥakam, the queen mother Ṣubḥ, or another very high-ranking individual. Neither al-Maqqarī nor Ibn Ḥayyān, who between them describe the physical construction and courtly life of Madīnat al-Zahrāʾ in ample detail, refer to any garden or residence that matches the appearance of the Small Garden. Doubtless the historians omitted it because few observers had ever seen it. In contrast, the upper and lower gardens were semipublic spaces that figured prominently in ceremonies and receptions.

In the upper garden, the beholder sat on the elevated platform of an axially placed pavilion or hall (the Salon Rico), raised above a garden too large to be encompassed in a single glance. But in the Small Garden, the beholder gazed at the garden from within the garden itself, enjoying nature on immediate terms and delighting in its smallest components. Its diminutive size and tight, closed properties discouraged the necessity for an emphatically articulated garden plan. Instead its plan was subordinated to the immediacy of the color and scent of the plants and flowers and the sound of the trickling water. The distinction between the upper-garden type, characterized by ample space and formal four-part partitioning, and the Small Garden, characterized by intimate scale and a more casual organization of slightly unequal halves, demonstrates that Madīnat al-Zahrāʾs architects were using well-developed, familiar types that could be modified without loss of legibility to the viewer.[57] Although these are the earliest surviving Islamic gardens in the western Mediterranean, we know that earlier Andalusian palace estates also had handsome, well-stocked gardens. Madīnat al-Zahrāʾs importance is not that it initiated a passion for gardens, but rather that it grafted that love onto an Abbasid-derived taste for spectacle and spectatorship, thereby creating a wholly new paradigm.

Miradors and the View

Although the Umayyad estates of Syria and Jordan were situated in artificial oases in which underground *qanāt*s and irrigation made agriculture and even pleasure gardens possible,[58] they lacked elevated vantage points from which to survey the surrounding cultivations. Similarly in al-Andalus, until ʿAbd al-Raḥmān's changes, the recreation estates in Cordoba's suburbs were generally built on the low-lying countryside bordering the river and did not have dramatic, far-reaching vistas.[59] In contrast, the Abbasids were exquisitely sensitive to the placement of architecture in landscape, emphasizing not just the view of nature but its view from a particular location—the mirador. The mirador, whether a poolside pavilion, three-iwan portal, throne room, or (later) tower, fixes the direction of gaze and dictates what is seen. For this reason the mirador's locus in the garden is at

the intersection of two crossed axes or one of the axes' terminal points, so that the path of vision follows the path of movement, the eye experiencing in an instant what the human body must traverse through time and space. Just as the king is raised on his throne or divan and looks down at his subjects, so, too, the mirador is elevated, directing the eye's gaze downward so that the garden is seen like a carpet from above. When the mirador is a place associated with a king (or caliph, or chief), such as a throne room, reception hall, or portal, the spatial or visual centrality of the mirador replicates the social centrality of the king. By such means, perception is guided by a sharply focused lens that objectifies the view of garden and landscape and signifies its owner. The mirador, as the origin of seeing, represents the subject/viewer—the king—and the view that is proffered is seen through his perspective, emphasizing by its breadth and its limits the extent of his lordship over the seen landscape, his domain.[60] In the words of Pierre Grimal, "Les jardins ne sont guère qu'une façon pour nous de prendre possession du visage dont il fait le portrait."[61]

In a discussion of eighteenth-century English landscape, John Barrell has elucidated the difference between private and public views: the private view is narrow, occluded, and recognizes objects individually without taking into account their relationship to each other or to a greater whole; the public prospect surveys the entire landscape and the people who inhabit it from a high point. A distinction is made between those who see (the subjects) and those who are seen (objects).[62] In al-Andalus, the panoramic view was not a privilege afforded to ordinary householders, but the ruler's exclusive prerogative, since he alone was responsible for conceptualizing and shaping the structure of the kingdom. In this way, the mission to direct or "oversee" a landscape was quite literally articulated by ʿAbd al-Raḥmān's right to "see over" it.

The opening up of space to allow long sight lines and sweeping views was more dramatic in the medieval Islamic context than a modern reader might initially realize. In the medieval environment, walls, doors, screens, and veils curtailed vision at every pass. Houses were not to be seen, except in a controlled manner by selected individuals and at select time; bodies were not to be seen, again except for a few individuals under controlled circumstances; and even in the supposedly public spaces of the city—the markets, *musalla*s, cemeteries, and parks—there were few occasions when long-range views encompassing large spaces and many people were possible. Streets were narrow and crooked, and there were far more blind alleys than true arteries through which to traverse the city.[63] Vision was a tightly controlled experience; it had social power and as such was not available to more than a small group of people in medieval Cordoba. Therefore, on those occasions when views were possible, they were highly charged with meaning.

The mirador not only provided a place for viewing, it enabled the very act of vision, simultaneously creating one person or place as the subject/viewer and another as the object. By distinguishing between subject and object and disciplining the act of perception, the frame created the relationship in which one was mutually dependent on the other. The object was presented as the created and the subject as the creator. The positioning of the patron as the earthly counterpart of God, the ultimate creator according to the Qurʾān, seems blasphemous, but we already know that ʿAbd al-Raḥmān approached the brink of acceptability on many other occasions, even crossing it, as we saw in Chapter Four, when he built a golden ceiling in one of his pavilions. Perhaps by marking his place in the Salon Rico with a blind niche—called a mihrab by a contemporary observer—he

intended to evoke the religious connotations of that architectural element, and thus implicitly to suggest his legitimate status as the representative of the Prophet.[64]

In the frame of the mirador, landscape and gardens were laid out as representations of nature; the fact that real trees, shrubs, and plants were displayed made the entire representation (including the limits set by the frame) seem "real" and "natural."[65] Yet the gardens were humanly selected collections of imported plants, carefully pruned and irrigated to survive the hot dry summers of al-Andalus and to yield unusually prolific amounts of flowers and fruit. If by "natural" we mean that which is untouched by human artifice, there was nothing natural about these gardens. Similarly, the landscape of farmlands and pasturage around Madīnat al-Zahrā᾽ was hardly natural: it was irrigated, manured, plowed, grazed, parceled, enclosed, and organized. The pleasing scene of productivity and order seemed God-given, as if this was the way al-Andalus was supposed to be under the correct and good stewardship of the king, his dynasty, and Islam; and accordingly disasters such as floods, droughts, and war were seen as anomalies interrupting the normal order of things. Thus human will was couched in terms of divine intention.

Through their enframing from strategic loci within the royal palace, landscapes became representations. In the mirador the act of representation was undisguised and acknowledged, for the arched and framed windows that stage-managed human vision were unabashed signals for scenic delight and visual spectacle. Less overt was the assumption that underlying the representation was a layer of the "real" and that this somehow preceded and validated the representation.[66] That the "real" layer was authentic, in other words, that this layer could be dissociated from human systems (meaning both systems of agriculture and semiotic systems of signage), was not questioned. In this manner the actual physical landscape was collapsed upon the constructed landscape of human desire.

The subject looked at landscape from a distance. This artificial separation between subject and object was important because the sense of being above or outside of the representation was an illusion that suggested the subject as its architect. The subject seemed to precede it as an author precedes the text and the artist precedes the work of art. But the act of making text or art is predicated on there being an institution already in place to receive, recognize, and call its existence into being.[67] The caliph/patron was as dependent upon his people/audience as they were on him, and they were partners in writing and reading the visual codes that served to legitimate and reinforce the system that defined their various positions. The frame that creates the object/view also creates the subject/viewer; thus the idea of priority—of being prior in time or space—is an illusion that was manipulated to enhance the caliph's pivotal and unique position. At Madīnat al-Zahrā᾽, the concept of spatial and temporal priority served to exalt the ruler; yet it depended upon the audience's recognition for validation. Who was that audience? To whom was the message of king-as-creator communicated? The texts reveal little; archaeology reveals even less. That it was a public message is evident, for the Salon Rico, of all the halls in the palace-city, was the only one with views and it was the only hall that fits the descriptions of the *majlis*(es) where ceremonies were held. One presumes that the audience consisted of the cultural and political elite who attended the festivities in the Salon Rico, since they were the people who could actually see the view through the eyes of

the caliph. The audience must also have included of the ordinary people who, below the palace, would occasionally look up to see the stone and stucco halls gleaming in the reflected sunlight.

Such questions ultimately lead us to ask about not only the viewer, the frame, and the view but about the relationship of these parts institutionally. We are far from being able to make a broad statement defining the institution of vision—the gaze—in medieval Islamic Spain. At this point, we can simply identify and analyze specific instances where a gaze was operative.

The construction of views to naturalize social hierarchy and serve state ideology became part of Islamic palace typology in Umayyad, taifa, Almoravid, and Nasrid al-Andalus and was transported abroad to the Maghreb where it appears in the stepped plan of the Dār al-Baḥr in the Qalʿa of the Banī Ḥammād, and to Afghanistan where it figured in Lashkar-i Bāzār's south palace and adjoining garden. In al-Andalus, ʿAbd al-Raḥmān III incorporated such views into the three-tiered plan of Madīnat al-Zahrā', drawing inspiration from Abbasid architectural models despite his inimical relations with that house, to magnify himself as king of al-Andalus, international potentate, and Commander of the Faithful.

6

LATER CORDOBAN PALACES AND GARDENS

And [al-Manṣūr] elevated himself almost to the level of kings in planning a palace where he, his family, and his followers would reside.
—Ibn Khāqān

ʿAbd al-Raḥmān III lived to an old age and his son al-Ḥakam succeeded him as a middle-aged man of forty-five years. Al-Ḥakam was apparently more interested in statecraft and books than in producing children; in his fifteen-year rule he and his Christian consort, Ṣubḥ, hatched only two sons. The first did not survive childhood and the second became the caliph Hishām at eleven years of age. When this child (b. Jumada II 354/June 965) inherited the kingdom in 366/976, the actual reins of government were handed over to a regent, the *ḥājib* Ibn Abī ʿĀmir, who, for his military successes against the northern Christian kingdoms, became known as al-Manṣūr (the Victorious). Whether the young caliph was unfit to rule or merely prevented from ever acquiring the skills and power necessary to do so will never be known. Al-Manṣūr conspired to continue as regent well past the age of the caliph's majority and managed to secure the position for his sons as well, so that the Amirids became dynastic regents.

Al-Manṣūr died in 392/1002 and was succeeded by his son ʿAbd al-Malik al-Muẓaffar (d. 399/1008). This al-Muẓaffar was succeeded by his brother Sanchuelo (d. 399/1009), who sorely tested the limits of the Amirid grasp of political power when he coerced the childless Hishām, by now practically a prisoner, into designating him as successor. While the people of Cordoba could accept the Amirids as regents, the thought of replacing the legitimate and noble Umayyad line with such upstarts must have been unbearably galling. Adding to the atmosphere of tension were the ethnic and class divisions among the population in which the more established Arabs and old Berbers took sides against the newer Berbers who had arrived in Spain from Africa to serve in the armies of ʿAbd al-Raḥmān III, and later of al-Manṣūr. The newcomers had no ties to the older community and attached their loyalty to their military chief—first al-Muẓaffar and then Sanchuelo—rather than to the impotent Hishām. As a group they had little in common with other Cordobans and so when the citizens of Cordoba backed Umayyad interests in the dispute over future succession, these Berbers took up a position in defense of their Amirid lords.

While Sanchuelo was away at war, one of the great-grandsons of ʿAbd al-Raḥmān III declared himself caliph under the name of Muḥammad II al-Mahdī (Hishām being a living but negligible presence on the political front). On 17 Jumada II 399/February 16, 1009, this Umayyad sent people

to sack the Amirid palace, thus initiating a civil war, or *fitna* (literally "disruption"). In the fighting that raged in Cordoba (and throughout al-Andalus) for the next two years, most of the suburbs and garden estates were looted and burned to the ground, many of the city's most distinguished citizens were killed or fled to safe havens elsewhere, and the caliphate was dealt a blow from which it never recovered. Without strong leadership, ethnic solidarity, or a clear sense of the Umayyad caliphate's ideological stance (it had been neither a committed member of the central caliphate nor a completely self-contained realm), Cordoba lost its privileged position as the seat of political power. The united and centralized state gave way to a network of regional taifa kingdoms (*mulūk al-ṭawāʾif*), each ruled by one of the former governors or a member of a noble family.

The dramatic political upheaval left its mark on garden design and symbolism. Until the civil war, Madīnat al-Zahrāʾ was the model for subsequent new palaces and estates located in the expanding ring of settlement around Cordoba. Although not much is known about these establishments—approximately ten of which were built between the date of al-Zahrāʾs foundation and its destruction in 401/1010[1]—the evidence suggests that some were built on natural rises in the land and enjoyed views of gardens and more-distant scenery. Garden symbolism was drawn from the earthly landscape, and garden typology continued to develop within the secular context of palatine architecture. It is not until after the civil war when a *waqf*-endowed public park was converted into a funerary garden that the theme of heavenly paradise was introduced to the garden. The change in meaning was profound: from an entirely worldly, even licentious context to one of piety and good works in order to gain a place in the paradise of eternity.

Al-ʿĀmirīya and al-Rummānīya

Of the estates built after Madīnat al-Zahrāʾ, nine date to the reign of al-Ḥakam, and one *munya* and one palace-city were built by the *ḥājib* al-Manṣūr (Fig. 49). Descriptions of their foundation and appearance are lacking for all except al-Manṣūr's celebrated Madīnat al-Zāhira, which has not been excavated, and the more obscure estate of al-Rummānīya, which was briefly surveyed in 1910 and has not been excavated since. Al-Rummānīya is important because the stepped topography, large pool with promenade, and siting of the manor house with a downward gaze toward the gardens and cultivated orchards identify it as one of the direct progeny of Madīnat al-Zahrāʾ.

The site of al-Rummānīya, al-Ḥakam's estate, is often confused with Alamiría (al-ʿĀmirīya), an entirely different estate owned by al-Manṣūr. The misunderstanding has a long history. In 1910 Velázquez Bosco excavated the ruins of a tenth-century estate three kilometers west of Madīnat al-Zahrāʾ.[2] He realized that it was not Madīnat al-Zāhira, because the location did not conform with written sources, and so he identified it as one of al-Manṣūr's other properties, the Munyat al-ʿĀmirīya. Velázquez Bosco was wrong, however, as Ocaña Jiménez showed when he identified the estate as al-Rummānīya.[3] But because Velázquez Bosco's identification was accepted for almost seventy-five years, all modern references to both al-ʿĀmirīya and al-Rummānīya must be used with caution.[4]

The misunderstanding began in the medieval period, when countless Arabic authors confused the names of Madīnat al-Zahrāʾ and Madīnat al-Zāhira—the two biggest landmarks outside the

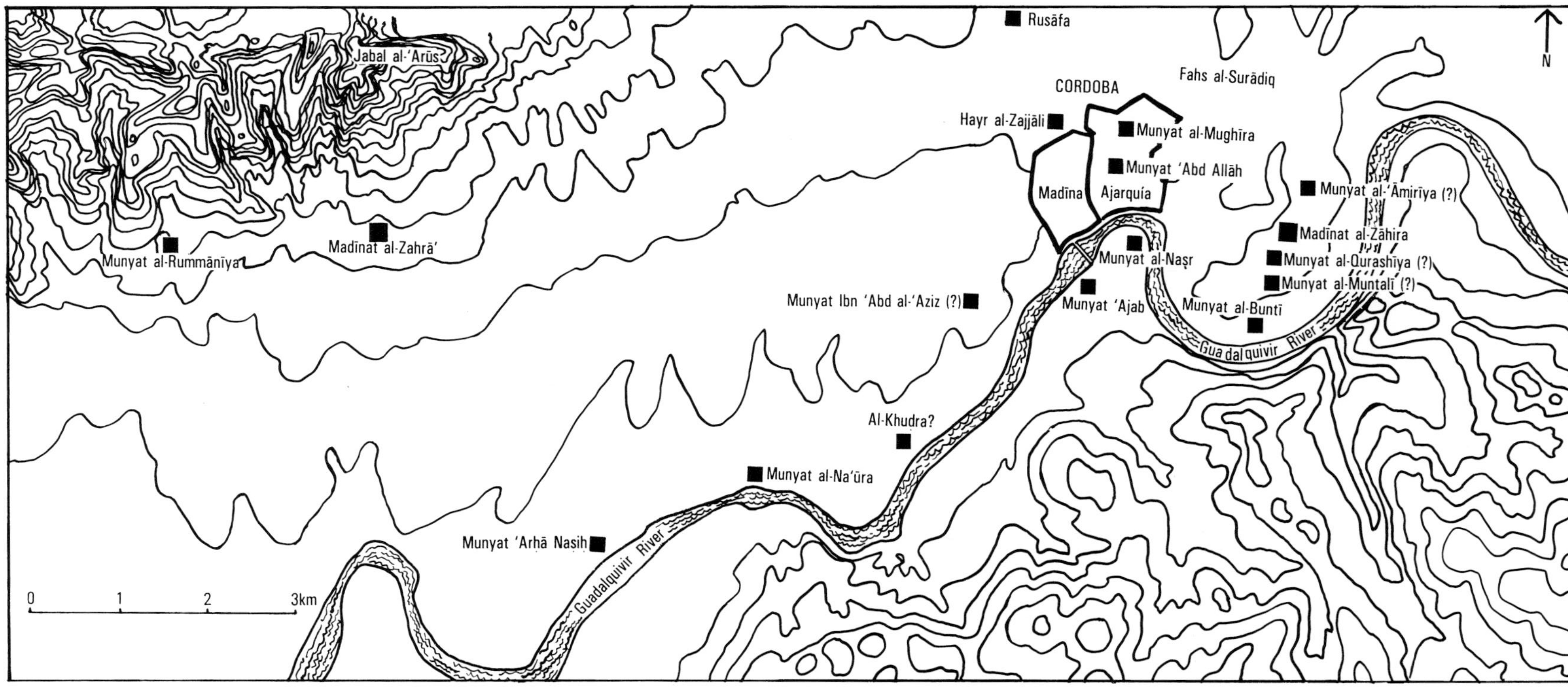

49. Map of the garden estates built around Cordoba before and after Madīnat al-Zahrā'

walls of Cordoba. In addition to erroneously substituting the name of one when the other was clearly meant, some authors referred indiscriminately to the palaces of "the Zāhirīya."[5] The confusion continued in the early nineteenth century when Conde offered the following account of Hishām's gift of the al-ʿĀmirīya estate to al-Manṣūr on the occasion of the latter's son's wedding, which was celebrated there in 376/978:

> In the spring of this year, the wedding of Abdelmelic, the son of Almanzor, and Habiba, the daughter of Abdala ben Yahye ben Abi Amer and Boriha, Almanzor's daughter, was celebrated in Cordoba: and there were great festivities and public banquets: the wedding festivities began in the beautiful garden of the Munya called Alameria, next to the palaces [*alcázares*] of the Zahriya, the Munya which the king Hisham gave to his Hajib Almanzor when he asked permission to celebrate the wedding there. The nobility of Cordoba attended these happy events: the lovely bride was led in triumph through the main streets of the city, accompanied by all the maidens whose families associated with hers, preceded and followed by the Qadi, and the witnesses, the Señores, Sheikhs, and gentlemen of the city: throughout the day the maidens, all of them armed with batons of ivory and gold, guarded the entrance of the pavilion [wherein sat] the bride. . . . All the gardens, woods, and fountains were lit, and the boats on its clear lakes resounded with sweet music.[6]

Unfortunately, this tantalizing account of gardens with ponds large enough for boats does not match any known Arabic text, and characteristically, Conde himself did not reveal his source. He wrote that the gardens of al-ʿĀmirīya were contiguous with the palaces of "la-Zahriya" but as this does not distinguish between the Madīnat al-Zahrāʾ west of Cordoba and the Madīnat al-Zāhira east of the city, it does not resolve the question of al-ʿĀmirīya's location. Ocaña Jiménez said that Conde's version was an elaboration and "clarification" of the account given by Ibn Bashkuwāl in *Al-Ṣila,* which mentioned a garden called Rabnalish. Ocaña Jiménez pointed out that there is an area known even today as Rabanales, but it is *east* of Cordoba, and thus al-ʿĀmirīya must have been on the east side of Cordoba, instead of the west, as Velázquez Bosco had believed.[7] This makes sense, for al-Manṣūr had strategically developed Cordoba's east side, building his own Madīnat al-Zāhira there to draw building attention and activity away from Madīnat al-Zahrāʾ, which was too closely identified with the Umayyads.

Al-ʿĀmirīya's landscape character and proximity to the river is evident from verses that were composed about it for al-Manṣūr by Ṣāʿid of Baghdad:

Behold the river nearby,
  gliding like a snake,
    while the birds sing praises,

in the shelter of the trees' limbs,
  and the branches drunkenly embrace
    in the swaying of their boughs.

And the gardens reveal the splendor
  of the daisy's smile
    and the tender narcissus gazes

at the anemone's cheek
while the gentle wind bears
the scent of sweet basil.

May you pass an eternal lifetime here
in happiness and peace![8]

This poem commends the *munya*'s trees, gardens, flowers, and fragrant herbs; another source tells about the elderly al-Manṣūr looking for medicinal plants at al-ʿĀmirīya, to soothe his pains.[9]

After disproving the al-ʿĀmirīya identification, Ocaña showed that the estate discovered by Velázquez Bosco was more likely to have been the estate called al-Rummānīya. It took its name from the Wādī al-Rummān, a stream that traversed the grounds, and a stream by the same name exists today west of Cordoba in the area of the site surveyed by Velázquez Bosco.[10] A contemporary account of the transfer to al-Ḥakam exists. It was a gift from the caliph's treasurer, the *fatā* (slave) Durrī the younger, in 362/973:

> It had been his own personal creation, his garden estate [literally, "the anchorage of his garden"], and he went to great lengths in its cost until its allurement whispered to all the desires of his master and gave him such pleasure that he was prompted to pass his days of leisure there and take restful promenades. In view of this, the *fatā* gave it, like a bride, at the moment of its completion, as a gift to the caliph, giving him everything in it, within and without, including the irrigated gardens [*basātīn*] and cultivated fields [*arāḍīn*], as well as male and female slaves, oxen, riding animals, and all its possessions, abundant riches and accumulated wealth. The caliph, his master, accepted it from him and evinced delight, and he ordered him to stay on as his inspector and supervisor there, lest its prosperity decline. This Durrī did.[11]

The motives for Durrī's lavish gift are obvious from the historical events that preceded it. Only a few months earlier he had fallen into disgrace and was publicly chastised by the *ṣāḥib* of Madīnat al-Zahrā', suspended from service and placed on a reduced salary, and ordered to move from his quarters at al-Zahrā' to the Cordoba Alcazar.[12] Although he was soon reinstated, he must have continued to worry about his standing at the court. Clearly the gift of al-Rummānīya was intended to regain the caliph's favor.

Several epigraphic fragments from al-Rummānīya are preserved in the Cordoba Archaeological Museum. One piece shows the letters *fī sanati kh-m-*. Ocaña read the last (incomplete) word as *khams,* or "five," and offered the translation "in the year 355 (965–66)," which he interpreted as the date of al-Rummānīya's building or at least its *terminus ante quem.*[13] If his reading of the inscription is correct, as I believe, the building was built at least eight years before it was given to al-Ḥakam II.

Al-Rummānīya was modeled on a smaller scale after Madīnat al-Zahrā' and was built on the lower slope of the same range of low mountains, some three kilometers beyond the palace city, well outside the suburbs ringing the capital. Like al-Zahrā', it was built in terraces—four, rather than three, in this case—each supported by thick stone retaining walls (Fig. 50).[14] The entire estate of

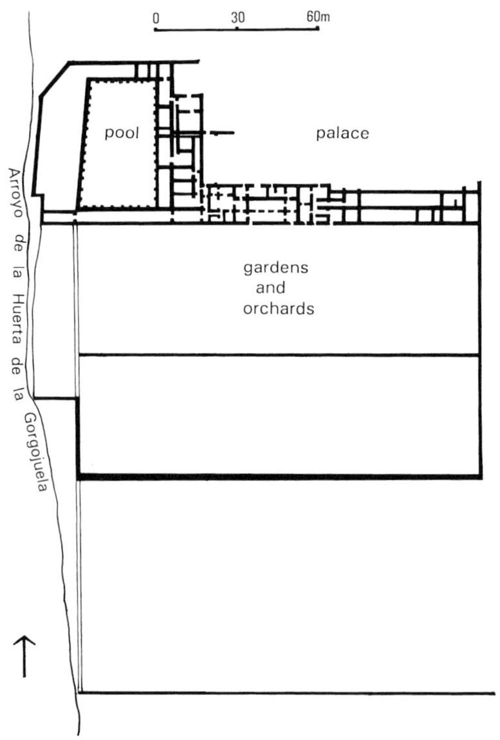

50. Plan of al-Rummānīya (after R. Velázquez Bosco)

four hectares was enclosed by a strong wall (two meters thick in places), the preserved sections of which consist of a base of three or four ashlar courses on which rise pillars of stone supporting rubble and concrete walls.[15]

The palace was built on the topmost level, overlooking the gardens that presumably grew on the lower terraces. At the time of excavation, few of the walls were still standing, so Velázquez Bosco's plan was based largely on the foundations. The central part of the palace was regular in plan: it had three parallel bays of equal width, crossed by two dividing walls creating square chambers in the ends of the rectangular bays. The square chambers were paved with marble slabs and probably vaulted, judging from their shape. This central body was flanked by two others of equal length. In front, a terrace paved with thick stone slabs opened onto the stairs or ramps descending into the gardens and buildings of the lower terraces. On each side of the central body, long narrow bays extended; they were probably stables. In the northwest was a series of small chambers bordering an enormous pool.

This pool, including part of the aqueduct that supplied it with water from the mountains above, is still in excellent condition. Constructed of ashlar masonry, it is 3 meters deep and almost rectangular, 49.7 meters by 28 meters with a total surface of 1,380 square meters.[16] From large stone corbels spring stone arches that formerly supported a flying walkway running completely around the pe-

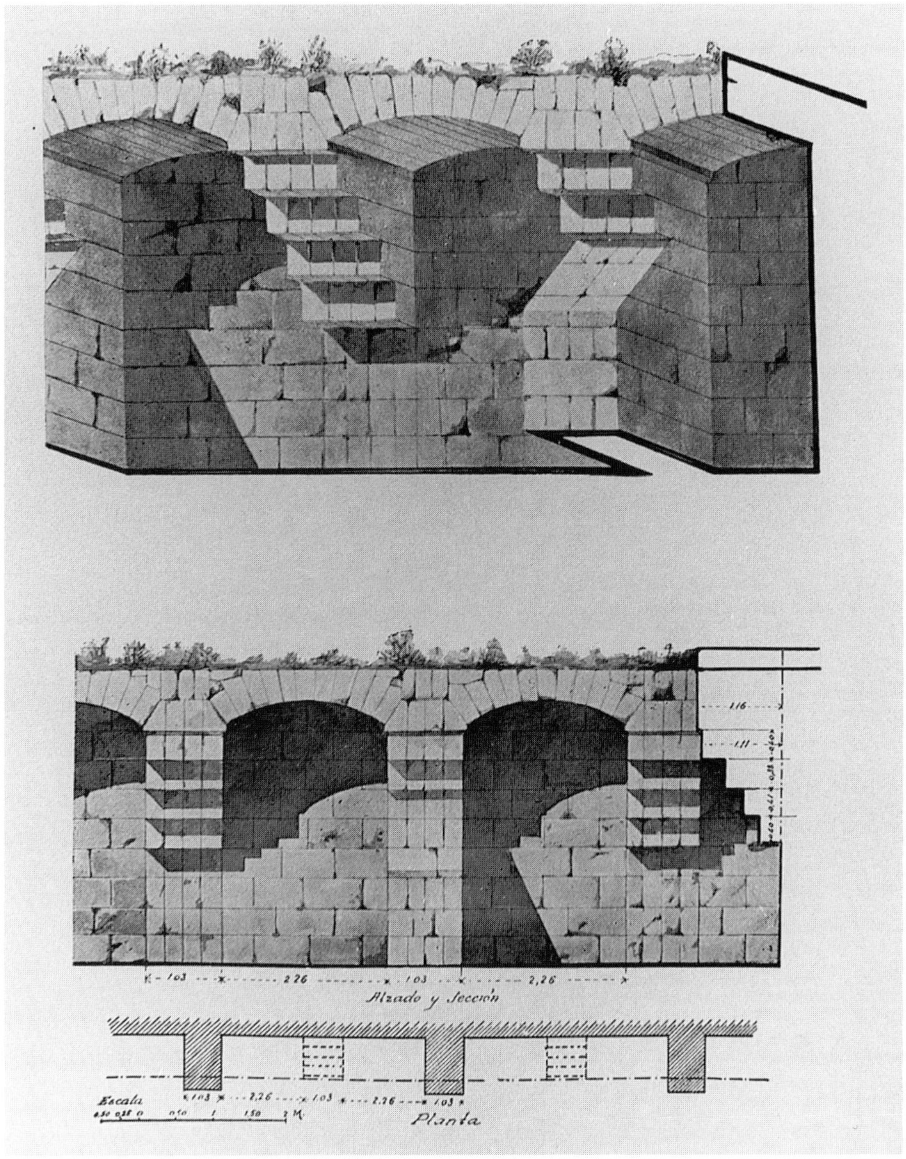

51. Drawing of the flying walkway at al-Rummānīya's pool (R. Velázquez Bosco)

rimeter of the pool (Fig. 51). A portion of the system of corbels and pavement still remains (Fig. 52). This surprising walkway, when a simple path around the perimeter would have sufficed, gives the pool a recreational aspect, and indeed its close proximity to the halls of the palace underscores its aesthetic role. Water from the mountains was collected here for irrigating the lower gardens; the pool's unusual depth also suggests that it could have held fish, as in one of the tanks at Madīnat al-Zahrā'.[17] Less than a hundred years later, gala nautical performances were held in the large pool in the Dār al-Baḥr at the Qal'a Banī Hammād (Algeria) (Fig. 53), but since no such thing was mentioned in connection to Cordoba, it is doubtful whether such entertainments were a part of Umayyad court life.[18] After the reconquest, the estate of al-Rummānīya came into the hands of the

52. The corbels supporting the flying walkway at al-Rummānīya

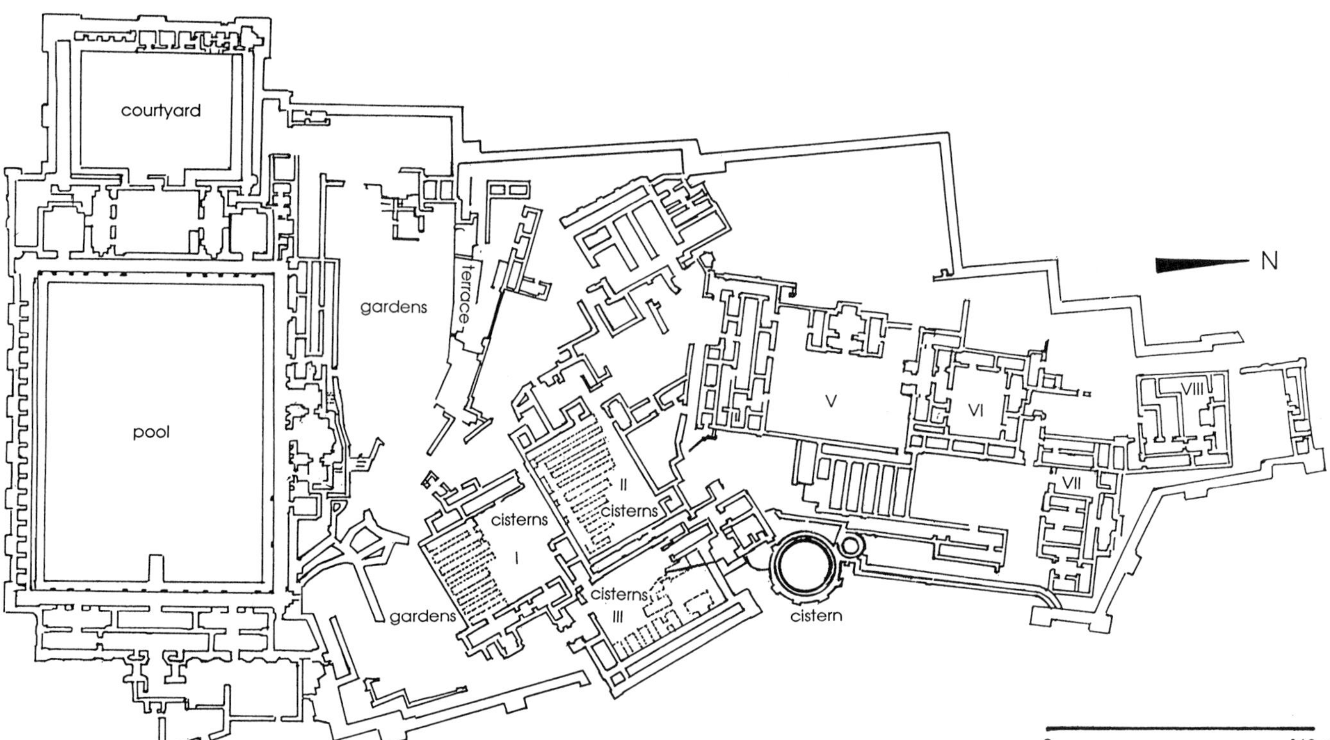

53. Plan of the Dār al-Baḥr at the Qal'a Banī Hammād (after De Beylié)

Fernández family of Cordoba, lords of Aguilar, and became known as Aguilarejo (and also variously Moroquil, Fontanar de la Gorgoja, and Gorgojuela). In 1910, when the state excavations at Madīnat al-Zahrā᾽ were delayed, Velázquez Bosco filled the idle days by making a quick survey of Aguilarejo/al-Rummānīya first. In 1926 most of the palace on the uppermost level was destroyed when a modern villa was built on the edge of the great pool; that house is now a ruined shell, and the estate has become a ranch where the cows are raised that produce the *toros bravos* for which Cordoba is famous. When the villa was built, a marble basin was unearthed, and in 1945, workers somewhere in the vicinity (the exact location is unclear) found another basin with similar but more complex decoration. Both basins are now in the Cordoba Archaeological Museum.[19]

Despite its poor condition, al-Rummānīya's importance to our knowledge of Hispano-Islamic architecture cannot be overestimated. It and Madīnat al-Zahrā᾽ are the only palaces from Umayyad Cordoba for which foundations and some standing fabric survive. Furthermore, the stepped design of al-Rummānīya, in which the buildings at the top have views over the rest of the estate, confirms that Madīnat al-Zahrā᾽ inspired profound changes in Hispano-Umayyad architectural design.

Other Estates

Other estates were built around Cordoba in the years after ʿAbd al-Raḥmān III assumed caliphal titulature, but unfortunately, aside from the fact that they are mentioned as *munya*s and thus belong to the category of garden palaces, little can be said about them. The Alhadra palace (from *al-khuḍra,* meaning "greenery" or "meadow") was a garden estate located between the Alcaide and Alameda, today part of the Cañito de María Ruiz on the west side of Cordoba. It is mentioned in a work written for King Fernando III, but there are few remains to be studied.[20]

The Munyat of al-Muṣḥafīya was built near Ruṣāfa, north of Cordoba, by Abū ʿUthmān Jaʿfar b. ʿUthmān al-Muṣḥafī (d. 372/982–83), who served as *ḥājib* to al-Ḥakam II throughout his reign. Al-Muṣḥafī held great power, serving as regent during the aging caliph's last illness, and conspiring with al-Manṣūr after the caliph's death to assassinate the caliph's brother, who was the logical heir, and instead to place young Hishām on the throne. He was soon displaced as *ḥājib* by his erstwhile ally and forfeited first his properties, including the *munya,* and then his life in 372/982–3. The *munya* was probably built between 350/961 (the beginning of al-Ḥakam's reign) and 368/979 (the year of al-Muṣḥafī's disgrace). Al-Maqqarī relates that when al-Muṣḥafī's grandson passed the estate one day he was prompted to lament: "Pause for a moment before al-Muṣḥafīya and weep for an eye without its pupil."[21] Nothing is known about the estate's architectural design.

The Munyat al-Mughīra was located on the east side of Cordoba near the Munyat ʿAbd Allāh and formed the nucleus of a suburb called Mughīra. Although the date and circumstances of its construction are not confirmed by documentary evidence, the *munya* may have been built in the third quarter of the tenth century by al-Ḥakam's brother, al-Mughīra, who was later executed by al-Manṣūr to prevent him from making a claim to succession.[22] The *munya* was located in the zone that was burned by the Berbers during the civil war, attacked along with Madīnat al-Zāhira in February 1009, precisely because of its association with the hated Amirids.[23] Ocaña Jiménez pointed out, however, that the Munyat al-Mughīra is mentioned in a later source when the Almoravids walled

the eastern side of Cordoba, called the Ajarquia, around the year 1125, so it was evidently not entirely destroyed by the Berbers; rather, they destroyed selectively, concentrating their attention on the Amirid houses and al-Manṣūr's own palace. The Berbers' leader was Muḥammad b. al-Mughīra, son of the man who probably built the *munya;* he may therefore have spared the district bearing the family name.[24]

Castejón suggested that the Munyat al-Mughīra and Munyat ʿAbd Allāh were situated in the place where the large gardens of the monasteries of San Pablo and San Augustino appeared on the 1811 map of Cordoba (marked P and A on Fig. 54).[25] Several archival documents lend credence to his theory: the "Huerta de San Pablo" (garden of San Pablo) is mentioned in documents dated as early as 1409, and private houses and a garden were granted by Alfonso XI for the establishment of the Monastery of San Augustin in 1328.[26] Both institutions were established on the site of what were formerly large gardens, or a garden estate. The noticeable continuity between the Islamic and modern configuration of streets and city gates is also true for the important buildings and public spaces. Public buildings generally maintained their public function: for example, Cordoba's congregational mosque and its courtyard were transformed into a cathedral without alteration of the amount of urban space allotted to them, and the palace gardens of the Muslim Alcazar served for the Alcazar built in 1328 by the Christian King Alfonso XI.[27] Since the Munyat ʿAbd Allāh and the Munyat al-Mughīra were the largest garden estates in Cordoba's Ajarquia quarter, it is quite likely that these *munya*s were identical to those gardens bequeathed to the religious orders.

Al-Dimashq (Damascus) Palace was built during the Umayyad period somewhere in the vicinity of Cordoba. "Modelled on the palaces of the Orient and raised up like the stars of the East," it was a handsomely embellished recreation palace with columns, stone pavements, courtyards, open terraces, and gardens.[28] It must have been one of the few palaces to survive the terrible destruction and burning during the *fitna,* the vizier of al-Muʿtamid, ruler of taifa Seville, visited there in the second half of the eleventh century and wrote:

> Any other palace next to al-Dimashq is a monstrosity,
> Because in it are gathered delicious fruit and the most exquisite perfumes;
> Its panorama [*manẓar*] is beautiful and its waters are pure;
> Its earth is sweet and its palace proud [*ashamm*].[29]

Manẓar, meaning "panorama" or "prospect," and *ashamm,* meaning "elevated" as well as "proud," are the kinds of words also used to describe the halls of Madīnat al-Zahrāʾ. Because al-Dimashq is described by the poet as surpassing all contemporary palaces and because we know that a new standard of luxury and beauty in architectural and landscape design was set at al-Zahrāʾ, al-Dimashq was probably one of the palaces built before the civil war but after 936.

Two miles west of Cordoba on the banks of the Guadalquivir is the Huerta de Valladares, the farthest of four gardens extending westward from the Huerta Maimón, which is located outside the city walls at the southwest corner of the medina. At the garden situated between the riverbank and the walled terrace, which is all that survives of the palace, remains from the Umayyad period were discovered. The surface survey made just prior to 1949 revealed walls of ashlar blocks measuring sixty by thirty-three by twenty centimeters and arranged in a pattern of one runner per four headers.[30] Similar treatment is seen in the stone walls at al-Rummānīya, built before 362/973, and in the

54. Map of Cordoba, 1811, with Munyas al-Mughīra (A) and ʿAbd Allāh (P) indicated (Biblioteca Nacional de Madrid)

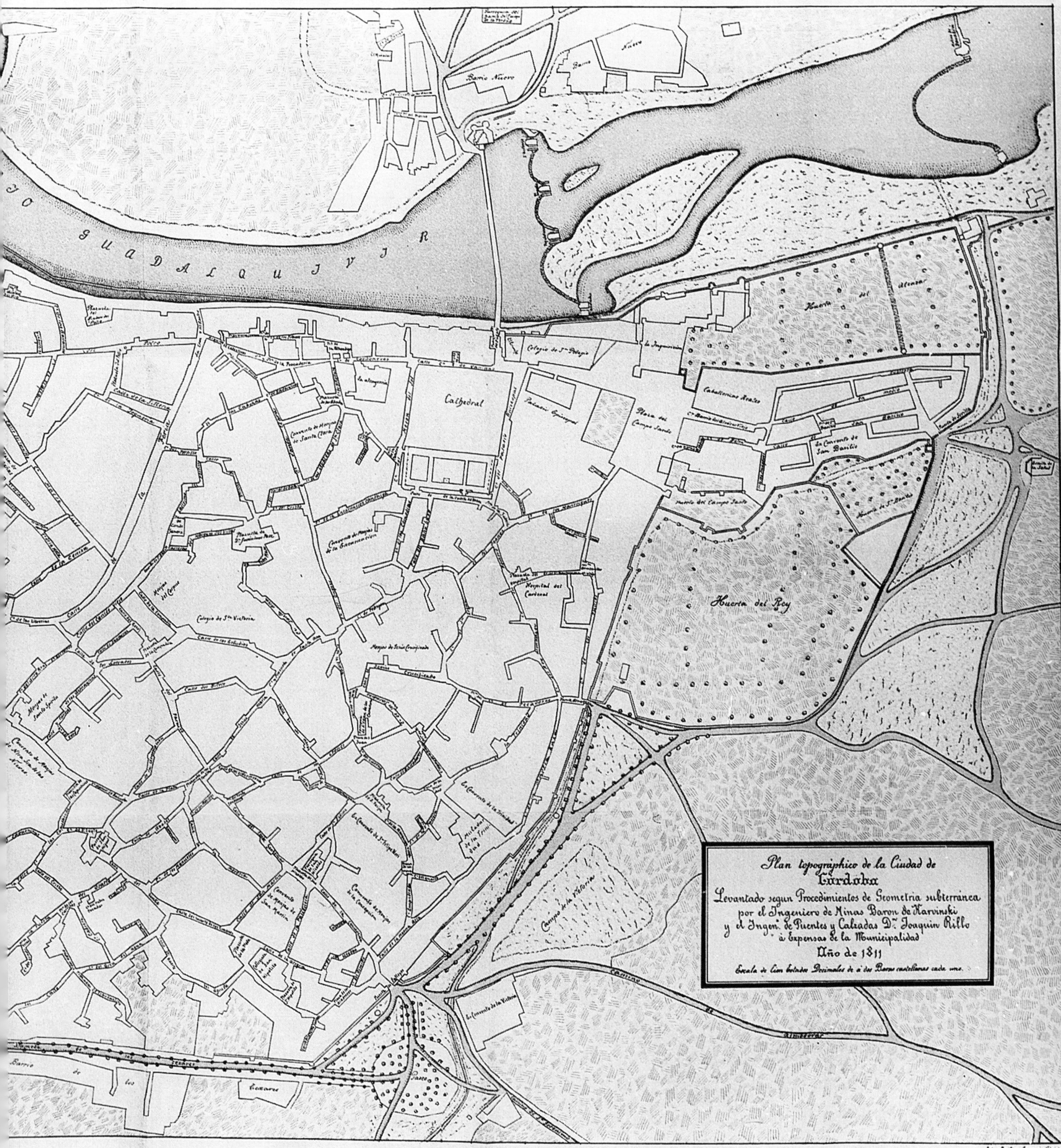
Plan topographico de la Ciudad de
Cordoba
Levantado segun Procedimientos de Geometria subterranea
por el Ingeniero de Minas Baron de Karvinski
y el Ingen.o de Puentes y Calzadas D.n Joaquin Rillo
à Expensas de la Municipalidad
Año de 1811
Guadalquivir
Barrio Nuevo
Cathedral
Colegio de Sn Pelagio
Plaza del Campo Santo
Huerta del Alcazar
Caballerizas Reales
Huerta del Rey
Hospital del Cardenal
Colegio de Sta Victoria
Campo de la Victoria
Barrio de los Tejares

stonework of al-Manṣūr's addition to the mosque.[31] The ornamental stone fragments found on the site were similar to the incised stone decoration at Madīnat al-Zahrā', except for one piece in which the linear motif was incised in channels, a technique not in evidence at Madīnat al-Zahrā' but employed in the stuccowork of al-Ḥakam II's addition to the Mosque of Cordoba.[32] Since both the stone-wall construction and the motifs of architectural ornamentation can be stylistically linked with construction carried out elsewhere under al-Ḥakam's patronage, it is plausible to date the garden at the Huerta de Valladares to al-Ḥakam's reign (961–76).

The ruins of another villa four miles from the road to the Castle of Albaida (which is five kilometers northwest of Cordoba) consists of ashlar blocks and pieces of marble and red stucco. The villa is a rectangular enclosure, connected by a paved road to the Ruṣāfa-Madīnat al-Zahrā' road.[33] Very little has been recovered from these sites, and sixty years after Castejón examined them, they are in a worsened state of deterioration due to farming and to house construction. On a visit to one of them several years ago, I saw in front of the modern farmhouse an enormous pile of discarded ashlar blocks that were clearly Umayyad. Only their location on the west side of Cordoba allows us to speculate that they may have been associated with ʿAbd al-Raḥmān al-Nāṣir and al-Ḥakam's development. Almost certainly these sites are the physical remains of some of the *munya* estates described in historical texts, but without an inscription or more information from the historical chroniclers, the link between the archaeological remains and the tenth-century life of the buildings is now lost.

The Munyat al-Qurashīya was designated by al-Rāzī as the *munya* at al-Shamāt or al-Shamāmāt (meaning either "melons" or something on the order of "scented"). Located somewhere along the banks of the Guadalquivir, probably east of Cordoba, it was owned by the brother of al-Ḥakam, Abū al-Ḥakam ibn al-Qurashīya (*ahl al-Qurayshī* being one of the honorific dynastic titles of the Umayyads).[34] It must have been built before 360/971 because when Jaʿfar Ibn ʿAlī and his brother Yaḥyā arrived from North Africa to the court of al-Ḥakam in the summer of that year, they camped on the east side of Cordoba at a distance from the city, while the women in their company stayed at this *munya*.[35] At one point they were instructed to leave this camp on the east side of Cordoba and to cross the city to new quarters in the Munyat Ibn ʿAbd al-ʿAzīz.[36] This indicates that the latter estate was located west of the city along the river, and possibly it corresponds to the remains that were found at a site along the river between the Alcazar and the Munyat al-Naʿūra.

The Munyat Arḥā' Nāṣiḥ was al-Ḥakam's favorite residence. The name means "mills of Nāṣiḥ," and it was situated on the right bank of the Guadalquivir River on the Seville-Cordoba road just before the entrance to the city.[37] On 11 Rajab 364/March 27, 975, al-Ḥakam, after suffering a stroke, left Madīnat al-Zahrā' attended by the principal dignitaries of the state. They stopped at the Arḥā' Nāṣiḥ, where they spent the night. The next day they proceeded to the Munyat al-Naʿūra, where they halted for midday prayer, and from there, met by attendants from the Alcazar, they left for Cordoba, where al-Ḥakam died several months later.[38] From this it is clear that the Munyat Arḥā' Nāṣiḥ was located south of Madīnat al-Zahrā' and west of the Munyat al-Naʿūra (see Fig. 49). On the banks of the Guadalquivir the remains of a foundation of ashlar blocks and of water channels have been found that might belong to this residence, but there is not enough evidence to confirm the identification. They could easily be the remains of the mills of Kulaib, built along the river by the son of ʿAbd al-Raḥmān I in the eighth century.[39]

Little is known about the Munyat al-Buntī. It was used as a guest house for important visitors and in 361/972 the Byzantine ambassador to the Umayyad court lodged there.[40] The name Buntī may derive from the word *puente* (bridge), indicating a location near a bridge and water course, but since Cordoba had a great many small bridges spanning numerous streams, this is not particularly informative. Like al-Buntī, the Munyat al-Aqraʿ, also known as the Munyat al-Najda, appears in al-Rāzī's chronicle only once: in 362/973, seventy deserters from the Berber troops of the Moroccan heretic Hasan Ibn Ḥanūn al-Hasanī were received with honor in Cordoba and were housed in the Munyat al-Aqraʿ.[41] That summer, a circumcision festival for the sons of those Berbers was held in the Munyat al-Muntalī, east of Cordoba. The caliph al-Ḥakam paid for the feast, and it was supervised by the *ḥājib* and *sāḥib* of Cordoba, al-Muṣḥafī.[42]

Madīnat al-Zāhira and Amirid Palaces

When al-Manṣūr came to power in 978, he redirected city growth from the west side of Cordoba, associated with the Umayyads, to the east, which he crowned with a new palace-city, encouraging his followers to settle in its vicinity, just as ʿAbd al-Raḥmān had done at al-Zahrāʾ. He had already built the estates al-ʿĀmirīya, the Dhāt al-Wādiyain (Having Two Streams), the Munyat al-Surūr, and Urṭānīya, but very little is known about them.[43] They were probably rather small, if elegant, country pleasances. Al-Manṣūr's most significant building was Madīnat al-Zāhira, a monumental palace-city that impressed the chroniclers with its splendor and size. Although there are many textual references to the new palace-city, begun in 368/978 and finished in 370/980–81, its location is still a matter of debate.

Madīnat al-Zāhira was first planned by al-Ḥakam and his *ḥājib* al-Muṣḥafī, but it was al-Manṣūr who ultimately built it.[44] According to al-Ḥimyarī, when al-Manṣūr rose to power, he came to fear the conspiracies of his enemies and assassination, and so purged the government of potential foes. He reoriented the city eastward, away from Madīnat al-Zahrāʾ:

> And he elevated himself almost to the level of kings in planning a palace [*qaṣr*] where he, his family, and his followers would reside, where the seat of government would be fixed and the administration of the political organization carried out, where he would gather his guards and staff and assemble tradesmen. Then he looked into the site of the city known as al-Zāhira, celebrated for its splendid buildings. He made it rise on the bank of Cordoba's great river and collected in it and endowed it with every kind of miraculous wonder. . . . He made it spacious and ample in the extent of its grounds [*basīṭa*], went to great lengths in the elevation of its walls, and was zealous in making its high and low areas level.[45]

Al-Manṣūr's palace-city was mostly built within two years. Its buildings were made of magnificent materials: gold, lapis lazuli, and such, so that "the sight wearied the eyes."[46] It was built along the river, and large waterwheels creaked along the riverbank and silos in the interior stored the grain gathered from the productive fields surrounding it. In addition to containing palaces, the new

city was ringed by pleasure pavilions.[47] The fountains of al-Zāhira were particularly spectacular. Abū Marwān al-Jazīrī described one of them in verse:

> In the center of the hall is a large basin of green water in which the tortoises continually make sounds.
>
> The water pours from the jaws of a lion whose mouth would seem to say something terrible, would it speak.
>
> It is of black amber and around its neck one sees a handsome necklace of pearls.[48]

The poet Ibn Hudhayl also described water basins that collected water from the mouths of "ʿĀmirī" lions with pearl necklaces and gold eyes, which of course recalls the fountain at the Munyat al-Naʿūra. He went on to describe the facade of a hall with arches like half-moons on marble columns,[49] a description that could serve equally for the facade of the Salon Rico.

The symbolic charge of fountains and gardens, synecdochic references to the prosperous cultivated landscape, was well understood and manipulated by the vizier. Madīnat al-Zāhira had a large pool adorned with a profusion of water lilies. One day, to impress visiting dignitaries, al-Manṣūr ordered that pieces of silver and gold be inserted into the lilies when they were still closed in the morning. In the afternoon, as the lilies opened to the sunlight, they were gathered on a tray and set before his guests, who were astounded to see that the flora of al-Andalus yielded silver seeds and golden pollen.[50] By means of this metaphor al-Manṣūr successfully demonstrated the natural bounty and riches of his kingdom.

Al-Manṣūr's Madīnat al-Zāhira rivaled the magnificence of Madīnat al-Zahrāʾ in its revetments, precious materials, ample grounds, and perhaps even the design of its halls. Indeed, there are marked ideological and symbolic parallels between the two cities. Al-Manṣūr drew artisans from afar and imported foreign building materials just as ʿAbd al-Raḥmān had done. Leveling "the high and low areas" of a vast expanse of land was an act signifying his colossal power over the land and its inhabitants, as ʿAbd al-Raḥmān's stepped terraces had been. By building such a palace, al-Manṣūr cunningly "elevated himself to the level of kings" and put himself in the place of the caliph.

He had risen from obscurity to attain the position of regent for Hishām. Even when Hishām reached his majority, he was quite unprepared to rule, and al-Manṣūr quickly took advantage of the power vacuum. The young caliph retained the empty signs of sovereignty—the invocation of his name in the *khuṭba* and the inscription of his name on coins and *ṭirāz* textiles—but it was al-Manṣūr who ruled the kingdom. Al-Ḥimyarī wrote that he snatched everything from Hishām but the caliphal titulature, installing his own officials in government positions and instructing that provincial communications, taxes, and revenues were to be sent directly to him. As al-Manṣūr's power increased, Hishām lost any hope of attaining independence, and he was made a virtual prisoner at Madīnat al-Zahrāʾ, "ignored as a nonentity, forgotten, his door closed and his person hidden from the public eye . . . and soon it got to the point where no one even knew the caliph any longer."[51]

In order to appropriate for himself the signs of sovereignty, al-Manṣūr had to keep the young caliph from sight—literally, the caliph was prevented from seeing ambassadors, dignitaries, and

the Cordoban public. At the same time, al-Manṣūr kept Hishām from being an object of vision. Except when it was absolutely necessary to maintain the fiction of Umayyad rule, Hishām did not emerge from al-Zahrā': he did not review troops prior to campaigns, witness executions, receive petitions for justice, or entertain musicians and poets in his court. Although a king appears to be the orchestrator of such events, he is also in some way the event itself, for such occasions are staged primarily to demonstrate before a large audience the political fact of hierarchies and dominance and to ensure the cooperation of the audience in the institution of monarchy. Hishām was removed from a visual relationship in which the people gazing at their king validated him as king and acquiesced to their position as his public, his subjects.

Al-Manṣūr stripped Madīnat al-Zahrā', so that Hishām was incarcerated in a remote half-empty palace under the watchful eyes of guardians. According to al-Ḥimyarī:

> From that moment onward, al-Manṣūr resided in the Palace of al-Zāhira and his power increased. With each day he expanded its constructions and decorated its halls until al-Zāhira reached a state of utter perfection and extraordinary beauty. The city did not cease to excel in its grace and good fortune, receiving word of one military victory after another. No banner was sent forth without returning in triumph, and no edict was issued without meeting with total success.[52]

Several modern historians have erroneously identified as al-Zāhira's the ruins found west of Cordoba at the site known as Cañito de María Ruiz, but the Arabic historians recorded that the future site of al-Zāhira, "Alush," was on the east side of Cordoba and on the banks of the Guadalquivir.[53] Al-Manṣūr, by concentrating building activity in the one area of Cordoba's environs that had not been inscribed with the Umayyad name, and by causing the western Umayyad zone to be neglected, redrew the lines of power in Cordoba, creating a sphere of influence that was expressed physically in his architectural patronage and territorial proprietorship. He moved the government offices to his new palace-city and gave his followers incentives to build there. Once built, al-Zāhira became the most fashionable place to live:

> He installed offices there for the government administrators, increasing the types of administrative positions; stables for all kinds of livestock; granaries on the interior; and mills in its open spaces. Then he made large land grants to his viziers, secretaries, senior military officers and *ḥājibs* who then built large houses and splendid palaces [*quṣūr*] in its shadow and made the area productive and profitable and built impressive parks [*manāzih*]. Before long the city grew; markets were established there and its wealth increased. People vied for houses near al-Zāhira or in its outskirts in order to be near the seat of power, and thus the extent of building activity continued until the new suburb's perimeters reached those of Cordoba.[54]

The family of Ibn Ḥazm (384/994–404/1064), one of the greatest men of letters in his day, joined the distinguished people who moved east from their house in the Balaṭ Mughīth on the west side of Cordoba, but when Ibn Ḥazm's father, who served as vizier to al-Manṣūr and his son, fell out of favor with the Amirids, the family returned to the old house on the west side.[55] Ibn Ḥazm, in

his treatise on love and friendship, describes a festive occasion that took place in the new house next to al-Zāhira: "The women stayed indoors for the first part of the day, then moved to a pavilion [*qaṣaba*] belonging to our house on an elevated site overlooking the gardens and providing a view from there onto the whole of Cordoba. It had bays with open windows, and the women began looking out of the latticework openings, shifting constantly from window to window for the varying views in each direction, different from each one. Then they descended to the garden."[56]

If this house's site gave it views over gardens and landscape, Madīnat al-Zāhira probably had an even greater panorama. That it was built on a height it also suggested by Ṣā'id's poem (cited above) in which the speaker looks down upon the river from al-'Āmirīya. We have already noted the likelihood of al-'Āmirīya being near the walls of Madīnat al-Zāhira. Ibn Bashkuwāl placed Madīnat al-Zāhira in the suburbs of the Ajarquia, the eastern side of Cordoba, walled by the Almoravids in the first quarter of the twelfth century.[57]

Ibn Ḥazm's pavilion, like that in the upper garden at Madīnat al-Zahrā', was a mirador with views toward nearby gardens and distant landscape. But there was a noticeable difference between them. The pavilion at Ibn Ḥazm's house offered many vistas, all of them onto the gardens, each one distinct, and each one seen through a *mashrabīya* (latticed) screen. We have only a slight idea of the architectural form of these pavilions, so it is difficult to assess if they were designed differently or whether the written description just makes it seem so. In any case, contrasting performances were enacted in each one. Instead of emphasizing the centrality of the pavilion and the primacy of the occupant both as viewer and object of the gaze, it is the viewers' movements and the multiplicity of views—no woman or view more significant than the next—that Ibn Ḥazm describes. Conversely, at Madīnat al-Zahrā' the viewer's place was fixed by the architecture of the Salon Rico and its facing pavilion to enhance the centrality of the viewer. Madīnat al-Zahrā's gardens are described in the context of ceremonies and the image is of static positioning and carefully constructed spatial hierarchy. The caliph was invariably seated in the exact center of the hall, his family and staff aligned in rows, the social status of each person present articulated by the relative proximity to the center and the caliph. For example, according to al-Rāzī's description of the celebration of the end of the Ramadan fast in 362/973 al-Ḥakam sat on the throne in the reception hall giving onto the gardens—probably in the "mihrab" niche in the Salon Rico (Fig. 55). The guests entered the hall according to rank: first the caliph's brothers, who saluted him and sat to his right and left; then, in line with the brothers, the viziers; below them the *ḥājib.* The great *fatā*s flanked the throne according to rank; beyond them stood the great *khalīfa*s, eunuchs, *kātib*s, *wasīf*s, and so on, the lower-ranking eunuchs extending from the hall to the esplanade running in front of it, followed by the surveyors (or mathematicians) (*aṣḥāb akhṭṭaṭ*), scribes, and others, all specially dressed and carrying decorated swords.[58] Such an event was very different from a social gathering at Ibn Ḥazm's house, where people moved about regardless of social rank, their physical relationship in constant flux, both with respect to each other and to their views of the garden.

Madīnat al-Zāhira was burned during the civil war that marked the collapse of the Umayyads and Amirids and destroyed much of Cordoba's suburban palace estates. Although its location within the area called the Ajarquia (or Madīnat al-Sharqīya, meaning "the east city") has been tentatively identified with the site of the Church of La Virgen de la Fuensanta (built in 1442) and a

55. The "mihrab" niche in the Salon Rico

56. Hypothetical location of Madīnat al-Zāhira

garden with the same name (Fig. 56), the theory has not been verified by excavations.[59] The only remaining vestige of the city is a basin in the Madrid Archaeological Museum.

Eleventh-Century Palaces

At least three estates were built after the civil war. One was a palace, famous for its rows of almond trees, built by Zubayr ibn ʿUmar al-Mulaththam at the end of the eleventh century when he was governor of Cordoba for the Almoravids.[60] The second postwar palace may have been built by the geometrician al-Ḥājj Yaʿīsh of Malaga, who moved to Cordoba sometime after 1160 to build and restore that city's palaces. In referring to this architect, al-Maqqarī mentioned a costly Almohad palace built on arches (or pilings) on the river. There are brick fragments embedded in the walls of a mill on the banks of the river near the bridge that might belong to this older structure.[61] Additionally there are references to the Munyat al-Habīb, the Castillo de Albaida, and the Jannat al-Maimun, but no dates are known for them. Finally, there was an important tomb garden belonging to the vizier al-Zajjāli, to which we shall return shortly.

Palaces and Gardens of the Imagination

Much of the poetry praising the beauty of the nature surrounding Cordoba acclaims palaces and estates that may never have existed, or if they did, were known to historians by more-mundane names. Ibn Zaydūn (394/1003–463/1070) mentioned, among the beautiful places of Cordoba, the hill of al-ʿUqāb, the palace al-Fārisī, the Maḥbas Nāṣiḥ, ʿAyn Shahda (or Shuhda, meaning "fountain of honey"), Musannāt Mālik where he drank with friends and bathed, and al-ʿAqīq (The Valley) where he spent several days with his beloved, the poetess Wallāda. In another long verse he praised the beauty of al-Jaʿfarīya, al-Jisr, al-Jawsaq al-Naṣrī, al-Waʿsāʾ, Maḍyaʿat al-Ḍawlāb, and Qaṣr Nāṣiḥ.[62] Many of these may have been complementary epithets that were not used by the historians, but at least two of the names can be associated with actual places in Umayyad Cordoba. Maḥbas Nāṣiḥ surely refers to the Arḥāʾ Nāṣiḥ: *maḥbas* means "flume"—the channeling of river water through the water-driven mill (*arḥāʾ*).[63] The Jawsaq al-Naṣrī may be a fanciful name for the Munyat al-Naṣr. Although the word *jawsaq* was seldom used in relation to Hispano-Islamic palaces, in the east this Persian word had the meaning of "palace" or "villa." Its application to the Munyat al-Naṣr may have implied eastern stylishness, and indeed we know that the interest in eastern fashion had already arisen circa 900 when the *munya* was remodeled.

Some of Ibn Zaydūn's names also occur in the works of other authors, a sign that they referred to real places. Al-ʿAqīq is mentioned among the recreation sites of Cordoba not only by Ibn Zaydūn, but also in verses by Abū al-Qāsim Ibn Hishām al-Qurṭubī, and in connection with al-Ruṣāfa in a poem by Qāsim ibn ʿAbbūd al-Riyāḥī.[64] Its exact location is unknown; perhaps it was not a private estate but simply an attractive place, like al-Rakīn, that was pleasant for outings and promenades. The Munyat al-Jaʿfar was the residence of Hishām II and the Munyat al-ʿUqāb was mentioned as the place where Sancho García's defense corps lodged when they were stationed in Cordoba.[65]

Ibn Zaydūn's fanciful names referred to actual places; that he listed so many, sometimes altering the names to make them more descriptive and more interesting, reflects the extent to which the palace estates and "beautiful places" of nature had permeated the poetic imagination. Love affairs transpired in gardens—Ibn Zaydūn had had secret meetings with Wallāda in the ruins of Madīnat al-Zahrā'—so did drinking parties; companionship with a friend was enjoyed during a stroll along the banks of a stream.[66] The loveliness of these palaces, with fountains, pools of water, and graceful channels traversing the thriving gardens, and with halls decorated with ornate stuccos and slender columns, became legendary in Cordoba, especially to the poets writing after the civil war. The former pleasure grounds and recreation estates of the city were not invented by Ibn Zaydūn, but in exile he idealized Cordoba's vanished beauty and through metaphor and fanciful names embroidered upon the charms of actual gardens that, as a resident of the city in the Amirid period, he had known well.

Tomb Gardens and the Theme of Paradise

The civil war was a significant turning point in Hispano-Umayyad history, and its effects were felt in the dividing up of the political landscape, as well as in the artistic and literary response to the new feelings of insecurity and regret for the waning of Spain's first golden age. Even in the glory days of the caliphate, ʿAbd al-Raḥmān III had been in an ideologically impossible situation, for his claim to the caliphate was founded on the premise of his being the rightful ruler of the *dār al-islām* (by its very definition a unitary concept) and his excluding the rights of all others to the caliphal title.[67] Yet, by contesting the Abbasid claim, he added another fissure to the edifice that had already cracked with the establishment of the Fatimids' Shi'ite caliphate.[68]

The second challenge to the integrity of the Umayyad caliphate and the stability of government came from the army. Following a precedent set by ʿAbd al-Raḥmān III, al-Manṣūr had recruited his army from the Berbers of North Africa. The Berber soldiers altered the ethnic stability of the kingdom; they had no ties to the older community of Arabs and more-established Berbers. Their loyalty was to al-Manṣūr rather than the caliph Hishām, so that when the citizens of Cordoba began a pro-Umayyad rebellion, these Berbers took up their position in defense of the Amirids. With no ties to the Umayyad past, they had nothing to lose by doing so.

Although the Amirids had wielded the power in Cordoba since Hishām's accession, angry protests were voiced when one of al-Manṣūr's sons, Sanchuelo, coerced Hishām into assigning him as heir. The protests grew to open rebellion, led by one of ʿAbd al-Raḥmān's grandsons, Muḥammad II al-Mahdī, and to full-scale civil war. In the fighting that raged in Cordoba for the next two years, most of the suburbs and garden estates were looted and burned to the ground, many of the city's most distinguished citizens were killed or fled to safe havens elsewhere, and the caliphate was dealt a blow from which it never recovered. With neither strong leadership, ethnic solidarity, nor a clear sense of the Umayyad caliphate's ideological stance (it had been neither a committed member of the central caliphate nor a completely self-contained realm), Cordoba lost its privileged position as the seat of political power. The united and highly centralized state gave way to a network of regional taifa kingdoms, each governed by one of the former governors or a member of a noble family.[69]

The former blithe confidence in the legitimate rule of the Umayyads and cultural superiority of Cordoba was violently shaken during the war; al-Andalus's prestige suffered and political contacts with rest of the world temporarily came to a halt. Scholarly interaction and trade continued unabated, however, since the Andalusian fascination with eastern arts and literature did not diminish.[70] Because of the continued admiration of eastern culture and the dispersal of Cordoban culture within al-Andalus, no true break with the past occurred. Umayyad cultural values flourished in the taifa courts, led variously by Berbers or Arabs, and were even stimulated to new heights as the kings vied to outdo each other in the brilliance of their courts and the splendor of their palaces. The taifa splintering and regrouping was a domestic phenomenon within the frontiers of al-Andalus, but it left the country vulnerable to attacks from the Christian north, and it coincided with other major upheavals elsewhere in Islam. In Baghdad, the Abbasids who had been manipulated since 945 by the Buyids became Seljuk puppets in 1055, and thus in Spain as well as in the very center of the Islamic world, non-Arabs held sway.[71]

The loss of unity and the division of the political landscape of the peninsula was reflected in the literature of eleventh-century writers such as Ibn Ḥazm. A prevailing sense of unease found expression in both poetry and garden iconography.[72] One of the changes affecting the gardens built in Cordoba was the reorganization of patronage. During this time of chaos, there was a lack of strong central leadership from the caliph or his vizier, and the architectural and garden patronage of the illustrious inhabitants of Cordoba was experimental in character. The ideological statements of the gardens of the new patrons were not dynastic in the former sense of a sovereign, a palace, and gardens with views onto his territory. Instead of being signs of a preoccupation with dynasty, which the civil war had destroyed, they were statements of personal taste and the individual's hope for an afterlife. Some gardens became expressions of the individual's desire for paradise, both on earth and in heaven. It is perhaps not coincidental, after the bloody war when so many men, women, and children in Cordoba died or were massacred in one of the many coups, that the theme now introduced should be eschatological: death and eternity.

Although plenty of nonroyal gardens existed, we have few descriptions of them. The garden of al-Zajjāli is a rare example of a nonroyal garden described by historians and with architectural inscriptions that were recorded. No trace remains of the garden itself, but its approximate location can be deduced from texts: outside the walls just west of the Bab al-Yahūd, north of the city.[73] Called the Ḥayr al-Zajjāli, it was first conceived as a pleasure garden. It was the property of a Berber family in Cordoba and became a public park in the eleventh century, when on the death of its owner, the vizier Abū Marwān al-Zajjāli, it was deeded by *waqf* as a mausoleum complex.[74] A *waqf* complex was a perpetual endowment that often incorporated tombs and pavilions and might include hospices, mosques, public drinking fountains, and educational centers. The obligatory performance (*wājib*) of the religious duty of charity and the non-obligatory but recommended (*mustaḥābb*) performance of good works could be achieved in the endowment of either secular or religious buildings. On a wordly level, the endowment benefited the donor, who could appoint his or her family members as trustees or use the trust to circumvent strict laws (mandated by the Qur'ān) of inheritance apportionment in order to favor or exclude particular heirs. On a spiritual level such an endowment also expressed faith in future continuity, both on earth (the dwelling of the body) and in paradise (the dwelling of the soul).

This tomb garden contained the sepulcher of al-Zajjāli and thereafter that of his friend, the poet Ibn Shuhayd, who died after him in 425/1035 at the age of forty-three.[75] A description of the hall's water channels, which flowed from one floor level to another in a smooth serpentine motion, and basins and polychromed pavilion, and the rows of trees with dense foliage and garden beds emphasized worldly beauty:

> Its courtyard is of pure white marble; a stream [*jadwal*] traverses it, wriggling like a snake. There is [also] a basin into which all waters fall. The roof [of the pavilion] is decorated with gold and blue and in these colours also are decorated the sides and various parts. The garden [*rawḍ*] has files of trees symmetrically aligned and its flowers smile from open buds. The foliage of the garden prevents the sun seeing the ground; and the breeze, blowing day and night over the garden, is loaded with scents. . . . Abū ʿĀmir [Ibn Shuhayd] enjoyed therein spells of well-being and rest both in the morning and afternoon. Fate gave him at that time whatsoever he desired, and the pleasures of sobriety and inebriation alternated with each other in his experience. He and the proprietor of the garden who is buried alongside him were companions in the youthful pursuit of the gratification of the senses and allies in joy.[76]

The description is not morbid and does not mention any religious motivation underlying the garden's creation. To the contrary, it was clearly a place for sensory pleasures and alcoholic intoxication. Continuing, the description states that al-Zajjāli and Ibn Shuhayd "were companions in death as they had been in life."[77] Ibn Shuhayd himself composed the epitaph for the tomb, recalling in its lines the pleasurable evenings spent in the garden in life, which in death vanished as if they had never been, and he begged God's mercy.[78] The references to life after death—the paradise promised by the Qurʾān to the faithful—are the only indications of the garden's association with piety and eternity, and they were added *after* the garden had already been created as a pleasance. The form preexisted; but its iconography changed.

This is the first recorded instance of an Andalusian pleasure garden associated with piety and paradise. The Muslim kings of Cordoba had traditionally been buried in a place in the Alcazar called the Rawḍa (not the same place as the Dār al-Rawḍa).[79] That the Rawḍa cemetery was within the city walls of Cordoba, not in the surrounding countryside, means that it was essentially an urban construction. The word *rawḍa,* meaning "garden," implies that the setting was cultivated, and certainly all the other cemeteries in Cordoba were open-air.[80] But we do not know to what extent they were gardened. Nothing indicates that they were irrigated or embellished with specially tended flowers and shrubs. There were no fountains, water basins, or bedded plants, and therefore, probably no axial compartments and no attempt to create order or an aesthetic composition. The royal Rawḍa was an open space, perhaps with trees among the burial markers, but it certainly was not a converted pleasure garden. As a cemetery, it had associations with the afterlife, but it did not partake of that particular formal garden typology that had developed within the context of palaces and recreation estates.

The addition of two graves (whether or not these were freestanding mausoleums is unknown) to the Ḥayr al-Zajjāli's pleasure garden was an important event in the development of garden iconography, for it brought together an explicitly worldly garden with the implied garden of paradise.

With only a single eleventh-century Andalusian funerary garden known, one cannot identify this as a widespread change in garden symbolism. But we can at least state that, while a paradisiac connotation was absent in palace gardens of the seventh through tenth centuries, a new aspect of meaning became available in the eleventh. The ramifications of the new iconographic possibility, in which gardens could serve a spiritual function, or more precisely could make specific reference to the Qurʾānic paradise, was not fully realized until more than two centuries later at the Alhambra.

PART THREE

THE GARDEN LEGACY

7

PALACES OF THE ELEVENTH AND TWELFTH CENTURIES

Oh al-Zahrā᾿s builder, how you waste your time in it! Why not proceed more slowly?
By God, how beautiful would be its brilliance if its flower would not wither!
—Mundhir b. Saʿīd

These verses, lamenting Madīnat al-Zahrā᾿s ephemeral splendor, were recited by the *qāḍī* Mundhir b. Saʿīd to ʿAbd al-Raḥmān III one day as they were walking in the gardens. But ʿAbd al-Raḥmān responded: "If over it wafts the breeze of memory and nostalgic yearning, and tender tears water it, then it will not fade."[1] The memory of Madīnat al-Zahrā᾿, and to a lesser extent its sister palaces, endured long after the buildings had disappeared and was an important legacy to western Islamic architecture. While in its time, Madīnat al-Zahrā᾿ reflected the concerns and ambitions of the two men who built its palaces and gardens, its meaning changed as the star of the Umayyad dynasty was eclipsed by the Amirid usurpers, and later, when Cordoba succumbed to a civil war and eventually to the Christian Reconquest. The site deteriorated and came to symbolize the sad new character of the Islamic political situation on the Iberian Peninsula. As the "readers" changed from the Umayyads and their subjects to the Amirids, taifa kings, Almoravids, Almohads, Christian conquerors, Nasrids, and ultimately the historians and archaeologists of the modern period, Madīnat al-Zahrā᾿ was perceived and remembered in different ways. Until twentieth-century excavations revealed its buried structure, its memory was preserved in literature, where it figured as a legendary place of courtly splendor, and in the later palatine architecture, for which it served as a conceptual model.

Madīnat al-Zahrā᾿ Remembered

Madīnat al-Zahrā᾿ lived in the memory of the poets and historians of al-Andalus long after its walls collapsed and weeds sprouted in the gaps where once there had been paving stones.[2] The tragic circumstances of Madīnat al-Zahrā᾿s destruction propelled it from an already fantastic place of

grandeur and magnificence into a truly mythological realm in which the human imagination enhanced the sumptuousness of its architecture and the brilliance of its inhabitants. Thus, although the architecture itself no longer could serve as a direct model for succeeding generations of builders, it provided an enduring and powerful conceptual paradigm. In this way, the palace acquired an even deeper significance as a ruin that it had enjoyed as the caliphal seat. Architectural memory depends on visual clues enriched by the imagination: ruins are powerful reminders of what was, allowing the mind's recollection to reconstruct the place as it might have and ought to have been.[3] In post-Umayyad al-Andalus, the ruins of Madīnat al-Zahrā᾽ remained for several centuries as a reminder of the splendor of the caliphate, evoking a time when the kingdom was unified under one king whose ancestry could be traced back (via Muʿāwīya I and ʿUthmān b. ʿAffān) to the Companions of the Prophet.

Al-Zahrā᾽ was burned on 23 Rabi I, 401/November 4, 1010, after the Berber rebels sacked it. Thereafter, it was the abode of birds and wild beasts: "The copper was pulled off the doors, the lead of the pipes and other materials taken away. With this ruin, the carpet of the world was folded up and the beauty that had been an earthly paradise was disfigured."[4] In the eleventh century when Cordoba was an independent taifa kingdom ruled by the Banū Jahwar, materials from the Umayyad palaces were sold, and this continued afterward, as evidenced by the Cordoban column capitals and mosque furnishings that were carted off to Seville, Granada, and Morocco.[5] The Umayyad palaces ultimately became quarries from which precious materials could be extracted for reuse in other palaces. One wonders if the columns, wooden panels, and objects thus obtained, in addition to their having manifest value as spolia, were especially prized as relics of the Umayyad palace.

Madīnat al-Zahrā᾽ was visited many times in the eleventh and twelfth centuries, the visitors often recording their responses to the devastation seen there. Like that of the Roman Forum, al-Zahrā᾽s ruin was a tangible reminder of the monumental architecture of a bygone age, and its deterioration was the inspiration for a flood of poetry on the tragedy of its decay. Poets composed despairing verses, and the scene of abandoned halls inspired jilted lovers to express the pain of heartache. The poet and philosopher Ibn Zaydūn, returning from self-imposed exile after the civil war, hid in the halls of the al-Zahrā᾽ palace where white lilies and red roses bloomed. From there he sent pleading poems to his beloved but fickle Wallāda in Cordoba, reminding her of former trysts in the gardens of al-Zahrā᾽:

> I remembered you in al-Zahrā᾽, while longing for you:
> The landscape was gay-looking and the earth shining with dew;
>
> The breeze of the evening was imbued with languor,
> As if its pity for me had filled it with sickness:
>
> The flower gardens smiled with their silvery waters
> Like collars loosened from the necks of fair maidens.
>
> It was a day resembling those of joy, now gone,
> When we were stealing pleasures, while Fate was fast asleep:

> Now I enjoy the view of flowers to which my eyes are attracted,
> And dew weighs heavily on them—their stems are drooping,
>
> Their eyes on seeing my constant sleeplessness,
> Seem to weep over my pain; their glittering tears fall one by one.[6]

A happier visitor was al-Muʿtamid, the taifa ruler of Seville and overlord of Cordoba. Muʿtamid and his courtiers made a day trip to the palace in 461/1068–89 while staying in Cordoba, and they gamboled about the fallen stones, drinking wine and reflecting upon the strange beauty of its ruins:

> They wandered from palace to palace, hacking away at the branches and brambles. They climbed to the topmost rooms, exchanging cups of wine among those high terraces [*shurufāt*] until they arrived finally in the garden [*rawḍa*] after having examined the ruins closely, their view [*iʿtibār*] increasing in increments as they went. In the garden they settled themselves on springtime carpets striped with white flowers and bordered with streams and water channels . . . overlooked by the ruins of those halls which, like bereaved mothers, mourn the devastation and the end of the joyful gatherings, now that the lizard plays among the stones and croaks on the walls. Nothing remained except holes and stones: the pavilions had collapsed and youth had become old age, as occasionally iron becomes soft and that which is new rots. All the while they drank cups of wine and wandered about, both enjoying themselves and yet pausing for reflection.[7]

The site was also visited by the Christians at that time, as is clear from a strange request made to al-Muʿtamid by the Christian king Alfonso VI. Al-Muʿtamid paid tribute to that king as part of a treaty agreement, but the treaty was ruptured when Alfonso demanded that his pregnant wife be allowed to visit the former Christian church in the Mosque of Cordoba and to take up residence in Madīnat al-Zahrāʾ, where she would benefit from the excellent air and from where she could make frequent visits to the mosque. Al-Muʿtamid was so angered by the request that he threw a desk at Alfonso's emissary, breaking his head open, and then had him crucified.[8] In the twelfth century Ibn al-ʿArabī visited Madīnat al-Zahrāʾ, and the Almohad caliph Yaʿqūb al-Manṣūr went there in 586/1190 to contemplate the remnants of the past. By then the palace-city was already a field of ruins, and he took away with him the female statue of al-Zahrāʾ (probably Roman spoils that had been reused by the Umayyads).[9]

After the conquest of Cordoba in 1236 by Ferdinand III of Castile, the identity of the site was gradually consigned to oblivion. In 1408 the grounds of "Córdoba la Vieja," as it was called, were ceded to the monks of San Jerónimo, who removed the ashlar blocks and marble for use in the construction of their monastery on the hill above al-Zahrāʾ. By the sixteenth century, the Islamic origins of Córdoba la Vieja had been forgotten. It was believed to be the foundation of the original Roman Colonia Patricia established by Marcellus.[10]

To Muslim visitors, the sight of these ruins gave rise to a sense of foreboding and doom, as if the fall of Cordoba foreshadowed the loss of all of al-Andalus to the Christian reconquerors. The ruins of the Umayyad palaces offered a presentiment of worse things to come, and in many cases

prompted the viewer to draw a moral conclusion. "What a lesson for the survivors!" wrote Ibn Ḥayyān,[11] and later authors recounted stories in which ʿAbd al-Raḥmān III and al-Manṣūr ignored warnings of imminent collapse. Ibn Ghālib told the fable of when ʿAbd al-Raḥmān, one sleepless night, climbed to the highest room in Madīnat al-Zahrāʾ, where a voice cautioned:

> O Lord of the palace, great and wonderful,
> Listen to my two-word warning!
> You are at the brink of leaving it
> For a pit two palms in breadth.[12]

Historians writing decades and even centuries after the fall of the Umayyads commented that Cordoba had fallen because of its rulers' extravagance and pride, which, no doubt, explains why the story of Madīnat al-Zahrāʾ's hall with the golden cupola was repeated so frequently by medieval historians.[13] ʿAbd al-Raḥmān's excessive use of gold and silver was a source of amazement and fascination to the chroniclers, but it was also seen as a harbinger of the ultimate fate of the Umayyad house. Ibn Shuhayd wrote: "I am sadly affected by the death which has befallen you. But was it not divine justice, since, during your life, you were so endlessly proud of your own splendor?"[14]

Similarly, al-Maqqarī wrote that a holy man exclaimed, upon seeing the opulence of Madīnat al-Zāhira: "O Palace of Kings! Every house in this country has contributed to thy ornament and perfection: thou shalt also (when in ruins) afford materials for every house."[15] The wreckage of Cordoba in 1009–10 was the first such experience in al-Andalus, and it was shocking. The decayed Roman and Visigothic palaces, temples, and churches that the early Muslims had encountered on the Iberian Peninsula did not provoke such melancholy in the Muslim consciousness, because Roman remains were regarded as foundations upon which to build the new order. They posed no reason for regret or nostalgia for a time when life was simpler and fortunes more secure. The Umayyad ruins, in contrast, symbolized the passing of a better age. Ibn al-ʿArabī, visiting Madīnat al-Zahrāʾ sometime in the last two decades of the twelfth century, was so moved by its desolation that he composed the following verses:

> Halls alongside of playgrounds gleam,
> but they have no occupants and they are in ruins.
>
> Birds are lamenting in them from every side,
> At times they are silent, other times cooing.
>
> I addressed one of the wingborn singers,
> who was sad at heart and aquiver.
>
> "For what do you lament so plaintively" I asked,
> And it answered, "For an age that is gone, forever."[16]

And in a similar mode Ibn Jahwar, the eleventh-century ruler of Cordoba, rued the empty halls of al-Zahrāʾ:

One day I asked the house of those who had passed on,
"Where are your inhabitants to us so dear?"
They replied, "They lived here for a short while,
Then they went away, but I know not where."[17]

Ibn Ḥazm, who was forced to leave Cordoba after the *fitna,* suffered terribly from homesickness for the city where he had grown up and where his father had served as vizier to the Amirids. When he asked a traveler for news of Cordoba, especially of his family's houses in the Balāṭ Mughīth quarter on the west side, he was told that the buildings were so deteriorated that they had all but vanished. The image of the neglected halls became for Ibn Ḥazm a tragic sign for the destruction of the Cordoba he once knew and for the passing of a time of peace, security, and happiness. His response was a profound statement of despair:

> It was as though the graceful palaces and embellished chambers that were as radiant as the sun, the beauty of their views erasing all cares, now that ruin and utter destruction was all around, were as the gaping mouths of wild predators announcing the annihilation of the world. . . .
>
> I seemed to see before my eyes the destruction of that noble citadel that I had once known as beautiful and prosperous, in the stable well-ordered atmosphere in which I had grown up; its courtyards once full of life, now empty.[18]

The abrupt decline and abandonment of a royal palace (in contrast to the Alhambra, which simply changed hands from Muslim to Christian owners) was a constant reminder of how quickly even the most stable of kingdoms can collapse. The fallen roofs of al-Zahrāʾ, the stripped walls and cracked pavements, represented the loss and ruin of all of al-Andalus and gave rise to a nostalgic yearning for an irretrievable time when Muslims ruled a unified al-Andalus and its territories were expanding under the capable leadership of ʿAbd al-Raḥmān, al-Ḥakam, and al-Manṣūr.

A poem by al-Sumaysir of Almeria (later of Ilbīra) addressed the palace as if it were a lover. But even as he rued the decay of the palace and all that it stood for, the poet realized the impossibility of resurrecting the past:

I stopped at al-Zahrāʾ weeping, looking at it
  I lamented its slow decay.
And I said, "O Zahrāʾ, come back." And she responded,
  "Who can return from death?"
I did not stop my crying, crying in that place.
  But the tears were of no avail; no, none at all.
Rather, they were the traces of tears shed by those
  hired to mourn the dead.[19]

In the eleventh and twelfth century, Muslims watched the erosion of the edges of al-Andalus, as piece by piece the country fell into Christian hands and the Muslim rulers were forced into

humiliating pacts with their enemies. From 1055 onward, the Christian Reconquest became a real threat as Fernando I of Castile and Leon besieged Saragossa, Toledo, and Badajoz, and made the taifa rulers his vassals. Nothing was more alarming than Alfonso VI's easy capture in 1085 of Toledo, already a tribute-paying state. It was an important moment because Toledo was the first Islamic kingdom to fall completely into the hands of a Christian king. The Christian menace so terrified al-Muʿtamid of Seville, the Afṭasī ruler al-Mutawakkil of Badajoz, and the Zirid ruler ʿAbd Allāh of Granada that they sought help from the Almoravid sultan Yūsuf Ibn Tāshfīn (r. 453/1061–500/1106) of Morocco. He entered Spain via Algeciras, pushing back the Christians in a celebrated victory at Zallāqa near Badajoz in 479/1086. He returned to Marrakesh but was asked to help a second time, and besieged Aledo without achieving a decisive victory. He again returned to Marrakesh, but when it became apparent that the ineffective taifa rulers were incapable of staving off the Christians without his support, he ousted them altogether, making himself ruler of Seville in 484/1091, Badajoz and Lisbon in 487/1094, Valencia in 495/1102, and Saragossa in 503/1110. Thus by the early twelfth century, Andalus was no longer autonomous but was an Almoravid province.

In the following century the Almoravids were expelled and were replaced by the Almohads, another Maghrebi dynasty ruling from both Marrakesh and Seville. By 1212 the Almohads were defeated by the Christians, so that by the mid-thirteenth century only the Nasrid kingdom of Granada (which included the cities of Almeria, Malaga, and Gibraltar) was left. With large portions of the peninsula occupied by the Christians, the theme of "paradise lost" reverberated in Arabic literature. In the decisive battle of Ecija (634/1234), the general al-Kalāʿī led his troops against the Aragonese, crying: "*ʿAn al-jannati tafirrūn?*"—"Are you going to flee from Paradise?"[20] For centuries afterward, Muslim writers would append to the names of Seville, Cordoba, Valencia, and other places the words *aʿādahā allāh bi-l-islām*—"May God restore it to Islam."[21]

Arabic historians dwelled more on the fall of Toledo to the Christians in the eleventh century than on the ultimate and final capture of Cordoba in 1236. Cordoba's moment of disgrace was the civil war, and its fall from power at that time was equated after the fact with the fall of al-Andalus to the Christian Reconquest. The taking of Toledo by Alfonso marked the beginning of the end of al-Andalus's self-rule, and Ibn Ghassāl's verses convey the sense of urgency felt by Muslims on the city's loss:

> O people of al-Andalus, spur your mounts,
> for our place here is but a deception.
>
> The fabric of the peninsula is unraveling from the
> edges, and the cloth even unravels from the center.
>
> We are in the midst of enemies we cannot get rid of.
> What kind of life is this, living in a basket of vipers?[22]

Likewise, lamenting the loss of Valencia after its conquest by El Cid in 483/1090, another poet wrote:

> A land whose dwellers were scattered by dire events,
> Fate's blows have scattered it by cruel blasts,

The hand of Destiny wrote on its courts:
You are not *you*, these dwellings are not *yours*.[23]

For Muslims, Madīnat al-Zahrā's legendary splendor came to represent a bygone era of stability, unity, and prosperity when the Umayyads ruled al-Andalus. Its subsequent deterioration was a reminder of the collapse of the Umayyad state and the internal decay of the fractious and ever shrinking taifa, Almoravid, and Almohad kingdoms. Thus, the palace-city was remembered in its prime as the pinnacle of Andalusian Islam, and as a ruin it became a symbol of paradise lost.

Palaces of Seville

In a poetry competition in the thirteenth century, al-Shaqundī captured the sense of both loss and gain when he described the taifa period as "the breaking of the necklace and scattering of its pearls."[24] The centralized Umayyad government had fallen apart, but a lasting cultural legacy was bequeathed to its taifa successors. Architecturally, the interest in material splendor, miradors, views, extensive and elaborate gardens was echoed to varying degrees in the palaces built after the *fitna* such as the Alcazaba of Malaga, the Naʿūra Palace of Toledo, the Aljaferia of Saragossa, and the Alhambra and Generalife of Granada. These attest to the continued importance of the landscape-garden-architecture paradigm that endured after the Christian Reconquest, particularly in Seville and the *carmen* gardens of Granada, and was carried across the Mediterranean by Andalusians emigrating to Tunisia and Morocco.

After two decades of unrest, assassinations, and coups, Cordoba became in the taifa period a republic ruled by an aristocratic Arab family, the Banū Jahwar (422/1030–401/1069), until it was absorbed by its ambitious neighbor Seville.[25] Economically depressed after the turmoil of the civil war, the city saw little building during the eleventh century; to the contrary, architecture was dismantled, as stone slabs, columns, and capitals from its ruined palaces were sold to builders in other cities.[26]

Taifa Seville was ruled by the ʿAbbadī family from 414/1023 until they were exiled by the Almoravids in 484/1091–92. By swallowing up smaller kingdoms, Seville became the most powerful of the taifa kingdoms, profiting from an advantageous location on the Guadalquivir River, the only navigable river in Spain, and near the center of al-Andalus with good routes to the rest of the taifa kingdoms and North Africa. Since the Arab ʿAbbadids designated themselves heirs to the Umayyads, Seville was one of the few taifa states to have an ideological basis for its existence.[27] It was the largest city in al-Andalus, having received most of Cordoba's émigrés after the civil war, and it maintained that preeminence until conquered by Castile in the mid-thirteenth century.

Seville had a palace zone that sprawled on either side of the city wall, as well as a number of suburban palaces. The palace in the medina consisted of the Alcazar and its gardens. On the other side of the city wall was the garden palace, the Buḥayra al-Kubrā, built outside the Bāb Jahwar and the Bāb Sharīsh to the southeast of the city (Fig. 57). The Buḥayra al-Kubrā was a drained lake that was planted by the taifa king al-Muʿtamid (r. 461/1069–484/1091) and later became known as the

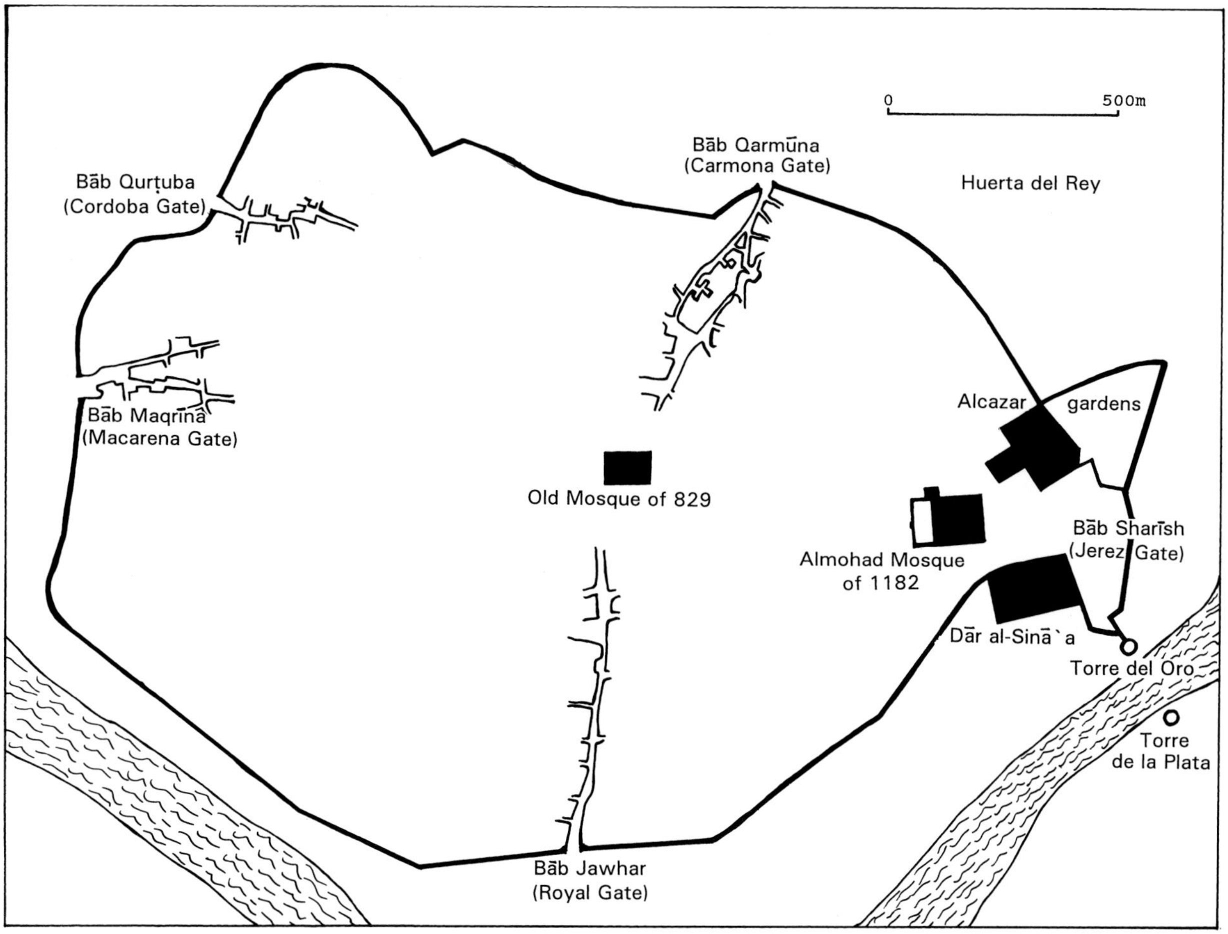

57. Plan of Seville (after Lévi-Provençal)

Huerta del Rey.[28] Amid the orchards and gardens he placed a pavilion, so that production and aesthetic enjoyment commingled. The relationship between the urban Alcazar and the Buḥayra was similar to that of Cordoba's Alcazar and gardens: the palace abutted the city wall and, for want of space in the medina, the gardens were located next to the Alcazar but outside the city wall.

The boundaries and character of the palaces of Seville's taifa complex are difficult to determine because of the paucity of textual data and because the subsequent rebuilding programs of the Almoravids and Christians almost obliterated the ʿAbbadid structures. But poetry of the period indicates that height was an important element of their design and that several of them were on rises overlooking the river or landscape. A poem by Ibn Khāqān mentioned several—al-Mubārak (the Fortunate), al-Waḥīd (the Unique), al-Zāhī (the Prosperous), al-Tāj (the Crown), and al-Zāhir (the Brilliant)—and a *risāla* by the poet Ibn Aḥmad consisted of a seven-part dialogue between the Mubārak and Mukarram palaces in which each applauded the beauty of its own architecture and gardens.[29] The Palace al-Mukarram praised its myrtles, palm trees, roses, narcissi, lilies, anemones, jasmine, stock, and violets, to which al-Mubārak responded with praise for its own intensely col-

ored poppies, marguerites, and other flowers that "attract the gaze and make the eyes dally." Ibn Aḥmad wrote of the palace al-Mukarram: "They have told me that your complex encloses adornment on two facades, the tiers of which hold a hall between two pools, both of great beauty, and the gardens of which are limpid and have branches embracing each other like lovers."[30]

Al-Mubārak had a central dome called al-Thurayya (the Pleiades), gardens, and fountains that included, possibly, the lion fountain described by Ibn Bassām.[31] It may have replaced the original Dār al-Imāra of the Umayyad period (built 301/913–14); but it is unclear whether al-Mubārak was located next to or in place of the older Umayyad building.[32] A small portion of one of al-Mubārak's courtyard gardens was discovered in the course of excavating a twelfth-century cross-axial garden from the Almohad period.[33] Rocío Lledó, who has made a study of the texts pertaining to the taifa palaces of Seville, believes that the palace al-Zāhī with its central domed hall called Saʿad al-Suʿūd (Joy of Joys), and its gardens, pools, and elephant fountain was associated with al-Mubārak Palace. She suggests that both belonged to one *qaṣr* that was part of an even larger complex, the relationship between the components of which resembled the relationship of the Alhambra's conglomeration of palaces. Al-Mubārak's primary function was residential, and it was the preferred dwelling of al-Muʿtamid. The palace al-Mukarram was devoted to administration. Ibn Aḥmad called it "the base of the caliphate, the stability of the chiefdom, and the seat of the legitimate dynasties."[34]

Al-Zāhir, variously called *qaṣr* and *ḥiṣn,* was the residence of the taifa king al-Muʿtaḍid (433–461/1041–42 to 1068–69) and was built before or during his reign and restored by his son, al-Muʿtamid, in 472/1079–80. Surrounded by olive groves, it was located on the slope of a steep hill forty meters above the river and four kilometers from the medina on the right bank of the Guadalquivir River. It fell into ruin after al-Muʿtamid was exiled and it was battered by Christian troops in 578/1182.[35] A century later the Almohad ruler Yūsuf Yaʿqūb al-Manṣūr rebuilt it with great halls opening out onto a view toward Seville and renamed it Ḥiṣn al-Faraj, meaning both "castle with a view" and "castle of pleasure."[36] A poem by Ibn Ḥamdīs praised the beauty of the palace and referred to figural representations painted on its walls.[37] The palace appears to have served both as a country retreat and as a semidefensive guard post.

For Seville of the Almoravid and Almohad periods there is more textual and archaeological documentation. The banks of the river were planted with gardens, orchards, and vineyards. Figs, cotton, and olives grew in the area known as the Ajarafe; the garden called the Jannat al-Musalla, south of the city, was planted with sugarcane.[38] In 567/1171, the Almohad caliph Abū Yaʿqūb Yūsuf built a magnificent group of palaces in the Buḥayra with funds from the state treasury and supplied them with water from a renovated Roman subterranean canal. Ibn Ṣāḥib al-Ṣalāt said that as soon as Abū Yaʿqūb Yūsuf's estate in the Buḥayra was built, "he took care to bring water to it to irrigate the trees in the orchard he had there. Outside the Bāb Qarmūna on the plain (*faḥṣ*) along the road which leads to Carmona was an ancient hole left from the construction of a canal which had been underground." The engineer al-Ḥājj al-Yaʿīsh examined it and, realizing it was an ancient *qanāt,* repaired it so that the people of Seville would have water.[39] This replaced the old system of hoisting water from the river.

For the Buḥayra's gardens Abū Yaʿqūb Yūsuf ordered special types of pear, plum, and apple from Granada and Guadix, and transported them in several convoys of mules. The sources state

that he took a great interest in the gardens and used to enjoy going out to watch the planting of olive trees.[40] In addition to hiring Aḥmad ibn Bāṣu, the leading architect in al-Andalus, he employed Abū al-Qāsim Aḥmad ibn Muḥammad, the *qāḍī,* and Abū Bakr Muḥammad ibn Yaḥyā, the *imām* of the mosque, "because of his trust in their knowledge of surveying, soil preparation, and cultivation to design for him everything concerning his palace constructions and the barren land surrounding them."[41] This is the first medieval Hispano-Islamic reference to what we would call a landscape architect. It is noteworthy that whereas Ibn Wāfid had achieved fame as a skilled agronomist in the eleventh century, Abū al-Qāsim and Abū Bakr were hired in the twelfth for their expertise in garden design.

The Buḥayra was a magnet for more building and it eventually grew to become a suburban quarter. In 1248 its palaces were burned during the Christian conquest of the city, and in later centuries, its gardens were filled in by urban expansion.[42] The Alcazar was also substantially altered after the taifa period, but some of its courtyard gardens have been discovered through archaeological excavations (Fig. 58). In the present-day Casas de Contratación, in an area that formerly belonged to the Alcazar, is a garden that dates to the twelfth century (it is uncertain whether it was built by the Almoravids or the Almohads). The almost square space (12.25 by 11m) is intersected by walkways that divide the garden into four quadrants (Color Plate 4).[43] These deep garden beds are two meters deep and decorated with elaborately painted stucco and intersecting blind arches of brick attached to the walls (Fig. 59). Pollen analysis determined the presence of jasmine and, planted in containers in the corners of each sunken quadrant, orange trees. At one end of the courtyard, the facade of a brick portico still survives, consisting of a large central arch flanked by three smaller arches on each side. At the other end of the garden the remains of an earlier garden from the eleventh-century Qaṣr al-Mubārak were excavated, consisting of three sunken flower beds, matched by three more that were obliterated by the later garden (Fig. 60).

Another garden courtyard, called El Crucero, also dates to the twelfth century (see Fig. 58). Its cross-axial plan is formed by walkways that divide the space into four deeply sunken quadrants, approximately five meters deep. It was largely destroyed by an eighteenth-century earthquake, but a seventeenth-century observer saw orange trees there, the tops of which barely reached the level of the paths.[44]

The Alcazar did not fare better than the suburban palaces; it housed the Christian rulers after the reconquest but was considerably remodeled. Although the result is a confusing mixture of taifa, Almohad, and Christian building, it is clear that a significant portion of the complex was devoted to open courtyards and gardens. The Alcazar's location on the edge of the dense medina precluded cultivation on a large scale, and in this sense it does not compare to the recreation palaces of Umayyad Cordoba. But outside the city walls, the Buḥayra provided the space for extensive gardens with collections of special plants obtained from afar, and at Qaṣr al-Faraj long-distance landscape effects were possible because the site of the palace was elevated to provide vistas. Although nothing is known about the layout of Seville's suburban gardens, the two Alcazar gardens show that by the twelfth century the cross-axial plan was used with complete assurance and featured elements of design that had matured in Cordoba: sunken garden beds divided by elevated walkways with water channels running along the axes and water basins marking the points of intersection.

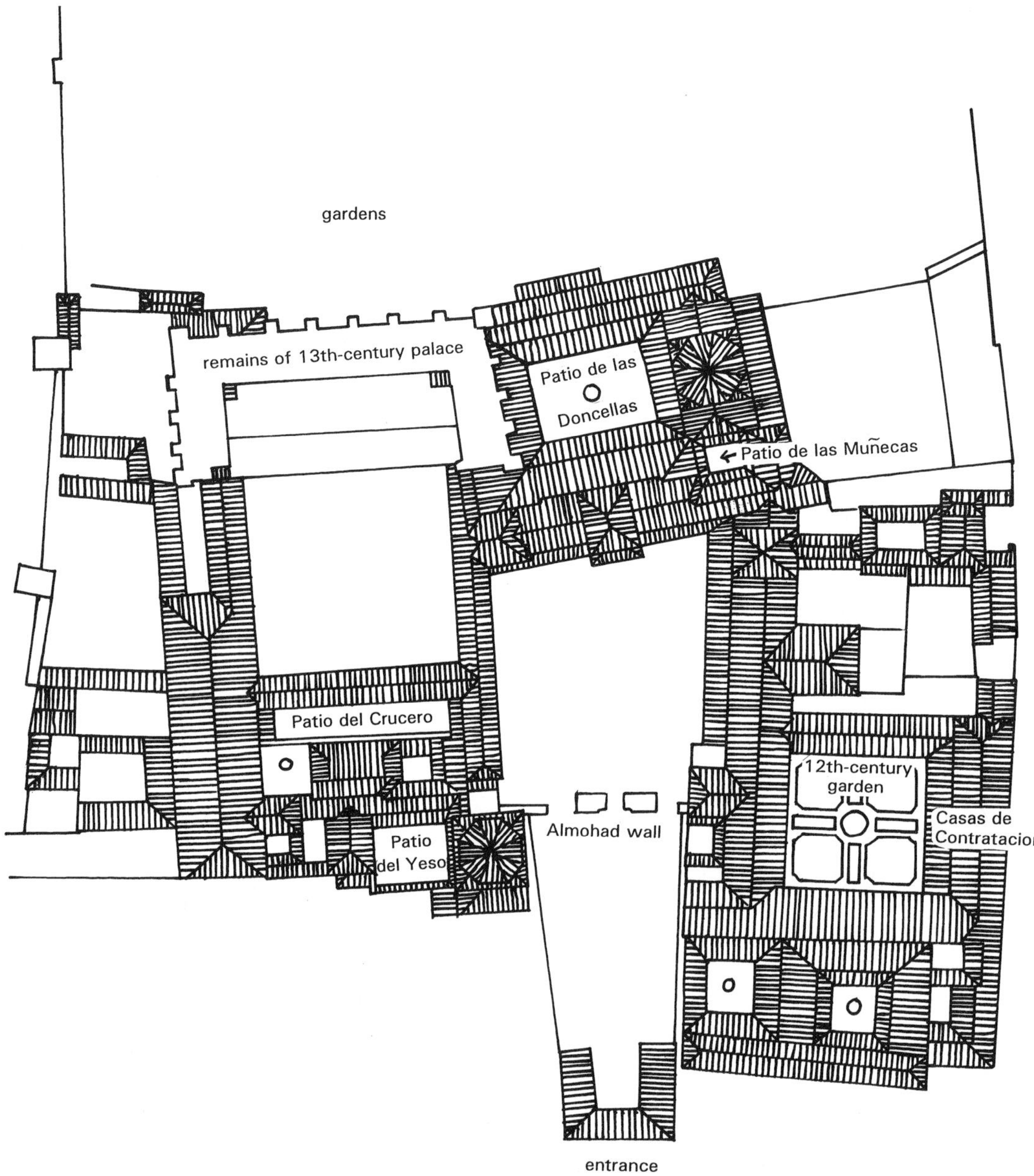

58. Plan of the Seville Alcazar and its gardens (after R. Manzano)

Not only the design, but the nomenclature as well, points to Cordoba as a source of inspiration for Seville's palaces. The name of al-Muʿtamid's al-Zāhir echoes al-Zahrāʾ and al-Zāhira, and a poem by that ruler states unequivocably, "Today my palaces envy those palaces of al-Zahrāʾ."[45] Seville's Abbadid rulers had more than just a fondness for the architecture of the past; during the taifa period the Arab Abbadids believed that they had special claim to the Umayyad political legacy. They and the Hammudids were the only taifa dynasties to insinuate aspects of caliphal titulature in

59. Sunken garden quadrants with blind arches in the present-day Casas de Contratación

60. Garden in the present-day Casas de Contratación with the remains of an eleventh-century garden at one end

correspondence and coinage,[46] and in 461/1069 al-Muʿtamid annexed Cordoba, taking possession of the grand old mosque and empty, ruinous Umayyad palaces that they then sought to re-create in Seville.

Palaces of Toledo

Seville's rival for prestige and power was taifa Toledo, ruled by the Dhū al-Nūn (Fig. 61). A Berber family and the former governors of Toledo, the Dhū al-Nūn became independent in about 407/1016 and ruled until Alfonso VI conquered the city in 478/1085. None of Toledo's royal palaces survive from this period, but they are known through descriptions in Arabic texts. Al-Maʾmūn (r. 435/1043–467/1075) built two renowned palaces, the first a magnificent structure with a fantastic crystal fountain/pavilion, the description of which, in al-Maqqarī's words, evoked ʿAbd al-Raḥmān al-Nāṣir's Madīnat al-Zahrāʾ:

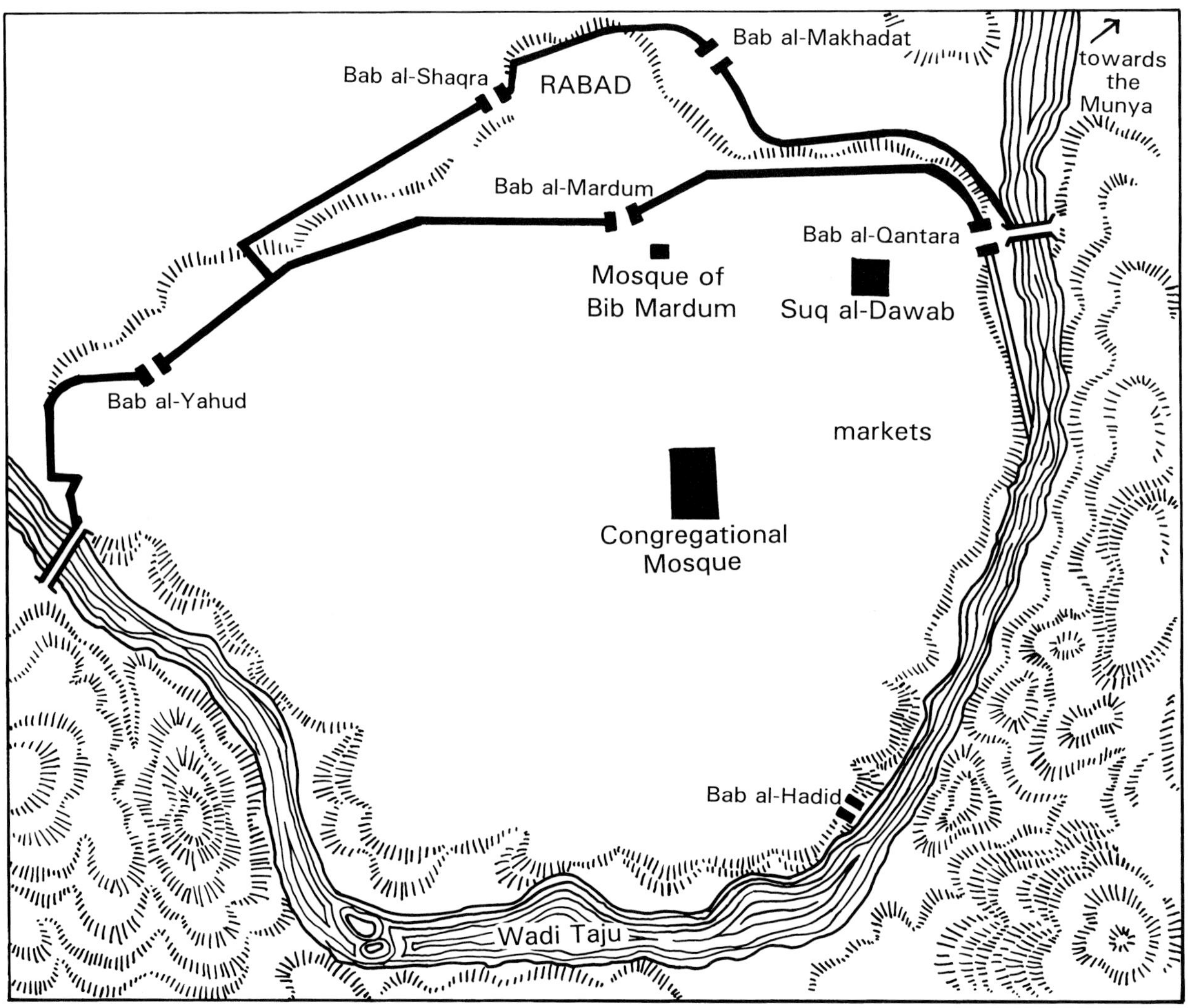

61. Plan of Toledo in the eleventh century (after Lévi-Provençal)

> There was an enclosure (*ḥayr*) in the middle of it and in the middle of the enclosure was a pavilion (*qubba*) of multicolored glass etched with gold. Water was conveyed to the top of the pavilion by a system devised by the engineers, so that from the top of the pavilion water poured down on all sides, covering the entire thing. The glass pavilion was enveloped by a veil of water that poured ceaselessly over the glass, and yet sitting inside of it al-Maʾmūn was untouched. [Sometimes] candles were lit inside of it so that a wonderful and astonishing spectacle was seen.[47]

Elsewhere al-Maqqarī stated that the pavilion was built in the middle of a lake (*buḥayra*).[48] The theatrical effect of the pavilion, in which the water cascading over the glass made it appear to be entirely of water and in which a person could sit in the fountain and yet remain dry, relied on illusionistic effects that had been experimented with in Madīnat al-Zahrā's upper garden. The upper garden's floating pavilion was carried to a conceit at Toledo, where the water not only appeared to surround the pavilion but, splashing over the glass, seemed to replace both glass and architectural structure in a magical trompe l'oeil. That Madīnat al-Zahrāʾ was the source for the idea is confirmed by al-Maqqarī himself, whose recollection of the Toledo pavilion was prompted by a long passage pertaining to "al-Nāṣir's majlis" at Madīnat al-Zahrāʾ.[49]

Another of al-Maʾmūn's palaces was a recreation estate with a hall called the Majlis al-Naʿūra. Torres Balbás believed that the *munya* was located across the river near the Alcántara Bridge.[50] The *majlis* had a pool with lion fountains spewing water, and to supply this and irrigate the gardens, water from the river was raised by a wheel, or noria (*naʿūra*—hence the name of the *majlis*), which creaked and "groaned like a she-camel after giving birth."[51] Although the *munya* served as the residence of Alfonso VI when Toledo was conquered relatively calmly by the Christians in 478/1085, it was largely destroyed twenty-five years later in the course of the Almoravid siege in the retaking of the city, and again in 1196 by the Almohads.

The Aljaferia of Saragossa

Saragossa was ruled by the Tujibids from 400/1010 until it was taken by the powerful Hudids in 431/1039–40. In addition to the Alcazar, located in the northwest corner of the city, there was a suburban palace one kilometer away, named the Qaṣr al-Suru, but popularly called Aljaferia after its patron, the second Hudid king, Aḥmad I Abu Jaʿfar, al-Muqtadir (441/1046–475/1082). The Aljaferia was built on an older foundation of which the tenth-century Torre de Trovador remains. The Aljaferia was greatly altered after the reconquest and has been much restored; very little of the original stucco remains, and the central garden has been completely reinterpreted by modern architects (Color Plate 5).[52] The site is flat and surrounded by a rectangular enclosure wall. Inside, the palace was divided into three parallel zones, the sides containing gardens or buildings of an ephemeral nature and the center containing the palace proper with reception halls, a garden, and a small, elegant oratory (Fig. 62), all of which have been significantly remodeled in recent decades. The central zone was organized around a rectangular gardened courtyard divided into two long halves

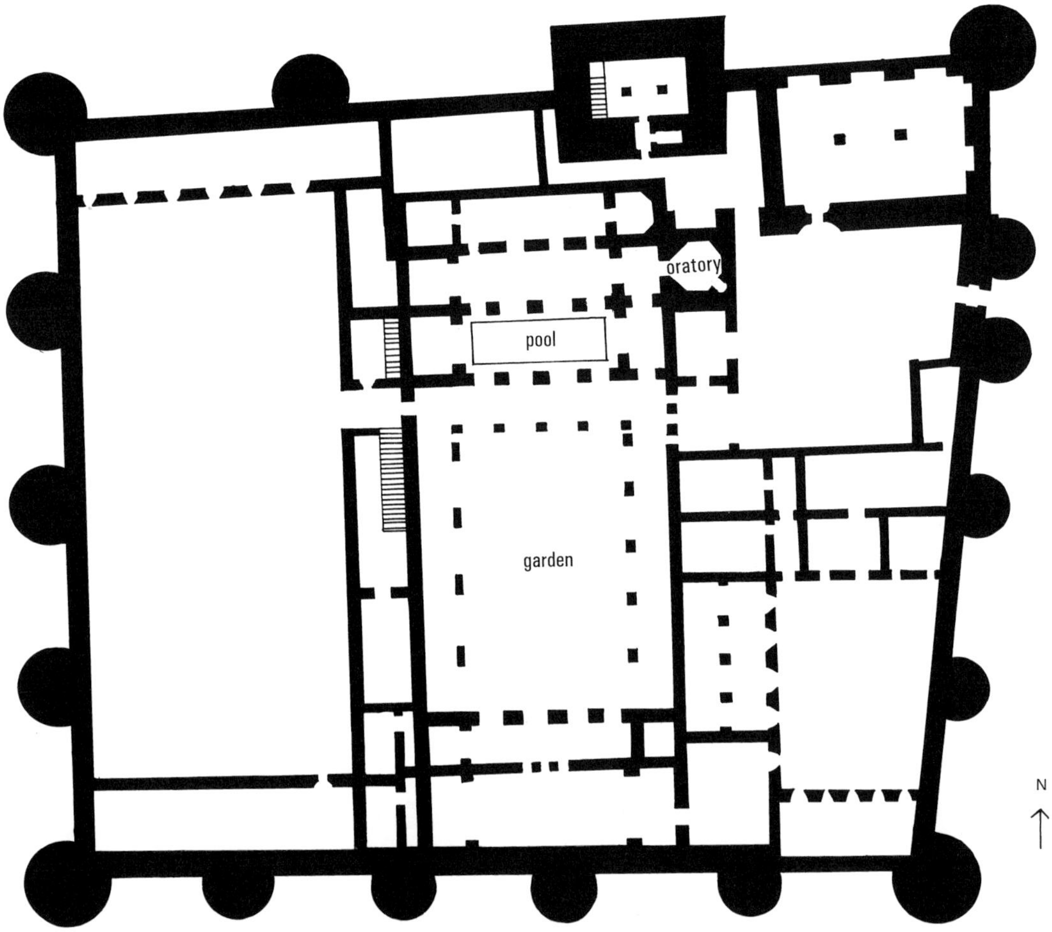

62. Plan of the Aljaferia

by a central narrow walkway, with the soil level being approximately half a meter below this walkway. At each end of the court were pools.

For reasons that scholars cannot agree on, the palace's simple plan is more typical of eastern Umayyad agricultural estates and palaces, such as Qaṣr al-Ḥayr East or Khirbat al-Mafjar, than of Umayyad Spain's hilltop castles. However, the decorative program of intricately interlacing polylobed arches forming screens along the courtyard facade (Fig. 63) and some of its column capitals (Fig. 64) were elaborations of motifs developed at the Mosque of Cordoba under al-Ḥakam II (Fig. 65). In the Aljaferia, the arcade motifs have been translated from an architectonic function, where columns and arches are weight bearing, to purely superficial and decorative service. The conversion of an architectural element such as these arches, or in other cases ribs and domes, from a supportive to an ornamental role is a characteristic of Islamic architecture that is by no means limited to the Iberian Peninsula or the eleventh century.

Perhaps the apparent contradiction between the rejection of Cordoban typology and emula-

63. The polylobed arcade at the south end of the courtyard in the Aljaferia

64. A column capital at the Aljaferia

65. The polylobed arches in the maqsura zone surrounding the mihrab in the Mosque of Cordoba (Girault de Prangey)

tion of Cordoban ornament can be explained by the Aljaferia's function. The Aljaferia was neither a grandiose palace-city nor a recreation estate but rather a fortress with thick impenetrable walls on the frontier with the Christian north. This defensive function distinguishes it from Madīnat al-Zahrā᾿ or the Samarra palaces, which used intricate spatial and institutional means for protecting the inhabitants, and links it with the so-called Umayyad desert estates of the seventh and eighth centuries. These had massive walls with limited points of ingress guarded by machicoulis, bent entrances, and portcullises that were adopted from earlier Roman, Byzantine, and Central Asian defensive practices. Yet, within the fortified exterior of an estate such as Khirbat al-Majfar, a bath-house with beautifully patterned mosaic floors, figural sculptures, and cascading domes provided a splendid stage for princely receptions.[53] The Aljaferia's richly appointed interior likewise hosted courtly gatherings.

The typological resemblance to eastern Umayyad fortified palaces was probably practical, but

the decorative debt to the Cordoban Umayyads was surely intended and ideological. Despite the fact that the Hudids were Berbers, they, like all the other taifa dynasties, wished to imply continuity with the Umayyad and Arab past not simply by possessing or rebuilding Cordoba (although the Abbadids did just that) but by inventing a "new Cordoba." Each taifa dynasty chose a different means of doing so: some, like the Hudids, were famed for the sophistication of literature produced under court patronage;[54] others inherited Cordoba's community of scientists, particularly botanical and agronomical experts; still others adopted the architecture of view and domain. No single taifa ruler reproduced the magnificence and intricacy of Cordoban architecture, because none of them were as powerful as ʿAbd al-Raḥmān III, al-Ḥakam II, and al-Manṣūr had been. Furthermore, while they were alike in measuring themselves against the golden age of the Umayyads—a unifying goal—they also sought to differentiate themselves from one another. Hence, despite the evidence of self-conscious adoption of older motifs and typologies, taifa architecture was by no means an unmediated reproduction of Umayyad architecture.

The Alcazaba of Malaga

Malaga, on the south coast of al-Andalus, was insignificant during the Umayyad period but gained importance as a trading port under its taifa rulers. A branch of the Berber Hammudi family ruled Malaga from 407/1016 until 450/1058 when it was annexed by the Berber Zirid ruler Bādīs of Granada. The Almoravids took the city in 483/1090. In addition to being known for its silk and brocades, Malaga was famed for its grapes (from which the renowned "Malaga wine" was made), pomegranates, almonds, and particularly figs. By the early thirteenth century al-Shaqundī wrote that it was densely planted with vines and orchards and that the fig trees were so heavily laden with fruit that their branches dipped to the ground.[55]

The Alcazaba of Malaga was built between 449/1057 and 455/1063 by Bādīs, and rebuilt under the Nasrids of Granada. It was situated at the foot of a hill at the edge of the seashore, with the Guadalmedina River to the west (Fig. 66). The palace was part of a larger defensive complex that included the fortress (*rābiṭa*) of Gibralfaro, built or refortified by the Nasrid ruler Yūsuf I (733/1333–755/1354), the imposing ruins of which survive today. Protectively stationed above the Alcazaba, the Gibralfaro looked down onto the harbor below, the most likely point of attack. It was well guarded and inaccessible with but a single point of entrance and large end towers; its asymmetrical plan conformed to the irregular site. Communication between the Gibralfaro and the Alcazaba was achieved through a covered passageway that ran between two walls.[56]

The Alcazaba was a walled enclosure measuring 126 by 40 meters, surrounded by an outer wall with rectangular projecting towers, and an inner second wall (Fig. 67).[57] It was built on a rocky site and adapted to the uneven topography by a system of communication via corridors that ran around the outside of the royal residential quarters and the workshops. The use of corridors, demanded by the irregular terrain, also served the mixed function of the complex—residential, administrative, and defensive—and kept the various types of traffic separate, routing some around the palaces and some into them. Water was lifted by noria from a deep well (at least forty meters in

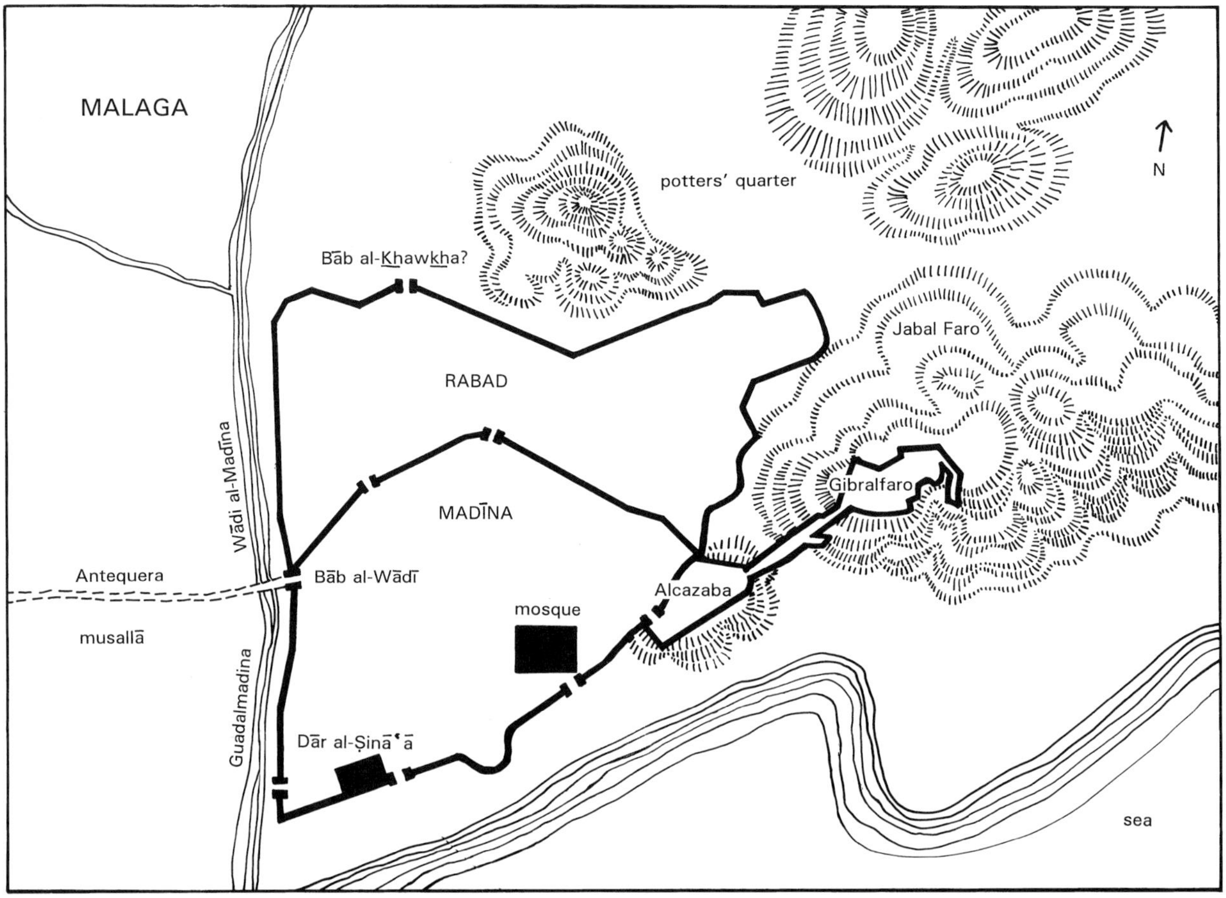

66. The plan of Malaga (after Lévi-Provençal)

depth) on the east side of the Alcazaba's outer enclosure, and presumably it was also collected in cisterns.[58]

As at al-Zahrā', the organization of the Alcazaba's halls on the sloping site exploited the possibilities for dramatic views. The governor's residence was on the upper part (though not on the summit, which held service quarters and workshops). It had a wide prospect over the gardens of the lower slope of the Alcazaba, the shore, and the sea, a combination of land and maritime panoramas praised by the poet al-Shaqundī.[59] The views could be seen from a small mirador, dating to the eleventh century, on the south side (Fig. 68).[60] It measured 2.5 meters square and was open on all sides and decorated with polylobate, interlacing arches similar to those marking the *maqṣūra* zone before the mihrab of the Cordoba Mosque. To enhance the visual breadth of field, the mirador was skewed slightly off axis from the hall and north-south courtyard to which it was attached. The photograph reproduced here (Fig. 69) was taken from a point between the Gibralfaro and the Alcazaba but gives an accurate sense of the dramatic overlook.

The courtyard was much rebuilt during the Nasrid and Christian periods and overly restored in the twentieth century, but judging by what remains, the courtyard of the eleventh-century palace

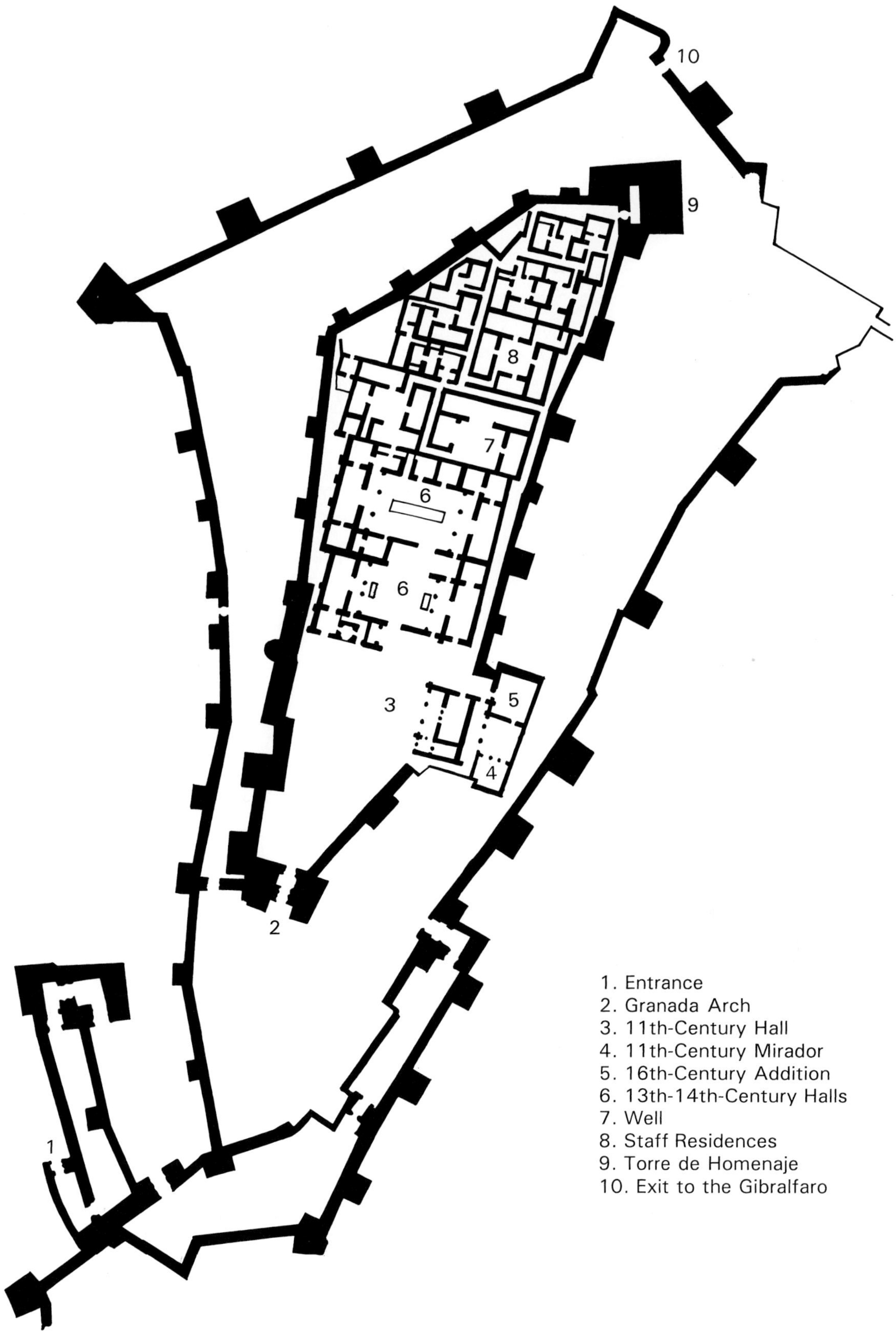

67. The plan of the Alcazaba of Malaga (after Torres Balbás)

68. The mirador at the Malaga Alcazaba

69. The panoramic view from below the Gibralfaro

belonged to the type seen in the small garden at Madīnat al-Zahrāʾ: rectangular with a hall running across each of the ends, opening onto the garden through a triple-arched entrance (Color Plate 6).[61]

In the thirteenth century, a *munya* called Sayyid was built outside of Malaga by the Almohad ruler Idrīs al-Maʾmūn just before he took the throne in 626/1229. Nearby was a cemetery where al-Maʾmūn was interred after his assassination in 630/1232.[62]

The Alcazaba and Estates of Almeria

Almeria was founded in 344/955–56 by ʿAbd al-Raḥmān III to satisfy al-Andalus's need for a seaport for Mediterranean trade. It quickly became the principal port of al-Andalus, reaching its greatest prosperity under the Almoravids when it received ships from Syria, Egypt, Byzantium, Genoa, and Pisa. It lay in an arid region surrounded by barren hills; its economy was oriented to the sea, and its income based on trading, textile production, and marble quarrying, some of which was used in Madīnat al-Zahrāʾs revetments, columns, and capitals.[63] In the eleventh century, the Banū Ṣumādiḥ, a taifa dynasty of Yemeni extraction, ruled Almeria and the eastern littoral. The Ṣumādiḥ reign was a time of political stability and economic prosperity for Almeria, and the second ruler, al-Muʿtaṣim (r. 443/1051-52–484/1091) built palaces such as the Alcazaba of Almeria as well as suburban recreation estates that, although now lost, were praised by the taifa poets.

Excavation attempts at the Alcazaba by Torres Balbás and Prieto Moreno in the 1950s and 1960s proved unsuccessful because the tenth- and eleventh-century layers were buried under fourteenth- and fifteenth-century buildings that were historically important in their own right. Furthermore, earthquakes in 1495, 1522, and 1550 had largely destroyed what was left of the taifa palaces. However, a text of al-ʿUdhrī, discovered in 1965, offered a description of al-Muʿtaṣim's palace in the Alcazaba.[64] He wrote that, from a hilltop site, it looked north toward a landscape of hills and south toward the coast (Fig. 70); fruit trees grew in a large orchard to the south in an area the length of which equaled the width of the Alcazaba; and this garden's south side was formed by a large hall. Progressing through the Alcazaba from west to east along the steep slope of the hill was a series of halls and gardens (Fig. 71). The administrative quarters were on the northern end, and farther along the south side was a great mansion with walls that were beautifully decorated with gilded designs. Still farther to the southeast was a large reception hall adorned with muqarnas (specifically *muqarnas bi-l-rufūf*) and a foundation inscription. Continuing downhill, there was a courtyard, the south side of which opened via gates decorated with double-arched windows to the rest of Almeria and the seashore.[65]

Al-ʿUdhrī mentions halls with the names al-Ḥāfa (meaning "the brink" or "edge," and referring perhaps to its location at the edge of the palace's elevated grounds) and al-Bahw (the courtyard) but it is not known whether these halls belonged to the Alcazaba or to another of al-Muʿtaṣim's palaces, perhaps in the suburbs of Almeria. Al-Muʿtaṣim built a cistern and canal system in Almeria between 419/1028–429/1038; it was prolonged in 458/1066 to reach the cistern west of the mosque and extended by canal to connect to the *qaṣr,* where it was lifted by a noria to provide water to the orchards and extensive gardens.[66] The noria was located in the northwest extremity of the precinct,

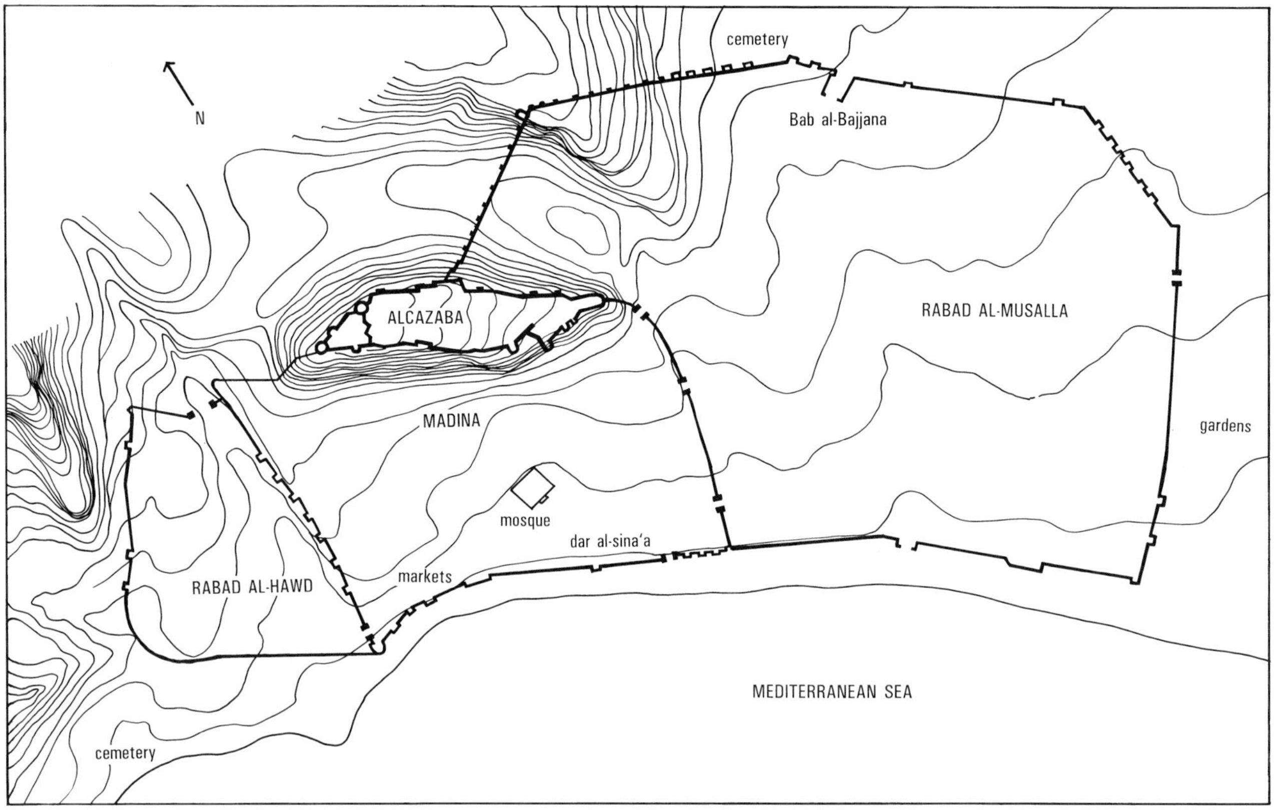

70. Plan of Almeria (after Lévi-Provençal)

emptied into a cistern, from there flowed downhill to the palace in the middle zone where a second cistern stored the water, and finally was released to the halls and gardens in the third and lowest sector below to the southeast.

Two panoramic views were provided for the residence, which on account of its rich decoration and grandeur has been identified as the quarters of al-Muʿtaṣim himself (Fig. 72).[67] At either end of the central courtyard (50 by 20.5 meters) were long chambers. The chamber at the southern end of the courtyard was divided into a simple A-B-A composition as at halls in Madīnat al-Zahrā' and al-Rummānīya. Its north side gave onto the courtyard via a triple-arched opening, and to the south three windows offered spectacular sea views. This corresponds with al-ʿUdhrī's description of "a portico with a balcony on top from which . . . one can observe the entire city of Almeria and the sea."[68]

At the other end of the courtyard, another long chamber, slightly skewed to fit the irregular contours of the hilly site, offered a view toward the courtyard through a portico with engaged columns as well as views toward the outside landscape. (The mirador projecting from the north side is an addition from the first half of the fourteenth century.) A paved walkway ran axially down the middle of the courtyard and in front of the chambers and around the interior of the courtyard's

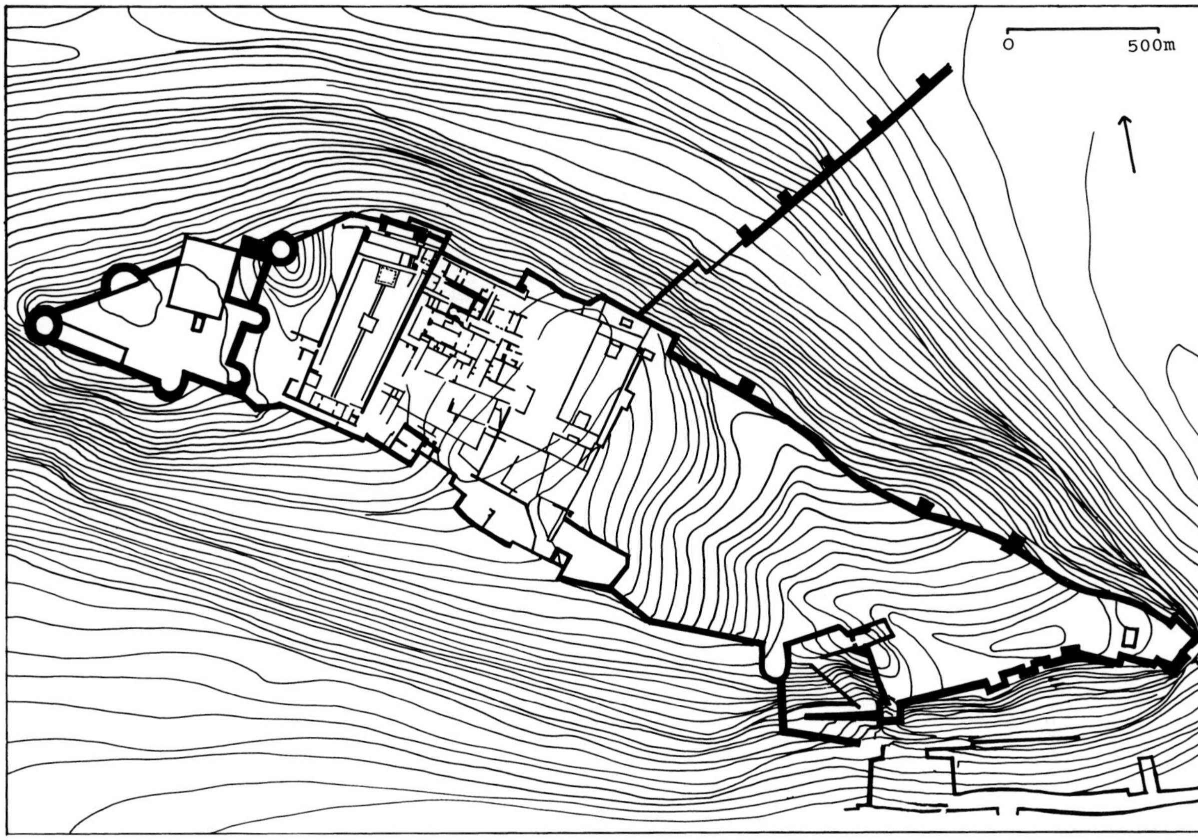

71. Plan of the Alcazaba of Almeria

enclosure walls. At the north end of the courtyard there was a rectangular pool, also surrounded by pavement, and in the middle (slightly off center) are the remains of a garden pavilion.[69]

Although defense mandated the hilltop location, the elevation of the site and the natural slope were also exploited for aesthetic purposes, thus continuing the interest in territorial views and formal palatine gardens first seen in Umayyad Cordoba. The Alcazaba contained a complex assortment of spaces serving administrative, agricultural, and ceremonial functions, as well as at least one royal residence. The halls of the latter were organized around a large garden endowed with walkways, a pool, and a central pavilion from which the surrounding plants and flowers could be seen and enjoyed. As at Madīnat al-Zahrāʾ where pavilions commanded views of gardens and territory, so, too, from either end of al-Muʿtaṣim's palace the ruler enjoyed prospects of mountains and the sea. Similarly just as the Umayyad's view of the agricultural landscape was an occasion to survey the economic base of the kingdom, Almeria's view of the port offered an economic prospect of its active and profitable Mediterranean trade.

Al-Muʿtaṣim also built other palaces in the countryside of Almeria. Little is known about the estates called Barja and Dalāya, but the Ṣumādiḥīya Palace was part of a large estate built beyond the suburbs surounding the city, among orchards watered by streams and canals, and with a great lake in its center around which were open reception halls. Al-ʿUdhrī wrote that varieties of sugar-

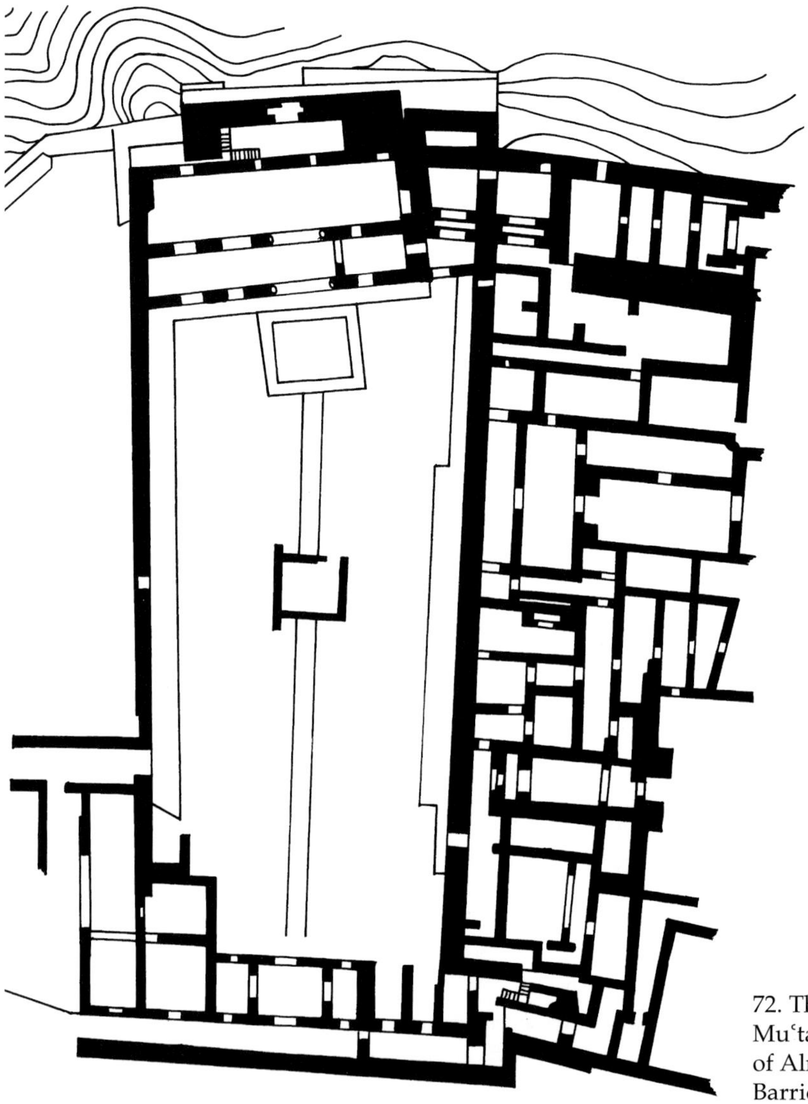

72. The residence of al-Muʿtaṣim in the Alcazaba of Almeria (after L. Cara Barrionuevo)

cane, banana, and other exotics were grown in its gardens, and that it had orchards and white marble pavilions.[70] While sitting in a majlis in that palace, al-Muʿtaṣim himself was inspired by the sight of a fountain to compose the following verse: "Look at the water how it split in spurting out, as if it were a spotted snake intent on fleeing!"[71] It has been suggested that al-Ṣumādiḥīya was located along the riverbank in the Valley of Pechina because that area was relatively green in contrast to the rest of generally arid Almeria, but no archaeological traces of such an estate have been found.[72]

Like Ctesiphon, Madīnat al-Zahrāʾ, and other great palaces, the Ṣumādiḥīya palace has its legend of land appropriation. According to the story, when al-Muʿtaṣim built the palace, his officials unbeknownst to him took a garden that belonged to two orphans. The protestations of their teacher went unheard, until one day as the ruler sat in his park he saw a piece of cane with its ends stopped

up floating along one of the canals that crossed the garden. Inside was a piece of paper on which was written the teacher's complaint. Al-Muʿtaṣim was moved by this and returned the land to the orphans, although in his so doing the symmetry of his palace was ruined.[73]

Like other taifa palaces, those of al-Muʿtaṣim were the descendants of Umayyad models and evince the same taste for luxury in a bucolic setting. The Ṣumādiḥīya palace was a country recreation estate with gardens of exotic plants where water was displayed in abundance, as if to deny its scarcity. Almeria, like Cordoba, had a countryside full of palaces—"pearls among emeralds" according to al-ʿUdhrī—but we have little information on them from which to draw comparisons.

The Castillejo of Monteagudo

The province of Murcia (in Arabic, Tudmīr) was variously either independent or ruled by other taifa states until it was taken over by the Almoravids in 484/1091. It was known for the quality and variety of its textile, carpet, and mat production and was praised by al-Shaqundī as "the city in al-Andalus most abounding in fruits of all sorts and aromatic plants and shrubs."[74] In the city of Murcia the texts tell us that there were a number of palaces, and archaeological remains have been found to support this. Recent excavations in the Convent of Santa Clara la Real in Murcia revealed a twelfth-century palace underneath one from the thirteenth century, both known as the Qaṣr Ṣaghīr. One of the halls of the later palace was superimposed on a cross-axial garden.[75]

Better known are the two fortified palaces in Monteagudo, a few miles from the city of Murcia. One, the Castillo de Monteagudo, dominates the land around it from a rocky hilltop; it was built on a platform created by buttress towers on the north side.[76] Below and four hundred meters to the northwest was a smaller castle called the Castillejo on top of a lower hill and surrounded by an enclosure wall with projecting towers (Fig. 73). The Castillejo probably dates to the period when Murcia was at the height of its importance under Muḥammad ibn Mardanīsh (1147–1172) (vassal of Alfonso VII and called Rey Lobo by the Christians) and may be his pleasance, the Qaṣr Ibn Saʿd mentioned in Arabic sources.[77] The palace, of which only the foundations remained for the excavators, was rectangular in plan, measuring sixty-one by thirty-eight meters with projecting quadrangular towers at either end (Fig. 74). It was entered on the northeast side through a portal flanked by two small towers; on the southwest side similar towers supported a balcony. Three or four meters below this side and about fourteen meters away, a second retaining wall added support to the foundations.

The palace's rooms were disposed around a central courtyard garden measuring thirty-three by eighteen meters. Paved walkways divided the courtyard into quadrants, the levels of which were sunken 1.4 meters below the level of the cross-axial walkway and surrounding galleries. At the intersection of the walkways was a fountain connected by water channels to the pools at either end of the courtyard. The courtyard may have been surrounded by a gallery, as Torres Balbás speculated, and at the ends of the courtyard, covering the pools, there may have been projecting pavilions. Perhaps these were prototypes of the porchlike pavilions in the Court of the Lions at the Alhambra, or simply extensions of the paved walkway, as in the case of the Small Garden at Madīnat al-Zahrāʾ.[78] Water was lifted to the palace by a noria, and vestiges of the tubes and canals by which the water was transported still remain.[79]

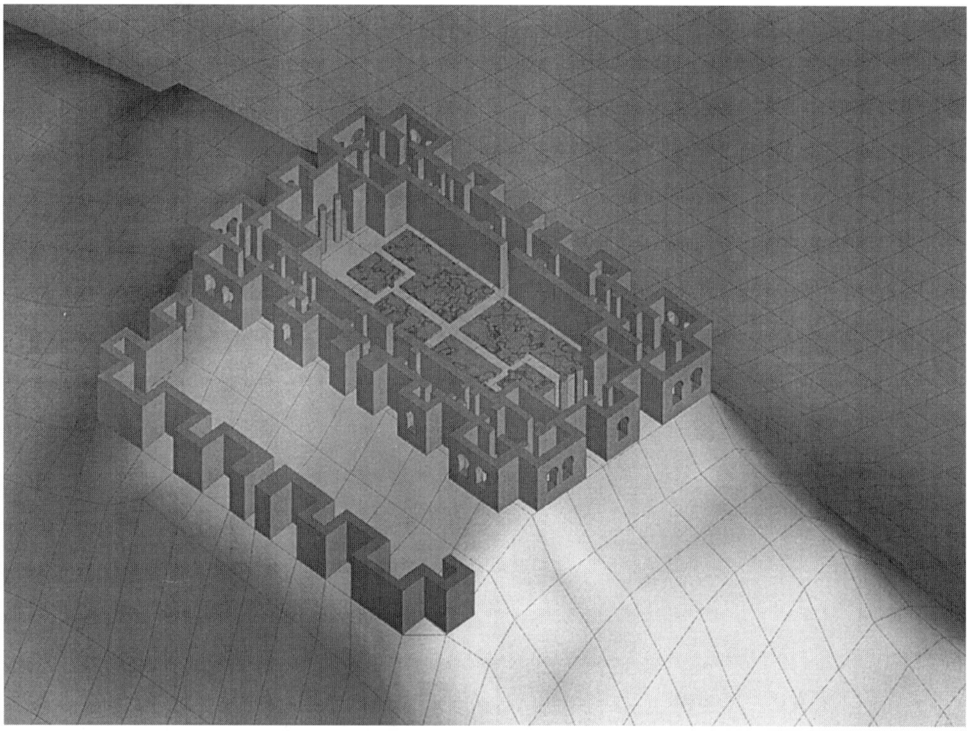

73. A computer-generated reconstruction of the Castillejo de Monteagudo (without its roof) (H. Wilke and D. Ruggles)

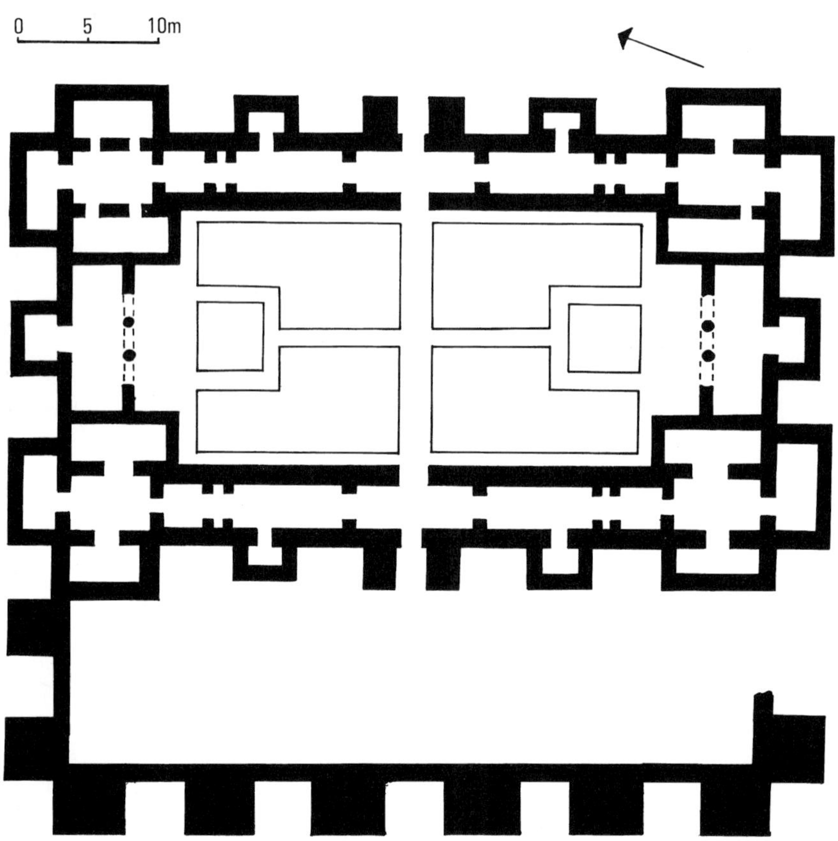

74. The plan of the Castillejo of Monteagudo

Like the Aljaferia, the Castillejo of Murcia was a relatively simple building resembling the plan of an Umayyad palace or agricultural estate. But like Abbasid and Hispano-Umayyad palaces, a large proportion of its interior space was devoted to an irrigated garden with watercourses and basins. The garden was traversed by walkways whose axial extensions terminated at the exterior walls in projecting towers that must have been pierced by windows offering landscape vistas that could have served equally for pleasure or defense (see Fig. 74). Thus, despite the simplicity of the organization of the Castillejo, the cross-axial garden plan, the situation on an artificially created terrace, and the panoramic prospects reveal an unmistakable Cordoban legacy.

Cordoban architecture influenced later palaces in a myriad of ways. The dazzling arts and learning of its court set a standard for cultural achievement that the taifa rulers strove to match and even surpass in their individual courts. For later poets and historians, the ruins of Cordoba's palaces was a nostalgic, if somewhat distant, symbol of all that was lost to the reconquest. Although there is no evidence that the derelict palace Madīnat al-Zahrā᾿ was directly studied by later generations of architects, it is quite clear that its design innovations had permeated Andalusian palatine typology even before the demise of the Umayyad house and were thus bequeathed to the taifas and Almoravids. The gardens that were such prominent features in the later palaces belonged to a continuous tradition stemming from the Umayyads of Syria, but the exploitation of elevation for landscape views at Malaga, Almeria, and Murcia's Castillejo reflects changes introduced by ʿAbd al-Raḥmān III. Al-Zahrā᾿'s innovations spread even as far as Algeria in the eleventh century to the Qalʿa Banī Ḥammād, where the main palace was built on sloping ground, with a terrace garden overlooking an enormous pool (see Fig. 53).[80] The Qalʿa, like Madīnat al-Zahrā᾿ and Madīnat al-Zāhira, was a large complex with numerous independent buildings, unlike the taifa palaces that, despite their grandiose claims, often consisted of single structures located near to the capital city in the manner of a fortress or citadel. The function and scale of the taifa palaces were distinctly different from their Cordoban ancestors, but the architectural means by which sovereignty was expressed was a direct and probably self-conscious legacy of Madīnat al-Zahrā᾿.

Al-Andalus was by no means the only agriculturally thriving land in the Islamic world at this time, for there were strong farming traditions in the Yemen and Iran. In the Mediterranean as well, ample evidence of a non-Andalusian typology of garden palaces can be seen in the 936 palace of Zīrī in Ashir (Algeria), built by an architect from Tunisia, and in the late ninth-century Tulunid gardens in al-Qaṭa᾿iʿ (Egypt). In the eleventh century the Fatimid palaces built along the Canal of Cairo had marble pavilions, pools, hunting parks and gardens colorfully planted with fruit trees and flowers.[81] But the architects of taifa Spain did not have to search that far afield for models for palace design. Although few of the monumental garden palaces of Cordoba remained after the fatal conflict of 1010, the architects who had been trained in Cordoba—or who were trained by masters from those workshops—quickly found employment in the taifa courts during the great political reshuffling of the eleventh century. Searching for architectural forms with which to publicly display power and dynastic legitimacy, the taifa rulers embraced the garden as the symbol of kingdom and the view as the symbol of sovereignty. Hence, Cordoba—even in ruins—remained a commanding image.

8

THE ALHAMBRA

In this garden I am an eye filled with delight and the pupil of this eye is, truly, our lord, Muḥammad [V].
—Ibn Zamrak

Granada began as a small hilltop fortress during the Umayyad period, at least as early as 276/889, and although nothing is left of this building, the community that grew up around its feet remained.[1] Granada was first peopled with inhabitants moved from nearby Elvira (Ilbīra) in 400/1009–10, by the leaders who founded the taifa Zirid dynasty.[2] The history of the dynasty is recorded in the memoirs written by the last Zirid king, ʿAbd Allāh, from his place of exile in the Maghreb. According to him, the people welcomed the new rulers and chose a new place of settlement on a high point dominating the area, moving everyone and everything to the new capital: "Their eyes lighted on a beautiful plain full of both rivers and trees. All the land around was watered by the Genil (*Wādī Shinīlī*) which flowed from the Sierra Nevada (*Jabal Shulayr*). They were quick to perceive that from its central position the mountain, on which is today the city of Granada, commanded all the surrounding country. . . . They were enthralled by the site and realized that it lay in the heart of a bountiful region."[3]

The Zirids and Their Viziers

The Zirids, of Ṣanhāja Berber stock, ruled Granada from 403/1013 until the Almoravids conquered the city in 483/1090. The third Zirid king, Bādīs b. Ḥabbūs (r. 429/1038–405/1073) was served by the viziers Ismāʿīl Ibn Naghrīla (also known by his Hebrew name Samuel Ha-Nāgīd) and his son Yūsuf. They were of a cultured Jewish family that had fled Cordoba in 1012, seeking refuge first in Malaga and then Granada. Samuel's career as a highly influential and capable vizier was in part due to his Cordoban sophistication, for like Ziryāb, who brought the refinement of Baghdad to the court of Cordoba in the ninth century, Samuel offered brilliant artistic taste and knowledge of *adab* (culture and etiquette) to Granada in the eleventh. According to legend, Samuel was an ordinary shopkeeper whose letter-writing skills were discovered by chance and propelled him into the world of literature and politics at the court of Granada.[4]

Samuel had a palace in Granada with spectacular fountains, and his own verses describe a fountain there similar to al-Maʾmūn's in Toledo: water poured down in the shape of a dome within which lanterns were set. His son Yūsuf inherited the position of vizier as well as his father's penchant for garden and architectural effects, designing for his father's house a garden with flowers in round beds encircled by a water channel and shaded by pomegranate and plantain trees.[5] Sometime between his father's death in 447/1056 and his own in 1066, Yūsuf built a second magnificent

palace. The poet Ibn Gabirol—himself from a Jewish family that had fled Cordoba for Malaga—described Yūsuf's as "a palace high above all its surroundings and built of precious stones; built to rise from a firm foundation, its walls fortified with towers" and surrounded by a "levelled plateau."[6] The buildings, he added, were paved with marble and alabaster and their walls decorated with openwork screens, like filigree. The palace courtyards and gardens were full of fruit trees, roses, beds of myrtle, palms, and shading-giving grape arbors, and had a fountain of lions spewing water into water channels that irrigated the plants, shrubs, and trees. Regarding this fountain Ibn Gabirol wrote:

> And there is a full sea, like unto Solomon's Sea,
> though not on oxen it stands,
>
> But there are lions, in phalanx by its rim,
> as though roaring for prey—these whelps
>
> Whose bellies are wellsprings that spout forth
> through their mouths floods like streams.
>
> And there are hinds embedded in the channels,
> hollowed out as water spouts
>
> To douse the plants in the beds,
> and upon the lawns to shed clear waters
>
> Wherewith to freshen the myrtle garden—
> they are like clouds sprinkling the treetops.[7]

Frederick Bargebuhr, who first translated Ibn Gabirol's Hebrew poem into English, argues that these are the same lions that are today in the Alhambra's Court of the Lions supporting a fourteenth-century inscribed basin (Color Plate 7). He cites a passage from ʿAbd Allāh's memoirs in which Yūsuf was criticized by his followers for "his construction of the Alhambra Fortress . . . where he intended to establish his residence when Ibn Ṣumādiḥ [an enemy from Almeria] had entered Granada."[8] This part of the Alhambra, according to Bargebuhr, was the Alcazaba al-Qadim, or the western part where we know a fortress had existed as early as the ninth century (Fig. 75). He then argues that the Alhambra that stands on the Sabika hill today is founded on and contains portions of the palace of the eleventh-century vizier, Yūsuf, on the basis of a statement in ʿAbd Allāh's memoirs to the effect that Yūsuf's palace was superior to the Zirid princes'.[9] We have seen other instances of viziers bestowing palace estates upon their lords (such as Durrī's gift of al-Rummānīya to al-Ḥakam in Chapter 6), so it is not impossible that the Alhambra should have passed from being a fortress to a Zirid vizier's palace and ultimately, in the thirteenth century, to the Nasrids' primary residence and seat of government. There was considerable construction on the Sabika hill, and it is possible that the Naghrīlas had a residence in close proximity to another Zirid palace (which in any case would have been secondary in importance to their palace in the Albaicín quarter of Granada), both of which were replaced by later Nasrid buildings.

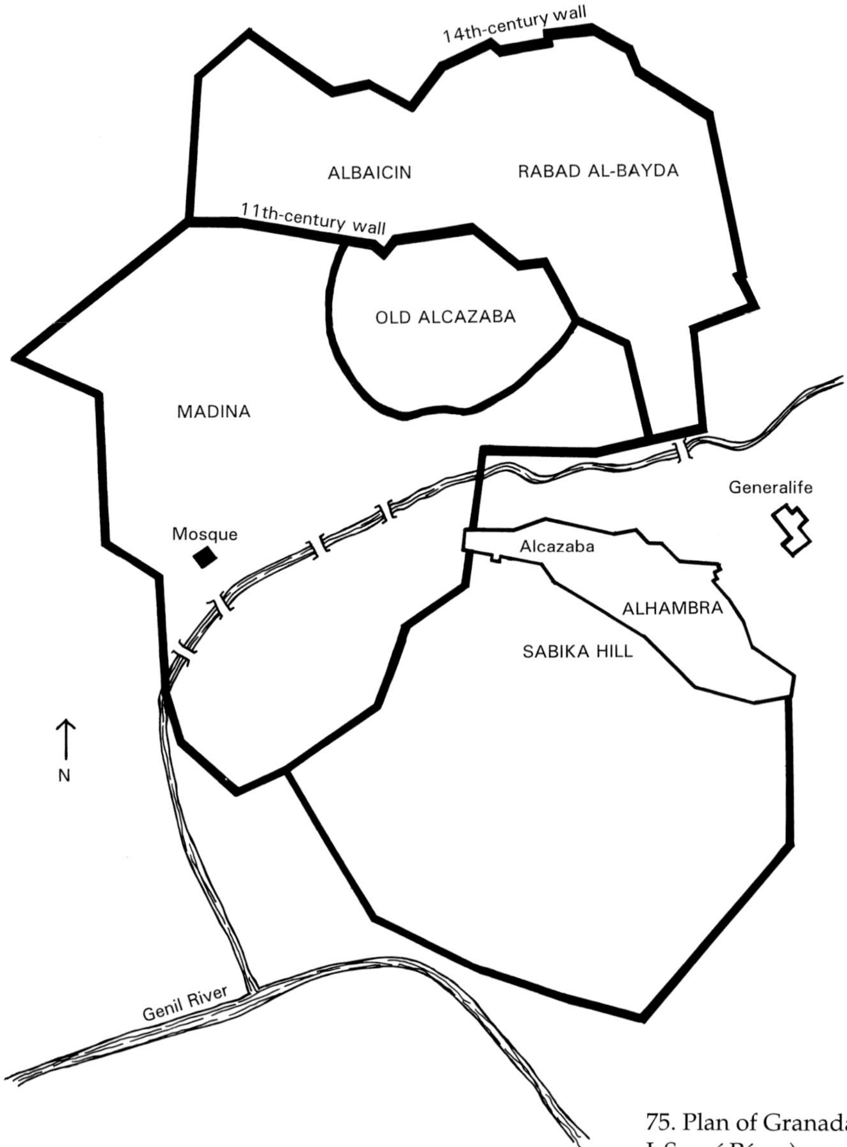

75. Plan of Granada (after J. Seguí Pérez)

But Bargebuhr's theory is deeply problematic. While the evidence does indicate that there was a palace belonging to Yūsuf somewhere on the Sabika hill, the most startling of Bargebuhr's conclusions was his attribution of the well-known lion fountain to the eleventh century. This fountain stands in the middle of the Court of the Lions at the crossing of the walkways that divide the space into quadrants. Water flows from the chambers and galleries on the north, east, south, and west sides of the court toward this fountain, which consists of twelve stone lion figures bearing a twelve-sided basin on their backs. Water spurts gently upward from the basin and spews as well from the mouths of the beasts into a shallow channel that surrounds them. The fact that the basin's inscrip-

tions mention the Nasrid rulers indicates a fourteenth-century date, but the lions might have carried a different basin earlier and may belong to an earlier period.

Bargebuhr maintains that these lions were the same described by Ibn Gabirol and that, while a new palace had been raised around them, they had not changed position since the eleventh century. But Ibn Gabirol's description of a lion fountain does not exactly match the Alhambra's fountain. Bargebuhr's original translation of the poem—on which he based his hypothesis—is as follows:

> And there is a full "sea," matching Solomon's Sea,
> yet not resting on ox;
> But there are lions, in phalanx on its rim,
> seeming to roar for prey.[10]

He later amended the translation to "lions, in phalanx *by* its rim" (emphasis added).[11] Hence, Ibn Gabirol's description is not of animals shouldering a basin, as is the configuration in the Alhambra, but rather of a basin with figural spouts emptying water into the basin from above, similar to the zoomorphic spouts that the sources described at Madīnat al-Zāhira and Munyat al-Naʿūra in Cordoba. Ibn Gabirol's poem demonstrates the continuity of the zoomorphic fountain motif from the Umayyad capital to taifa Granada, which is not surprising, given that both the Naghrīlas and Ibn Gabirol came from Cordoba, but it does not prove that the Alhambra's fountain is the one described by Ibn Gabirol.

Bargebuhr saw the tenth century in al-Andalus as a brilliant period of "learned laity, minded to poetry . . . congregating in garden symposia."[12] According to him, the eleventh century continued the achievements in poetry and the arts but shrugged off faded associations with the east for a new self-confidence, humanism, and "renaissance-like individualism."[13] The flourishing humanism of the taifas then disappeared under the stern Almoravids and Almohads but was revived by the Nasrids. Bargebuhr's mapping of the human spirit in this way seemed to justify his proposed chronology of the Alhambra. Because that palace's refined architectural taste, sensual appreciation for nature, and freestanding sculpture (otherwise rare in medieval Islam) was more like the earlier Umayyad and taifa palaces than the solid Almohad constructions, Bargebuhr believed that it must have been built during the eleventh century and went to great lengths to justify that date, pointing to ashlar blocks in the foundations that might be eleventh century. In Yūsuf Ibn Naghrīla's poetry, he quite rightly saw a sketch of an eleventh-century palace inspired by Umayyad architecture and believed that it described the Alhambra in its earliest phase. However, while these similarities demonstrate a clear typological debt, there is not enough concrete evidence to conclude that the Naghrīla palace actually begot the present Alhambra. The old ashlar blocks still evident in the foundations may have belonged to fortifications rather than to a palace, and the poetry is not a reliable source of physical description. As one critic stated, "Medieval Hebrew and Arabic courtly poems are not literally but typologically descriptive."[14]

There can be little doubt, however, that the Naghrīla Palace, which was styled after the magnificent palaces of Umayyad Cordoba, provided the Nasrids with a model of palatine splendor, complete with gardens, fountains, elevated buildings, and attractive vistas. The parallels between

Yūsuf's palace and Madīnat al-Zahrā' are many: both were luxuriously appointed, had halls adorned with porticoes and stucco arabesques, and had elevated sites overlooking a flat plain. Additionally, the emphasis on water in the form of large tanks, fountains that were like natural springs, and channels traversing the gardened courtyards reveals the resemblance to the Cordoban prototype. The palaces that stand today at the Alhambra are entirely thirteenth- and fourteenth-century in date and do not need to be explained in terms of a missing model. Their typological debt is not to Yūsuf's vanished palace but, like most other royal palaces in al-Andalus, quite directly and deliberately to that venerable ancestor, Madīnat al-Zahrā' itself. The Nasrids chose the model of Umayyad Cordoba to evoke their Arab past, an ethnic distinction that differentiated them from the Berber Almohads, their predecessors, and gave them a legitimacy that was sorely needed as they balanced themselves between Christian Castile and the Berber Merinids of Morocco.

The Nasrids

The Nasrids came to power in 629/1232 in the wake of the defeat of the Almohads at the battle of Las Navas de Tolosa in 609/1212. While the remaining Islamic kingdoms succumbed in quick succession to the armies of the Christian north, the Nasrid kingdom, which grew from Granada to include Almeria and Malaga, survived as a tributary to Castile. Granada's peculiar tenacity was due not so much to its own internal strength but to the strain on Castile's resources in repelling the Merinids, who invaded several times from Morocco, and to the disruption in Castilian leadership when Alfonso X's son Sancho led a rebellion against him.[15] But once the Nasrids were ensconced, delicately balancing themselves between predators to the north and south, and faced with paying heavy tribute to Castile, their key to success and survival was to make the kingdom prosper. And indeed, Ibn al-Khaṭīb in the first half of the fourteenth century said that gardens enveloped Granada like "a mother surrounded by children, with luxuriant herbiage adorning her sides as if she had donned a necklace," and that *munyas* "encompassed the city like bracelets."[16] In addition to the palace-gardens of the Alhambra, he mentioned the orchards of al-Mays, al-Maʿrawī, Ibn Kāmil, and at least a dozen others, all endowed with fertile land, irrigation, shady trees, and excellent plants.[17] He mentioned livestock corrals, pigeon houses, irrigation canals, 130 water mills, and "villas of such magnitude and prohibitive cost that none but a member of the royal family could afford to own them, for some yield crops worth half a thousand dinars notwithstanding the low prices vegetables fetch in this city."[18] The Nasrid rulers succeeded in enriching themselves and their Castilian overlords to the satisfaction of both, and Granada gained renown for its wealth and refined living standards.

The first Nasrid sultan (also referred to as *malik* [king] in inscriptions) was Muḥammad I, called Ibn al-Aḥmar (r. 629/1232–671/1272), and it was probably he who began construction of what would eventually become the Alhambra palace complex. Of his descendents, the greatest patrons of architecture belong to the fourteenth century: Muḥammad III (r. 701/1302–708/1309), Ismāʿīl I (r. 713/1314–725/1325), Yūsuf I (r. 733/1333–755/1354), and Muḥammad V (r. 755/1354–760/1359 and 763/1362–793/1391).

When the Nasrids entered Granada they established themselves first at the old Zirid palace in the Albaicin, which lay just outside the north side of the eleventh-century city walls, while they built or rebuilt a new fortress-residence on the northwestern part of the Sabika hill. This was the Alcazaba, a military complex largely dating to the thirteenth century although probably built on the foundations of an older Zirid *qaṣba.*[19] The primary sources conflict with respect to the foundation of the Nasrid Alcazaba. Although an anonymous Arabic manuscript stated that Ibn al-Aḥmar "laid out the foundations" of the Alhambra in 1238, a structure called the *ḥiṣn al-ḥamrā'* ("red fortress" or "fortress of the Alhambra") existed in Granada already by the end of the ninth century, and traces of older masonry confirm that there existed something on the present site of the Alhambra prior to the thirteenth.[20] The Alcazaba is in poor condition now, and even in its own day probably offered little of architectural interest, but it is important as the germ of further growth on the Sabika hill.

During the reign of Muḥammad I or possibly of his son Muḥammad II (671/1273–701/1302), the Alhambra was fortified, water brought from the nearby hills, and an official Nasrid residence established there. Ibn al-Khaṭīb and Ibn al-Jayyāb state that Muḥammad III made the Alhambra his official residence and built numerous palaces there.[21] Certainly by the fourteenth century the Alhambra was not an isolated hilltop palace-city, for it was downhill from other aristocratic estates whose existence is confirmed by historical texts and archaeology. Nor was the Alhambra a single entity, for within its irregular enclosure there were several semi-independent palaces, many of them adjoining each other. The walls formed a palatine city approximately 740 meters long and 220 meters at its widest point;[22] it was served by paved access roads and entered by monumental portals, and it had its own congregational mosque and baths.

Although the Alhambra complex was built continuously during the thirteenth and fourteenth centuries, most of the older structures were dismantled to build the new ones and even those halls that remained were redecorated with fresh plaster ornament and Arabic inscriptions. The fact that the complex was periodically renewed and was its own source of spolia makes the chronology of construction difficult, though not impossible, to determine. In modern literature, the palatine buildings are usually discussed in order of function and present-day access, proceeding from the Mexuar to the Comares palace, Lions Palace, Partal, and then the Generalife, but since we are concerned with the development and meaning of the gardens, it is more logical to treat each existing palace in the approximate order of construction, beginning with the scant remains from the thirteenth century. Although the Generalife is outside the Alhambra's city walls, it was spatially and functionally an annex of the palatine precinct and that is how it is treated here.

The Abencerrajes, Generalife, and San Francisco Palaces

The Abencerrajes Palace, named after the powerful Abencerrajes family, was located in the middle of the walled precinct's southern perimeter and was surrounded by smaller residences (Fig. 76). It was built in the thirteenth century, the tower and some of its inscriptions surviving until at least 1804.[23] It was toppled in 1812 by the French and what remained was not properly preserved until excavations were carried out around 1970 by Pavón Maldonado. The architectural remains are in

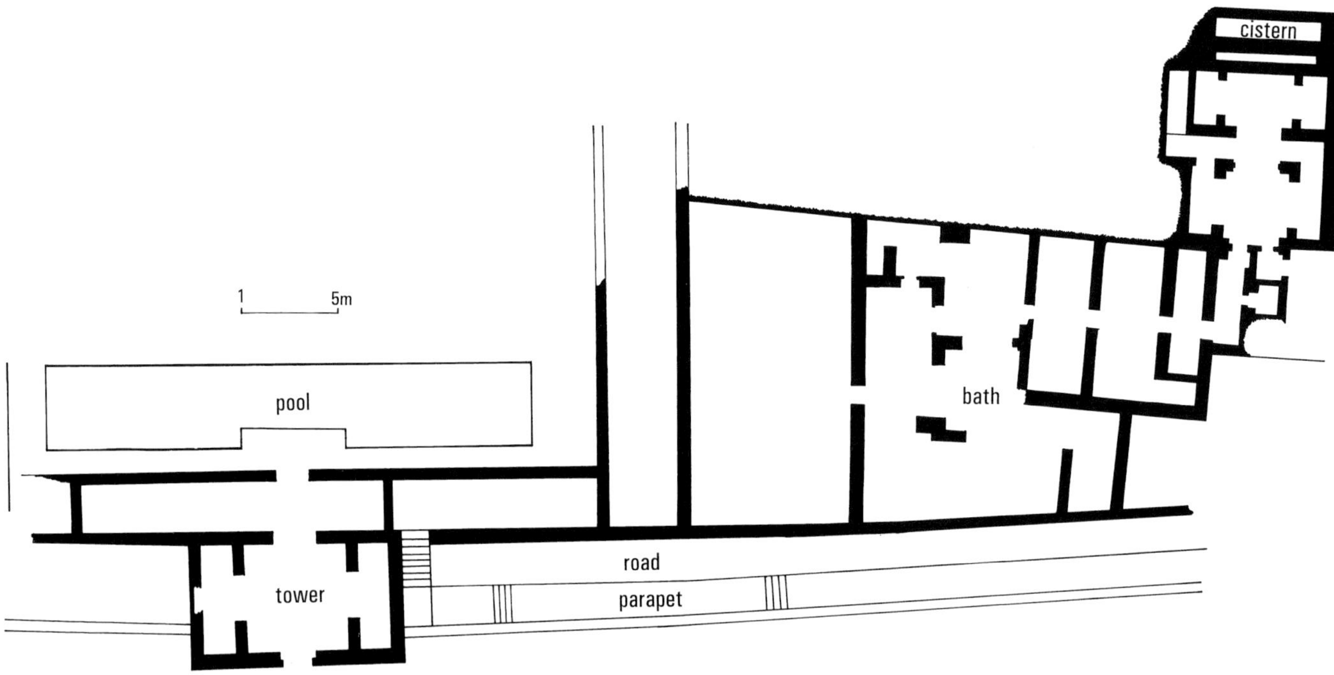

76. Plan of the Abencerrajes Palace at the Alhambra (after B. Pavon Maldonado)

two parts separated by a road.[24] The eastern part consisted of a two-story brick dwelling with a private cistern and bath with tiled floors and walls as well as plaster walls painted red, as at Madīnat al-Zahrā' and various other Cordoban palaces. A second smaller bath was located nearby. The western part was dominated by the salient Abencerrajes Tower (or Torre de la Contaduría), a mirador with a vertiginous outlook. At the foot of this tower, inside the palace walls, there was a large rectangular pool (15.17 by 4.43 meters) surrounded by a walkway that, on the tower side, projected into the pool like a small pier with steps leading from either side of it down into the water. The pool was surrounded on three sides by large rooms with stone pavements; the fourth side had no walls and probably opened toward a garden.

The palace's pool and tower recall the Generalife's Acequía Court, the Partal, and the Court of the Myrtles, with the exception that the Abencerrajes pool runs east-west whereas in the others it runs north-south. The fact that the Abencerrajes Palace predated the others demonstrates that the combination of pool/courtyard/mirador was not a late development but was a formula already in use by the Nasrids in the thirteenth century. While the Nasrid period is often regarded as the pinnacle of Islamic civilization in Spain, a time of intense creative energy and in which the most beautiful and sophisticated garden-palaces were erected, archaeological evidence at the Abencerrajes Palace suggests that the Nasrids inherited more than they invented. Unfortunately, the Abencerrajes Palace is the only proof of this, for the other early palaces and houses—which might have strengthened this theory—were either obliterated by the later constructions of Yūsuf I and Muḥammad V or systematically despoiled to provide those palaces with rich architectural materials.

The Generalife (Fig. 77) was a summertime pleasance built by Muḥammad III during the first decade of the fourteenth century on the side of the Santa Elena hill where at least two other palaces were located.[25] The dates of these, the Alijares and Dār al-ʿArūsa palaces, are uncertain and almost nothing remains of them today, but they appear to have been built sometime after the Generalife and were already in ruins when the Venetian traveler Andres Navagero saw them in 1524–26.[26] Unlike the Alhambra, which was an enclosed urban complex with small gardens, the Generalife is draped gracefully in terraces along the side of a hill with outward-looking views, gardens, fresh breezes, and an abundance of cool mountain water (Fig. 78). The nucleus of the palace is surrounded by larger orchards, the original character of which is well known.[27] The Generalife was served by two canals, the Acequía del Tercio and Acequía del Rey, and amply irrigated, receiving approximately four times as much water as the Alhambra.[28] The palace was divided into several parts: the Acequía (canal) Court, Bóveda de Laureles (laurel arbor), water stairway, Huerta de la Mercería, and cypress garden, in which is included the so-called Garden of the Sultana, which is entirely modern in both fabric and design.[29]

The Acequía Court (Fig. 79) was excavated after a terrible fire destroyed major parts of the Generalife in 1958, exposing hitherto unknown architectural fabric to view.[30] The enclosed court, which was on an esplanade cut into the side of the ravine, consisted of four garden quadrants formed by a long north-south axis and a short east-west axis, punctuated at their intersection by a fountain (Fig. 80). The court was limited to the east by a long hall that also served as a buttress wall separating it from the gardens on the level above. Along the west side was a gallery with a projecting mirador that looked across the ravine for a spectacular view of the Alhambra. At the court's south end was a three-storied residence for the harem, and at the north end was a pavilion with outlooks toward the Albaicin quarter (Figs. 81 and 82). After the fire, the original pavements demarcating the four slightly octagonal quadrants were found at a depth of about seventy centimeters below the present pavements. The garden's original soil layer was discovered to be undisturbed between a coarse rocky underlayer and the modern top layers. It was less than half a meter thick, indicating that the garden consisted of a carpet of fairly low plants, with some deeper pits made for the roots of shrubs and small trees. Indeed, Navagero saw myrtle bushes and orange trees there in the early sixteenth century.[31] Also during the excavations, a pipe was discovered under the pavements, linking the central fountain with the mirador in the west wall. Perhaps the mirador once had a sunken basin like the one in the kiosks of the Court of the Lions at the Alhambra (see Fig. 105).

The two rows of water jets that play in the Acequía Court today are not original. But water was supplied both from the Acequía del Tercio and a waterwheel in a tower in the Huerta de la Mercería; perhaps such an excessive amount was needed for an extravagant fountain display. The idea of a high-spouting jet was not as completely foreign to the aesthetic of the Acequía Court as modern historians believe, for Navagero described a small courtyard on a lower level—perhaps the Patio de Polo (see below)—with a fountain that shot water ten yards ("diez brazas") into the air.[32]

A water stairway still links the Patio de la Sultana with a small open terrace at the highest part of the palace (Color Plate 8). The stairway descends in a straight line through a sloped bank of small trees, pausing at small circular terraces, in the center of each of which is a shallow basin with a water jet. Additionally, water runs in a channel carved in the top of the handrails, the speed of its

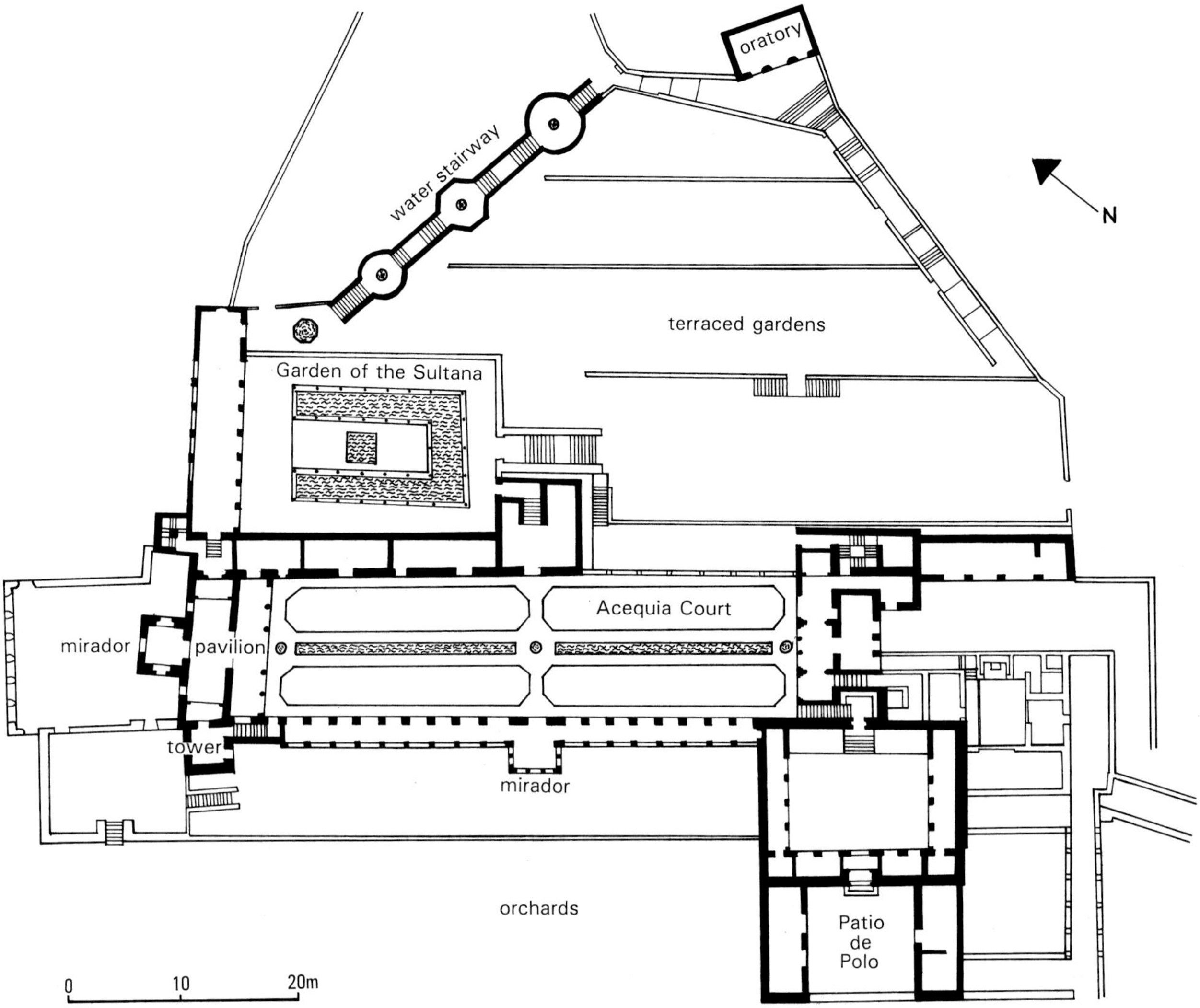

77. Plan of the Generalife Palace and gardens (after J. Seguí Pérez

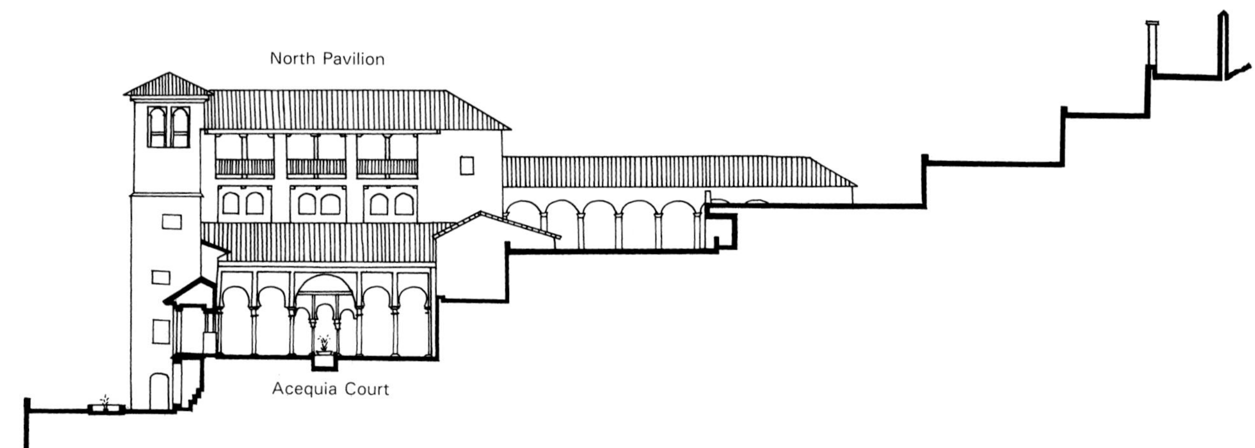

78. Section of the Generalife: from the east through the Acequía Court and sloping down to ravine (after J. Seguí Pérez)

79. The Acequía Court

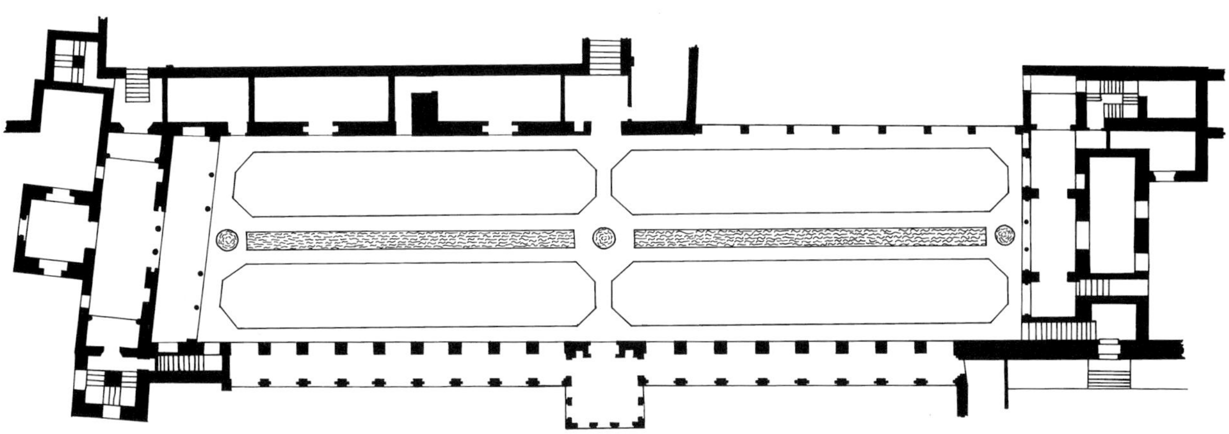

80. Plan of the Acequía Court

81. Acequía Court, the north pavilion

82. Acequía Court, oblique view of the north pavilion (courtesy of the Fine Arts Library, Harvard)

course checked by tiered depressions or cups, transforming the balustrade into an enchanting miniature cataract. Navagero reported that both the little torrents of water and the terraces' jets could be controlled by a water lock so that they could be held back or released at whim, soaking the unsuspecting visitor to the merriment of all witnessing the spectacle.[33] Navagero visited the Alhambra and Generalife only thirty-two years after the Christian conquest of Granada, during which time the Generalife was scarcely touched, and there can be little doubt that his account provides an accurate reflection of the gardens during their Nasrid phase.

The Generalife had its own baths: at the south end of the cypress garden were discovered the remains of a hypocaust system.[34] The palace had no formal reception hall, since official state business was not carried out there, nor did it have its own congregational mosque. But it did have a small private mosque or oratory mentioned by European visitors such as Henríquez de Jorquera (1594–1646), who referred to a small and very old hermitage called Santa Elena on a hilltop near the walls of the Alhambra.[35] This oratory may have been the diminutive structure at the head of the Generalife's water stairway that was ultimately rebuilt as a pavilion, since a former director of the Alhambra had personally communicated to Bermúdez that the pavilion had very old foundations (see Fig. 77). That this structure, so opportunely placed as a garden kiosk-mirador, could have served first as an oratory is not so farfetched as it might seem, since, as we shall see, there were at least three other Nasrid oratories with garden and landscape views.

On the south side of the palace were walled, terraced orchards. A sunken and covered walkway ran through these, descending from the Torre de los Picos to the Puerta del Hierro of the Alhambra to a cluster of defensive towers in the southwest corner of the Generalife. This entrance into the Generalife was gained through the so-called Patio de Polo, an open courtyard with a central fountain, and up a stairway to the Patio de la Acequía. The direct route between the two palaces was intended for the convenience and privacy of the royal residents; visitors from the outside would have entered the Generalife on its south side.[36]

Across the ravine in the northwestern part of the walled Alhambra complex was a palace that looked toward the Generalife's mirador in the Acequía Court. It was built by Muḥammad III in the early fourteenth century,[37] and was remodeled thereafter by Yūsuf I and Muḥammad V.[38] It was largely demolished and rebuilt as a monastery known as the Convento de San Francisco immediately after 1492, receiving the remains of Queen Isabel after her death in 1504 until they were moved in 1521. The monks left in 1835, and in the twentieth century it was converted into a hotel; today the Islamic remains are identified simply as the palace of the Convento de San Francisco.

The buildings of the Nasrid palace and Isabelline monastery were excavated and repaired by Torres Balbás in 1927–28, although because one end of the palace was on privately owned land, he could not examine its entirety.[39] The excavated portion of the Nasrid palace (Fig. 83) consisted of a mirador and a long narrow courtyard with a central watercourse and a gallery at the eastern end, the whole resembling, in his words, a smaller version of the Generalife's Acequía Court. On the other side of the gallery there was a large water tank from which water was supplied to the courtyard. The few surviving inscriptions offered simply the Nasrid motto, There is no conqueror but God.

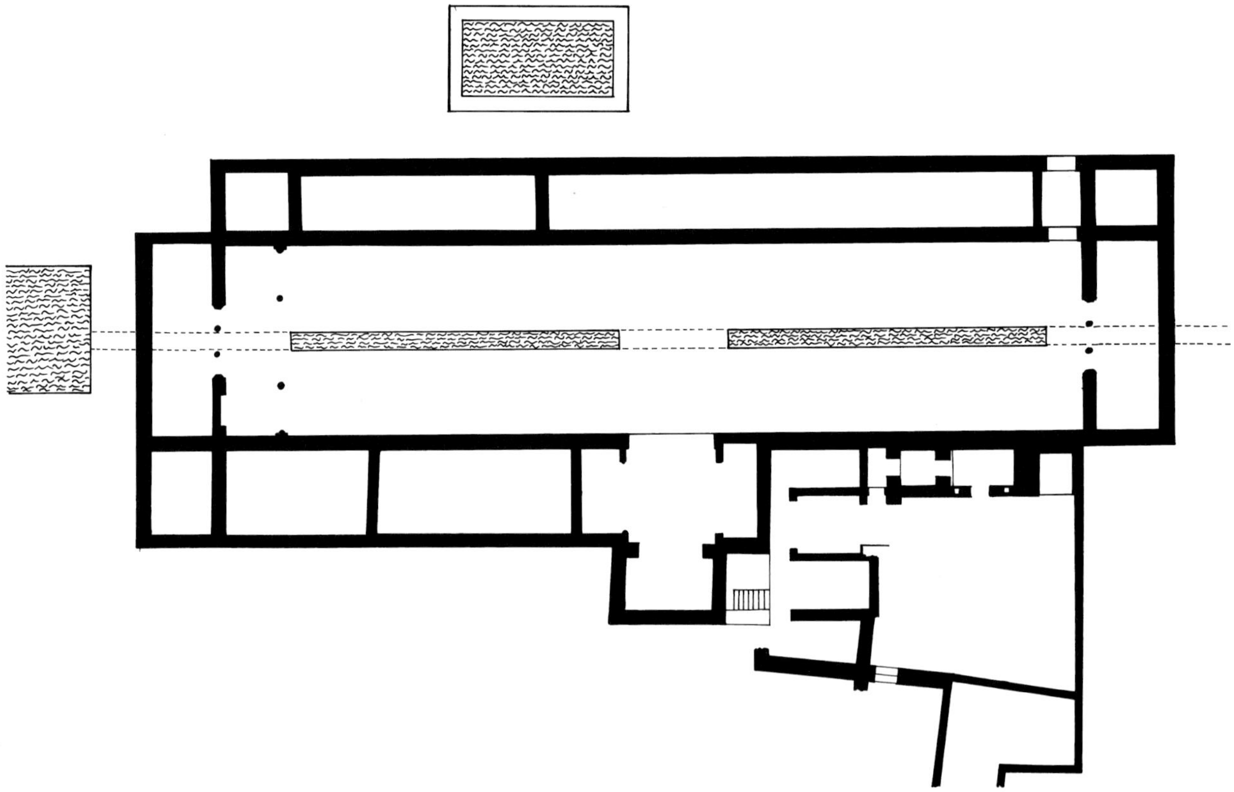

83. Plan of the palace of the Convento de San Francisco (after J. Seguí Pérez)

The Partal and Tendilla Palaces

In the center of the northern side of the palace city was the Partal Palace, built during the reign of Muḥammad III at the beginning of the fourteenth century (Fig. 84).[40] Although formerly the palace was completely enclosed and surrounded by other houses, today there are open gardens (of modern design) and of the original architecture only the northern portico and the nearby Torre del Mihrab remain (Fig. 85). The portico, called the Torre de las Damas, stands at one end of a large rectangular pool, its present isolation in jarring contrast to its original, more coherent environment. Previously it faced a matching portico to which it was united by lateral walls and a central courtyard in much the same manner as the Court of the Myrtles (which postdated it). The wooden ceiling in the tower was removed by a German collector in the nineteenth century and is now in the Museum für Islamische Kunst in Berlin. The Torre de las Damas retains little of its original stucco and ceramic wall decoration but what remains is the most refined of the Alhambra.[41] It is pierced on its courtyard side by five large arches on pillars, today restored with marble columns.[42] The north facade is interrupted by a rectangular salient with five windows at the courtyard level and a row of smaller windows above, admitting light to the airy space. The salient is a mirador with a greater

84. The Torre de las Damas

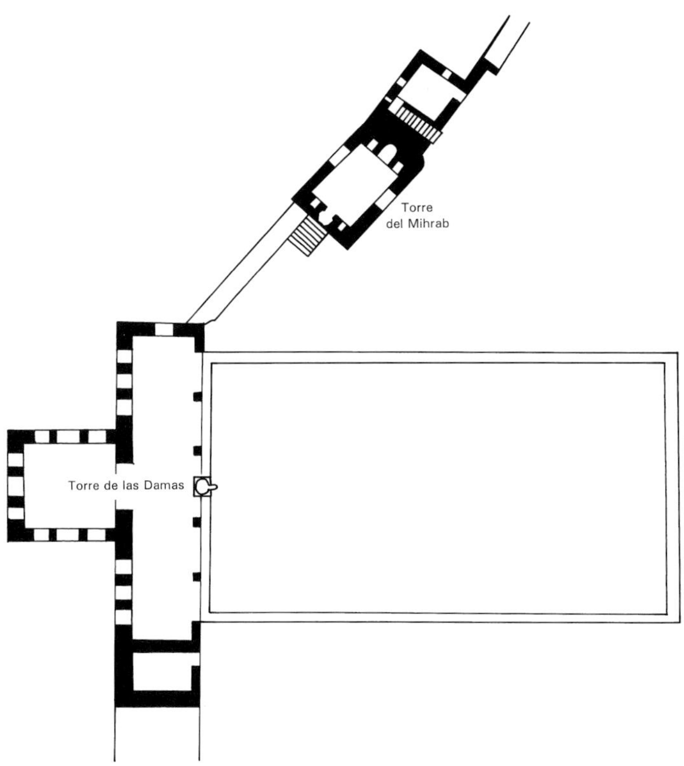

85. Plan of the Partal Palace and Torre de las Damas (after J. Seguí Pérez)

than 190-degree prospect of the surrounding landscape, and it is flanked on either side by three smaller miradors in the form of slightly projecting arched niches. At the western end of this building, stairs lead to a two-story tower with fifteen windows that enjoys the same extensive vistas of the Darro River valley and Albaicin quarter.

The Torre del Mihrab, or Mihrab Tower, which stands just south of the Torre de las Damas, was an addition by Yūsuf I (Color Plate 9).[43] It is a freestanding structure with an oratory on its north side oriented to Mecca, and on the south side a house known as the Casa de Astasio de Bracamonte after its sixteenth-century owner (Fig. 86). There is no means of access between the two, which is in part due to the fact that the Casa de Bracamonte was a slightly later addition.[44] The separation of spaces and the chronology of construction indicate that the oratory was intended to serve not the occupants of the house but the Partal Palace, which it faces. The exterior stucco that originally would have masked the brick fabric of the building is unfortunately long gone.

Through a door on the west side one enters into a rectangular room divided into two parts by means of an arch on engaged columns. Opposite the entrance is the mihrab: a deep, faceted niche with an octagonal vault decorated with stucco panels of fine floral and geometric designs and framed by a Kufic inscription (Fig. 87). This stucco is original and contains verses from the Qur'ān admonishing the believer to pray regularly. Similar exhortations are inscribed on the impost blocks of the mihrab arch (Qur'ān, VII:205) and elsewhere in the oratory. Inside the mihrab niche is a longer Qur'ānic inscription (XVII:78–81).[45]

On the wall perpendicular and to the left of the mihrab there is a shallow niche with a double framed window (*ajimez*); regrettably most of the stucco in this area is not original.[46] This double window is mirrored by an identical one on the opposite wall. Above, on all four walls of the chamber, are ten smaller windows, two of which were walled up when the Casa de Bracamonte was added. From the little mosque's elevated position, perched on the walls of the palace-city, which itself occupies a hilltop, the windows on the north side offer a splendid view of the river valley and hills surrounding the Alhambra (Fig. 88). As Torres Balbás commented, were it not for the presence of the mihrab, one might identify this as a garden pavilion built, like the Torre de las Damas, expressly for gazing at landscape;[47] but it is in fact a place where prayer and the enjoyment of nature are conjoined.

The merger of mosque and pavilion, although unusual in the Islamic world, is not an oddity in the Granadine context. In addition to this and the Generalife's oratory pavilion, there was the oratory attached to the Mexuar in the Alhambra (Fig. 89). Because its original interior was destroyed by an explosion in 1590, one cannot address the inscriptions or the ornament enframing its windows. However, its location parallels that of the Partal oratory, and sitting on the palace's precinct walls its windows offered broad views of the Albaicin. Last, there was an oratory that served the madrasa built by Yūsuf I and supervised by the *ḥājib* Riḍwān in 750/1349 (Fig. 90). Although the madrasa was mostly destroyed in 1722–29, the oratory still survives, embedded like a gemstone in the more modern building that faces the cathedral. This oratory gave onto a garden via *ajimez* windows on either side of the mihrab, and indeed a fragment of epigraphic poetry from elsewhere in the madrasa instructs the viewer: "Behold this garden (*rawḍ*)."[48]

86. Section drawing of the Torre del Mihrab and Casa de Bracamonte (after L. Torres Balbás)

87. The interior of the Torre del Mihrab

88. The view from the window in the Torre del Mihrab, c. 1870 (J. Laurent, courtesy of the Fine Arts Library, Harvard)

89. The oratory adjoining the Mexuar

Southeast of the Partal was the last palace built in the royal walled city, called the Palace of the Conde de Tendilla after one of its postconquest owners (Fig. 91). It dated to the reign of Yūsuf III (r. 810/1408–820/1417). (Although appearing out of chronological order in this discussion, it is described briefly here in order that I may devote the remainder of the chapter to the Comares and Lions palaces.) The palace was described by the German traveler Hieronymus Münzer when he visited it in 1494 as "sumptuous and superb," but because it was demolished two hundred years later by Philip V and its reusable materials sold, there is little to see today.[49] The only visible remains are its foundations, the hypocaust floor of the baths, and a fountain. It was located on the highest ground of the Partal area and its tower overlooked the courtyard and garden in one direction and the exterior landscape in the other.[50] The plan of this courtyard resembled that of the earlier Comares Palace and the palace's situation between garden and exterior landscape with a mirador-tower at the spatial and visual threshold resembles that of its precursors, the Partal, Comares, and Lions palaces.

90. The oratory in the Madrasa of Granada

The Comares and Lions Palaces

The two palaces that in the present day have come to symbolize the Alhambra, the Nasrids, and sometimes even all of al-Andalus are the Comares and Lions palaces, each centered around a handsome garden courtyard (Fig. 92). After the building of these two, few major changes (except for the Palace of the Conde de Tendilla) were made to the architecture of the Alhambra until Charles V razed a large portion to build his round Renaissance palace and the gardens were restructured according to a later neoclassical European taste. Thus, the present-day plan of the complex (Fig. 93) gives a fairly accurate idea of the Alhambra in the time of Muḥammad V in the late fourteenth century.

As it stands today, the Comares Palace is largely the work of Ismāʿīl I, Yūsuf I, and Muḥammad V and was finished in 1370. But there are traces of older walls that suggest that the fourteenth-

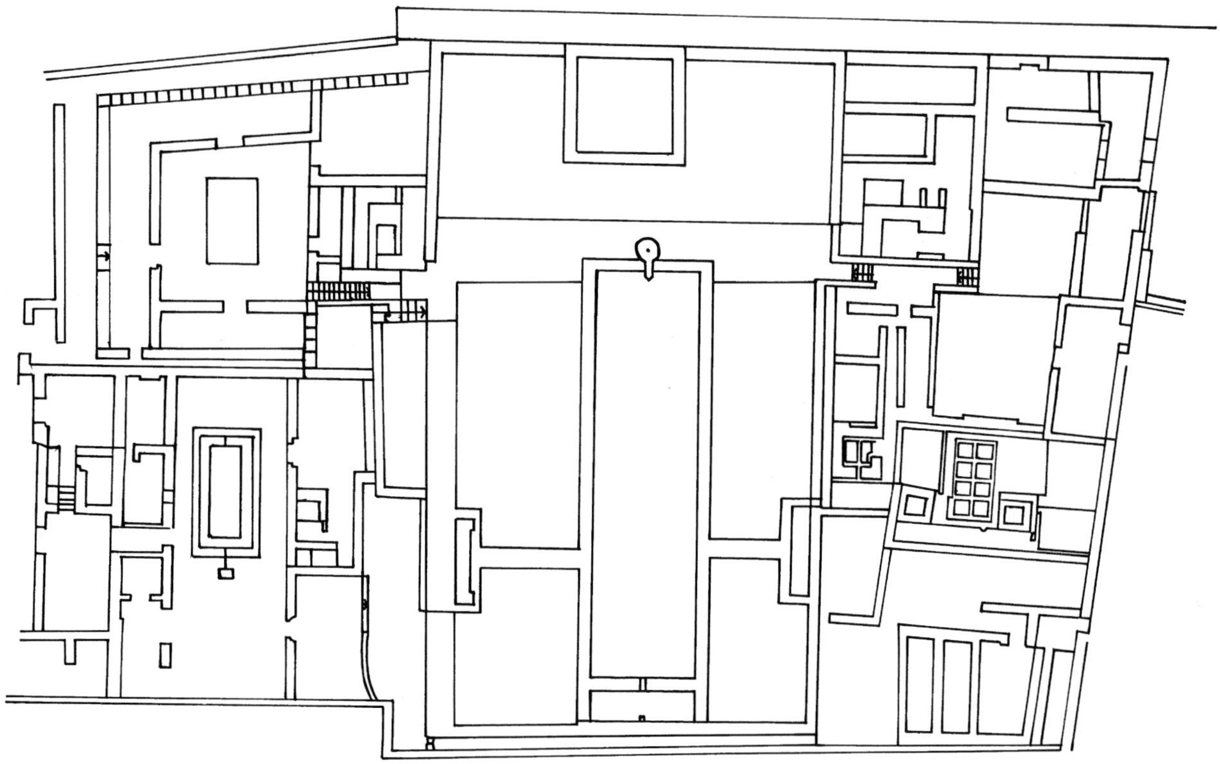

91. Plan of the Palace of the Conde de Tendilla (after J. Seguí Pérez)

century rectangular courtyard enclosed by halls and a tall tower conformed to the plan of an earlier structure, perhaps from the reign of Muḥammad III.[51] The Comares palace consisted of several courtyards, the main one being the Court of the Myrtles. This was preceded by the Mexuar (*mashwar,* or council) Court where ordinary state business was seen to and the so-called Patio of the Cuarto Dorado where the sultan on occasion presented himself enthroned against the stunning backdrop of the court's richly decorated south wall and overhanging eave (Fig. 94). This small patio with its high walls is a compressed and intimidating space that is alleviated by a single shallow water basin. The wall opposite the throne dias has three arches through which one passes into a small chamber called the Cuarto Dorado (Golden Chamber) (Fig. 95). The Cuarto Dorado has a large wall niche with a window on an axis with the throne at the patio's south wall. This window provides a view outward to the exterior countryside and inward toward the enclosed paved courtyard, whose only reference to nature is its solitary basin. The axial alignment of the throne in the courtyard with the mirador in the Cuarto Dorado reflected more than a love of symmetry; it expressed spatially the social order of Nasrid al-Andalus, the sultan being at the generating point of the visual field that opened toward his kingdom and subjects.

A similar juxtaposition of interior and exterior views occurs in the adjoining and much larger Court of the Myrtles (Fig. 96). This large court is almost entirely taken up by a large rectangular

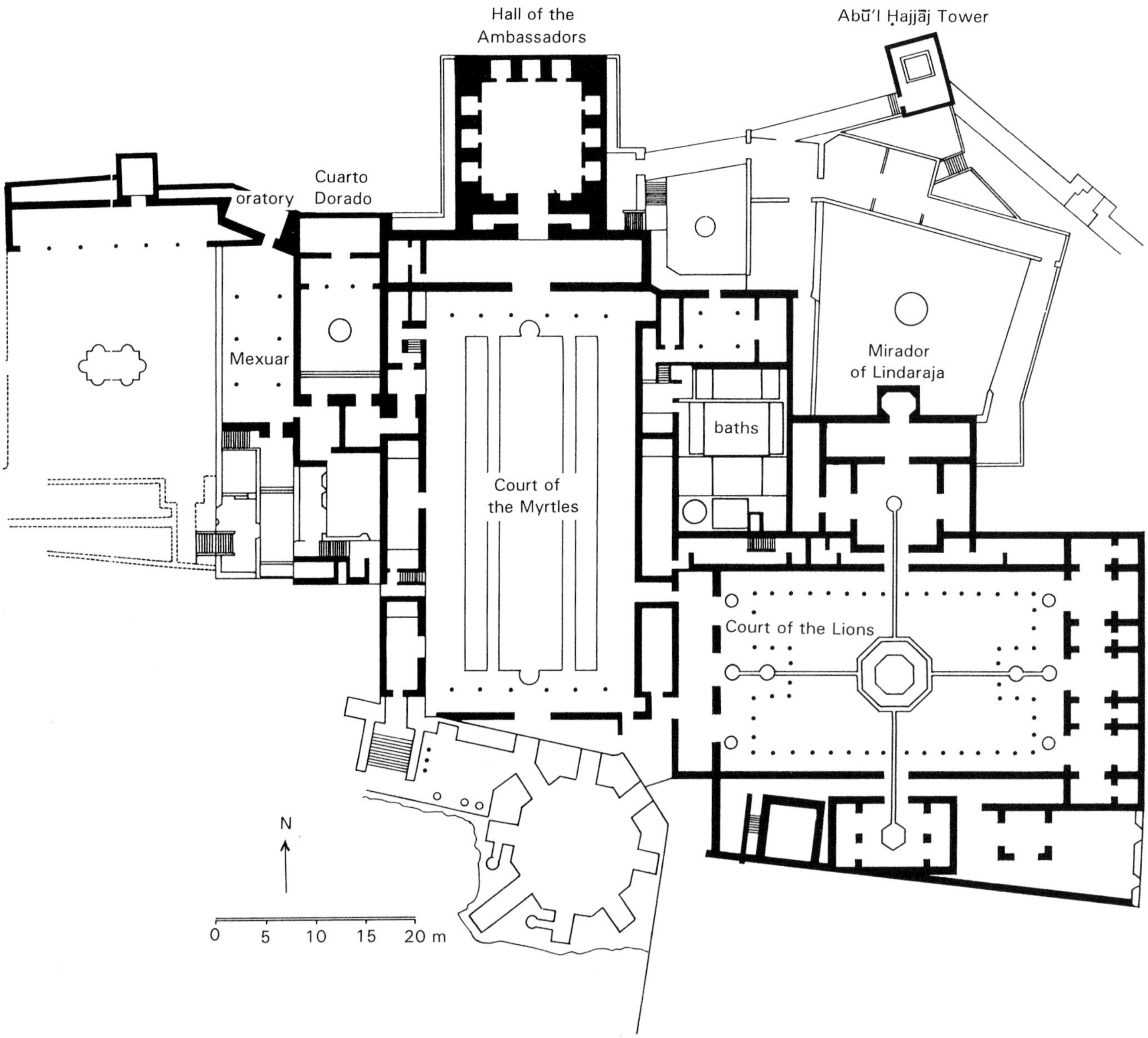

92. Plan of the Comares and Lions palaces

basin (*birka,* whence comes one of the names of the court, al-Birka; it is also called Patio de los Arrayanes, this last word meaning "myrtles"), measuring 36.6 by 23.5 meters. The rows of myrtle shrubs that run along the east and west sides of the pool recall Ibn Luyūn's suggestion that the ideal garden have a pool planted with evergreens.[52] The modern planting of this garden, unlike that of so many others, approximates its historical appearance, for when Navagero saw the beds a few decades after the conquest, they were planted with both myrtles and orange trees.[53] The long thin

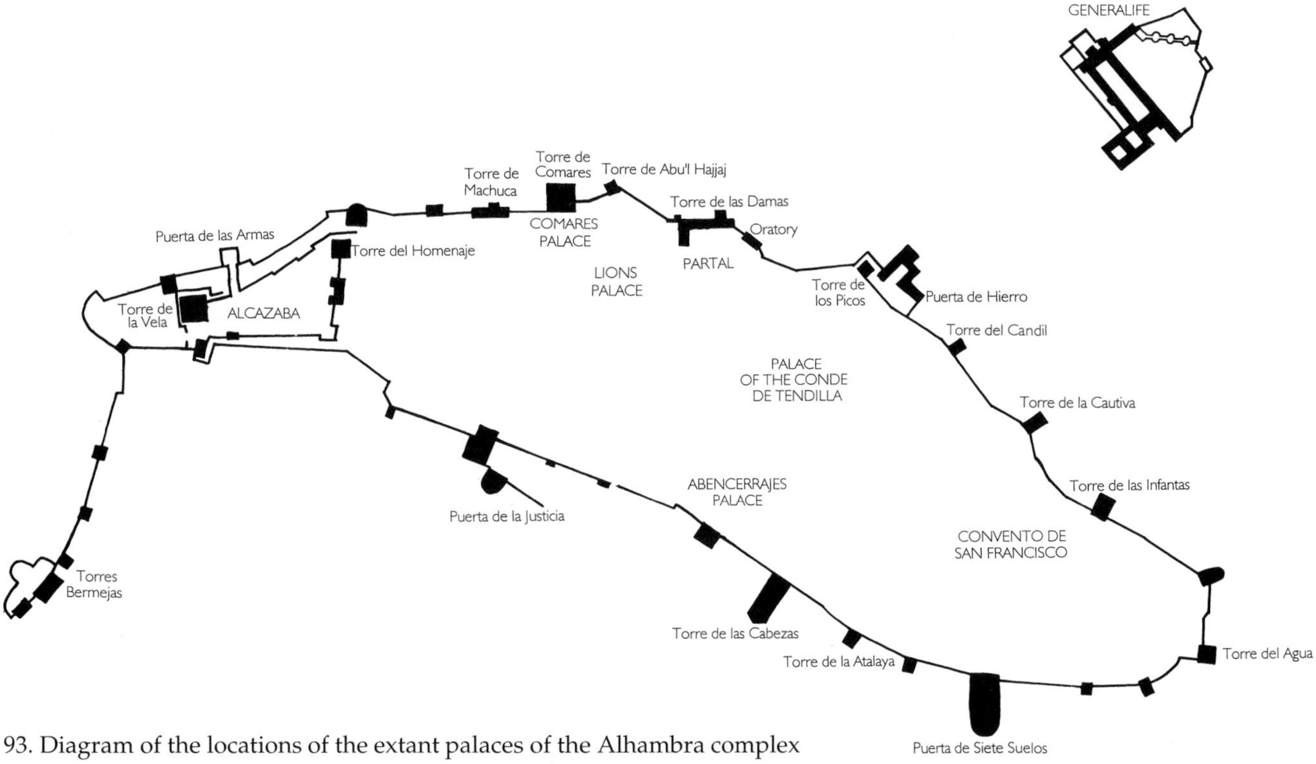

93. Diagram of the locations of the extant palaces of the Alhambra complex

94. Patio of the Cuarto Dorado, south wall

95. Patio of the Cuarto Dorado, the arcade on the north side

96. The Court of the Myrtles

97. Water basins in the Court of the Myrtles

beds of vegetation are framed by narrow channels of water sunken into the marble pavement. At either end of the pool there are small basins from which water spouts gently upward to fall back into the basin and trickle along a short open channel into the main pool (Fig. 97). The brief vertical axes of these burbling jets contrast with the horizontal sheet of silvery water on which the surrounding architecture is mirrored and add dynamism to the otherwise placid environment. The basin's circular shape alleviates the severe rectangularity of the larger pool and linear shrubbery beds, and it imitates the undulating ring of a waterdrop falling onto the surface and radiating outward in gentle ripples.

The courtyard is enclosed at either end by galleries of seven arches on marble columns that appear doubled when reflected in the pool's surface. The east and west walls consist of discreet two-story apartments, probably for the four wives of the sultan.[54] Through openings in these walls one enters the Court of the Myrtles from the Patio of the Cuarto Dorado and leaves it for the adjoining Lions Palace. The Court of the Myrtles is a self-contained space, yet it opens dramatically at the north end in what James Dickie has aptly termed a "dilated mirador,"[55] the so-called Hall of the Ambassadors, begun by Yūsuf I and finished by Muḥammad V (Fig. 98). This hall occupies the upper part of the Comares Tower, which projects from the main wall of the palace-city. The Hall of the Ambassadors was the state reception hall where the sultan met official delegations and entertained the notables of Granada, and its size and sumptuousness reflect the importance of diplomacy to the Nasrids, who survived more by negotiation than by military strength.

The hall is large, square, and taller than it is wide (11.3 meters square by 18.2 meters high). In each of its walls there are three large alcoves (Figs. 99 and 100). Those on the three outer walls form small chambers that open to the exterior, like miradors within the larger mirador, and they have dramatic, elevated views of the city and valley that lie at the Alhambra's feet (Fig. 101). Above these alcoves runs a clerestory of smaller windows that illuminate the hall. The airy interior is hand-

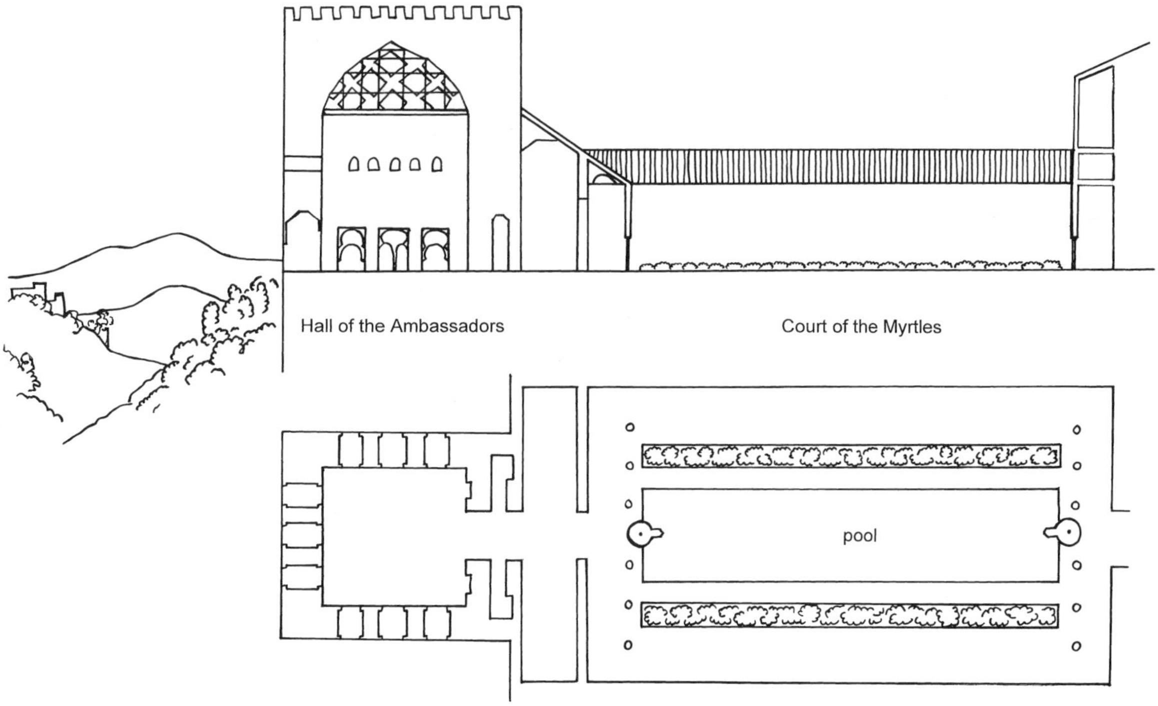

98. Section and plan of the Court of the Myrtles and Hall of the Ambassadors (after Prieto-Moreno)

99. The Hall of the Ambassadors

100. Central alcove in the Hall of the Ambassadors, c. 1870 (J. Laurent, courtesy of the Fine Arts Library, Harvard)

101. The Comares Tower and its view (courtesy of the Fine Arts Library, Harvard)

somely decorated with a tiled dado and floor, stucco walls, and an enormous cove vault, meticulously assembled of geometrically cut, wooden pieces inlaid with mother-of-pearl stars, the whiteness of which gleams against the darker background of wood like the stars of the night sky. The metaphor of a celestial canopy and the cosmos that is suggested visually is emphasized by the inscriptions. Those that run just below the vault contain the complete Sūrat al-Mulk (Sura 67), which begins: "Blessed be He who holds the (reigns of) Kingship in His hand, who has power over every thing" (verse 1).[56] The sura describes God's power in creation and his constant surveillance and protection. The allusion to the seven heavens, over which God is supreme, is reinforced by the geometrical and stellar design of the wooden vault, which consists of six rows of stars rising to the seventh component, a central domelet.[57] The theme of watching—"He is an observer of all things" (verse 19)—and of sustaining—"Who else could provide you with sustenance if He were to with-

hold His provision?" (verse 21)—had a secular dimension as well, for from the mirador the sultan surveyed his people and provided for them, much as God provided for the believers.[58]

The central niches are more intricately ornamented than are those in the corners, and an inscription indicates that the sultan sat on a throne in the central niche on the north side on the axis that ran through the Court of the Myrtles and the Hall of the Ambassadors. Thus during state receptions his subjects and visitors would look at him and at his domain simultaneously so that the sultan and the backdrop—his kingdom—united in the viewer's eyes to become a single entity.[59] The ruler was precisely positioned within the hall's architectural space and on a visual continuum extending from viewer to landscape that articulated the centrality and primacy of his role as Nasrid sultan. Moreover, his two identities as an individual living in a finite temporal context and as timeless institution within a geospatial context were simultaneously combined.[60]

The far-reaching power of the sultan was symbolized also in the unadorned exterior of the tower that forms part of the palace's enclosure wall. From it the sultan and his court had a sweeping view of the city below, whereas the people living there or walking in its environs, although exposed to view themselves, could see little of the life and ceremonies inside the palace. The tower's stark forbidding rectilinear mass loomed, aggressively visible as a symbol of royal presence, omniscience, and above all, watchful surveillance (Fig. 102). By such means architecture projected the sovereign authority of the patron and was imbued with his identity.[61]

Adjoining and, to some extent, replicating the Comares Palace is the Lions Palace, a late addition to the Alhambra, built between the years 1370 and 1390 by Muḥammad V (see Fig. 92). Replacing an older garden from Yūsuf I's reign, it was squeezed between the Comares Palace and the royal cemetery (*rawḍa*) on artificially leveled land.[62] Whereas in the first half of the fourteenth century the cupolas and towers in the old garden, cemetery, and nearby areas were visible from afar, as testified to by Ibn al-Khaṭīb, by the second half of the century they were obscured by the newly erected Lions Palace.[63] With its construction, this part of the Alhambra became more crowded and urban in character.

It is difficult to ascertain the Lions Palace's precise function, especially vis-à-vis the Comares Palace, since adjoining parts were obliterated by the palace of Charles V in the sixteenth century. Nonetheless, many theories have been put forth for the reason for duplicating palaces in this manner. The first can be dismissed summarily: unlike the relationship between the Generalife and Comares palaces, there was no significant seasonal variation between the Lions and Comares palaces. The second theory suggests that the Comares Palace was public and the Lions Palace private, since the former had a reception hall and was closer to the "public" council chamber, the Mexuar. However, since the Comares Palace was already divided between the ceremonial area and the residential chambers along the sides of the Court of the Myrtles, the more "private" character of the Lions Palace simply duplicated that which the Comares Palace already had. The fundamental problem with the theory of divided spaces is that the concepts of private and public are not functionally explanatory terms in Islamic architecture. In the Islamic Mediterranean in this period, privacy was achieved by means of bent entrances, latticed window screens (*mashribīya*), and directed sight lines. In other words, privacy was a visual attribute rather than a functional designation permanently

102. The Comares Tower seen from below (Girault de Prangey)

ascribed to a room. To some degree, any room visited or inhabited by the sultan was, by virtue of his presence, temporarily public, and while visitors were received in the Hall of the Ambassadors, the Comares Palace could at any time be closed off—made private—simply by preventing them from entering through the courtyard of the Cuarto Dorado.

The most convincing explanation for the Lions Palace was Georges Marçais' theory that the palaces were successive creations in the sense of Madīnat al-Zahrā᾿ and Madīnat al-Zāhira, or the various Abbasid palaces of Samarra.[64] But unlike those earlier palaces, the Lions Palace did not supplant a preexisting structure, in other words, the Comares Palace. Rather, it was a visually separate addition that, when built, transformed the older building into an "antechamber" which then preceded the Lions Palace spatially, much as Ismāʿīl and Yūsuf preceded Muḥammad V historically.

The apparent separation of private and public that resulted was simply a factor of the progressively limited access as one moved from the outer rooms toward the palace interior.

The plan of the Lions Palace dovetails neatly with Comares and the baths. Although in general the courtyards of the Alhambra and Generalife palaces run along a north-south axis, the Lions Palace runs east-west in order to accommodate preexisting buildings. The palace is organized around a central rectangular courtyard (28.5 by 15.7 m) containing a garden divided axially by paved walkways into four equal quadrants (Fig. 103). The garden is surrounded by an arcade whose floor level is slightly higher than the garden's paths, with projecting kiosks at the east and west ends (see Color Plate 7). The slender columns, in groups of one, two, and three, that support the attenuated arches of the gallery and kiosks diminish the apparent mass of the architecture and disguise the distinction between interior and exterior space, so that architecture and garden are interpenetrating and continuous. The elegantly carved stucco contributes to this effect because the carved relief of rhythmic lines and dense vegetal designs creates sharp contrasts between light and dark that give the sense that the solid wall is a perforated screen, like a *mashribīya* (Fig. 104). The stylized motif of interlaced arches that fills the rectangular spaces between the arches and their frames is indeed derived from a screen: it is a highly elaborate descendent of the overlapping polylobed arches surrounding the mihrab and adjacent bays in al-Ḥakam's addition to the Mosque of Cordoba (see Fig. 65).

This play between interior and exterior and between positive and negative space is continued by the water channels that flow from the surrounding chambers to the center of the courtyard. Under the east and west galleries jets spurt upward from sunken basins and flow into the basins under the kiosks from where they flow in narrow channels embedded in the floor pavement, cascading gently and over the drop of less than fifteen centimeters to the level of the garden pavements (Fig. 105). On the north side of the courtyard is the chamber called the Hall of the Two Sisters (the aforementioned Sala de las Dos Hermanas) and on the south side is the Hall of the Abencerrajes, both famed for their ornate muqarnas vaults, the almost irrational complexity of which dematerializes the mass of the domes overhead so that they appear like sparkling, rotating, cosmic canopies (Fig. 106). Indeed verses in each chamber refer to the Pleiades, the Gemini, "the stars in the heavens," and "the heavenly spheres whose orbits revolve."[65] Below the dome in each chamber there is a large basin from which the water flows in channels like those emanating from the kiosks, meeting them at the fountain of lions in the garden's center. The liquid ribbons of water from the surrounding chambers that run across the porticos and ultimately into the open garden are a unifying element that binds the disparate spaces together (Fig. 107).

The garden was planted with orange trees, and in 1502 the French visitor Antoine de Lalaing saw there six tall enough to stand beneath.[66] The original layers of soil were disturbed for the sake of architectural restorations carried out in the courtyard in the late nineteenth century, but Gómez Moreno observed the medieval soil level was approximately eighty centimeters below the present level.[67] The depth of the quadrants almost matches the Generalife's Acequía Court, and as in that earlier garden, the sunken vegetation and embedded water basins were intended for viewers seated on carpets or low cushions at floor level. Thus positioned, their glance skimmed the surface of the garden so that with the exception of the orange trees, it was the tops of the brightly colored flowers

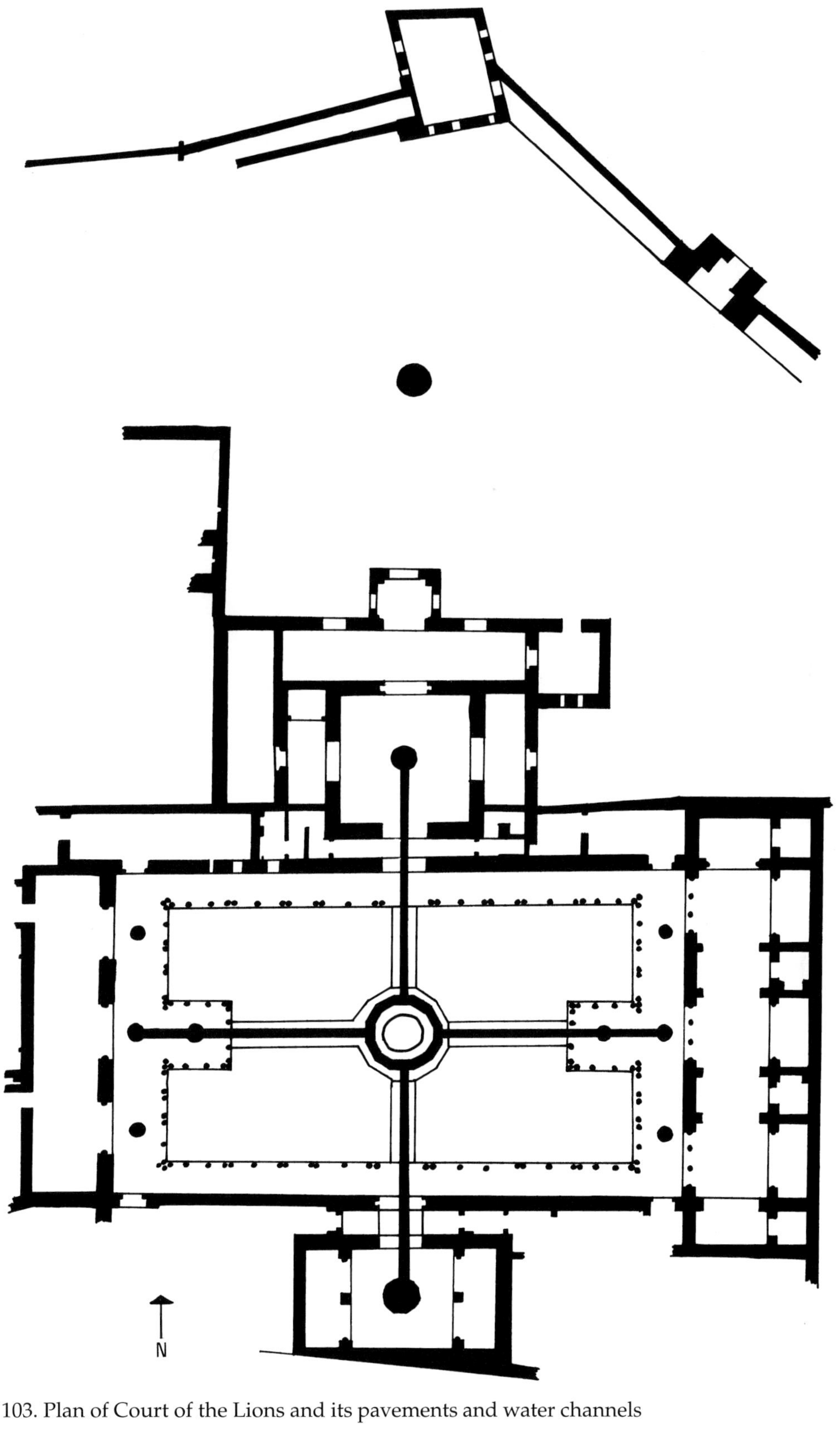

103. Plan of Court of the Lions and its pavements and water channels

104. Carved stucco in kiosk in the Court of the Lions

reaching upwards to the sunlight that were seen, rather than plants in profile or clumps of plants, as in modern European and American gardens.

Although the exact plantings in these gardens are not known today and probably will not be learned until the day that paleoarchaeological techniques such as seed flotation are employed (and it is questionable how useful such techniques will be in these gardens that were replanted in the centuries after the reconquest by patrons with very different tastes), the depth and shape of the garden beds evince a notable preference for flat surface effects and straight lines. This same aesthetic can be seen in the gardens represented in the paintings in a manuscript of the *Bayāḍ wa Riyāḍ* (Vatican Ar. 368), a love story set in Iraq, but written here in Maghrebi script and attributed variously to thirteenth- or fourteenth-century Spain on the basis of similarities to figural imagery in Spanish textiles and Nasrid architecture. The series of miniatures shows enclosed gardens with towers, pavilions, pools, trellised vines, and the crisp outline of an occasional cypress and leafy fruit tree (Color Plate 10), and throughout there is a clear preference for clean forms and gardens with neatly defined parts.

In the miniature showing a wounded, bleeding Riyāḍ on the left, there is a pool with a flying walkway or rim (reminiscent of the tank at al-Rummānīya in Cordoba) and in the background a

105. Water basin and channels in kiosk in the Court of the Lions

tree growing in a low garden. To either side of the water tank there are steps leading down to another garden with sunken beds, the vegetation indicated by a solitary plant set in grass or a ground cover to the right and a climbing vine or espalier tree to the left. The clearly delineated trunk of this vine rises to a horizontal trellis supported on stakes.[68] Across from Riyāḍ, on the opposite side of the water tank, there is a kiosk under the arch of which are two older women, one of whom is seated with her hand resting on a latticed balustrade from which she overlooks the rest of the garden. Many of the paintings in this manuscript depict garden scenes with windowed towers, rivers, and a waterwheel; usually the low ground cover is rendered as vertical green strokes

106. Muqarnas vault in the Hall of the Abencerrajes

bearing red dots, a rather formulaic way of representing a flat garden bed with a low carpet of flowering plants.

These paintings, although valuable as unique visual representations of Islamic Mediterranean gardens, are a problematic source of information on Nasrid gardens because the manuscript lacks the beginning and end pages that might have supplied the date and place of manufacture and there are no other illustrated manuscripts of this type with which to compare it.[69] Paintings that have been pegged as late Almohad or early Nasrid because of similarities in style to textiles and architecture must be used cautiously as a source of information about style in another medium, in this case gardens.

107. Water basin and channels in the Hall of the Abencerrajes (Garzón, courtesy of the Fine Arts Library, Harvard)

108. The lions fountain, with a detail of its inscribed rim.

The fountain of twelve lions that gives the Lions Palace its name has been the subject of considerable iconographic and archaeological analysis (Fig. 108). Scholars do not agree on whether the animal statues date to the eleventh century (and possibly Ibn Naghrīla's palace) or the fourteenth century, contemporary with the courtyard itself. The basin resting on the lions' haunches is fourteenth-century and, although it may have replaced an older basin, the fact that it was made expressly for the lion fountain is demonstrated by its poetic inscription, one verse of which states: "Truly, what else is this fountain but a beneficent cloud pouring out its abundant supplies over the lions underneath?" The poem addresses the Nasrid rulers and exclaims, "May the blessings of God forever be with you! May He make your subjects obedient to your rule, and grant you victory over all your enemies."[70]

The lion is an age-old symbol of sovereignty and power and is employed here in that general sense. More specific, however, may be a reference to Solomon, "the King-Prophet who had become in mediaeval Jewish and Muslim legend the prince *par excellence*."[71] Solomon was known for fantastic gardens and palaces full of architectural illusion. His temple had a large basin, a "molten sea," that rested on the backs of twelve oxen arranged in a ring (1 Kings, 7:23–26), and for the Queen of Sheba he made a gold-and-ivory throne on a raised platform with twelve lions lining the six steps (1 Kings, 10:18–20). The Solomonic interpretation of the Alhambra's lions was developed by Bargebuhr, who made his claim on the basis of Ibn Gabirol's poem, which mentions "a full 'sea,' matching Solomon's Sea" with lions rather than with oxen. But as explained earlier, the link between the eleventh-century vizier's palace and the Nasrid Alhambra cannot be proved, and the link between the Hebrew poem and the lion fountain is purely circumstantial; given the abundance of poems annotating the architecture and in situ objects such as basins, the lack of an explicit reference to Solomon in the lions fountain is strange, if such an interpretation were intended. Even if such an inscription had existed on an earlier basin, the fact that it was not reiterated on the fourteenth-century replacement indicates that that particular iconography did not prevail among the Nasrids. Grabar suggests that "by the fourteenth century in Andalusia, the creation for a prince of a garden with a fountain surrounded by handsomely decorated buildings can be considered an automatic gesture without compelling meaning,"[72] and the same should be said of the lion fountain. When we reject the likelihood of Ibn Gabirol's Hebrew poem being a description of the Alhambra's lions, the Solomonic connotation fades from a specific evocation to one of a myriad of princely themes current in Andalusian court culture from the Umayyads to the Nasrids and having a very long genealogy in the Mediterranean and Persian world.[73]

The Lindaraja Mirador and Inscriptions

Above the porticoes on the north and south sides of the Court of the Lions there are second-story chambers with windows that look down into the courtyard (Fig. 109). These are self-contained living quarters similar to the two on each side of the Court of the Myrtles. The chamber on the north side has, in addition to its courtyard vista, a view in the opposite direction directed through the Hall of the Two Sisters to a mirador giving onto the large garden of the Lindaraja (Fig. 110). Such views in which interior and exterior were united in the eyes of the viewer were common at the Alhambra, as we have already seen in some of the halls of the Generalife, Partal, Cuarto Dorado, and Comares palaces. But the penetration of this view through the hall, across the Lindaraja garden and extending beyond the walls of the palace-city to the Albaicin and distant mountains is the most dramatic and unexpected juncture in Andalusian architecture of an interior, enclosed space with the exterior landscape because, unlike the aforementioned halls, the Court of the Lions is not perched on the palace-city's perimeter walls but stands well inside. The Lindaraja Mirador is thus a threshold that brings together at the same time as it makes evident the separation of the palace from the surrounding landscape. Like the water channels that unite the side chambers with the Court of the Lions garden, vision in the mirador binds garden and landscape in the eyes of the beholder (Fig. 111).[74]

109. The second-story chambers overlooking the Court of the Lions, c. 1870 (J. Laurent, courtesy of the Fine Arts Library, Harvard)

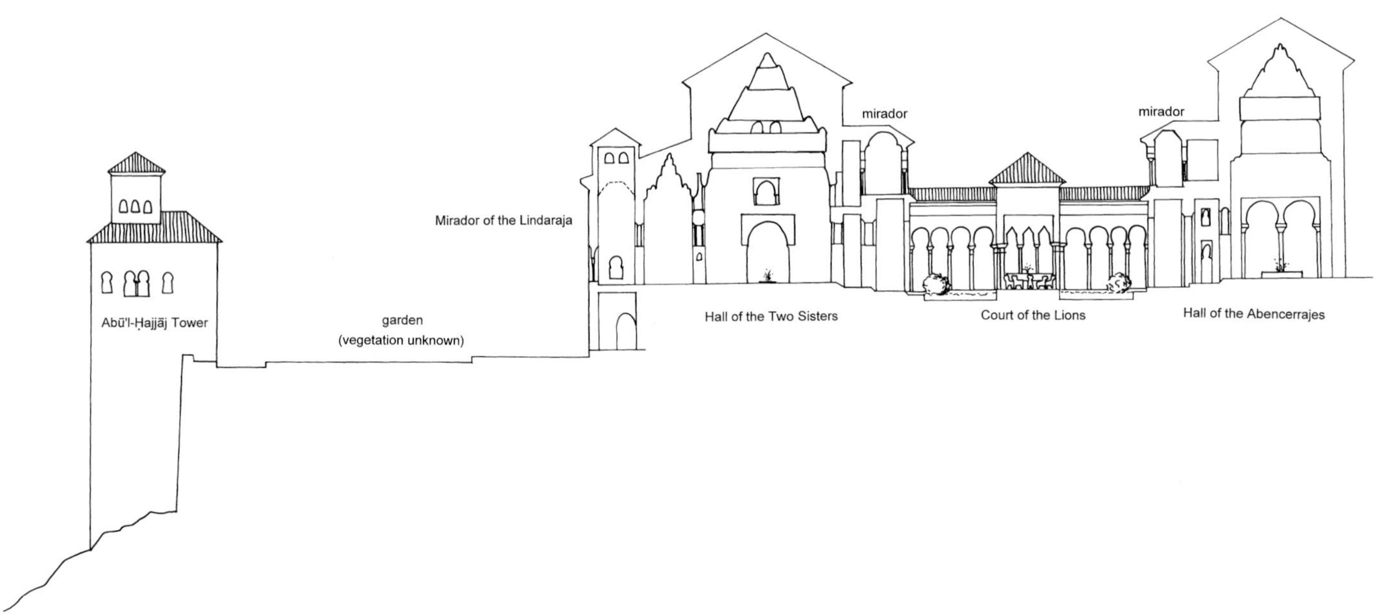

110. Section of the Court of the Lions and the Lindaraja Mirador (after Prieto-Moreno)

111. The view through the Hall of the Two Sisters to the Lindaraja Mirador and beyond (Garzón, Courtesy of the Fine Arts Library, Harvard)

The Lindaraja Mirador (*Lindaraja* translates as "the eye of the house of ʿĀʾisha") is on level with the Hall of the Two Sisters but, because of the topography of the Alhambra's site, projects at a second-story level into the garden below. The mirador is a box with single windows on each side and a double *ajimez* window in front, and above, a row of stained-glass windows that admit a jewel-like radiance into the elegant chamber decorated with a colorfully tiled dado and ornately carved plasterwork (Color Plate 11). Formerly the garden that the mirador overlooked had views of the exterior landscape that were only minimally limited by the Tower of Abū'l Ḥajjāj (Torre del Peinador de la Reina), but in the sixteenth century the walls were built up by Charles V, enclosing the garden and blocking vision.[75]

The Lindaraja Mirador's interior is revetted with poetic inscriptions in stucco, and similarly there are verses on the walls and fountains of the Comares, Lions, Partal, and Generalife palaces, the baths, and the towers.[76] The poets were Ibn Jayyāb (672/1274–749/1348) who wrote nine poems for the Alhambra and numerous others that were never inscribed or, if they were, do not survive as inscriptions today; Ibn al-Khaṭīb (713/1313–776/1374) who wrote at least two poems for the Comares Palace; and his protégé Ibn Zamrak (733/1333–795/1393) wrote the greatest number of poems found today at the Alhambra.[77] The Alhambra is the only extant western Islamic palace accompanied by an inscribed program of poems such as occurs here and is a unique case of a building clothed with texts that purport to explain the meaning of its architectural forms.[78] In the frames surrounding the entrance and windows of the Lindaraja Mirador, there is a poem by Ibn Zamrak in which the mirador describes its relation to the garden below, speaking in the first person:

> In this garden [*rawḍa*] I am an eye [*ʿain*] filled with delight and the pupil [*insān*] of this eye is, truly, our lord,
>
> Muḥammad [V], praiseworthy for his bravery and generosity, with fame outstanding and virtue graceful;
>
> He is the full moon on the empire's horizons, his signs are lasting and his light brilliant.
>
> In his abode he is none other than the sun, the shade from which is beneficent.
>
> In me he looks from his califal throne toward the capital of his entire kingdom.[79]

The verse plays with the word *ʿain,* which has the double meaning of "eye" and "spring" (or "well"). When it first appears here, *ʿain* seems to mean "spring," a reference perhaps to a garden fountain; but in its second appearance, coupled with *insān* (pupil), it means "eye." In the poem's metaphor, the mirador is an eye that is identified with the sultan Muḥammad V, and the view of that sovereign eye (or "I") is of garden, city, and kingdom. The mirador positions the viewer and frames the view, thus establishing the structural relationship of subject and object, as discussed at the end of Chapter 5. The poem confirms the mirador's positioning function so that the device is played out in words as well as in architecture; moreover, it makes the metaphor specific to Muḥammad V and his capital.

This is not the first example of an Arabo-Andalusian inscription anthropomorphizing the object it adorned. The device is common in Arabic rhetoric and is called *fakhr.*[80] An intricately carved

112. Earthenware jar with *sgraffito* inscription (in the Ayuntamiento de Valencia)

ivory pyxis (Hispanic Society) from Madīnat al-Zahrā' in the tenth century has a short poem encircling its lid, one line of which states: "I am a receptacle for musk, camphor and ambergris."[81] From the Almohad period there is a rather plain ivory casket (in the Instituto de Valencia de Don Juan, Madrid) with an inscription running around its lid that states, "With beauty I did wonders that are radiant all the while I was surrounded by gardens and embellished with plants and flowers."[82] From the same period comes a painted earthenware jar (Ayuntamiento de Valencia) with bands of inscription that proclaim, "Behold excellence, for you see the results before your eyes. . . . In me, by God's grace, is art made beauty"[83] (Fig. 112). A Nasrid ivory pyxis (Cabildo Metropolitano de Zaragoza) has an inscription encircling its body that begins, "Truth is in me like something stored in a pyxis."[84] These objects and others demonstrate that personification was common in Andalusian inscriptions from the tenth through thirteenth centuries.[85]

Eventually the device of personification was used for architecture also, but we do not know when this happened because today the Alhambra is the only surviving building in western Islamic lands with such a poetic program.[86] Whether or not it was the first is impossible to answer at present. However, a likely link between architecture and poetic inscriptions is the poem written for the taifa ruler of Seville in which the poet put self-congratulatory words into the "mouths" of the two competing reception halls so that one addressed the other: "They have told me that your . . . gardens are limpid with branches that embrace each other like lovers" (see pages 142–43).[87] The Seville poem was clearly written after the construction of the halls, since it was able to describe them in detail. The inscriptions at the Alhambra were presumably likewise written after the architecture and inserted in the bands framing the doors, windows, and niches, substituting for, or perhaps erasing the formulaic Nasrid motto, There is no conquerer but God.

By the fourteenth century, poems praising architecture were common on the walls of Nasrid buildings, and a great many more were written for future inscription that never received that privilege. For instance, Ibn Jayyāb's *Dīwān* contains verses describing a cupola of Yūsuf I that either was never built or was demolished; or equally possibly, the poet may have hoped for but failed to

achieve the recognition of having his words permanently placed on the palace walls.[88] Poets composed their works and recited them orally at court; if good enough, poems would circulate, enjoy repeat performances, and perhaps be immortalized in written form, either as a complete poetic cycle such as Ibn al-Khaṭīb's *Diwān* or in the histories and biographies of authors such as al-Maqqarī.

The Alhambra was not the only complex with monumental inscriptions. Ibn Zamrak wrote that he authored many of the poems not only in the palaces and gardens of the Alhambra, but in those of Alijares and elsewhere on the Sabika hill.[89] Ibn al-Khaṭīb wrote epigraphic poems for a palace of his own in the village of Ainadamar near Granada.[90] It is regrettable that none of these other buildings survive and that so little is known about them, but in any case it is unlikely that any of the inscriptions was as extensive as the Alhambra's program, of which thirty-one epigraphic extracts remain in situ, some of them quoted at considerable length or even the entirety of long poems. Twenty-five of these refer directly to the architecture on which they were written.[91]

Some of the Alhambra's poems are written in the impersonal voice of the third person, as the poem by Ibn Jayyāb in the entrance to the Generalife, which begins, "Over this perfect palace of singular beauty shines the greatness of the Sultan . . ."[92] But eleven others employed the "I" voice, in which the architecture itself seems spontaneously to speak.[93] For example, running around the perimeter of the Hall of the Two Sisters, a poem by Ibn Zamrak begins, "I am the garden which beauty adorns" and framing a niche in the entrance to the Sala de la Barca, a poem by Ibn Jayyāb begins, "I am a mihrab" (Fig. 113).[94] By accepting the anthropomorphizing device, the poem's reader agrees to suppress the "objective" voice of the author—the living poet—and to pretend that it is the building itself that gives utterance.

These secular poetic inscriptions differ significantly from Qur'ān excerpts written on the walls of mosques and other buildings and from the inscriptions commemorating the foundation of buildings. The Qur'ān has a recognized divine authorship and when the first-person plural "we" occurs, the reader knows that it is God who speaks. When inscribed on the Alhambra's walls, verses from the Qur'ān or even the ubiquitous Nasrid motto, There is no conqueror but God, reminded the viewer of unquestionable tenets of religious faith that were already familiar. In an entirely different way, the author of a foundation inscription is similarly manifest. By publicly stating the patron and date of a building on its facade or in an equally prominent place, foundation inscriptions commemorate authorship for the present and future. While it is true that such inscriptions can lie by making false claims (an example being the insertion of Muḥammad V's name in parts of the Alhambra that were built by his predecessors), this only proves the power of the written word in establishing agency: one inscribes a statement on the assumption that it will be believed. In Qur'ānic architectural inscriptions, where the "we" voice occurs, the text and divine author are known and no one confuses the author with the building; in foundation inscriptions the building does not speak for itself but is recorded by an agent (presumably the patron). To some extent, any inscription written directly on the wall has a privileged relationship to the building that is quite unlike a text written about but not directly on a building, such as a *waqfīya* (deed of endowment) or a historical description. But the poetic inscriptions of the Alhambra do not just exist in relation to the architecture, they are the very voice of the building.

The issue of voice as the marker of the subject and its place in the chronological sequence of

113. Niche in the wall of the entrance into the Sala de la Barca from the Court of the Lions

the oral and the written is complex and is a topic of considerable debate in the fields of linguistics, literature, anthropology, and psychology. Dependent upon the question of whether the signified (the concept) precedes the signifier (the verbal or visual representation of it through sound or written letters), is the question of whether speech precedes the written word, and whether writing is a visual representation of speech. Derrida has cast the issue as one of presence and absence: in the act of speech the signifier (sound) and signified (concept) seem to fuse (what Derrida calls "s'entendre parler"), whereas in writing the reader has to supply the concept to signs that do not in and of themselves have meaning. In speech, the self is immediately present, and in writing, it is momentarily absent; speech is thus about presence whereas writing about absence.[95] A chronology of precedence is implied.

In the case of the Alhambra's mural inscriptions, the architecture evidently preceded the poetry, since the poems describe specific places and views. The Lindaraja poems described the mirador, its view, and the viewer. To cite another example, in the Hall of the Two Sisters and the Hall of the Abencerrajes, on the north and south sides of the Lions Palace respectively, there are verses that refer to the Pleiades, the Gemini, "the stars in the heavens," "the heavenly spheres whose orbits revolve," gardens, and white marble columns.[96] Both chambers are vaulted with ornate muqarnas (see Fig. 106), the almost irrational complexity of which dematerializes the mass of the domes overhead so that they appear like sparkling, rotating, cosmic canopies. The parallels between the poetry

and the actual architecture are too close to be accidental: the poem reads as a description of the halls, enriched with metaphor and hyperbole.

But perhaps to ask if the building preceded the poetry or if the oral recitation preceded the written inscription is to cast the question too narrowly, implying, as in the case of representation and the "real" landscape, an elusive priority. The critical issue is not to discover the moment of origin or to locate the level of the real but instead to understand the machinery of the address, the nature of speech and silence. The building was certainly not unintelligible without the annotative texts (or "soundtrack"), or we would have to conclude that earlier palaces lacking inscriptions were mute and incapable of establishing a dialogue with their viewers, a patently untenable notion. Ultimately, both the architecture and the poetry are forms of address that mark a presence: the mirador, whether by its physical fabric or its text, compels us—the reader/viewer—to enter into a relationship with it in which the subjective and objective positions are firmly established.

The poems are unsigned. Although members of the court knew the poet of the Lindaraja verses to be Ibn Zamrak, the inscriptions, because they lack signature and speak in the first person, deny any author but the building itself. The building addresses its readers naturally and with authority, its words carved in bands enframing niches, similar to the placement of Qur'ānic text around mosque mihrabs (Fig. 114). The poems appear to shift authorship and agency upon the building;

114. The mihrab and enframing inscription in the Mosque of Cordoba

yet ultimately, both the words and building seem authorless, appearing miraculously at the patron's behest, so that agency is not so much negated as subsumed within the sultan's role as the supreme worldly patron.

That Muḥammad V is placed at the center of a visual trajectory that encompasses the horizons of his kingdom seems as natural and logical as the view itself in which the frame's selection of a particular place and perspective seems inalienable from the object seen, the architect's intention masked by the apparent artlessness of the scene. The function of this personification device is the same as the frame: it masks the artificiality and vulnerability of the sultan's position as head of his diminished fourteenth-century kingdom and represents it as right and inevitable. The creation of a fixed place for viewing gardens and for framing the sovereign viewer was not new, but was the culmination of architectural ideas begun at Madīnat al-Zahrā᾽ four hundred years earlier. However, the inclusion of poetry to explain the view was an innovation that made possible an almost mystical conflation of individual look (the view from the mirador) and all-seeing gaze (the light shed by the moon and sun) in which the sultan was posited impossibly as the generator of both.

The Lindaraja's written text directed the viewer's attention to one aspect of meaning already inscribed in the architecture and recognized by the viewer. We are meant to accept the building as the spontaneous author, and the sultan its natural rather than designated occupant. Thus the mirador and poem present a circular, self-fulfilling system of signs in which the sovereign authority that engenders it is then confirmed by it. The self-conscious manner of referring in speech and words to the mirador's function suggests that the manipulation of the view, the positioning of the viewer, and the constructed relationship between subject/viewer and object/landscape had by this time become a familiar trope.

9

ILLUSION AND PARADISE

If you ask them: "Who created the heavens and the earth?" they will answer: "The Mighty and All-knowing created them." He who made the earth a bed for you, and laid out tracks upon it so that you may find the way.

—Qur'ān (43:9–10)[1]

Granada was one of the most prosperous regions in Spain, agriculturally rich with fertile plains, green orchards, and vineyards. Visitors in the Nasrid period such as al-ʿUmarī, Ibn Baṭṭūṭa, ʿAbd al-Bāsiṭ b. Khalīl b. Shāhīn al-Malaṭī, and Münzer described with delight the abundance of beautiful estates with gardens and pavilions.[2] But these enchanting gardens of miradors and fountains were innovative with respect neither to form nor to symbolism. In Part One of this book I argued that the form of the earliest gardens in Islamic Spain was drawn from the utilitarian organization of the greater agricultural landscape. Agricultural practice did not change significantly after the initial burst of manual writing in the eleventh century, although production shifted from basic crops such as grains to more specialized and profitable items such as dried fruits and silk.[3] Major changes occurred only after the reconquest and the expulsion of Muslims. Nor was the design and concept of the palace garden significantly altered after its formative phase: the Nasrids relied on large tanks of water, linear and quadripartite layouts, axes marked by water channels, and sunken beds, and all of these devices were extant and in use under their predecessors, the Umayyads, taifas, Almoravids, and Almohads. The thirteenth and fourteenth centuries, therefore, were not a period of invention but of the continuation of practices that had led to the agricultural prosperity of al-Andalus in the late ninth and early tenth century.

However, while the Nasrids did not invent the idea of a sovereign's palace of gardens and panoramic views, they did refine it and heightened the drama of the already existing typology. One of these refinements was the addition of epigraphic poetry (discussed in the previous chapter); another was the manipulation of theatrical illusion. Finally, they built oratories with windows framing views of gardens and landscape, so that the mirador, from having been an instrument of sovereignty and power, now provided a glimpse of paradise anticipated.

Theater and Illusion

Two kinds of drama were offered in the views of contained domestic space and exterior landscape at the Alhambra. One was the slowly unfolding spectacle of landscape that changes from winter's snow-capped mountains to the fresh green of spring and summer's yellow maturity. The other was

the more self-consciously staged theater of the courtyard garden, where the delight taken by medieval Andalusians in metaphor and paradox is fully evident. A variety of devices stimulated the senses and the mind, but water was primary among them. At Madīnat al-Zahrā' and the Alhambra's Court of the Myrtles, fountains and pools provided illusory reflections of the surrounding architecture and, when propelled in jets and channels, animated an otherwise inert environment.

A common illusion was the apparent dematerialization of a material or object. Solid substances seemed to melt and flow, as in the verse by Ibn Zamrak: "A running stream evokes the illusion of a solid substance for the eyes, so that we wonder which one is fluid."[4] The water channels in Ibn al-Khaṭīb's recreation estate, called the Fountain of Tears, were compared to the bright tails trailing comets, an instance of allusion or verbal simile rather than a true visual deception.[5] But unmistakable examples of visual illusionism occur at Madīnat al-Zahrā''s pavilion in the upper garden, which seemed afloat, and in al-Ma'mūn's Toledo palace, where a glass cupola became a cascading fountain. Water also transformed the Generalife's garden stairway into a surprising torrent, and at Madīnat al-Zāhira, water lilies produced miraculous buds of solid silver and gold. At the Alhambra, the stellar patterns of the wooden and stucco vaults suggested heavenly canopies, rotating as the sun's rays moved throughout the day. These artifices gave pleasure in the simplest sense as entertainments but they may have been read on a variety of other levels, speaking to a highly cultivated audience accustomed to simile and metaphor in which nothing is quite what it seems.

A theatrical performance featured in many of the Nasrid palaces was that of the animal sculpture come to life. The illusion was achieved by forcing water through the stone or metal animal body so that it gushed through the maws, thus endowing the fountain with both movement and sound. Madīnat al-Zāhira had a fountain with a lion "whose mouth would seem to say something terrible, would it speak": the suggestion of growling must have been enhanced by the fact that lion shared its basin with croaking (presumably live) tortoises.[6] In Yūsuf Ibn Naghrīla's palace in Granada the lions also seemed to roar. The Munyat al-Naʿūra in Cordoba had a lion spout with jewelled eyes, and Madīnat al-Zahrā' had a faceted basin with animal figures spewing water on each side.[7] Perhaps the freestanding bronze stag (no. 500, Museo Arqueológico Provincial de Córdoba) excavated at the latter was attached to such a fountain (Fig. 115). In the mountains above Madīnat al-Zahrā', a large stone elephant fountain (in situ until recently) emitted water into a rectangular tank belonging to the irrigation system of an agricultural estate (Figs. 116 and 117). In taifa Toledo, al-Ma'mūn's garden palace had lion figures from which water "poured like pearls," and in one of al-Muʿtamid's palaces in Seville a silver elephant similarly spewed water into a large pool.[8] A poet in the court of Saragossa between approximately 1110 and 1118, when it was governed in the name of the Almoravids, described a lion fountain as "the lion of the firmament, from whose mouth the Milky Way is spouting."[9] The Ḥammādids of the Maghreb evidently acquired the same penchant for animal fountains, for sources describe crouching lions with golden bodies illuminated like fire by the sun, spewing liquid gold in the al-Manṣūrīya palace in Bougie; also mentioned are the remains of a cast bronze quadruped from Beni-Khalled, dated to the tenth century, and various relief sculptures of lions on basins and vessels from the Qalʿa Banī Ḥammād.[10] Poems written for the palaces of the Norman kings in Palermo attest to the presence of stone lion fountains there as

115. Bronze stag from Madīnat al-Zahrā᾿ (courtesy of the Museo Arqueológico de Córdoba)

well.[11] Such zoomorphic themes were common in the Islamic palaces throughout the western Mediterranean.

In Granada there is the fountain, discussed in Chapter 8, in the form of a large duodecogonal basin resting on twelve lions standing in the center of the Court of the Lions at the Alhambra (Fig. 118). In addition to these famous and well-studied beasts, there were two spouts in the form of seated lions in the hospital of the Albaicin quarter in Granada, now moved to the Torre de las Damas's basin in the Partal,[12] and there were two stone lions from the Casa de Moneda which was originally one of Muḥammad V's palaces in the Alixares quarter of Granada. A lion fountain that is half destroyed but with its inner water pipe still visible is today in the Convento San Francisco in the Alhambra. Additionally, Ibn al-Jayyāb described a basin fed by water channels and surrounded by lions spewing water into it, in a palace of Muḥammad III in the Najd quarter on the banks of the Genil River.[13] And, although for reasons already stated the *Bayāḍ wa Riyāḍ* manuscript must be used with caution, one of its paintings (see Color Plate 10) shows a garden pool with spouts in the shape of horses' heads.

The animal motif was common in the Umayyad palaces and was transmitted from Cordoba to the taifa kingdoms as a result of the diaspora of artisans, literati, and statesmen after the *fitna*. Sculptures of beasts such as lions, stags, and elephants appeared thereafter many times in both al-Andalus and the Maghreb as princely symbols referring to the hunt—a royal privilege—and to power and domination. And as we saw in the preceding chapter, they could also be references to specific mythic characters.

116. The elephant fountain near Cordoba

117. The elephant fountain and its pool

118. Lions fountain in the Court of the Lions

Poetry and Performances

Generally, artistic conceits such as the roaring lion were evident to the viewer, but in other cases poetry called attention to the illusion. For example, on the basin of the lion fountain were verses that described the basin as solid ice from which the water seemed to melt, and continued: "Yet it is impossible to say which of the two is really flowing. / Don't you see how the water from above flows on the surface, notwithstanding how the current underneath strives to oppose its progress?" (see Fig. 108). The poet then compared the overflowing water to a lover's tears and concluded:

> For truly, what else is this fountain but a beneficent cloud pouring out its abundant supplies over the lions underneath?
>
> Like the hands of the Caliph when he rises in the morning to distribute plentiful rewards among his soldiers the lions of war.[14]

Similarly, around the outer rim of the basin in the Lindaraja Garden, verses proclaimed the water to be like liquid pearls and the marble on which it fell like ice.[15]

The poetic devices of metaphor and simile were familiar to the well-educated audience that heard them, and the success of both the poetry and hydraulic tricks depended on the existence of an already primed audience educated in science and the arts. Indeed, the ingenuity of the fountains

was an entertaining offshoot of the more practical sciences of hydraulics, geometry, astronomy, and the engineering of machines such as clocks and waterwheels. The display of cleverness and wit on the part of the architects, engineers, and poets was predicated on the audience's ability to "read" it, and more than this, rested on the assumption of a shared cultural milieu that bound them together as a class and a culture. The king was the primary patron of this audience, admittance to which was controlled by him. The members, through events such as poetry contests and learned symposia, and through theatrical spectacles such as illusionistic waterworks, formed an elite circle in which they cooperated in making him the ultimate arbiter of taste.

The verses encircling the fountain in the Court of the Lions were extracted from a much longer *qaṣīda* by Ibn Zamrak.[16] The selection of a short excerpt in this manner suggested that the audience knew the entire poem, an assumption of common cultural formation similar to that implied by the geometrical symbolism in the ceiling of the Hall of the Ambassadors. Clearly both were intended for a select audience versed in the literary and scientific arts who could understand the significance of the quotations and metaphors. A necessary attribute for ministers of state, sovereigns, scholars, magistrates, and musicians—and for any man or woman who wished to make a mark in the Nasrid court—was skill in *adab,* which included exquisite literary eloquence. Therefore, the audience and the authors of the visual and verbal competitions staged at the Alhambra were usually one and the same. Such poetic inscriptions reflected an already shared appreciation for literature, but also demanded it. Thus, a standard of intellectual cultivation was established that, like the visual screening to distinguish private from public, defined social categories of those who were "in" and those who were "out."

In addition to being *au courant* with the latest in literature and art, the audience was united by a shared frame of reference to myth and history. They would have recognized the Solomonic references in the lion fountain at the Alhambra and other palaces, and would have seen that Ibn al-Khaṭīb's glass pavilion with cascading water in his recreation estate outside of Granada was a deliberate evocation of al-Ma'mūn's Toledo.[17] Through such references to the past, patrons could suggest continuities that served, for some, to legitimitize and aggrandize sovereign authority, and for others to suggest refinement and connoisseurship, necessary attributes in a society where political advancement was achieved through *adab.*

The question of historicism is an important one. On the one hand, the evocation of bygone grandeur through architectural imitation or literary revival linked the present with the past, associating contemporary figures with the glory of distinguished or heroic predecessors. On the other, the literary performances and works of art happening there and then in the royal palace, if good enough to capture the imagination of the court, would reprise again and again in the future. For example, the *qaṣīda*s recited by poets at festivals were a form of theater staged in present time; the mediocre attempts were immediately forgotten, but because the best works gained a popularity that ensured reiteration in subsequent performances, quotation by the learned, and possibly inscription on the sultan's palace walls, they achieved immortality. Many of the poems of the Alhambra were composed for oral performance and then given the honor of permanence on palace walls.[18] Thus, poetry could serve to mark a specific moment, such as the opening of a new hall in the palace,

and to immortalize a specific monarch, as well as to provide a collective reference to all such celebrations presided over by the monarch or his descendants.[19]

The Garden as "Paradise on Earth"

Like the sculptural, architectural, and literary allusions, the symbolism of gardens worked because it was recognized by its audience. The symbolism in courtyard gardens, as I have already explained, used artifice to make constant reference to nature, so that a trickling fountain evoked a spring and a carefully tended bed suggested the cultivated landscape of fields and orchards. In this way the garden became a metaphor for an entire landscape transformed by human enterprise and skill. The fundamental elements of agriculture were taken up by the garden, where they became carefully orchestrated compositions of form, color, texture, and light, the structure of the cultivated landscape reduced to its simplest, purest forms. Thus the simple divisioning of the land into regular plots became the formal four-part plan; irrigation canals and wells were elaborated into ornamental channels and gushing fountains; and reservoirs for water storage became large pools.[20] The function was the same, whether in the farm or the ornamental garden, but the latter was charged with greater (or more self-conscious) meaning. Water, in particular, appeared in the garden in lavish displays, since the fountains and pools were supplied in quantities exceeding the normal demands of irrigation. The abundance of vibrantly colorful and sweetly scented plants juxtaposed in gardens and utterly dependent upon irrigation signified the luxury of having more than enough to satisfy one's basic needs. Finally, the role of the garden occupant was transformed from one requiring active participation and hard work into one offering contemplation and pleasure.

Of course these gardens, while making reference to the bounty of the earth, also suggested paradise in the sense of an ideal space that is completely fertile, comfortable, beautiful, and endless. In a good garden, the natural occurrence of weeds, drought, insect infestation, and damaging bacteria, viruses, and fungi are discouraged by attentive cultivation and by rooting out the offenders and replacing them with healthier specimens. But the fact that in nature, green plants will eventually turn brown and die is denied in the garden. Its purpose is to present nature not in its coarse reality but as an ideal in which plants are always growing or at their peak, and in which life triumphs over death. In this sense, then, all of the gardens discussed in this book are paradisiac. This is not to say, however, that all of these gardens were intended to evoke the eternal paradise described in the Qur'ān as the reward of the believers. It is difficult to know the intentions and interpretations of medieval viewers of the Andalusian palace gardens, but a careful look at the words that they used to describe them indicates that, at least in the first few centuries, Qur'ānic references are absent.

In Cordoba through the tenth century, I have found no explicit conceptual link between the gardens of the *munya*s of Cordoba and the Qur'ānic concept of paradise as a garden of shade-giving trees and flowing rivers. Rather, palace gardens were sensual places of worldly pleasure and arenas for political ceremonial. Underscoring this is a story related by al-Khaṭīb al-Baghdādī: when a vis-

iting Byzantine dignitary criticized Caliph al-Manṣūr's Baghdad for its lack of gardens, he replied, "We were not created for frivolity and play."[21] The narrative was clearly a post facto invention to explain the move from Baghdad to the suburban palaces, but it demonstrates unequivocably that gardens were not associated with piety and serious endeavors.

The courtyard of the Mosque of Cordoba had been planted with trees since the ninth century.[22] But whether the insertion of vegetation into that religious context was intended to connote paradise is cast in doubt by the fact that jurists argued about the permissibility of allowing trees to adorn a mosque courtyard.[23] More probably, the rows of trees kept the dust from rising from the courtyard's unpaved floor and provided cooling shade during the long hot summer. It is not until the early eleventh century at the Ḥayr al-Zajjāli that the wordly celebration of life met the pious commemoration in death and the hope for eternity. The shift occured in a *waqf*-endowed mausoleum garden when the theme of the soul's attainment of paradise was added to the already fixed garden typology. Having thus been introduced, the paradisiac theme began to appear in nonfunerary contexts such as the Munyat al-Naʿūra in taifa Toledo, about whose garden Ibn Khāqān wrote: "Oh what a landscape! When you behold its beauty it recalls the beauty of eternal Paradise (*jannat al-khuld*)."[24] But even here, paradise is invoked only as a standard of beauty; nothing indicates that the garden was intended to *re-create* the ultimate paradise.

Too little is known about the garden context of tenth- and eleventh-century Muslim tombs to make broad conclusions about their symbolism and meaning. In al-Andalus, the only archaeologically retrieved tomb is that of the Nasrid dynasty in the Alhambra; outside the walls of the Court of the Lions, the excavators unearthed numerous graves and the foundations of a two-chambered structure, one half of which consisted of a cupola on piers (Fig. 119).[25] Planting, inscriptions, and architectural decoration are not known. In any case, this cemetery dates to the thirteenth and fourteenth centuries, by which point the tomb garden in the rest of the Islamic world was well beyond its formative phase. One can speculate that the theme of the afterlife was incorporated into garden iconography when the garden, which was part of the vocabulary of palace architecture, merged

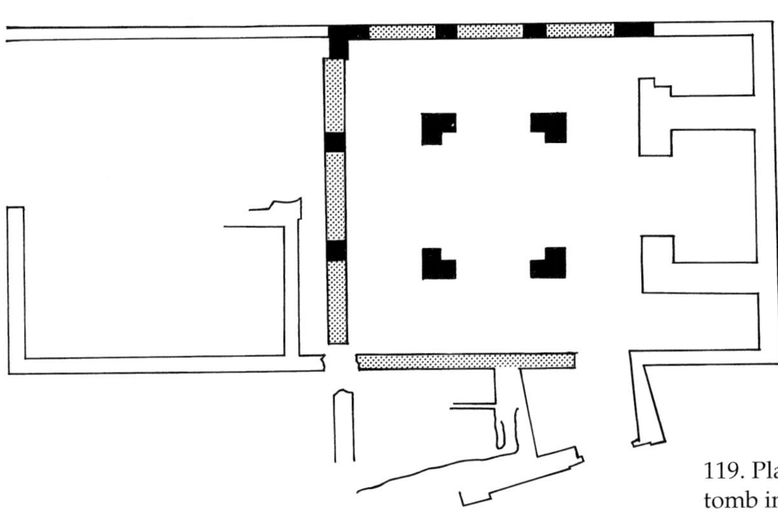

119. Plan of the royal cemetery and tomb in the Alhambra

with the vocabulary of the tomb complex.[26] The precise point of intersection—the tomb—was in its turn also a merger of distinctly separate architectural ideas, for as the eternal resting place of the patron the tomb combined the Islamic concept of eternity with the secular and practical notion of dwelling.

The question of paradise symbolism in gardens is complicated by the fact that the Arabic word for paradise, *janna* (pl. *jinān*), has the additional meaning of "garden." In some usages the double meaning presents no conflict, as when cities were equated with paradise (*janna*) and al-Andalus as a whole was said to be a paradise on earth.[27] However, there are many occasions when *janna* was used only in the sense of "garden" and did not attribute a paradisiac dimension to the gardens described. For example, when the geographer Idrīsī noted that Toledo was surrounded by *jinān* and *basātīn* (gardens), he was describing features of the physical landscape; and when the biographer of the agronomist Ibn Wāfid recorded that he tended al-Maʾmūn's *janna* in Toledo, he was referring to an experimental field garden.[28] When Ibn Saʿīd described al-Ruṣāfa as having "an expanse of spacious gardens [*jinān*]," his emphasis was clearly the achievements of the earthly patron and not paradises created by God.[29] It is telling that, when equating Toledo's eleventh-century Munyat al-Naʿūra with paradise (*janna*), this same poet added the adjective "eternal" (*khuld*) so as to distinguish between the garden as a generic and earthly entity and the specific garden of eternal paradise. Similarly, al-Shaqundī, in praising Almeria, quoted an anonymous poet as saying, "It is a land where if you walk the stones are as pearls, the dust as musk, and the gardens [*al-riyāḍ*] paradises [*janān*]."[30] Clearly the narrators did not unilaterally conflate gardens with paradise, although nonetheless *some* gardens could be described in both earthly and paradisiac terms.

The problem with attributing a paradisiac meaning to all Islamic gardens, whether palatine or funerary, early or late, Mediterranean or eastern, is compounded by the fact that a great many of the surviving gardens are indeed explicitly paradisiac. Historically, the most impressive extant Islamic gardens were those built by the Mughals, many of them for funerary contexts where an eschatological and pious theme was certainly present. The gardens surrounding the mausoleum evoked those of fruit trees, shade, and cooling waters that the deceased's soul was supposedly to enjoy in his or her afterlife. In many tomb gardens, the link between earthly and heavenly gardens was explicitly stated; for example, over the entrance to Akbar's tomb (Sikandra, 1613), there is the inscription: "These are the Gardens of Eden: enter them to dwell therein eternally."[31] The Tāj Mahal (Agra, begun 1631) is replete with inscriptions referring to the Day of Judgment and paradise. The cenotaph of its patron, Shāh Jihān, calls him *firdaus āshyānī* (Dweller in Paradise) and its many Qurʾānic inscriptions refer to paradise, such as:

> "But O thou soul at peace,
> "Return thou unto thy Lord, well-pleased, and well-pleasing unto Him.
> "Enter thou among my servants,
> "And enter thou My Paradise."
> (89:27–30)[32]

But just because the theme of paradise prevailed in Mughal mausoleum gardens of the seventeenth century, can we assume that it was present in earlier gardens? The paradisiac theme does not

seem to have developed until the very end of the reign of Bābur, who, when he sought retreat from his life as military commander and king in the third decade of the sixteenth century, retired to a garden called the Bāgh-i Zar Afshan.[33] However, because the history of Islamic gardens was written to explain such monuments as Humāyūn's Tomb and the Tāj Mahal and other nonfunerary gardens of the same period in Iran and Central Asia, and was, moreover, written before the gardens of Madīnat al-Zahrā᾿ and Syrian Ruṣāfa were known, the iconography of these relatively late gardens has been taken as universally applicable to all Islamic gardens. In short, an iconography of *the* Islamic garden was drafted on the basis of a limited set of monuments and one immutable text—the Qur᾿ān—instead of more historically contextualized iconographies of different Islamic gardens nuanced by such factors as region, patron's class, function (palatine or funerary), and political ideology.

Linguistically, because the study of Islamic art is the child of archaeology and "oriental" languages, it reflects philological practices of the nineteenth century. Philologists and historians have tended to view Islamic culture from the standpoint of its texts, giving special privilege to the Qur᾿ān, as the text that marked the birth of the religion and led to the standardization of Arabic as a written language. Indeed, Islamic art is highly textual in character, for meaning is often conveyed through textual inscriptions rather than through pictorial representations. Even in inscriptions having a limited repertoire, such as the Qur᾿ānic excerpts placed around the mihrab in a mosque, the selection chosen for quotation (in full or simply as an abbreviated reference) can convey considerable meaning of both a religious and a political nature. This privileging of the textual over the visual has affected our reading of garden symbolism by encouraging historians erroneously to use the Qur᾿ānic description of paradise to explain earthly gardens.

The philologist notes that the Persian and Arabic words for "paradise"—*firdaus* and *janna*—are synonymous with "garden," and that paradise and garden are therefore inseparable concepts. And furthermore, because the Qur᾿ān describes paradise as a garden, the relevant passages in that text must be the key to the meaning of real gardens. The Qur᾿ān describes the afterlife of the faithful as follows:

> Announce to those who have done good deeds, glad tidings of gardens (*janna*) under which rivers flow, and where, when they eat the fruits that grow, they will say,: "Indeed they are the same as we were given before." (2:25)

And:

> The semblance of Paradise promised the pious and devout (is that of a garden) with streams of water that will not go rank, and rivers of milk whose taste will not undergo a change, and rivers of wine delectable to drinkers, and streams of purified honey, and fruits of every kind in them, and forgiveness of their Lord. (47:15)[34]

Because the Qur᾿ānic paradise is a garden with four rivers, implying a cross-axial plan, countless authors have assumed that all quadripartite gardens must therefore be direct reflections or anticipations of this heavenly paradise.[35] Yet the conclusion that the Qur᾿ān supplied the blueprint

for Islamic gardens is methodologically fallacious. That text provided neither the concept nor the layout of Islamic gardens, for shade-giving trees, water, and four-part divisioning existed prior to Islam; and the very image of paradise as a garden owes much to preexisting Jewish and Christian conceptions of Eden and heaven.

My study of Andalusian gardens has yielded no evidence for an explicit association between the humanly constructed palatine garden and heavenly paradise in the eighth through tenth centuries. To the contrary, gardens belonged to the world of luxury and personal vainglory that was, on more than one occasion, castigated as the work of the devil.[36] Whereas the foundation of a mosque for the worship of God was an act of piety, the creation of a garden was not. And while Cordoban mosques had courtyards, they were little more than enclosed spaces with ablution fountains and possibly some trees. On the other hand the landscapes and gardens lauded by the poets and geographers were lush, fragrant, sensuous places that had the power to evoke other desirable locations in the imagination. They were also irrigated and productive places for picking delicious fruit and enjoying the simple loveliness of nature.[37] In this sense their meaning was certainly Qur'ānic, because that text says that the world and all its beauty is of God's making:

> It is He who grew the gardens [*janna*], trellised and bowered, and palm trees and land sown with corn and many other seeds, and olives, and pomegranates, alike and yet unalike. So eat of their fruit when they are in fruit, and give on the day of harvesting His due, and do not be extravagant, for God does not love those who are prodigal. (6:141)[38]

And elsewhere, on the subject of agriculture:

> It is He who sends down water from the skies, and brings out of it every thing that grows, the green foliage, the grain lying close, the date palm trees with clusters of dates, and the gardens [*janna*] of grapes, and of olives and pomegranates, so similar yet so unlike.
> Look at the fruits, how they appear on the trees, and how they ripen.
> In all these are signs for those who believe. (6:99).[39]

These and the passage on the creation of the heavens and the earth, quoted at the beginning of this chapter, talk of the earth not as a reflection of the paradise to come but as a thriving natural environment given life by God and given to humankind. The use of the word *janna* in these passages is illuminating because, whereas in the selections quoted earlier *janna* clearly meant "paradise," here it is used to refer to a productive earthly garden stocked with familiar flowers and fruit from the domestic landscape of which God is the steward. The Qur'ān states that all landscape, gardens, architecture—in short all the materials of this earth—are the realm of God; but they are not necessarily the realm of the afterlife. If the Qur'ān itself distinguishes between the garden that is paradise and gardens that are simply gardens, so must historians.

Like the rest of the built environment, gardens ought to be studied within specific historical and geographical frameworks. Yet, the same historians who are meticulous in differentiating between the various political and regional contexts of architecture too often mistakenly try to

interpret all Islamic gardens on the basis of seventeenth-century exemplars. Moreover, the emphasis on the Qurʾānic description of paradise as a garden has served to collapse all of Islamic culture into a monolithic and unchanging entity, the primary character of which is religious. It assumes that the Muslim religion as it is practiced is ahistorical, whereas the existence of multiple schools of Islamic law and a vast literature of *ḥadīth* (sayings of the Prophet) and *tafsīr* (Qur'ān commentary) indicates that there was considerable room for disagreement in the reading of primary religious texts, and that the interpretation was shaped by contemporary social and political conditions such as sectarianism and regional practices. The earliest Islamic gardens were likewise the product of local practice and owed much to late Roman (including Byzantine) and Mesopotamian (Achaemenid and Sasanian) forerunners. Gardens with axial plans and fountains existed long before Islam, and thus in neither their form nor their symbolism could they have been drawn from a Qurʾānic archetype. Islamic societies attached the idea of a Qurʾānic paradise to living gardens after the typology of the garden was already formalized. In this sense, the tomb garden of al-Zajjālī in Cordoba is a fitting example for our study, since, there too, the paradisiac and eschatological meaning was added to an already built, fully functional garden.

It is difficult to pinpoint the precise moment when the paradisiac inflection was introduced, and indeed I suspect that the merger occurred not due to a single patron's innovation—the Zajjālī tomb was hardly a major monument—but as a result of a proliferation of mausoleum building throughout Muslim lands. Tombs were preferably open walled and often surrounded by open spaces to accommodate visitors wishing to pray, lament, or absorb *baraka* (blessing) through proximity to the deceased. When the surrounding space was gardened, visitors naturally understood it within the tomb's eschatological theme as a reference to paradise. No doubt builders surrounded tombs with gardens with that specific symbolism in mind; but the vocabulary of plants, water, and axes defined by channels or walkways that they employed had been developed earlier in a very different context for the display of political power and the positioning of the sovereign in the physical and social space of the palace, landscape, and kingdom.

Two important things happened with the proliferation of tombs, tomb gardens, and their paradisiac symbolism. First, all gardens whether in cemeteries or palaces eventually acquired the potential meaning of "paradise on earth." Second, the theme of paradise-on-earth was carried with the tomb into other buildings to which tombs were attached, such as mosques. (I am distinguishing here between references to paradise in mosques and in commemorative monuments such as the Dome of the Rock in Jerusalem and the Great Mosque of Damascus where gardens were represented as vegetal motifs rendered in mosaic, ceramic, and painted decorations, and the actual installation of gardens as architectural spaces.) Hence, at the Alhambra, at the Generalife, and in Granada's Nasrid madrasa we find places for prayer with windows next to or flanking the mihrab itself, inviting the worshipper to avert his or her eyes from the *qibla* (the direction of Mecca) and the *dār al-baqāʾ* (the hereafter) in order to contemplate the sunlight, singing birds, and fertile landscape of the here-and-now, or *dār al-fanāʾ*. The appearance of these mirador-mosques in the fourteenth century suggests that, by then, the concepts of paradise-as-a-garden and the-garden-as-paradise had been thoroughly integrated.

Conclusion

Just as the forms, techniques, and symbolism of architecture were subject to change, the form and symbolism of gardens developed and changed from one historical period to another and from one geographical region to another. In this study I have examined six centuries of gardens built for palaces or recreation estates in Muslim-ruled al-Andalus, where gardens not only were important architectural elements but where entire palaces were designed to dominate and thus respond to the greater landscape context. Considered individually, these garden-palaces can reveal only a limited amount about the development of the landscape and the garden as an architectural response to that development. But as a collective body, even brief nuggets of information such as is available for al-Ruṣāfa and the minimal remnants of foundations at the Castillejo of Monteagudo contribute to a fuller understanding of how the Andalusian landscape was regarded and valued.

I have suggested that the aesthetic valuation in the formative period of Hispano-Islamic gardens was the measurement of the conceptual distance between the land as a "pure" physical entity and its transformation into a cultivated landscape. This aesthetic measure was inextricably bound to the conviction that Muslim rule was just and divinely sanctioned—hence the immense productivity of al-Andalus. Because the successful florescence of the kingdom was interpreted in a way that supported the institutions of power, particularly the emirate and caliphate of the Umayyads, landscape cultivation and gardens were used by those and all subsequent rulers to express the legitimacy of their rule. Among other attributes of sovereignty, such as the minting of coins, the manufacturing of arms, and the bestowal of *ṭirāz* and robes of honor as a sign of favor, the garden was a necessary adjunct to the audience hall, for as the king sat in state in his hall, he looked from it to his kingdom—literally, the surrounding landscape—the latter thus providing the perimeter in relation to which he was defined as the center.

In these Andalusian gardens, the political meaning reverberated more loudly than the religious. In its formative period, garden iconography appears to have been primarily agricultural and economic, having more to do with the celebration of earthly success than with the hope for eternal bliss. Any paradisiac meaning in the early centuries referred to ideals of nature and humankind's place on earth. Specific Qur'ānic symbolism of the garden as an earthly anticipation of the ultimate reward of the believers was not attached to the garden until, as settings for tombs, gardens were associated with death and thus the afterlife. Subsequently, some of the formal vocabulary of the garden—notably the mirador—was introduced with the tomb into other building types. Without wishing to create an artificial distinction between religious and secular architecture (for surely tombs were both), we can propose that the result was that forms developed for the palatine ("secular") context were transferred to the spiritual context. This parallels the transfer of other architectural elements such as the dome and salient tower from palatine and defensive architecture to the mosque, as analyzed in studies by Oleg Grabar and Christian Ewert.[40]

The miradors and gardens of the Alhambra exemplify the shift from a symbolism derived from the agricultural landscape to the symbolism of the Qur'ānic paradise, and from the worldly to the spiritual. By the time the Alhambra reached its Nasrid zenith in the fourteenth century, the lands

of Islamic Spain were seriously threatened by the encroaching Christian kingdoms. As the size of Muslim-ruled al-Andalus shrank and confidence in Muslim rule began to wane, the patrons of architecture clung to the forms and motifs of the Umayyad period, regarded as a golden age of Muslim ascendance on the Iberian Peninsula. The repertoire of architectural forms did not change significantly, but the meanings and the perceptions of them did. The most striking example of this is the mirador, which changed from a signifier referring to the active relationship of the powerful, sovereign viewer to his territory of gardens and endless vistas, to a signifier referring to the memory of that relationship (Color Plate 12).

The confident expansionism of the Umayyads constitutes the formative period of Hispano-Islamic architectural and landscape typology, when form and meaning evolved in tandem. But while the Umayyad forms were elaborated in taifa palaces of the eleventh century, the circumstances that had produced them were slowly disintegrating. The kingdom slowly lost its ideological force, as witnessed in the nostalgic poetry, and survived as an appendage to first the Almoravid and then the Almohad conquerors from Morocco. By the time of the Nasrids, its domestic politics were volatile, and its diplomatic relationships were cautious. Although some new artistic forms were introduced—most notably the muqarnas and the lambrequin arch—these were admixtures to the aesthetic vocabulary which had been developed earlier in the course of constructing the Mosque of Cordoba and the garden-palaces of the Umayyads. Thus, the Alhambra, which is the largest, best-preserved, and most impressive surviving monument of Islamic Spain, pays homage in almost every aspect to its ancestor, Madīnat al-Zahrāʾ. Despite the many differences that set the palaces of al-Andalus off from one another, they shared a mythic concept of the sovereign as creator and steward of the land, expressed in the visual continuities that united architecture with garden.

NOTES

Introduction

1. Marçais, "Les jardins de l'Islam," in *Mélanges d'histoire et d'archéologie de l'occident musulman,* 2 vols. (Algiers, 1957), I: 233–44.

2. Dickie, "The Islamic Garden in Spain," in *The Islamic Garden,* ed. E. B. MacDougall and R. Ettinghausen (Washington, D.C., 1976), 89–105, and "The Hispano-Arab Garden: Notes Toward a Typology," in *The Legacy of Muslim Spain,* ed. Salma K. Jayusi (Leiden, 1992), 1016–35.

3. Torres Balbás, "Patios de crucero," *Al-Andalus* 23 (1958), 171–92; his chronology has been revised by D. F. Ruggles, "Il giardini con pianta a croce nel Mediterraneo islamico," in *Il giardino islamico: Architettura, natura, paesaggio,* ed. Attilio Petruccioli (Milan, 1993), 143–54.

4. For a historiography of the site excavations, see Antonio Vallejo Triano, "Madīnat al-Zahrā', pasado, presente y futuro," in *II Congreso de Arqueología Medieval Española* (Madrid, 1987), I: 205–18; Klaus Brisch, "Madīnat al-Zahrā' in der modernen archäologischen Literatur Spaniens," *Kunst des Orients* 4 (1963), 3–41; and D. F. Ruggles, "Historiography and the Rediscovery of Madīnat al-Zahrā'," *Islamic Studies* 30 (1991), 129–40.

5. Hernández Giménez, *Madīnat al-Zahrā': Arquitectura y decoración* (Granada, 1985). The prologue, by Antonio Fernández-Puertas, is immensely useful in making sense of the text.

6. See Lucie Bolens, *Agronomes andalous du Moyen-Age* (Geneva and Paris, 1981); S. M. Imamuddin, "Al-Filāḥah (Farming) in Muslim Spain," *Islamic Studies* 1 (1962), 51–89; Joaquín Vallvé, "La agricultura en al-Andalus," *Al-Qanṭara* 3 (1982), 261–97; and Andrew Watson, *Agricultural Innovation in the Early Islamic World: The Diffusion of Crops and Farming Techniques, 700–1100* (Cambridge, 1983).

7. A-Maqqarī, *Analectes sur l'histoire et la littérature des Arabes d'Espagne,* [*Nafḥ al-ṭīb*], ed. R. Dozy et al., 2 vols. in 3 (Leiden, 1855–61; London, 1967). Ibn ʿIdhārī, *Histoire de l'Afrique du Nord et de l'Espagne musulmane intitulée Kitab al-Bayan al-mughrib,* ed. Lévi-Provençal and G. S. Colin, vols. I and II (Leiden, 1948–51) (cited hereafter as *Al-Bayān,* I and II); for translation, see Ibn ʿIdhārī, *Histoire de l'Afrique et de l'Espagne intitulée al-Bayano l'Mogrib,* trans E. Fagnan, 2 vols. (Algiers, 1901–4); volume III of Ibn ʿIdhārī's Arabic text was published separately as *Al-Bayan al-mughrib, Histoire de l'Espagne musulmane au XIe siècle,* ed. E. Lévi-Provençal (Paris, 1930) (cited hereafter as *Al-Bayān,* III.).

8. Al-Rāzī, *Anales palatinos del califa de Córdoba al-Ḥakam II por ʿĪsā Ibn Aḥmad al-Rāzī (360–364 H./971–975 J.C.),* trans. E. García Gómez (Madrid, 1967); Anon., *Una crónica anónima de ʿAbd al-Raḥmān III al-Nāṣir,* ed. and trans. E. Lévi-Provençal and E. García Gómez (Madrid and Granada, 1950); Ibn Ḥayyān, *Al-Muqtabis* (see Bibliography).

9. See, for example, the memoirs written by the Zirid king himself: ʿAbd Allāh al-Zīrī, *Mudhakkirāt al-amīr ʿAbd Allāh, al-musammāt bi-kitāb al-Tibyān,* ed. Lévi-Provençal (Cairo, c. 1955); *The Tibyān,* trans. and annotated by Amin T. Tibi (Leiden, 1986).

10. Andres Navagero [Andrea Navaggiero], *Viaje por España (1524–1526),* trans. Antonio M. Fabie (Madrid, 1983); Antoine de Lalaing's account in M. Gachard, ed., *Collection des voyages des souverains des Pays-Bas* (1876); Jerónimo Münzer, *Viaje por Espãna y Portugal (1494–1495)* (Madrid, 1991).

11. F. Bargebuhr, *The Alhambra: A Cycle of Studies on the Eleventh Century in Moorish Spain* (Berlin, 1968).

12. Shack, *Poesie und Kunst der Araber in Spanien und Sizilien,* 3 vols. (Berlin, 1865).

13. Pérès, *La poésie andalouse,* 2d ed. rev. (Paris, 1953).

14. María Jesús Rubiera Mata, *La arquitectura en la literatura árabe* (Madrid, 1981); 2d ed. (1988).

15. Biblioteca Apostolica Vaticana, Rome, Vat. Ar. 368; reproduced in Alois Nykl, *Historia de los amores de Bayād y Riyād* (New York, 1941).

16. Renata Holod, "Luxury Arts of the Caliphal Period," in *Al-Andalus: The Art of Islamic Spain* (New York, 1992), 41–47; and 190–201, entries 1–4.

17. See, for example, the works of Laura Mulvey, *Visual and Other Pleasures* (Bloomington, 1989); Kaja

Silverman, "Fassbinder and Lacan: A Reconsideration of the Gaze, Look, and Image," *camera obscura*, no. 19 (1989), 55–89; Louis Marin, *Portrait of the King* (Minneapolis, 1988); John Tagg, *The Burden of Representation: Essays on Photographies and Histories* (Amherst, 1988); and Nicholas Green and Frank Mort, "Visual Representation and Cultural Politics," *Block* 7 (1982), 59–68.

1. History and Landscape

1. Ramón Menéndez Pidal, ed., *Historia de España*, 4 vols. (Madrid, 1940), III:xvii; Joseph F. O'Callaghan, *A History of Medieval Spain* (Ithaca, 1975), 70–71.

2. José Orlandis, *Historia del Reino Visigodo Español* (Madrid, 1988), 279. For an analysis of the way that twentieth-century scholars have weighed the Roman and Visigothic contributions to history, see Jerrilynn D. Dodds, *Architecture and Ideology in Early Medieval Spain* (University Park, 1990), 9–11.

3. Orlandis, *Historia*, 261.

4. The largest villas were to be found in the fertile Duero Valley to the north, which was more heavily Visigothic than Baetica, the southern portion of the peninsula, which had smaller estates of no more than two thousand hectares (Orlandis, *Historia*, 259–60).

5. Orlandis, *Historia*, 126–30.

6. The name al-Andalus appeared as early as 98/716–17 in a bilingual coin struck in Cordoba. For discussion of the etymology of this name, see Heinz Halm, "Al-Andalus and Gothica Sors," *Der Islam* 66 (1989), 252–63, and "L'Origine du nom *Al-Andalus*," in *Proceedings of the Fourteenth Congress of the Union Européenne des Arabisants et Islamisants*, II, ed. A. Fodor (Budapest Studies in Arabic, 15–16), 49–55. My thanks to Jonathan Bloom for these references.

7. Thomas Glick and others doubt the historical authenticity of the accounts of the conquest of al-Andalus. See Glick, *Islamic and Christian Spain in the Early Middle Ages* (Princeton, 1979), 31–33.

8. *Mozarabic Chronicle of 754*, in Kenneth B. Wolf, *Conquerors and Chroniclers of Early Medieval Spain* (Liverpoool, 1990), 132.

9. John Boswell, *The Royal Treasure: Muslim Communities Under the Crown of Aragon in the Fourteenth Century* (New Haven, 1977), 1–3. On the other hand, John Williams points to the lack of surviving Visigothic artifacts in the south as evidence of destruction by the invading Muslims ("Orientations: Christian Spain and the Art of Its Neighbors," in *The Art of Medieval Spain*, [New York, 1993], 12–25).

10. Glick, *Islamic and Christian Spain*, 31–33.

11. Gabrieli, "Omayyades d'Espagne et abbasides," *Studia Islamica* 31 (1970), 93–100.

12. Vallvé, "Agricultura," 268–72.

13. Claudio Sánchez-Albornoz, "Pequeños propietarios libres in el reino astur-leonés. Su realidad histórica," in Sánchez-Albornoz, *Investigaciones y documentos sobre las instituciones hispanas* (Santiago, 1970), 178; Glick, *Islamic and Christian Spain*, 146–53.

14. Jaime Vicens Vives, *An Economic History of Spain* (1969), 107. See also Ibn ʿAbdūn's *ḥisba* manual regarding the projected estimation of harvest yields (Lévi-Provençal, *Séville musulmane au début du XIIe siècle: Le traité d'Ibn ʿAbdūn* [Paris, 1947], 10; and *Trois traités hispaniques de ḥisba* [Cairo, 1955], 5–6).

15. In dry farming areas (*muzāraʿa*) the landlord and tenant farmer contributed equal portions of seed, the farmer did the actual cultivating and reaping, and the two divided the harvest. In irrigated lands (*musāqā*), the farmer only received one-third of the crop; and in orchard land (*mughārasa*), the percentage of crop received by each varied. There were often clauses protecting the farmer in the event of drought, flood, plague, or war (Vallvé, "Agricultura" 295–96; these Arabic terms are supplied by Vallvé). On the subject of agricultural catastrophes (*jāʾiḥa*), Lévi-Provençal relates a legal case in which the plaintiff's fields suffered from a plague of parasites following the rains; the presence of Muslim and Christian armies, which hindered irrigation; and a band of ravenous rabbits. The experts who were consulted on the matter decided that the farmer should be allowed an abatement in taxes of one-quarter to one-third of the amount he would normally have paid (*Histoire de l'Espagne musulmane* (Paris, 1950–53), III:269–70).

16. Pedro Chalmeta, "Un formulaire notarial hispano-arabe du IV/Xe siècle: Glanes économiques," *Revista del Instituto Egipcio de Estudios Islámicos en Madrid* 23 (1985–86), 181–202. Also S. M. Imamuddin, *The Economic History of Spain* (Dacca, 1963), 48.

17. Taxation was similarly regulated. Ibn ʿAbdūn noted that professional estimators determined the amount of tax to be paid on the basis of preharvest calculations. In the case of olive cultivation, he maintained that the actual tax should be 25 percent less than the estimators' assessment in order to allow for the possibility of calamitous weather or an

onslaught of disease. Additionally, the tax should be based on the amount of oil pressed, not on the actual olive harvest, and "in the case of cereals, the harvest should not be counted until the sheaves of wheat are gathered in ricks, and after the deduction of the declared rise in prices at the time of the harvest. This was the procedure of the people of Cordoba—may God protect them." (Lévi-Provençal, *Séville musulmane,* 10; and *Trois traités,* 5–6.)

18. Chalmeta, "Un formulaire notarial," 198–99.

19. Georges Duby, *Rural Economy and Country Life in the Medieval West* (Columbia, 1968), 22–27.

20. James Ruffner and Frank Bair, eds., *The Weather Almanac,* 4th ed. (Detroit, 1984), 332.

21. Ibn ʿIdhārī, *al-Bayān,* years 302/915, 310/922, and 311/923; French trans. Fagnan, *Histoire de l'Afrique,* II:276, 301–4.

22. Ibn Ḥayyān, (*Muqtabis* v), *Crónica del califa ʿAbdarraḥmān III an-Nāṣir entre los años 912 y 942,* Spanish trans. M. J. Viguera and F. Corriente (Saragossa, 1981), 132; see also 142 for the campaign against the rebel outpost of Bobastro.

23. Ibn Ḥayyān, *Crónica* (v), 69.

24. Ibn Ḥayyān, *Crónica* (v), 253–54.

25. For an example of an agricultural estate, see Oleg Grabar et al., *City in the Desert: Qasr al-Hayr East* (Cambridge, 1978). Regarding the historical transformation of a Middle Eastern landscape, see Georges Tchalenko, *Villages antiques de la Syrie du nord,* 3 vols. (Paris, 1953), and A. Reifenberg, *The Struggle Between the Desert and the Sown: The Rise and Fall of Agriculture in the Levant* (Jerusalem, 1955).

26. The distinction between inhabited and uninhabited land was noted by Ibn Ḥawqal, Ibn al-Faqīh al-Hamadhānī, Ibn Baṣṣāl, and Ibn Luyūn. The demarcation between the two, however, changed in the eleventh century when uncultivated land was no longer viewed as barren and useless but rather as a blank screen awaiting the signature of agricultural development. (Ibn Ḥawqal, *Biblioteca Geographorum Arabicorum* [*Kitāb Ṣūrat al-arḍ*], vol. II, 3d ed., ed. J. H. Kramers [Leiden, 1967]; *Configuration de la Terre,* French trans. J. H. Kramers and G. Wiet, 2 vols. [Paris, 1964], I:107; Ibn al-Faqīh al-Hamadhānī, *Description du Maghreb et de l'Europe au IIIe/IXe siècle,* ed. and French trans. M. Hadj-Sadok [Algiers, 1949], 52; Ibn Baṣṣāl, *Kitāb al-Filāḥa, Libro de Agricultura,* ed. and Spanish trans. J. M. Millás Vallicrosa and M. Aziman [Tetouan, 1955], 64; Ibn Luyūn, *Ibn Luyūn: Tratado de Agricultura,* Spanish trans. Joaquina Eguaras Ibáñez [Granada, 1975], 37.) See also André Miquel, *La géographie humaine du monde musulmane jusqu'au milieu de XIe siècle,* 5 vols. (Paris, 1967–88), esp. vol. I, 8, and vol. III, 1.

27. Al-Maqqarī, *Analectes,* I:126; loosely trans. in Pascual de Gayangos, *The History of the Mohammedan Dynasties in Spain,* 2 vols. (London, 1840–43), I:84–85.

28. The creation of Islam as a cultural and political body has been treated by, among others, Oleg Grabar, *The Formation of Islamic Art* (rev. ed., New Haven, 1987); Fred M. Donner, *The Early Islamic Conquests* (Princeton, 1981); and Michael Morony, *Iraq After the Muslim Conquest* (Princeton, 1984).

29. There is no consensus regarding the possibility of climatic change in the western Mediterranean. See Brent Shaw, "Climate, Environment, and History: The Case of Roman North Africa," in *Climate and History,* T. Wigley, M. Ingram, and G. Farmer, eds., (Cambridge, 1981), 379–403.

30. In addition to Grabar, Morony, and Donner, already cited, see Marshall Hodgson, *The Venture of Islam,* 3 vols. (Chicago, 1974).

31. Juan Zozaya, "Fortifications in Al-Andalus," in *Al-Andalus: The Art of Islamic Spain,* 63–73; Lévi-Provençal, *Hist. Esp. Mus.* III:59–66; and *Inscriptions arabes d'Espagne* (Paris and Leiden, 1931), I:134, 47.

32. Vallvé, *La división territorial de la España musulmana* (Madrid, 1986), 252.

33. The disposition of agricultural zones in concentric rings around the city in which both the value of the land and the value of the goods produced there diminish according to the distance from the center conforms to an economic model of agrarian production posited by Johann H. von Thünen, *Der isolirte Staat in Beziehung auf Landwirthschaft und Nationalökonomie* (Hamburg, 1826); 2d ed. French trans. Jules Laverrière, *Recherches sur l'influence que le prix des grains . . .,* (Paris, 1851). I am grateful to Professor Robert Hunt for drawing this text to my attention.

Although predating it, von Thünen's model reminds us of Walter Cristaller's *Central Places in Southern Germany* (Englewood Cliffs, 1966) which places economic activity within a spatial frame whose center is the urban marketplace.

34. Thomas Malthus, *An Essay on the Principle of Population,* expanded 2d ed. (London, 1803). More recent work on the Malthusian model of population growth was published by the Club of Rome, Donella H. Meadows, ed., *Limits to Growth,* 2d ed. (New York, 1974).

35. Ester Boserup, *The Conditions of Agricultural*

Growth: The Economics of Agrarian Change Under Population Pressure (Chicago, 1965).

36. Ibn ʿIdhārī wrote that Cordoba's population swelled during al-Manṣūr's rule due to Berber immigration (*Histoire de l'Afrique du nord* [*al-Bayān*], ɪɪ:287–88; *Histoire de l'Afrique et de l'Espagne,* ɪɪ:478–79). Leopoldo Torres Balbás calculated that, based on mosque amplifications, the number of Muslim males in Cordoba grew from almost 5,000 in the last quarter of the eighth century to more than 24,500 in the last quarter of the tenth ("Ampliación y tamaño de las mezquitas," *Al-Andalus* 21 [1956], 339–52). Elsewhere he calculated the population based on houses per hectare and persons per house (*Ciudades Hispanomusulmanes,* 2d ed. [Madrid, 1985], 93–111). See also María Luisa Avila's interesting though problematic study of Andalusia, 961–1058, using the dates in medieval biographical dictionaries (*La Sociedad Hispanomusulmana al Final del Califato* [Madrid, 1985]).

37. Thomas F. Glick, "Hydraulic technology in al-Andalus," in *The Legacy of Muslim Spain,* ed. S. K. Jayyusi (Leiden, 1992), 974–86.

38. Watson, *Agricultural Innovation,* passim.

39. J. A. García de Cortazar, *La época medieval* (*Historia de España,* vol. ɪɪ), 7th ed. (Madrid, 1980), 63.

40. Glick, "Comment on Paper by Watson," *Journal of Economic History* 34 (1974), 77.

41. For a summary of descriptions in praise of al-Andalus by medieval geographers, see Imamuddin, "Al-Filāḥah," 51–54.

42. Ibn Khurradādhbih, Ibn al-Faqīh al-Hamadhānī, and Ibn Rustih, *Description du Maghreb,* 10–11, 30–77; Lévi-Provençal, *Hist. Esp. Mus.* ɪɪɪ:234–53; Hadj-Sadok, *Encyclopaedia of Islam,* new ed., ɪɪɪ: 839–40.

43. Ibn Khurradādhbih, Ibn al-Faqīh al-Hamadhānī, and Ibn Rustih, *Description du Maghreb,* 36–37, 52–53.

44. Ibn Ḥawqal, *Configuration de la terre,* ɪ:107–16; *Bibl. Geogr. Arab.,* ɪɪ:108–17.

45. Al-Muqaddasī, *Description de l'occident musulman au IVe–Xe siècle,* ed. and trans. Charles Pellat (Algiers, 1950), (Arabic) 36; (French trans.) 37.

46. Lévi-Provençal, "La ʿDescription de l'Espagne' d'Ahmad al-Rāzī," *Al-Andalus* 18 (1953), 64–65, 69. This geographer was the father of the historian ʿĪsā' who wrote the chronicle of al-Ḥakam II's reign.

47. Al-Shaqundī, in al-Maqqarī, *Analectes,* ɪɪ:143; Spanish trans. E. García Gómez in al-Shaqundī, *Elogio del Islam Español* (Madrid, 1935), 95.

2. Botany and the Agricultural Revolution

1. For discussion of the term *fitna* and its Qur'ānic implications, see Peter Scales, *The Fall of the Caliphate of Córdoba* (Leiden, 1994), 2–4.

2. Glick accepted the medieval Arabic emphasis on the roles of the old and new Berber and Arab factions (*Islamic and Christian Spain,* 182–5). Peter Sales, however, has pointed out that the medieval emphasis on a Berber-Arab dichotomy may reflect the political mindset of the taifa period and cautions that the historiography of the *fitna* took a different tack according to whether the writers were Arabs or Berbers (*Fall of the Caliphate,* 5).

3. David Wasserstein, *Rise and Fall of the Party-Kings* (Princeton, 1985), 99–106; Rachel Arié, *Historia de España:* ɪɪɪ, *España musulmana (VIII–XV),* 27.

4. ʿAbd Allāh al-Zīrī, *Mudhakkirāt al-Amīr ʿAbd Allāh,* 16; trans. in Wasserstein, *Rise and Fall of the Party-Kings,* 99.

5. Al-Shaqundī, in al-Maqqarī, *Analectes,* ɪɪ:128.

6. Ibn Saʿīd, in al-Maqqarī, *Analectes,* ɪ:304.

7. Al-Khushanī (writing in the third quarter of the tenth century), *Aljoxani, historia de los jueces de Córdoba,* trans. Julian Ribera (Madrid, 1965; reprint of 1914 edition), 176–77.

8. Ibn Hishām al-Lakhmī (twelfth century) quoted in Julio Samsó, "Ibn Hisām al-Lajmī y el primer jardīn botánico en al-Andalus," *Revista del Instituto Egipcio de Estudios Islámicos en Madrid* 21 (1981–82), 135.

9. Al-Maqqarī, *Analectes,* ɪ:305. It is worth noting here that whereas al-Maqqarī refers to seeds, al-Khushanī—who is the original tenth-century communicant—referred to a sprig.

10. Samsó, "Ibn Hisām al-Lajmī," 138–39.

11. Samsó, "Ibn Hisām al-Lajmī," 140; Emilio García Gómez, "Sobre agricultura arábigo andaluza," *Al-Andalus* 10 (1945), 134, translating a passage from Abū al-Khayr's *Kitāb al-filāḥa.*

12. Additionally, there is the case of citron, which spread with the Mediterranean diaspora of Jewish communities because it was used in the celebration of the holiday the Feast of Booths (Leviticus 23:40); knowledge of citron cultivation possibly paved the way for later orange and lemon cultivation (Erich Isaac, "The Citron in the Mediterranean: A Study of Religious Influences," *Economic Geography* 35 [1959], 71–78).

13. Walter Horn and Ernst Born, *The Plan of St. Gall,* 3 vols. (Berkeley and Los Angeles, 1979).

14. Horn and Born, *Plan of St. Gall,* II:181, 203, 205, 211–12.

15. The gardens followed close on the heels of herbal texts such as *Buch der Natur* (1475) and *Grant Herbier* (1526) (Arthur W. Hill, "History and Function of Botanical Gardens," *Annals of the Missouri Botanical Garden* 2 [1915], 190–91).

16. Jean Sermet, "Acclimatation: Les jardins botaniques espagnols au XVIIIe siècle et la tropicalisation de l'Andalouse," in *Histoire économique du monde méditerranéen 1450–1650, Mélanges en l'honneur de Fernand Braudel* (Toulouse, 1973), 558.

17. Watson, *Agricultural Innovation.* See chapters on the "agents" and "medium" of diffusion, 87–98.

18. Ibn Ghālib, *Kitāb farḥat al-anfus,* extract ed. Luṭfī ʿAbd al-Badīʿ in *Majallat maʿhad al-makhṭuṭāt al-ʿarabiyya* (Cairo), 1 (1955), fasc. 2, 295; Ibn Ḥawqal, *Configuration de la terre,* 112–13.

19. Ibn al-ʿAbbār, *Kitāb al-takmila,* II:551, notice 1557.

20. Ibn Ṣāḥib al-Ṣalāt, *The History of the Moroccan Empire in Maghrib, Andalusia, and Ifriqiya,* vol. III of *Tārīkh al-mann bil-imāma,* (Arabic edition) ed. Abdul Hadi Attazi (Beirut, 1964), 477; *Al-Mann bil-imāma,* trans. A. Huici Miranda (Valencia, 1969), 190.

21. Max Meyerhof, "Esquisse d'histoire de la pharmacologie et botanique chez les musulmans d'Espagne," *Al-Andalus* 3 (1935), 29.

22. Despite earlier confusion regarding the two names, the second of which was thought to be a Romanized corruption of the first, it is now believed that the names refer to two entirely different people. The existing Latin and Hebrew-Arabic manuscripts of the *Calendar* that we read today are a compendium compiled by a third party (R. Dozy, ed., *Le Calendrier de Cordoue,* new ed. in Arabic and Latin with French trans. by Charles Pellat [Leiden, 1961]). See also E. Lévi-Provençal, *Hist. Esp. Mus.,* III:239–43; Samsó, "La tradición clásica en los calendarios agrícolas hispanoárabes y norteafricanos," in *Actas del II Congreso Internacional de Estudios sobre las Culturas del Mediterráneo Occidental (1975)* (Barcelona, 1978), 177–86; Angel C. López, "Vida y obra del famoso polígrafo cordobés del siglo X, ʿArīb Ibn Saʿīd," in *Ciencias de la Naturaleza en al-Andalus,* I:317–47.

23. The Castilian version of Ibn Wāfid's manual is given in J. M. Millás Vallicrosa, "El *Libro de Agricultura* de Ibn Wāfid y su influencia en la agricultura del Renacimiento," *Al-Andalus* 8 (1943), 281–332.

24. Charles Pellat published a set of Egyptian calendars that include Christian feast days, and he believes that the writer of the *Calendar of Cordoba* consulted such Coptic calendars in addition to Muslim *anwāʾ* (*Cinq calendriers egyptiens* [Cairo, 1986]). It is likely that the Christian calendar appeared where there was a mixed population of Muslim and Christian patrons.

25. Samsó, "La tradición clásica," 177–86.

26. J. C. Webster, *Labors of the Month in Antique and Medieval Art to the End of the Twelfth Century* (Princeton, 1938), 37–56; Nils E. Enkvist, "The Seasons of the Year," in *Commentationes humanarum litterarum* 22, no. 4, (Helsingfors, 1957).

27. Lynn White, *Medieval Technology and Social Change* (Oxford, 1962, reprinted 1965), 56–57, 69; and George Duby, *Rural Economy and Country Life in the Medieval West* (Columbia, 1968), 22–27. The practice of three-field crop rotation improved upon the older method of two fields rotating between cultivation and fallow. Under the new system, the first field was planted in the fall with grain, the second was planted in the spring with oats, barley, or legumes, and the third was left fallow. The next year the first field was planted with a spring crop, the second left fallow, and the third with a winter crop. The third year the first field was left fallow, and so forth. The advantages of three-field rotation were many: productivity increased because labor was distributed throughout the year instead of concentrated in moments of peak effort; the likelihood of famine was reduced, since crop diversification diminished the risk of a natural disaster destroying an entire year's harvest; and human diet was improved by diversity and the increased consumption of legumes.

28. Sources on the Dioscorides manuscript are M. M. Sadek, *The Arabic Materia Medica of Dioscorides* (Quebec, 1983), 7–53; C. E. Dubler, *La "materia médica" de Dioscórides,* 6 vols. (Barcelona, 1953), esp. vol. I, chap. 2; and Meyerhof, "Esquisse," 1–41.

29. Dubler, *Dioscórides,* I:41–45, and Bolens, *Agronomes,* 40.

30. Dubler, *Dioscórides,* I:50. The first Arabic translation of *De Materia Medica* was achieved in Baghdad during the reign of the al-Mutawakkil (847–61) by Stephan ben Basil (Iṣṭifān b. Bāsīl) and the caliph's personal physician Ḥunayn ibn Isḥāq. First it was translated from the Greek into Syriac by Ḥunayn; a different translation from Greek to Arabic was made by Stephan; finally Stephan's Arabic translation was revised by Ḥunayn. See Sadek, *Dioscorides,* 12, for detailed chronology of the Byzantine translations of Dioscorides.

The earliest surviving Arabic Dioscorides manuscript copy is dated 475/1083 and is in Leiden (Univ. Lib. cod. or. 289) (Sadek, 12).

31. Ibn Abī Uṣaybiʿa (in his biographical entry for Ibn Juljul), *ʿUyūn al-Anbāʾ fī ṭabaqāt al-aṭibbāʾ*, 2 vols. (Cairo, 1882), II:46–49; French trans. Sylvestre de Sacy, *Relation de l'Egypt par Abd Allatif* (Paris, 1810), 495–89, and Meyerhof, "Esquisse," 8–11.

32. Millás Vallicrosa, "Caracteres de la ciencia hispanoárabe," (1949) reprinted in *Estudios sobre historia de la ciencia española,* vol. I (Madrid, 1987), 23–41.

33. Ibn Abī Uṣaybiʿa, *ʿUyūn al-Anbāʾ*, I:230.

34. Ibn Abī Uṣaybiʿa, *ʿUyūn al-Anbāʾ* I:43.

35. Dubler, *Dioscórides,* I:51; Max Meyerhof and G. F. Sobhy, eds. and trans., *The Abridged Version of "The Book of Simple Drugs" of al-Ghâfiqî,* fasc. 1–4 (Cairo, 1932–40), 19; Ildefonso Garijo, "El tratado de Ibn Yulyul sobre los medicamentos que no mencionó Dioscórides," in *Ciencias de la naturaleza en al-Andalus, Textos y estudios,* ed. E. García Sánchez, (Granada, 1990), I:57–70.

36. Ibn Abī Uṣaybiʿa, *ʿUyūn al-Anbāʾ*, II:46–48.

37. For more extensive listing, see B. Lewin, "Adwīya," in *Encyclopaedia of Islam,* new ed., I:212–14.

38. Meyerhof, "Esquisse," 12.

39. Meyerhof, "Esquisse," 13.

40. Abulcasis probably acquired the *nisba* (descriptive name) al-Zahrāwī because he was born or grew up at al-Zahrāʾ. *Al-Taṣrīf* was partially translated in Toledo by Gerard of Cremona in the second half of the twelfth century, by which means it reached the Christian West (Sami Khalaf Hamarneh and Glenn Sonnedecker, *A Pharmaceutical View of Abulcasis al-Zahrāwī in Moorish Spain* [Leiden, 1963], 13–16).

41. Meyerhof and Sobhy, *Abridged Version of al-Gāfiqī,* 20.

42. Meyerhof and Sobhy, *Abridged Version of al-Gāfiqī,* 23.

43. Meyerhof and Sobhy, *Abridged Version of al-Gāfiqī,* 31–36; Ibn al-Bayṭār, *Al-Jāmīʿ li-mufradā al-adwiya wa-l-aghdhiya* (Bulak, 1291 A.H.); French trans. L. Leclerc, "Traité de Simples," in *Notices et extraits de la Bibliothèque Nationale* (1877–93), nos. xxiii, xxv, xxvi, xxx.

44. Miguel Forqada, "Ṣāʿid al-Bagdādī y los antecedentes de la agronomía andalusí," *Al-Qanṭara* 16 (1995), 163–71; and Ibn ʿĀṣim, *Kitāb al-anwāʾ wa-l-azmina al-qawl fī-l-suhūr,* ed. and Spanish trans. M. Forqada, in *Fuentes Arábico-Hispanas* 15 (Barcelona, 1993).

45. Claude Cahen, "Notes pour une histoire de l'agriculture dans les pays musulmans médiévaux: Coup d'oeil sur la littérature agronomique musulmane hors d'Espagne," *Journal of the Economic and Social History of the Orient* 14 (1971), 66.

46. For a list of Persian botanicals, see Miguel Asín Palacios, *Glosario de voces romances, registradas por un botánico anónimo hispano-musulman (siglos XI–XII)* (Madrid and Granada, 1943), xvi; and Meyerhof and Sobhy, *Abridged Version of al-Gāfiqī,* 6–30.

47. In 1990 Toufic Fahd stated that he would publish a critical edition in three volumes of *Al-Filāḥa al-nabaṭīya,* in Publications of the Institut Français de Damas. As the *Nabaṭīya* has been the subject of heated debate among Arabists and historians of medieval Islamic science, one hopes that Professor Fahd's forthcoming study will resolve the issue of the author's name and nationality, and the sources from which he drew his agronomic information.

48. Millás Vallicrosa, "La tradición de la ciencia geopónica hispanoárabe," *Archives Internationales d'Histoire des Sciences* 34 (1955), 119–21; reprinted in *Estudios sobre la historia de la ciencia española,* 2 vols. (Madrid, 1987). The *Nabaṭīya* was discovered in the nineteenth century by the Russian scholar D. A. Khvolson, who believed its claim to antiquity.

49. The *Nabaṭīya* appeared in the *Kitāb al-anwāʾ* of Ibn ʿAṣim (d. 403/1013). See M. Forqada, "Ṣāʿid al-Bagdādī," 169.

50. López, "ʿArīb Ibn Saʿīd," 317–47.

51. According to a brief reference by G. S. Colin in 1965 ("Filāḥa: Muslim West," *Encyclopaedia of Islam,* new ed., II:901–2), Abulcasis's agricultural manual was discovered some years earlier by Henri Pérès, who intended to publish it; however, nothing further has appeared. See also Expiración García Sánchez, "Agriculture in Muslim Spain," in *The Legacy of Muslim Spain,* ed. S. K. Jayyusi, (Leiden, 1992), 987–99.

52. García Sánchez, "Agriculture in Muslim Spain," 988; López, *Kitāb fī tartīb awqāt al-girāsa wa-l-magrūsāt: Un tratado agrícola andalusí anónimo* (Granada, 1990).

53. Millás Vallicrosa discovered the Arabic manuscript that matched the Spanish-Castilian translation by "Abel Mutariph, Abel nufit" (Ms. 10106, Bibl. Nac. Madrid, originally found in the library of the Toledo Cathedral, Ms. 96–40). Millás Vallicrosa, "La traducción castellana del *Tratado de Agricultura* de Ibn Wāfid," *Al-Andalus* 8 (1943), 281–332; reprinted as "El *Libro de Agricultura* de Ibn Wāfid y su influencia en la agricultura del Renacimiento," in *Estudios sobre la historia de la ciencia española,* 2 vols.

(Madrid, 1987); "Un manuscrito árabe de la obra de Agricultura de Ibn Wāfid," *Tamuda* 2 (1954), 87–96; and "Nuevos textos manuscritos de las obras geopónicas de Ibn Wāfid e Ibn Baṣṣāl," *Tamuda* 2 (1954), 339–44. Regarding the attribution of the Castilian version of "Abel nufit," see Dubler, "Fuentes árabes," *Al-Andalus* 6 (1941), 145 ff.

54. Ms. 833, Escorial Library (Meyerhof, "Esquisse," 13).

55. Ibn al-ʿAbbār, *Kitāb al-takmila li-kitāb al-ṣila,* II:551, biographical notice 1557.

56. Ms. 4764, Paris Bibl. Nat., fol. 64v–161, dated 1038 (1628–29) in Maghrebi script. That it is copied from a Spanish manuscript is evident in the use of Romance names for the months (Millás Vallicrosa, "Aportaciones para el estudio de la obra agronómica de Ibn Ḥajjāj y de Abū-l-Jayr," *Al-Andalus* 20 [1955], 87–105 [reprinted in *Estudios,* II:153–81]).

Bachir Attié, who has tried to form a new chronology for the agricultural manuals based largely on Ibn al-ʿAwwām's citations, believes that Abū al-Khayr flourished in the second half of the eleventh century and was a slightly older contemporary of Ibn Baṣṣāl, and that he wrote his manual c. 1070–75 (Attié, "L'Ordre chronologique probable des sources directes d'Ibn al-ʿAwwām," *Al-Qanṭara* 3 [1982], 299–332). G. S. Colin puts Abū al-Khayr as a medical student in Seville in 494/1100 ("Filāḥa: Muslim West," 901).

57. Abū al-Khayr, *Kitāb al-Filāḥa ou le livre de la culture,* extracts trans. into French by A. Cherbonneau, ed. Henri Pérès (Algiers, 1946).

58. Abū al-Khayr, *Kitāb al-Filāḥa,* 13.

59. Abū al-Khayr, *Kitāb al-Filāḥa,* 15.

60. Ibn Baṣṣāl, *Kitāb al-Filāḥa.*

61. Colin, "Filāḥa: Muslim West," II:901. Colin assumed that, because of the lack of citations, Ibn Baṣṣāl relied solely on own personal experiences, but I doubt this.

62. Millás Vallicrosa, biography of Ibn Baṣṣāl in *Libro de agricultura,* 13.

63. Ms. Arab. 80, Codera collection, Real Academia de la Historia, extracted in *Kitāb al-Filāḥa,* ed. and trans. Millás Vallicrosa and Aziman, 33–34.

64. Ibn Bassāl, *Kitāb al-Filāḥa,* 34.

65. Ibn Bassāl, *Kitāb al-Filāḥa,* 41.

66. Ibn Bassāl, *Kitāb al-Filāḥa,* 64.

67. Ibn Bassāl, *Kitāb al-Filāḥa,* 68.

68. Millás Vallicrosa, "La traducción castellana," 281–332.

69. Bachir Attié, "La bibliographie de *al-Muqniʿ* de Ibn Ḥaǧǧāǧ," *Hespéris-Tamuda* 19 (1980–81), 47–74, and "L'Ordre chronologique," 327–28; Millás Vallicrosa, "Aportaciones," 87–105.

70. Ibn al-ʿAwwām, *Le livre de l'agriculture,* trans. (French) J.-J. Clément-Mullet, 2 vols. in 3 (Tunis, 1977), I:216–17, 335.

71. Bachir Attié, "L'Ordre chronologique," 317–21.

72. Unpublished edition prepared by Joaquina Eguerras of the Escuela de Estudios Arabes de Granada. See also Millás Vallicrosa, "Un nuevo manuscrito de la obra agronómica de al-Ṭignarī," *Tamuda* 1 (1953), 85–86; Bolens, *Agronomes andalous,* 31; and Attié, "L'Ordre chronologique," 329–30.

73. Millás Vallicrosa, "La tradición de la ciencia," 128; and Attié, "L'Ordre chronologique," 329.

74. Attié, "L'Ordre chronologique," 330.

75. Ibn Luyūn, *Tratado de agricultura.* Ibn Luyūn's biography (Abū ʿUthmān Saʿad Ibn Abī Jaʿafar Aḥmad b. Ibrāhīm b. Luyūn al-Tukhībī) is given in Ibn al-Qāḍī, *Al-Hijāl,* ed. I. S. Allouche (Rabat, 1939).

76. Ibn Luyūn, *Tratado,* (Arabic) 37.

77. Ibn Luyūn, *Tratado,* (Arabic) 61 on rows, and 183–84, (Spanish trans.) 40 on beds. These figures match Dozy's definition of the word *ḥawḍ,* which in his *Supplément aux dictionaires* he says is an agrarian surface measure of twelve by four cubits. Dozy himself derives this definition from medieval Andalusian agricultural manuals, however, so the *Supplément* must be used with caution.

78. "Mimmā shafahahu bih ahl al-tajriba wa-l-imtihān." Cited in Colin, "Filāḥa," 902.

79. Ibn Luyūn, *Tratado,* (Arabic) 61 and 87–88.

80. Ibn Luyūn, *Tratado,* (Arabic) 171–75; trans. James Dickie, "The Islamic Garden in Spain," in *The Islamic Garden,* ed. E. B. MacDougall and R. Ettinghausen (Washington, D.C., 1976), 94.

81. Ibn Wāfid in Millás Vallicrosa, "Traducción," 304. My thanks to Professor Richard Kagan for his help in translating this passage.

82. One is reminded of the Plan of St. Gall, which offers a treasure of information on medieval monastic life, urban planning, architecture, and even gardening but, unfortunately, cannot be applied to a surviving site. One is left wondering to what extent the plan refers to actual monastic life and architecture and to what extent it refers merely to an ideal that was never realized. See Horn and Born, *Plan of St. Gall.*

83. García Gómez, "Traducciones Alfonsies de agricultura árabe," *Boletín de la Real Academia de Historia* 181 (1984), 387–97.

84. Johannes Pedersen, *The Arabic Book* (1946),

trans. G. French (Princeton, 1984), 62; citing Ibn ʿAbd Rabbih, *Al-ʿiqd al-farīd* (Cairo, 1322/1904), 183.

There is evidence to suggest that at least one of the mills next to the great bridge of Cordoba was devoted to papermaking (Oriol Valls I Subirà, "El paper al al-ándalus i a la corona d'aragó," in *Actas del II Congreso Internacional de Estudios sobre las Culturas del Mediterráneo Occidental* [*Barcelona, 1975*] [Barcelona, 1978], 442–43).

85. Valls I Subirà, "El paper," 443, citing A. Mez, *El renacimiento del Islam* (Madrid and Granada, 1936).

86. Pederson, *The Arabic Book,* 120, citing Ibn Ḥazm and al-Maqqarī.

87. Lévi-Provençal, *Hist. Esp. Mus.*, III:313–14.

88. Abū al-Khayr, *Kitāb al-filāḥa,* 26.

89. Al-Maqqarī, *Analectes,* II:104.

90. On the other hand, it is not necessarily true that written texts mirrored oral tradition. See the study of a Yemeni almanac by Daniel M. Varisco, *Medieval Agriculture and Islamic Science* (Seattle, 1994), 8.

91. Mary Carruthers, *The Book of Memory: A Study of Memory in Medieval Culture* (Cambridge, 1990).

92. M. Forqada, "Ṣāʿid al-Bagdādī," 163–71.

93. Al-Maqqarī, trans. Gayangos, *History* I:62–3.

94. Juan Vernet, *La cultura hispanoárabe en oriente y occidente* (Barcelona, 1978). Georges Duby notes that the writing of practical manuals flourished in Europe in the thirteenth century (*Rural Economy and Country Life,* 88–89). This is considerably later than al-Andalus and is one of many indicators that Europe's agricultural expansion and intensification occurred later than al-Andalus.

95. According to Ibn Abī Uṣaybiʿa, the eagerness of the botanists who glossed the magnificent Byzantine Dioscorides was entirely due to their desire to gain favor with ʿAbd al-Raḥmān III (*ʿUyūn al-Anbāʾ*, 47–48).

96. Watson, *Agricultural Innovation,* 101; Lucie Bolens, *La cuisine andalouse* (Paris, 1990).

97. Watson, *Agricultural Innovation,* 101.

98. Lévi-Provençal, *Séville musulmane,* (Arabic) 5.

99. Jürgen Jakobi, "Agriculture Between Literary Tradition and Experience," in *Timurid Art and Culture,* ed. Lisa Golombek and M. Subtelny (Leiden, 1992), 203.

100. Al-Rāzī, *Anales,* 169–70 = Ibn Hayyān, *Al-Muqtabis fī akhbar,* 135–6. See Bibliography for explanation of the relationship of these texts.

101. J. Boardman, "The Olive in the Mediterranean. Its Culture and Use," in *The Early History of the Mediterranean,* ed. J. Hutchinson et al. (Oxford, 1977), 187–94.

102. Michael Brett, review of Watson, *Agricultural Innovation in the Early Islamic World,* in *Bulletin of the School of Oriental and African Studies* 48 (1985), 126–28.

103. Glick, "Comment," 74–78. Also, Jeremy Jones, "A Green Revolution?" *Journal of African History* 25 (1984), 343–44.

104. Antonio García Maceira, *Apuntes y noticias sobre la agricultura de los árabes españoles* (Zamora, 1876), 10–11. By *morisco,* the speaker meant the population of Moors or Muslims, or more accurately the people of Moorish descent, remaining in Spain after the reconquest.

105. García Maceira, *Apuntes y noticias,* 8.

106. García Maceira, *Apuntes y noticias,* 8–9.

107. See Karl W. Butzer et al., "Irrigation Agrecosystems in Eastern Spain: Roman or Islamic Origins?" *Annals of the Association of American Geographers* 75 (1985), 479–509; and Glick's commentary, "Hydraulic technology in al-Andalus," 976.

108. Glick, "Hydraulic technology in al-Andalus," 974–86.

3. Palaces and Estates of Cordoba, 711–936

1. Karl Wittfogel, *Oriental Despotism* (New Haven, 1957).

2. For example, the papers given by McGuire Gibson, James A. Neely, Eva Hunt, and Robert C. Hunt at the symposium *Irrigation's Impact on Society,* in the collection of that title, ed. T. Downing and M. Gibson (Tucson, 1974). For an assessment of Wittfogel's contributions and flaws, with twenty years' hindsight, see Glick, *From Muslim Fortress to Christian Castle* (Manchester, 1995), 65 ff.

3. Boserup, *Conditions of Agricultural Growth.*

4. Glick, *Islamic and Christian Spain,* 69–70. See also Maurice Lombard, "L'evolution urbaine pendant le haut moyen âge," *Annales: Economies, Sociétés, Civilisations* 12 (1957), 7–28, reprinted in *Espaces et réseaux du haut moyen âge* (Paris and the Hague, 1972).

5. Lombard, "L'evolution urbaine," 63.

6. García Gómez, "Notas sobre topografía cordobesa en los 'Anales de al-Ḥakam II' por ʿIsa Rāzī," *Al-Andalus* 30 (1965), 334. Lévi-Provençal defined them as recreation villas, often endowed with open parks or *ḥayr,* belonging to the aristocracy and mem-

bers of the Marwanid family (*Hist. Esp. Mus.*, III:335).

7. Al-Muqaddasī, *Description de l'occident musulmane,* 38–39.

8. For *qaṣr,* Dozy gives the definitions of "caserne" and "village entouré d'une muraille" (*Supplément aux Dictionnaires Arabes,* 3d ed. [Leiden, 1967]). Lane defines *qaṣr* as "a palace; a pavilion or kind of building wholly or for the most part isolated, sometimes on top of a larger building" and also a "mansion, or house" (*An Arabic-English Lexicon* [London, 1867]). Kazimirski offers the meanings of "château, palais," "prison, cachot," and "restriction" (*Dictionaire Arabe-Français* [Beirut, 1860]).

9. María Jesús Rubiera Mata, *La arquitectura en la literatura arabe,* 121.

10. For example, Ibn Ḥazm, *Ṭawq al-ḥamāma,* ed. and trans. (French) Bercher (Algiers, 1949), 250.

11. "Awal mā nadhkaru min al-muntazahāt muntazah al-khulafā' al-marwānīya wa hua qaṣr al-Ruṣāfa" (Ibn Sa'īd in al-Maqqarī, *Analectes,* I:304). Al-Nuwayrī refers to al-Zahrā' as one of several *mustanzihāt* (*Nihāyat al-'arab,* I:66).

12. Unfortunately, al-Rāzī's text on the topography of Cordoba, which would doubtless have contained considerable information on the exact location of suburban aristocratic residences and *munyas*, has never been found. Ibn Ḥazm alluded to it in al-Maqqarī, *Analectes,* II:118; Lévi-Provençal, *Hist. Esp. Mus.*, III:357. Instead, most of the available information on the *munyas* comes from the authors reproduced in al-Maqqarī.

13. Jean-Gérard Gorges, *Les villas hispano-romaines: Inventaire et problématique archéologiques* (Paris and Talence, 1979). For the most part, the excavated remains of these villas are scant, consisting of a few floor mosaics or enough wall and pavement to allow a very tentative reconstruction of part of a floor plan.

14. Ibn 'Idhārī, *al-Bayān,* II:1–15.

15. Ibn 'Idhārī, *al-Bayān,* II:14; al-Idrīsī, (*Nuzhat al-Mushtāq*) *Description de l'Afrique et de l'Espagne,* ed. and trans. (French) R. Dozy and M. J. de Goeje (Leiden, 1866; reprinted Amsterdam, 1969), 187.

16. Ibn Ḥawqal did not mention Roman ruins among Spain's assets. Ibn Faqīh referred to the Islamic conquest of the Visigoths in his geography but does not mention the architecture as much as the contents of two buildings: one housing the fabled Table of Solomon, and the other containing a prophetic picture of turbaned Arab conquerors (*Description du Maghreb et de l'Europe au IIIe = IXe siècle,* ed. M. Hadj-Sadok [Algiers, 1949], 36–39).

17. The excavators concluded that it was either a case of the Islamic reuse of Visigothic spolia or else the site itself was Visigothic and was remodeled in the Islamic period [Anon., "Los hallazgos de Turruñuelos," *al-Mulk* 4 (1964–65), 167–68].

18. Jerrilynn D. Dodds, *Architecture and Ideology,* 100 and passim; and personal communication.

19. Dodds, *Architecture and Ideology,* 94–106, and "The Great Mosque of Córdoba," in Dodds, ed., *Al-Andalus: The Art of Islamic Spain,* 11–25.

20. For a discussion of architecture mythology, see Rubiera Mata, *Arquitectura en la literatura.*

21. Al-Maqqarī, *Analectes,* I:302.

22. Gayangos, *History,* II:208.

23. *Akhbār Majmū'a,* in *Collección de obras arábigas de historia y geografía que publica la Real Academia de la Historia,* vol. I, ed. and trans. (Spanish) Emilio Lafuente y Alcántara (Madrid, 1867), (Arabic) 10–12, (Spanish trans.) 23–25.

24. *Akhbār Majmū'a,* (Arabic) 21, (Spanish trans.) 33.

25. Al-Maqqarī, *Analectes,* II:6–8; Spanish trans. in *Akhbār Majmū'a,* appendix, 194. In 714, Mughith was entrusted with delivering the news of the taking of Toledo to the Umayyad Caliph al-Walīd in Damascus, but he returned to Cordoba, where he remained.

26. *Akhbār Majmū'a* (Arabic) 21, (Spanish trans.) 33. Rafael Castejón asserted that the palace was a Roman construction but did not explain why ("Nuevas identificaciones en la topografía de la Córdoba califal," in *Actas, Primer Congreso de Estudios Arabes e Islámicos (Córdoba, 1962)* [Madrid: 1964], 374 n. 15).

27. *Akhbār Majmū'a,* (Arabic) 21, (Spanish trans.) 33; also Lévi-Provençal, *Hist. Esp. Mus.*, III:376.

28. Al-'Udhrī, *Fragmentos geográfico-históricos de al-Masālik ilā ŷamī' al-mamālik,* ed. 'Abd al-'Aziz al-Ahwani, (Madrid, 1965), 121–23.

29. The Alcazar's south facade and the esplanade were erased by the building of the Seminario de San Pelagio and a patio associated with the Bishop's Palace sometime at the end of the sixteenth or beginning of the seventeenth century, according to Castejón, "Córdoba califal," *Boletín de la Real Academia de Córdoba* 8 (1929), 279–80, and Lévi-Provençal, *Hist. Esp. Mus.*, II:130–32.

30. Lévi-Provençal, *Hist. Esp. Mus.*, II:131.

31. Lévi-Provençal, *Hist. Esp. Mus.*, II:131.

32. Castejón, "Córdoba califal," 279–80; and Lévi-Provençal, *Hist. Esp. Mus.,* II:131.

33. Lévi-Provençal wrote that the Alcazar was divided into three zones (*Hist. Esp. Mus.,* II:131), referring to the reader to Castejón. The latter, however, admits "De la distinción interior del Alcázar, no se puede hoy colegir nada, apesar de las diversas menciones" ("Córdoba califal," 280).

34. Lévi-Provençal, *Hist. Esp. Mus.,* II:130–32; Ibn Bashkuwāl in al-Maqqarī, *Analectes,* I:302–3.

35. Ibn Khaldūn, in al-Maqqarī, *Analectes,* I:380; trans. Pascual de Gayangos, *The History of the Mohammedan Dynasties,* II:467 (145, n. 39). Also in Ibn Khaldūn, *Al-ʿIbar wa-dīwān,* 7 vols. (Bulak, 1867), IV:144.

36. Rubiera Mata, *Arquitectura en la literatura,* 123; citing Ibn Ḥayyān, *al-Muqtabis,* ed. Maḥmūd ʿAlī Makkī (Beirut, 1973), 111–18.

37. Al-Rāzī, 271–72 = Ibn Ḥayyān, 229–31. Lévi-Provençal believed that the Alcazar was so densely built up by the tenth century that al-Nāṣir had to demolish older structures to create space for his Dār al-Rawḍa (*Hist. Esp. Mus.,* II:132). However, it is also possible, as Vallvé believes, that the addition was a semi-independent structure on the west side of the Alcazar (*División territorial,* 251).

38. Ibn Saʿīd in al-Maqqarī, *Analectes,* I:304.

39. According to Lévi-Provençal, in part I (unpublished) of *Muqtabis,* al-Rāzī says that Ruṣāfa was actually built earlier by Razīn al-Burnusī, a Berber chieftain in the army that conquered Cordoba in the early eighth century. Al-Rāzī's version of the founding of Ruṣāfa is unique. However, Lévi-Provençal, whose plan to publish an edition of *Muqtabis* (I) never reached fruition, says that mild support for al-Rāzī's statement is given by the persistence of Razīn's name in regional toponymy, as for example, the Masjid al-Razīn in the western suburb of Cordoba (Lévi-Provençal, *Hist. Esp. Mus.,* III:374, citing lost manuscript of *Muqtabis,* folios 244v–245v.). The *Akhbār Majmūʿa* referred to a site one mile north of Cordoba called the Qalaʿ Tudmin (fortress of Teodomiro, a Visigothic name), and this may be the same place as Ruṣāfa (Castejón, "Nuevas identificaciones," 384–86). See also Manuela Marín, "Al-Ruṣāfa, 4. In Muslim Spain," *Encyclopedia of Islam,* new ed. (1994), VIII:631–3.

40. Castejón, "Nuevas identificaciones," 384–86. Although he uncovered pavements, he discovered no decorative fragments or plasterwork and concluded that the palace was a plain, unadorned structure. Alternatively, it is possible that he was erroneously excavating an auxilliary building of lesser importance.

41. Ibn ʿIdhārī, *al-Bayān,* vol. II, (Arabic) 60; Fagnan, French trans. 85–86; Gayangos, *History,* II:86; al-Nuwayrī, *Nihāyat al-ʿarab,* (Arabic) 17–18, (Spanish trans.) 16. This is my translation. The poem closely parallels verses attributed to ʿAbd al-Malik, the Syrian-born governor of Seville in the time of ʿAbd al-Raḥmān I (trans. Gayangos, *History,* II:77 n. 4).

42. On the pre-Islamic origins and subsequent development of the Syrian Ruṣáfa, see M. Mackensen et al., *Resafa I: Eine befestigte spätantike Anlage vor den Stadtmauern von Resafa* (Mainz, 1984). A garden belonging to Hishām's palace was excavated by the German Archaeological Institute of Damascus in 1990 (Thilo Ulbert, "Ein umaiyadischer Pavillon in Resafa-Ruṣāfat Hišām," *Damaszener Mitteilungen* 7 [1993], 213–31); this is not the same area of the site that Katharina Otto-Dorn identified as Hishām's palace ("Grabung im Ummayadischen Ruṣāfah," *Ars Orientalis* 2 [1957], 119–33).

43. Ruggles, "Il giardini con pianta a croce nel Mediterraneo islamico," 143–54.

44. Al-Maqqarī, *Analectes,* I:304.

45. Al-Maqqarī, *Analectes,* I:304.

46. For example, overseeing the execution of prisoners (*Akhbār Majmūʿa,* [Arabic] 110, 115, [Spanish trans.] 101, 105).

47. Ibn Saʿīd in al-Maqqarī, *Analectes,* I:304.

48. The princess was al-Bahaʾ (d. 305/918); see Lévi-Provençal, *Hist. Esp. Mus.,* I:267; and *Esp. Mus. Xe siècle,* 224.

49. Ibn Ḥawqal, *Configuration de la Terre,* (French trans.) 112; *Bibl. Geog. Arab.* II, (Arabic) 110–11.

50. Ibn ʿIdhārī, *Al-Bayān,* ed. Fagnan, II:355; Lévi-Provençal, *Hist. Esp. Mus.,* I:102–3; al-Maqqarī, *Analectes,* I:255.

51. Ibn ʿIdhārī, *Al-Bayān,* III:102; Lévi-Provençal, *Hist. Esp. Mus.,* III:374.

52. Al-Rāzī wrote that it was used to receive allies from North Africa on that date (Al-Rāzī, 64 n. 26 = Ibn Ḥayyān, 43).

53. Al-Maqqarī, *Analectes,* I:309. Ibn Saʿīd claimed that it was used for military reviewing (*furja*), but this word also can mean "pleasure."

54. Torres Balbás inferred from this term that the Umayyad princes had a country house there, but while envoys camped in tents within an enclosure, there is no mention of a permanent residence (*Ciudades,* 139); E. García Gómez called it merely an "es-

planade" in "Notas sobre topografía," 357–59; Lévi-Provençal, *Hist. Esp. Mus.*, III:89, 374–75, citing the now missing first part of Ibn Ḥayyān's *Muqtabis*, folio 169r.

55. Lévi-Provençal, *Hist. Esp. Mus.*, III:381–82.

56. Rafael Castejón, "Córdoba califal," 291, 301; Torres Balbás, *Ciudades*, 140.

57. Lévi-Provençal, *Hist. Esp. Mus.*, III:379–80.

58. Ibn Ḥayyān, *Chronique du règne du calife umayyade ʿAbd Allāh à Cordoue* (*Muqtabis* III), ed. M. M. Antuña (Paris, 1937), (Arabic) 38–39.

59. Al-Ḥimyarī, perhaps citing Ibn Ḥammāla, in al-Ḥimyarī, *La péninsule ibérique*, entry no. 180, pp. 187, 226–27.

60. The poet was ʿUbayd Allāh b. Yaḥyā (d. 298/911), cited in al-Ḥimyarī, *La péninsule ibérique*, 187.

61. Lévi-Provençal, *Hist. Esp. Mus.*, III:380–81, citing the now lost part I of Ibn Ḥayyān's *Muqtabis*.

62. Al-Rāzī, *Anales palatinos*, 44–46, n. 3–4; García Gómez, "Notas," 338–39.

63. Ibn ʿIdhārī, *Al-Bayān*, II:91 (Arabic); al-Nuwayrī, *Nihāyat al-ʿarab*, (Arabic) 42, (Spanish trans.) 45.

64. Al-Nuwayrī, (Arabic) 42, (Spanish trans.) 45.

65. Ibn Ḥayyān, *Al-Muqtabas* (V), ed. P. Chalmeta, F. Corriente, and M. Ṣubḥ (Madrid, 1979), (Arabic) 57; *Crónica del califa ʿAbderraḥmān III An-Nāṣir entre los años 912 y 942*, trans. M. J. Viguera and F. Corriente (Saragossa, 1981), 54.

66. In Ibn al-Khattānī, *al-Tashbihāt*, ed. I. Abbas (Beirut), 70, cited in Rubiera Mata, *Arquitectura en la literatura*, 124–25.

67. Lévi-Provençal, *Hist. Esp. Mus.*, III:381 n. 4, citing Ibn Ḥayyān (I), folio 246r.

68. Al-Rāzī and Ibn Bashkuwāl in al-Rāzī, 194 = Ibn Ḥayyān, 153; al-Maqqarī, *Analectes*, I:304; Rafael Castejón, "Cordoba califal," 327; reiterated by Lévi-Provençal, *Hist. Esp. Mus.*, III:373.

69. Ibn Ḥayyān, *Muqtabis* (III), ed. Antuña, (Arabic) 38–39.

70. Ibn Ḥayyān, *Muqtabis* (III), ed. Antuña, (Arabic) 38–39.

71. Al-Maqqarī, *Analectes*, I:231. For detailed commentary see Ruggles, "A Source of Wood for Madīnāt al-Zahrāʾ?" *Al-Qanṭara* 12 (1991), 573–76.

72. Al-Maqqarī, *Analectes*, I:231; trans. Gayangos, *History*, II:153–54.

73. Ruggles, "A Source of Wood," 573–76.

74. Al-Maqqarī, *Analectes*, I:229.

75. Al-Rāzī in al-Maqqarī, *Analectes*, I:304; Ibn al-Khāṭib, *Aʿmāl al-aʿlām*, partial edition in Lévi-Provençal, *Histoire de l'Espagne Musulmane d'Ibn al-Haṭīb* (Rabat, 1934), 120.

76. Al-Maqqarī, *Analectes*, I:380.

77. Except that in *al-ʿIbar* [IV:144], Ibn Khaldūn refers to al-Munīf as a *qaṣr*.

78. Al-Rāzī, 271–72 = Ibn Ḥayyān, 229–30.

79. Lévi-Provençal, *Hist. Esp. Mus.*, II:132, III:375. This theory is echoed by García Gómez, "Notas," 324.

80. Al-Rāzī, *Anales palatinos*, 190, 322.

81. Ibn Ḥayyān (citing al-Rāzī), *Crónica* (V), 67–68.

82. Al-Rāzī, 87 n. 35, 252 n. 215 = Ibn Ḥayyān, 212.

83. Castejón, "Excavaciones en el cortijo El Alcaide. ¿Dar al-Naura?" *Al-Mulk* 1 (1959–60), 163–66; see also Hernández Giménez, *Arquitectura y Decoración*, 176–82.

84. Al-Maqqarī, *Analectes*, I:371. Fragments of this aqueduct were discovered in 1925.

85. Ibn Ḥayyān, *Crónica* (V), 317; *Muqtabas* (V), ed. P. Chalmeta, 424.

86. Ibn Ḥayyān, *Crónica* (V), 359; *Muqtabas* (V), ed. P. Chalmeta, 248–49.

87. Al-Rāzī, 252 = Ibn Ḥayyān, 212.

88. Ibn Ḥawqal, *Configuration*, (French trans.) I:110–1, (Arabic) II:111; al-Maqqarī, *Analectes*, I:298.

89. When Cordoba's markets were expanded in 971/361, the mule stables were moved from the al-Muṣāra—formerly the outermost edge of the settled area—to a place near the prison at al-Naʿūra (Al-Rāzī, *Anales palatinos*, 87). Thus, although in the ninth century the area around Munyat al-Naʿūra had been open countryside, by the third quarter of the tenth century it marked the edge of urban development.

90. Quoted in al-Maqqarī, *Analectes*, I:304.

4. Madīnat al-Zahrāʾ

1. Quoted in al-Maqqarī, *Analectes*, I:344.

2. Hernández Giménez, *Madīnat a-Zahrāʾ: Arquitectura y Decoración*.

3. Joaquín Vallvé, *La División territorial*, 257.

4. Or "ḥādiratayn"; Al-Rāzī, 117 = Ibn Ḥayyān, 93.

5. Gabrieli, "Omayyades d'Espagne et Abbasides," 93–100.

6. Richard Bulliet, *Conversion to Islam in the Medieval Period: An Essay in Quantitative History* (Cambridge, 1979). For a calculation of the size of

Cordoba's Muslim population based on mosque expansions, see L. Torres Balbás "Ampliación y tamaño," 339–52.

The available data enables us only to assess the number of adult males in a medieval Islamic community, although from that figure the rest of the population can be calculated. However it takes more than a decade for a generation of children to mature, so that a male convert's children may not register in the historical data until many years after the father adopts Islam. The point is self-evident: I include it here merely to stress the fact that ʿAbd al-Raḥmān III and his contemporaries surely knew that they were in the midst of an accelerating trend toward adoption of the faith, even before the numbers registered statistically in the historians' calculations.

7. Ibn ʿIdhārī, *Al-Bayān,* I:158. Also, Jonathan M. Bloom, "The Origins of Fatimid Art," *Muqarnas* 3 (1985), 20–21.

8. Lévi-Provençal, *Hist. Esp. Mus.* III:480–81.

9. David Wasserstein has argued that the caliphal institution stayed intact and unitary but that the Fatimids and Umayyads made competing dynastic claims to its office (*The Caliphate in the West* [Oxford, 1993], 10).

10. Glick, *Islamic and Christian Spain,* 36.

11. Lévi-Provençal, "Un échange d'ambassades entre Cordoue et Byzance au IXe siècle," *Byzantion* 12 (1937), 1–24; reprinted in Lévi-Provençal, *Islam d'occident: Études d'histoire médiévale* (Paris, 1948), 79–107.

12. Lévi-Provençal suggests that the Abbasid form of political organization may have been learned indirectly from intermediaries, the Aghlabids of Ifriqiya, with whom the Umayyads had more frequent and closer contact than that with the Abbasids (*Hist. Esp. Mus.,* III:7). On Aghlabid administration, see Marçais, *La Berbérie musulmane et l'orient au moyen age* (Paris, 1946), 57 ff.

13. Regarding the political organization of al-Andalus, see Lévi-Provençal, *Hist. Esp. Mus.,* III: 1–53.

14. Al-Maqqarī, *Analectes,* II:83–90; Lévi-Provençal, *Hist. Esp. Mus.,* I:268–72. Ziryāb's itinerary led him via the Aghlabid capital at Kairouan; indeed, Ifriqiya (Tunisia) was one of the avenues through which the Hispano-Umayyads acquired familiarity with Abbasid culture.

15. Most, but not all, of the textual references to Madīnat al-Zahrāʾ have been collected and translated by Rosario Castejón in "Madinat al-Zahra en los autores árabes," *Al-Mulk* 1 (1959–60), 63–106; and 2 (1961–62), 119–56. However, a number of important authors are omitted, notably Ibn Ḥayyān, al-Rāzī, Ibn Ḥawqal, Ibn Ghālib, and al-ʿUdhrī.

16. Ruggles, "Arabic Poetry and Architectural Memory in al-Andalus," *Ars Orientalis* 23 (1993), 171–78.

17. Al-Maqqarī, *Analectes,* I:346, 373.

18. Ibn Ḥawqal, *Bibl. Geo. Arab.,* II:111; al-Maqqarī, *Analectes,* I:344, citing Muḥyī al-Dīn Ibn al-ʿArabī.

19. Ana Labarta and Carmen Barceló, "Las fuentes árabes sobre al-Zahrāʾ: Estado de la cuestión," *Cuadernos de Madīnat al-Zahrāʾ* 1 (1987), 95.

20. Al-Maqqarī, citing Muḥyī al-Dīn Ibn al-ʿArabī, who said that he heard it directly from "one of the learned men of Cordoba," *Analectes,* I:344.

21. Zakarīyā ibn Muḥammad Qazwīnī, *Āthār al-Bilād* (Beirut, 1960), 440–41. A Spanish translation may be found in Rubiera Mata, *Arquitectura en la literatura,* 41–42, who points to the similiarity between the two fables. According to the story, Parvīz built a park stocked with birds and animals that had taken a thousand men seven years to build. One day Shirīn asked him to build her a palace there that would surpass all others, and because she was the most beautiful woman in the world, he built it for her.

22. Al-Maqqarī, citing Muḥyī al-Dīn Ibn al-ʿArabī, *Analectes,* I:344.

23. R. Castejón, *Excavaciónes del plan nacional,* 14–17.

24. Vallejo Triano, "La infrastructura exterior de Madinat al-Zahraʾ," paper presented at the International Congress of the History of Art, (Berlin, 1992), unpublished.

25. For example, in the hamlets of Alameda del Obispo, Alcolea, Cortijo del Alcaide, and Villarrubia (Gorges, *Les villas hispano-romaines,* 248–52).

26. Ambrosio de Morales, *La crónica general de España,* vol. II of 3 (Alcala de Henares, 1574), 124–25.

27. Al-Maqqarī, *Analectes,* I:374. Ibn ʿIdhārī, *Al-Bayān* II:247; French trans. Fagnan, II:382. ʿAbd al-Raḥmān is mentioned as riding on horseback to personally observe the paving of the road between Madīnat al-Zahrāʾ and the Munyat al-Naʿūra in spring 330/942 (Ibn Ḥayyān, *Crónica* [V], 359).

28. Ibn Ḥayyān, *Crónica* (V), 323–28. *Akhbār Majmūʿa,* (Arabic) 156, (Spanish trans.) 135.

29. Al-Maqqarī, *Analectes,* I:375; al-Maqqarī, *Azhār,* II:270; Ibn Khāqān, *Maṭmaḥ al-anfus* (s.l., 1907), 45.

30. Al-Maqqarī, *Analectes,* I:373, 374. Al-Maqqarī also refers to the second man merely as Ḥasan (*Azhār,* II:270), and Ibn ʿIdhārī calls him Ḥasan al-Qurṭubī (*Al-Bayān,* II:246).

31. For example, the names of Jaʿfar ibn ʿAbd [al-Raḥmān]; a stone carver, Fataḥ al-Naqqāsh; and someone referred to as Shakar al-Fatā al-Kābir are discussed in Manuel Ocaña Jiménez, "Capiteles epigrafiados de Madīnat al-Zahrāʾ," *Al-Andalus* 4 (1936), 158–66.

32. Saʿd, Muḥammad b. Saʿd, Saʿīd al-Aḥmar, Rashīq, Muẓaffar, Fataḥ, Aflaḥ, and other incomplete or undecipherable names are discussed in Ocaña Jiménez, "Inscripciones árabes descubiertas en Madīnat al-Zahrāʾ en 1944," *Al-Andalus* 10 (1945), 154–59.

33. Al-Nuwayrī, *Historia de los musulmanes,* (Arabic) 61, (Spanish trans.) 54–55. Ibn Ghālib confirms the presence of Christian slaves at Madīnat al-Zahrāʾ, although he does not mention their numbers ("La descripción de Córdoba," 674).

34. Al-Maqqarī, *Analectes,* I:370.

35. Al-Maqqarī, *Analectes,* I:370; *Azhār,* II:265.

36. Ibn Bashkuwāl cited in al-Maqqarī, *Analectes,* I:345.

37. Ibn ʿIdhārī, *Al-Bayān,* II:246; al-Maqqarī, *Analectes,* I:346, 373; Ibn al-Khaṭīb, *Histoire de l'Espagne Musulmane* (Rabat, 1934), 43.

38. Al-Maqqarī, *Analectes,* I:373; *Azhār,* II:269. Ibn Ghālib notes five hundred loads each of plaster and lime ("La descripción de Córdoba," 674).

39. Ibn Khallikān, *Wafayāt al aʿyān,* II:38; al-Maqqarī, *Analectes,* I:372–73; *Azhār,* II:268; Ibn ʿIdhārī, II:246. Ibn al-Khaṭīb quotes a figure of 4,324 columns (*Histoire,* 43), and Ibn Ghālib's figures differ as well ("La descripción de Córdoba," 674).

40. Al-Maqqarī, *Analectes,* II:372. Ibn Ghālib, "La descripción de Córdoba," 674.

41. Ibn ʿIdhārī, *Al-Bayān,* ed. Dozy, II:246; al-Maqqarī, *Analectes,* I:374. With 4,313 columns the total cost came to 34,504 dinars, or 3,000 pesetas in 1960, according to Rosario Castejón, "Madinat al-Zahra en los autores árabes," 70–71.

42. One hundred almudies of Qasimīya dirhems or less, according to some, but one of the staff at Madīnat al-Zahrāʾ calculated the cost at three hundred thousand dinars for the twenty years of ʿAbd al-Raḥmān's residence at the palace (al-Maqqarī, *Analectes,* I:374). Ibn Ghālib noted three hundred thousand gold dinars, or fifteen million for the entire duration of the construction ("La descripción de Córdoba," 674).

One third of the revenues was apportioned to the army, and another third was stored against times of famine and drought (Ibn Ghālib, "La descripción de Córdoba," 674; al-Maqqarī, *Analectes,* I:374). The revenues amounted to 5,480,000 dinars from the kingdom of al-Andalus and 875,000 from the caliph's own properties. Booty from military conquests was not included in these figures, since it was never numerically assessed (al-Maqqarī, *Analectes,* I:374). A slightly lower figure of 765,000 from the caliph and market taxes is given by Ibn ʿIdhārī (ed. Dozy, II:247), cited in Rosario Castejón, "Madinat al-Zahra en los autores árabes," 148.

43. I am grateful to Cecil L. Striker for pointing this out.

44. In *Analectes,* al-Maqqarī cites Ibn Ḥayyān and his sources (I:372–73) regarding the number and provenance of the columns and Ibn Faraḍī (I:370) regarding the numbers and types of skilled and ordinary workers.

45. The written figures vary. Ibn Khallikān (in al-Maqqarī, *Analectes,* I:344) claimed that the city measured 2,700 by 1,500 cubits (one cubit being the equivalent of 47 cm, according to Rosario Castejón, "Madinat al-Zahra en los autores árabes," 71–72), or 1,269 by 705 meters. Al-ʿUdhrī also underestimated the size of the site as being 1,900 by 1,090 cubits (*Fragmentos,* 123). Ibn Ḥayyān, on the other hand, was either very misinformed or was misquoted by al-Maqqarī, who attributed to him the grossly inaccurate figure of 2,700 by 990,000 cubits (al-Maqqarī, *Analectes,* I:345).

46. Al-Idrīsī, *Description,* 212; al-Ḥimyarī, *La péninsule ibérique,* 95.

47. Al-Nuwayrī, *Historia,* I:62.

48. Al-Rāzī, 68 and 153 = Ibn Ḥayyān, 50 and 120; al-Maqqarī, *Analectes,* I:344; *Akhbār Majmūʿa,* 132.

Lévi-Provençal, who believed the Cordoba figure to be the Virgin Mary, was led to conclude that the Islamic historians' identification of the figure at Madīnat al-Zahrāʾ as the concubine al-Zahrāʾ was an attribution invented post facto (*Hist. Esp. Mus.,* II:135–36).

49. Rosario Castejón, "Madinat al-Zahra en los autores árabes," 74. The presence of abundant Roman sculptural fragments and pieces of Roman sarcophagi at Madīnat al-Zahrāʾ supports Castejón's

theory. See also Basilio Pavón Maldonado, "Influjos occidentales en el arte del califato de Córdoba," *Al-Andalus* 33 (1968), 213.

50. Ibn ʿIdhārī, *El anónimo de Madrid y Copenhague* (abridged version of Ibn ʿIdhārī's fourth volume), ed. and trans. (Spanish) A. Huici Miranda (Valencia, 1917), (Arabic) 60–61, (Spanish trans.) 64.

51. Al-Maqqarī, *Analectes,* I:252.

52. For example, when King Ordoño was received in the court of al-Ḥakam in April 351/962, he was met by a reception committee at the walls of the city. The group passed on horseback between two rows of soldiers who were dressed in full regalia, until they reached the Bāb al-Aqbāʾ. There the reception committee dismounted, allowing Ordoño and his highest-ranking men to continue on horseback to the Bāb al-Sudda where his men dismounted. Only Ordoño entered the Dār al-Jund riding (al-Maqqarī, *Analectes,* I:252–53).

In contrast, when the Maghrebi chieftain Jaʿfar Ibn ʿAlī came to Cordoba to submit to al-Ḥakam in 360/971, he was regarded as a political prisoner and as a sign of his diminished status, was made to dismount outside the Bāb al-Sudda (Al-Rāzī, 64–69 = Ibn Ḥayyān, 43–50).

53. Ibn ʿIdhārī, *Al-Bayān,* II:247.

54. Ibn Ghālib, citing al-Rāzī and other authors, "La descripción de Córdoba," 674. Vallvé translates *riyāḍāt* as "mausolea," but as there is no historical mention of burials at al-Zahrāʾ, a better translation is "gardens."

55. Al-Rāzī, 88 = Ibn Ḥayyān, 66.

56. Al-Maqqarī, *Azhār,* I:260–61; Ibn Ghālib, *Kitāb farḥat al-anfus,* 301. The mint had been transferred from Cordoba to al-Zahrāʾ by ʿAbd al-Raḥmān in 336/947 (Ibn ʿIdhārī, *Al-Bayān,* II:214).

57. Al-Rāzī, 185 = Ibn Ḥayyān, 146.

58. Ibn Khaldūn in al-Maqqarī, *Analectes,* I:380.

59. Ibn Ḥayyān, *Crónica* (v), 41.

60. Ibn Ḥayyān, *Crónica* (v), 201, 203.

61. Al-Maqqarī, *Analectes,* I:373; Ibn al-Khaṭīb, *Histoire,* 44; elsewhere al-Maqqarī gives eight hundred as the figure for loaves consumed (*Azhār,* II:270).

62. Al-Maqqarī, *Analectes,* I:346; al-Nuwayrī, *Historia,* I:62.

63. Ibn Khaqān, *Maṭmaḥ al-anfus,* 50, Spanish translation in Rosario Castejón, "Madinat al-Zahra en los autores árabes," 151.

64. For example, the Dār al-Jund is called variously the Gran Salón, Salón Oriental, Salón Septentrional, Salón Occidental, Majlis al-Gharbī, and Schlichter Empfangssal (to distinguish it from the Reiches Empfangssal), and Salon Rico (Mercedes Lillo Alemany, "Sobre los patios de Madīnat al-Zahrāʾ," in *Actas de las Jornadas de Cultura Arabe e Islámica [1978]* [Madrid, 1981], 264 n. 7).

65. Al-Maqqarī, *Analectes,* I:251.

66. Al-Maqqarī, *Analectes,* I:252–54.

67. Al-Maqqarī, *Analectes,* I:372.

68. Ibn al-Ḥasan al-Nubāhī, cited in al-Maqqarī, *Analectes,* I:377–78; also al-Nubāhī, *Kitāb al-marqaba,* 71; al-Maqqarī, *Azhār,* II:280–82.

69. Al-Maqqarī, *Analectes,* I:346; al-Nuwayrī, *Historia,* I:62.

70. Al-Maqqarī, *Analectes,* I:346.

71. Al-Maqrīzī, *al-Khiṭāṭ,* II:108–9 cited in Rubiera Mata, *Arquitectura en la literatura,* 82–86. This Tulunid garden employed fanciful effects such as gilded palm trunks and piped water that in turn were modeled on Abbasid gardens.

72. Al-Maqqarī, *Analectes,* I:377–78; *Azhār,* II:280–82; al-Nubāhī, *Histoire,* 71.

73. Al-Maqqarī, *Analectes,* I:251.

74. Al-Rāzī, 99 = Ibn Ḥayyān, 76.

75. Al-Rāzī, 99 = Ibn Ḥayyān, 76. Although the precise wording is "*fī al-majlis al-sharqī minhā,*" I believe that the qualifier *minhā,* which refers to the Dār al-Mulk, indicates that this is not the great reception hall called the Majlis al-Sharqī and mentioned in the context of the Saṭḥ al-Mumarrad. Rather, the author is referring simply to an ordinary chamber on the eastern side of the Dār al-Mulk complex which, if excavation evidence has been interpreted correctly, is in the western half of the Qaṣr.

76. Al-Nuwayrī, *Historia,* 64. It is an oft repeated topos. See Ibn Ghālib in "La descripción de Córdoba," 676–67; Dozy, *Recherches sur l'histoire et la littérature de l'Espagne pendant le moyen âge* (Leiden, 1881), I:245–56; Luis Seco de Lucena, "Los palacios del taifa almeriense al-Muʿtasim," *Cuadernos de la Alhambra* 3 (1967), 18; and regarding Ctesiphon, al-Qazwīnī, *Āthār al-Bilād,* cited in Rubiera Mata, *Arquitectura en la literatura,* 39–41.

77. Ibn al-Faraḍī in al-Maqqarī, *Analectes,* I:370–1.

78. Hernández Giménez, *Madīnat al-Zahrāʾ,* 42–43.

79. Antonio Fernández Puertas, prologue to Hernández Giménez, *Madīnat al-Zahrāʾ,* xxii. Also communication with present director of excavations, Antonio Vallejo.

80. Since the *ḥājib* died in 971, the Dār al-Jaʿfar can

be dated before then (Hernández Giménez, *Madīnat al-Zahrā'*, 67–71).

81. Al-Rāzī, 88 = Ibn Ḥayyān, 66.

82. R. Castejón, *Excavaciones del plan nacional*, 19–21.

83. Excavations were begun by Velázquez Bosco and continued by Castejón (R. Castejón, *Excavaciones del plan nacional*, 37–40).

84. R. Castejón, *Excavaciones del plan nacional*, 27–29.

85. R. Castejón, *Excavaciones del plan nacional*, 29–33.

86. Hernández Giménez, *Madīnat al-Zahrā'*, 72.

87. Fernández-Puertas writes that the stairs led to an upper story (prologue to Hernández Giménez, *Madīnat al-Zahrā'*, xxiii). R. Castejón believed that they led to the caliphal quarters (*Excavaciones del plan nacional*, 31).

88. Ocaña Jiménez, "Capiteles de la residencia califal de Medina Az-Zahra: Estudios de sus inscripciones," *Boletín de la Real Academia de Córdoba* 32 (1931), 215–26.

89. Manual Gómez-Moreno, *Ars Hispaniae*, vol. III, *El arte árabe español hasta los almohades, arte mozárabe* (Madrid, 1951), 160.

90. The Salon Rico was excavated during the 1944 season by Hernández Giménez, Emilio Camps, and Rafael Castejón. Although the roof and walls were collapsed and buried under layers of soil and debris, and the columns and other valuables were missing from the interior, most of the rubble from the structure was lying on the floor, in some places as deep as five to six meters. Included in this were marble chips from the columns. (Rafael Castejón, "Nuevas excavaciones en Madīnat al-Zahrā': El salon de 'Abd al-Raḥmān III," *Al-Andalus* 10 [1945], 147–54).

91. Water runoff was a critical planning problem at Madīnat al-Zahrā'. During the rainy season, water did not percolate into the soil but stayed on the surface and flowed downhill (Hernández Giménez, *Madīnat al-Zahrā'*, 34]. To prevent erosion in the gardens and damp in the buildings, the site was planned with an extensive network of runoff channels and underground drains.

92. Rafael Castejón, "Nuevas excavaciones en Madīnat al-Zahrā'," 149.

93. Gómez-Moreno, *Ars Hispaniae* III, 84.

94. Gómez-Moreno, *Ars Hispaniae* III, 84.

95. Hernández Giménez, *Madīnat al-Zahrā'*, pp. 125–53; Christian Ewert, "Elementos decorativos en los tableros parietales del Salón Rico de Madīnat al-Zahrā'," *Cuadernos de Madīnat al-Zahrā'* 1 (1987), 27–60, with excellent photographs of the decorative panels.

96. Rafael Castejón, "Nuevas excavaciones en Madīnat al-Zahrā'," 149.

97. Al-Maqqarī, *Azhār*, II:260; Ibn 'Idhārī, *Al-Bayān*, II:228.

98. A. Vallejo Triano, "Madinat al-Zahra': La realidad arqueológica y las fuentes documentales," in *Actas de las I Jornadas de Cultura Islámica (Toledo, 1987)* (Madrid, 1989), 125–26.

99. A. Vallejo Triano, "El baño próximo al Salón de 'Abd al-Raḥmān III," *Cuadernos de Madīnat al-Zahrā'* 1 (1987), 141–65.

100. Hernández Giménez, *Arquitectura y decoración*, 62.

101. Personal communication from Antonio Vallejo Triano.

102. Rafael Castejón, "Las excavaciones de Madinat al-Zahra de 1967 a 1969," *Boletín de la Asociación Española de Orientalistas* 6 (1970), 207.

103. Personal communication from A. Vallejo Triano. The stairs have not been thoroughly excavated and are not indicated on the plan.

5. Madīnat al-Zahrā', Samarra, and the View

1. Ulbert, "Ein umaiyadischer Pavillon," 213–31.

2. Pérès, *Esplendor*, 33, 59–62; Reynold A. Nicholson, *A Literary History of the Arabs* (originally 1907), (Cambridge, 1966), 415–17; Alois R. Nykl, *Hispano-Arabic Poetry and Its Relations with the Old Provençal Troubadours* (Baltimore, 1946), 16–17; and Linda Fish Compton, *Andalusian Lyrical Poetry and Old Spanish Love Songs: The "Muwashshaḥ" and Its "Kharja"* (New York, 1976), passim.

3. Maqrīzī, *al-Khiṭāṭ*, cited in Rubiera Mata, *Arquitectura en la literatura*, 84–86.

4. Maqrīzī, *al-Khiṭāṭ*, cited in Rubiera Mata, *Arquitectura en la literatura*, 84–86; al-Khaṭīb, *Ta'rīkh Baghdad* [Cairo, 1931] I:100–4, Spanish translation in Rubiera Mata, 69–74. Rubiera Mata (57–59) notes that these stories echo the fabulous palace of Iram, which had gem-studded rivers, and palms with golden branches and leaves of fruit of jacinth, emeralds, and pearls.

5. Al-Maqqarī, *Analectes*, I:372.

6. Lévi-Provençal, *Hist. Esp. Mus.*, II:148.

7. S. M. Stern, "An Embassy of the Byzantine Emperor to the Fatimid Caliph al-Muʿizz," *Byzantion* 20 (1950), 239–58; reprinted in Stern, *History and Culture in the Medieval Muslim World* (London, 1984).

8. The Islamic centers were better known than were Christian ones, for Muslim travelers set their sights on attaining the Islamic pilgrimage centers Mecca and Medina first, followed by Baghdad, Cairo, Kairouan, and the other great Islamic cities. In the ninth and tenth centuries only a small proportion went to Constantinople and Rome.

In North Africa, the geographer al-Muqaddasī noted the parallels between Baghdad and the Fatimid capital of Ṣabra-Manṣūrīya (near Kairouan), which, like the former, was circular in plan, with oriented gates, and with the ruler's residence and the congregational mosque in the center (Al-Muqaddasī, *Aḥsan al-taqāsīm fī maʿrifat al-aqālīm*, ed. de Goeje [*Descriptio imperii moslemici*] [Leiden, 1877], 266, cited in Bloom, "Origins of Fatimid Art," 28).

9. Ibn Ghālib, *Farḥat al-anfus*, 281; and cited again in al-Maqqarī, *Analectes*, II:104.

10. Al-Maqqarī, *Analectes*, II:118; trans. Gayangos, *History* I:186.

11. Gayangos, *History*, II:151.

12. Ibn Ḥawqal, *Configuration de la terre*, 111; *Bibl. Geog. Arab.*, II (3d ed., 1967), (Arabic) 110.

13. E. Herzfeld and F. Sarre, *Erster vorläufiger Bericht über die Augraben von Samarra* (Berlin, 1912) and Ernst Herzfeld, "Mitteilungen über die Arbeiten der zweiten Kampagne von Samarra," *Der Islam* 5 (1915), 196–204, excerpted and trans. by K. A. C. Creswell (with Herzfeld's review and approval), *Early Muslim Architecture*, II:232–42, 265–70. See also Henri Viollet "Description du palais de al-Moutasim à Samara" and "Fouilles à Samara," *Memoires de l'Academie des inscriptions et belles-lettres*, ser. I, vol. XII, pt. II, (1909, 1911), 567–94, 685–7171. For a complete bibliography, see Alastair Northedge, "An Interpretation of the Palace of the Caliph at Samarra," *Ars Orientalis* 23 (1993), 143–70.

14. J. Lassner, *The Shaping of ʿAbbasid Rule* (Princeton, 1980), 169–75, 184–203; and "The Caliph's Personal Domain: The City Plan of Baghdad Reexamined," in *The Islamic City: A Colloquium*, ed. Albert Hourani and S. H. Stern (Philadelphia and Oxford, 1970), 103–18.

15. Anon. *Una crónica anónima*, (Arabic) 59, (Spanish trans.) 151–52; Ibn Ḥayyān, *Crónica* 184.

16. Gabrieli, "Omayyades," 93–100.

17. *Murūj*, ed. Barbier de Meynard, I:362, ed. Pellat, II:192; cited in Gabrieli, "Omayyades," 93–100.

18. Lévi-Provençal, *Hist. Esp. Mus.*, III:6–10, 488–96. Also Gabrieli, "Omayyades," 93–100.

19. Al-Rāzī, 239–40 = Ibn Ḥayyān, 198–99.

20. Al-Khaṭīb, *Taʾrīkh Baghdad* I:100–4; trans. in G. LeStrange, "A Greek Embassy to Baghdad in 917 A.D.," *Journal of the Royal Asiatic Society* (1895), 35–45.

21. Lévi-Provençal, *Hist. Esp. Mus.*, I:271–72.

22. Pérès, *Esplendor*, 50; al-Maqqarī, *Analectes*, II:97; Ibn al-ʿAbbār, *Takmila*, notice 2114.

23. Ziryāb went via the Aghlabid court in Kairouan (Lévi-Provençal, *Hist. Esp. Mus.*, I:269). To name some others: the historian al-Warrāq (b. 292/904–5) spent most of his life in Kairouan before going to al-Ḥakam II's court (M. Antuña, "Ibn Ḥayyān de Córdoba y su historia de la España musulmana," *Cuadernos de Historia de España* 4 [1946], 58). In the late tenth century Ibn Ṣāʿid went from Baghdad, to the Fatimid court in Cairo, ending up in al-Manṣūr's court in Cordoba in 380/990 (Régis Blachère, "Un pionnier de la culture arabe orientale en Espagne au Xe siècle: Ṣāʿid de Bagdad," *Hespéris* 10 [1930], 15–36).

24. He paid people four hundred dirhems to settle near Madīnat al-Zahrāʾ, and they complied eagerly [Ibn Saʿīd, *Kitāb al-Mughrib*, 174, marginal numbering]. Ibn Ḥawqal gave the same information and noted that the countryside between al-Zahrāʾ and Cordoba eventually became so crowded that the houses formed a continuous line.

25. Richard Ettinghausen and Oleg Grabar, *The Art and Architecture of Islam, 650–1250* (Harmondsworth, 1987), 78–79; J. M. Rogers, "Samarra: a Study in Medieval Town-Planning," in *The Islamic City: A Colloquium*, eds. A. H. Hourani and S. M. Stern (Philadelphia and Oxford, 1970), 119–55, 120, 142–43.

26. Grabar, *Formation of Islamic Art*, 67.

27. Al-Yaʿqūbī, *Biblioteca geographorum arabicorum* (*Buldān*), ed. de Goeje (Leiden, 1870–94) 266–67; trans. in K. A. C. Creswell, *A Short Account of Early Muslim Architecture* (Aldershot, 1989), 367. The caliph pronounced this after moving into the new city of al-Jaʿfarīya, north of Samarra, where he lived for nine months before being assassinated in 247/861.

28. For example, al-Khaṭīb's *History of Baghdad* describes a reception ceremony in which all the treasures of the Abbasid palace were brought forth, including thousands of beautifully worked hangings, gold brocades, embroideries, and carpets; hundreds of handsome horses with gold and silver saddles,

four elephants in silk brocade, and one hundred lions; ten thousand gilded breastplates and as many helmets, shields, bows, and ornamented weapons; and a fabulously crafted tree of gold and silver branches with gold and silver singing birds; and many more wonders, trans. in Grabar, *Formation of Islamic Art,* 168–171.

29. Ettinghausen and Grabar, *Art and Architecture of Islam,* 86.

30. Al-Yaʿqūbī, *Les Pays* (Cairo, 1937), 11; *Bibl. Geo. Arab.,* 238.

31. Al-Maqqarī, *Analectes,* I:344.

32. Al-Ḥimyarī, *La péninsule ibérique,* (Arabic) 80.

33. Al-Yaʿqūbī, *Les Pays,* trans. (French) Wiet 47; *Biblio. Geo. Arab.* (VII), 257.

34. Descriptions of the remains of this site were recorded in 1898 and 1901, summarized in Creswell, *A Short Account of Early Muslim Architecture,* 131–34.

35. G. Le Strange, *Baghdad During the Abbasid Caliphate* (Oxford: 1900), chaps. 2 and 3.

36. Rogers, "Samarra," 152, citing Yāqūt, *Muʿjam al-buldān,* and Qazwinī, *Nuzha.* The elevation of buildings for the purpose of giving a perspective onto the grounds below was by no means an Islamic innovation. Roman villas and imperial baths often occupied high positions and had large windows from which views of gardens or the sea could be appreciated. Persian palaces such as the ʿImārat-i Khusrau at the Qaṣr-i Shīrīn and the Ḥaush Kuri (591–628) stood on high terraces from which the surrounding gardens could be viewed (Ralph Pinder-Wilson, "The Persian Garden: *Bagh* and *Chahar Bagh,*" in *The Islamic Garden,* ed. E. MacDougall and R. Ettinghausen [Washington, D.C., 1976], 72–73).

37. Excavated 1911–13 and published in preliminary form by Ernst Herzfeld, "Mitteilung über die Arbeiten," 196–204; translated and summarized by Creswell (and corrected by Herzfeld), *Early Muslim Architecture,* II:232–45. The most recent treatment of the palace is Northedge, "Palace of the Caliph," 143–70.

38. Numerous historians have confused this portal with the Dār al-ʿĀmma (Hall of Justice) also mentioned by al-Yaʿqūbī, but they were distinct buildings. The Dār al-ʿĀmma was in the southern part of the complex whereas the Bāb was on the west side (Northedge "Palace of the Caliph," 152–53).

39. Northedge, "Palace of the Caliph," 146.

40. Northedge, "Palace of the Caliph," 145.

41. Northedge, "Palace of the Caliph," 150.

42. Balkuwārā was excavated by Herzfeld in the summer of 1911 and published only in the form of a preliminary report (*Erster vor laüfer Bericht über die Ausgrabungen von Samarra* [Berlin, 1912]) which the author never revised or completed but which was edited and included in Creswell, *Early Muslim Architecture,* II:265–70. Thomas Leisten is preparing a final report for future publication.

43. Yasser Tabbaa has pointed out that the only surviving fountain from Samarra pertained to the Great Mosque ("The Medieval Islamic Garden: Typology and Hydraulics," in *Garden History: Issues Approaches, Methods,* ed. J. D. Hunt (Washington, D.C., 1992), 307.

44. Creswell, *Early Muslim Architecture,* II:265–70, citing Herzfeld.

45. Creswell, *Early Muslim Architecture,* II:265–70, citing Herzfeld.

46. Herzfeld, trans. in Creswell, *A Short Account of Early Muslim Architecture,* 366. Alastair Northedge questions Herzfeld's ability to see the Qaṣr al-ʿĀshiq and the Qubbat al-Sulaibīya (personal communication, May 17, 1996).

47. G. LeStrange, "Description of Mesopotamia and Baghdad, Written About the Year 900 A.D. by Ibn Serapion," *Journal of the Royal Asiatic Society* (1895), 33–76 and 255–315.

48. Government of Iraq, Department of Antiquities, *Excavations at Samarra 1936–1939* (Baghdad, 1940), 4–8.

49. For example, the case of a natural stream that was allowed to course through the villa of Manilius Vopiscus, in Zoja Pavlovskis, *Man in an Artificial Landscape: The Marvels of Civilization in Imperial Roman Literature* (Leiden, 1973), 17 and passim; also Pierre Grimal, *Les jardins romains* (2d rev. ed., Paris, 1969), 293–99.

50. Gorges, *Villas hispano-romaines,* 241; Alexander G. McKay, *Houses, Villas, and Palaces in the Roman World* (Ithaca, 1975), 74–77.

51. Al-Nuwayrī, *Historia,* 62.

52. See "mirador" in *Webster's New Collegiate Dictionary* (1977).

53. Ibn Ḥayyān, *al-Muqtabis,* ed. El-Hajji, 21. See also al-Maqqarī, *Azhār,* II:260.

54. Hernández Giménez, *Arquitectúra y Decoracíon,* 61–62. The mirador theory has been echoed most recently by Alfonso Jiménez Martín, "Los jardines de Madīnat al-Zahrāʾ," *Cuardernos de Madīnat al-Zahrāʾ* 1 (1987), 81–92.

55. The Alhambra's Comares Tower in particular (Hernández Giménez, *Arquitectura y Decoración,* 62).

56. Ruggles, "The Mirador in Abbasid and Hispano-Umayyad Garden Typology," *Muqarnas* 7 (1990), 78–79.

57. James Dickie argues for the existence of two garden types in the Alhambra, built three centuries later: one derived from the Roman "villa rustica," the other from the Roman "villa urbana" ("The Alhambra: Some Reflections Prompted by a Recent Study by Oleg Grabar," in *Studia Arabica et Islamica* [Beirut, 1981], 127–49). This distinction is problematic, however. Even as early as the first century B.C.E., the terms "urban" and "rustic" did not refer to discreet types, because by that time the Roman house/villa had expanded into the landscape, so that the distinction between open and closed spaces was no longer clear (Bettina Bergmann, review of Elisabeth B. MacDougall, ed., *Ancient Roman Gardens*, in *The Journal of the Society of Architectural Historians*, 48 [1989], 387–89).

58. Grabar, *Formation of Islamic Art*, 31–32.

59. Al-Ruṣāfa may be an exception because the presumed site occupied a hill with views of Cordoba; however, the excavations under the present government-run parador were by no means conclusive and the precise location of the palace has not been ascertained. The Arabic deescriptions of the site did not emphasize views or mention the building of artificial terraces.

60. For a discussion of the semiotic significance of landscape view and perspective in an altogether different context, see Nicholas Green, *The Spectacle of Nature: Landscape and Bourgeois Culture in Nineteenth-Century France* (Manchester, 1990); and the chapter on Constable's landscape paintings in Ann Bermingham, *Landscape and Ideology: The English Rustic Tradition 1740–1860* (Los Angeles and Berkeley, 1986).

61. Pierre Grimal, *Les jardins romains*, 2–3.

62. John Barrell, "The Public Prospect and the Private View: The Politics of Taste in Eighteenth-Century Britain," in *Reading Landscape: Country-City-Capital*, ed. Simon Pugh (Manchester, 1990), 19–40.

63. For a provocative comparison of vision and the gaze in nineteenth-century North Africa and Europe, see Timothy Mitchell, *Colonising Egypt* (1988) (Berkeley and Los Angeles, 1991), 1 and 2.

64. In the first 150 years of Islam, the word *miḥrāb* did not refer primarily to a niche in a mosque. Its meaning ranged from a covered sitting place (in the Qur'ān) to a reserved place of honor or, in residential architecture, to "a row of columns with their intervening spaces" (R. B. Serjeant, "Miḥrāb," *Bulletin of the School of Oriental and African Studies* 22 [1959], 439 ff.). But by the mid-tenth century, "mihrab" was the accepted term for a prayer niche. Used at Madīnat al-Zahrā' to describe the frame for the caliph, it is clearly the older sense of the word that ruled. But the religious connotation must also have hovered, so that the Umayyad caliph's "honored sitting place" in the reception hall was thus associated with the single most highly charged place in the mosque that resonated with the privilege of princes, the Prophet's presence, and God's light (Sūrat al-Nūr 24:34). See also Estelle Whelan, "The Origins of the *Miḥrāb Mujawwaf*: A Reinterpretation," *International Journal of Middle East Studies* 18 (1986), 205–23.

65. Regarding the frame as the marker of the discursive field, see John Tagg, *Grounds of Dispute* (Minneapolis, 1992), 30–31.

66. Mitchell (*Colonising Egypt*, 60) discusses this with respect to vision and urban space. He refers to Derrida's discussion of the ontological relationship between "discourse and inscription," (Derrida, "The Double Session," in *Dissemination*, trans. Barbara Johnson [1972] [Chicago, 1981], 191); also see Peter Brunette and David Wills, "The Spatial Arts: An Interview with Jacques Derrida," in *Deconstruction in the Visual Arts* (Cambridge, 1994), 15–18.

67. Derrida in Brunette and Wills, "Interview with Derrida," 15–18.

6. Later Cordoban Palaces and Gardens

1. Most historians give 422/1031 as the date of the end of the Umayyad dynasty and this is literally correct; however, the Umayyads had lost power as a result of the civil war, and during or soon after 1010, taifa dynasties, beginning with the Hammudids of Malaga and the Zirids of Granada, began to spring up.

2. It was in the area of Moroquil. Ricardo Velázquez Bosco, *Medina Azzahra y Alamiriya* (Madrid, 1912).

3. Ocaña Jiménez, "Las ruinas de 'Alamiría,' un yacimiento arqueológico erróneamente denominado," *Al-Qanṭara* 5 (1984), 365–81.

4. Although Velázquez Bosco's identification was accepted by Lévi-Provençal and Rafael Castejón, it was *not* accepted by Manuel Gómez Moreno, Leopoldo Torres Balbás, Henri Terrasse, or Christian

Ewert (Gómez Moreno, *Ars Hispaniae,* III:166; Henri Terrasse, *L'art hispano-mauresque des origines au XIIIe siècle* [Paris, 1932], 166–67). Terrasse, as early as 1932, challenged the attribution of "al-ʿĀmirīya" to al-Manṣūr, saying that in style it more resembled Madīnat al-Zahrāʾ. He also pointed out that most of the Islamic texts place al-ʿĀmirīya near Madīnat al-Zāhira, which was on the *east* side of Cordoba. Ewert gave a paper in 1979 on Arab palace typology at the IV Congreso de Estudios Extremeños in which he spoke of the lack of evidence to support the identification of this palace with al-ʿĀmirīya.

5. For example, al-Ḍabbī, *Bugyat al-multamis fī taʾrīkh riyāl ahl al-Andalus,* ed. F. Codera and J. Ribera in *Biblioteca Arábico Hispana,* vol. III (Madrid, 1885), no. 1545.

6. José Antonio Conde, *Historia de la dominación de los árabes en España* (Madrid, 1820; the 1874 edition cited here), 128–29.

7. Ibn Bashkuwāl, *al-Ṣila,* 207; Ocaña Jiménez, "Las ruinas de 'Alamiría,'" 373–74.

8. Al-Maqqarī, *Analectes,* I:384.

9. Rafael Castejón, "Alamiría," *Boletín de la Real Academia de Córdoba* 70 (1954), 150–57.

10. Al-Rāzī, 136 = Ibn Ḥayyān, 106; Ocaña Jiménez, "Las ruinas de 'Alamiría,'" 376–77.

11. Al-Rāzī, 136–37 = Ibn Ḥayyān, 106–7.

12. Al-Rāzī, 136 = Ibn Ḥayyān, 103.

13. Ocaña Jiménez, "Las ruinas de 'Alamiría,'" 380, pl. 2.

14. The site was published by Ricardo Velázquez Bosco in *Medina Azzahra y Alamiriya;* Samuel de los Santos et al., "Las ruinas de Alamiría," in *Anales de la Comisión de Monumentos Historicos y Artísticos de Córdoba* (Cordoba, 1926), 17–21; and Rafael Castejón, "Alamiría," 150–57.

15. Rafael Castejón, "Alamiría," 150–57.

16. Santos et al., "Las ruinas de Almaría," 17–21.

17. Al-Maqqarī, *Analectes,* I:373; al-Maqqarī, *Azhār,* II:270; Ibn al-Khāṭib, *Aʿmāl,* 44.

18. L. de Beylié, *La Kalaa des Beni Hammad, une capitale berbère de l'Afrique du Nord au XIe* (Paris, 1909), 60; Rafael Castejón, "Alamiría," 150–57; *Kitāb al-Istibsār* cited in Golvin, *Recherches archéologiques à la Qalʿa des Banū Hammād* (Paris, 1965), 58. For a discussion of the similarities between the Qalʿa, al-Rummānīya, and Madīnat al-Zahrāʾ, see Ruggles, "Vision and Power at the Qala Bani Hammad in Islamic North Africa," *The Journal of Garden History* 14 (1994), 28–41.

19. Rafael Castejón, "Alamiría," 150–57.

20. Rafael Castejón, "Córdoba califal," 298–99.

21. Al-Maqqarī, *Analectes,* I:307; Pérès, *Esplendor,* 138; on al-Muṣḥafī's career, see Lévi-Provençal, *Hist. Esp. Mus.,* II:205–217.

22. Lévi-Provençal, *Hist. Esp. Mus.,* II:206–8.

23. Ocaña Jiménez, "Notas sobre la Córdoba de Ibn Ḥazm," *Al-Mulk* 3 (1963), 53–62.

24. Ocaña Jiménez, "Notas sobre la Córdoba"; Ibn Bashkuwāl in al-Maqqarī, *Analectes,* I:304.

25. Rafael Castejón, "Córdoba califal," 327; Lévi-Provençal, *Hist. Esp. Mus.,* III:373.

26. Archivo Histórico Nacional, Sección Clero, folder 487, no. 9, dated Cordoba, August 1, 1409; cited in José M. Escobar Camacho, *Córdoba en la Baja Edad Media* (Cordoba, 1989), 221, 225. San Augustin's garden is mentioned in the Real Academia de la Historia, Colección Morales, C-14, 316–21, and in the Archivo General de Obispado de Córdoba, *Protocolo general . . . deste . . . Convento de Santo Augustín,* folio 25r, dated Cordoba, February 16, 1328; cited in Escobar Comacho, *Córdoba,* 240–47.

27. The Alcazar became the Bishop's Palace. Its grounds provided the site for the Christian Alcazar, which still stands today (Rafael Castejón, "Nuevas identificaciones en la topografía," 371–89, esp. 376).

28. Al-Maqqarī, *Analectes,* I:306–7. Lévi-Provençal proposed that Dimashq (Damascus) was another name for the Ruṣāfa Palace, but there is simply no evidence for this (*Hist. Esp. Mus.,* I:136 n. 1).

29. The vizier was Ibn ʿAmmār, in al-Fatḥ Ibn Khāqān, *al-Qalāʾid,* 84; reproduced in al-Maqqarī, *Analectes,* I:306–7, where it says that the verses had also been attributed to the *ḥājib* Abū ʿUthmān Jaʿfar ibn ʿUthmān al-Muṣḥafī; discussed in Pérès, *Esplendor,* 133.

30. Rafael Castejón, "Vestigios de alcázares musulmanes en Córdoba," *Boletín de la Real Academia de Córdoba* 20 (1949), 213–22.

31. Velázquez Bosco, *Medina Azzahra y Alamiriya,* pl. 8 and 9.

32. The stuccos around the mihrab of the Mosque of Cordoba were restored in 1815 by Furriel, so they may be of dubious value in ascertaining dates of construction. See Rafael Castejón, "Vestigios de alcazares musulmanes," 82.

33. Rafael Castejón, *Córdoba califal," 327–28.*

34. Lévi-Provençal, *Hist. Esp. Mus.,* III:189.

35. Al-Rāzī, 64 n. 25 = Ibn Ḥayyān, 43.

36. Al-Rāzī, 64 n. 26 = Ibn Ḥayyān, 43.

37. Al-Idrīsī, *Description,* (Arabic) 207–8, (French trans.) 256. Ibn ʿIdhārī also mentioned a Qaṣr Nāṣiḥ

on the outskirts of Cordoba, which must be the same site (*Al-Bayān*, III:42).

38. Al-Rāzī, 251–52, n. 214, 215 = Ibn Ḥayyān, 211–12.

39. Lévi-Provençal, *Hist. Esp. Mus.*, III:378 and I:163, citing Ibn Ḥazm, *Jamharat al-ansāb*, 86.

40. The Banū Hasanī were the nephews of the Moroccan rebel Ibn Ḥanūn, and their arrival in Cordoba after deserting the Berber rebels was cause for celebration (Al-Rāzī, 140 = Ibn Ḥayyān, 109–10).

41. Al-Rāzī, 93 n. 49.

42. Al-Rāzī, 124 n. 85 = Ibn Ḥayyān, 96.

43. Ibn ʿIdhārī, *al-Bayān*, II:398–99. Lévi-Provençal believed that the Dhāt al-Wādiyain was located where the Arroyo Fuensanta stream empties into the Guadalquivir, and noted that the name Urṭānīya was derived from the Hispano-Roman "Huertanilla" (*Hist. Esp. Mus.*, III:381 n. 4). Additionally, al-Manṣūr's son ʿAbd al-Malik al-Muẓaffar (d. 399/1008) built a new palace called the Ḥājibīya about which nothing is known (Ibn ʿIdhārī, *al-Bayān*, III:62).

44. Al-Ḥimyarī, *La péninsule ibérique*, (Arabic) 80, (French trans.) 100.

45. Al-Fatḥ ibn Khāqān, quoted by al-Ḥimyarī, *La péninsule ibérique*, (Arabic) 80–81; quoted almost verbatim in al-Maqqarī, *Analectes*, I:380–81.

46. Al-Ḥimyarī (quoting al-Fatḥ Ibn Khāqān), *La péninsule ibérique*, (Arabic) 81, (French trans.) 101.

47. Al-Ḥimyarī (quoting al-Fatḥ Ibn Khāqān), *La péninsule ibérique*, (Arabic) 81, (French trans.) 101.

48. J. M. Continente, "Abū Marwān al-Ŷazīrī, poeta ʿāmiri," *Al-Andalus* 34 (1969), 131.

49. Quoted by Ibn Kattānī in *Kitāb al-tashbīhāt*, ed. I. Abbas (Beirut), 79, cited in Rubiera Mata, *La arquitectura en la literatura*, 69.

50. Al-Maqqarī, *Analectes*, I:349.

51. Al-Ḥimyarī, *La péninsule ibérique*, (Arabic) 82; on the *khuṭba*, coinage and *ṭirāz*, see al-Maqqarī, *Analectes*, I:258.

52. Al-Ḥimyarī (quoting al-Fatḥ Ibn Khāqān), *La péninsule ibérique*, (Arabic) 82, (French trans.) 103.

53. Rafael Castejón, "Córdoba califal," 324; Ibn Ḥayyān, cited in al-Ḥimyarī, *La péninsule ibérique*, (Arabic) 80, (French trans.) 100.

54. Ibn Ḥayyān, cited in al-Ḥimyarī, *La péninsule ibérique*, (Arabic) 81–82.

55. Ibn Ḥazm, *Le collier du pigeon* (*Ṭawq al-ḥamāma*), ed. and trans. L. Bercher (Algiers, 1949), 168–69, 242.

56. Ibn Ḥazm, *Le collier*, 282.

57. Cited by al-Maqqarī, *Analectes*, I:304; see also Escobar Camacho, *Córdoba en la Baja Edad Media*, 32–36.

58. Al-Rāzī, 152–53 n. 127 = Ibn Ḥayyān, 119–20.

59. Lévi-Provençal wrote that al-Zāhira was located one kilometer from the medina walls at the site where now is located the church, citing as his source of information a manuscript of the *Aḥkām Kubrā*, folio 212v, in the Rabat Library (*Hist. Esp. Mus.*, III:373).

60. Torres Balbás, "Los contornos de las ciudades hispano-musulmanas," *Al-Andalus* 15 (1950), 453; al-Maqqarī, *Analectes*, I:307, 384; Pérès, *Esplendor*, 138.

61. This information comes from an anonymous chronicle called the *Anónimo de Madrid y de Copenhague*. A poor photograph of the mill is reproduced in L. Torres Balbás, *Ars Hispaniae* IV (Madrid, 1949), 30.

62. Ibn Zaydūn, *Dīwān*, 153–54, and 56–57, 276 (cited in Pérès, *Esplendor*, 135–37).

63. Pérès, *Esplendor*, 135–37.

64. Al-Maqqarī, *Analaectes*, I:313, 356, cited in Pérès, *Esplendor*, 137; see also Claudio Sánchez-Albornoz, *La España musulmana según los autores islamitas y cristianos medievales*, 2 vols. (Buenos Aires, 1946), I:339.

65. Ibn ʿIdhārī, *al-Bayān*, III:42, and II:311. See also Lévi-Provençal, *Hist. Esp. Mus.*, III:381 n. 4.

66. Ibn Ḥazm, *Ṭawq al-ḥamāma*, 168–69, 250, 256.

67. Even in the ninth century, however, the emir was addressed as "Son of the caliphs," according to Ibn al-Faqīh al-Hamadhānī (*Description du Maghreb*, 36–37).

68. Wasserstein, *The Rise and Fall of the Party-Kings*, 27–29, 34.

69. Wasserstein, *The Rise and Fall of the Party-Kings*, 104–5.

70. Wasserstein, *The Rise and Fall of the Party-Kings*, 184–85.

71. Gabriel Martínez-Gros, *L'Idéologie Omeyyade* (Madrid, 1992), 15.

72. See Ruggles, "Arabic Poetry and Architectural Memory in al-Andalus," 171–78.

73. James Dickie, *El-Dīwān de Ibn Shuhayd al-Andalusī, 382–426 H = 992–1035 C., Texto y Traducción* (Cordoba, 1975), 59–60.

74. Ibn Khāqān, *Qalāʾid*, 152–53, reproduced in al-Maqqarī, *Analectes*, I:419–20; Pérès, *Esplendor*, 134–35; Torres Balbás, *Ciudades*, 142.

75. *Al-Dhakhīra*, 1–1°–288, cited in Dickie, *Dīwān*, 62.

76. Ibn Khāqān, *Qalā'id*, 153, trans. by James Dickie, "The Islamic Garden in Spain," 92–93.

77. Ibn Khāqān, *Qalā'id*, 153, cited in Dickie, *Dīwān*, 66.

78. Ibn Shuhayd, Arabic and trans. in Dickie, *Dīwān*, 124–25.

79. Lévi-Provençal, *Hist. Esp. Mus.*, I:138 ('Abd al-Raḥmān I's burial in the Rawḍa in 788/172) and 191 (al-Ḥakam I buried next to his father, Hishām I, in the Rawḍa in 822/206). In regard to the interment of 'Abd Allāh in 912/300, the cemetery was also referred to as the *rawḍat al-khulafā'* (Anon. *Una crónica anónima de 'Abd al-Raḥmān III al-Nāṣir*, 92–93). The fact that the first tomb was that of 'Abd al-Raḥmān I makes it plain that the Rawḍa cemetery was not the same place as the Dār al-Rawḍa built in the tenth century by 'Abd al-Raḥmān III.

80. In the eleventh century cemeteries were places for prayer, but also for meeting friends and romantic rendezvous, and in some cities, prostitution (Torres Balbás, *Ciudades*, 238–39, 256–58).

7. Palaces of the Eleventh and Twelfth Centuries

1. Al-Maqqarī, *Analectes*, I:379.

2. The following section on poetry was published, in slightly different form, in Ruggles, "Arabic Poetry and Architectural Memory in al-Andalus," 171–78.

3. Charles W. Moore, William J. Mitchell, and William Turnbull, Jr., *The Poetics of Gardens* (Cambridge, 1988), 10.

4. Ibn Ḥayyān cited by Ibn Bassām, *Al-dakhīra fī maḥāsin ahl al-Jazīra*, in García Gómez, *Algunas precisiones sobre la ruina de la Córdoba omeya," al-Andalus* 12 (1947), 281.

5. Ibn Ḥayyān, cited in Ibn Bassām, *Al-dakhīra*, in García Gómez, "Algunas precisiones," 284–86.

6. Reproduced in Arabic in García Gómez, *Qasidas de Andalucía* (Madrid, 1940), 47; this trans. by Nykl, *Hispano-Arabic Poetry*, 117–18.

7. According to al-Fatḥ Ibn Khāqān, who got his information from the vizier Abū al-Ḥasayn ben Sirāj, cited by al-Maqqarī, *Analectes*, I:411–12.

8. Anon., "Córdoba según al-Ḥimyarī," *Al-Mulk* 1 (1959–60), 23–24.

9. Ibn 'Idhārī, *al-Bayān*, cited in Hernández Giménez, *Madīnat al-Zahrā'*, 182–82. Already by the second quarter of the twelfth century, Madīnat al-Zahrā' was on the verge of disappearing altogether according to al-Idrīsī (*Description de l'Afrique*, 212, 262–63) and al-Ḥimyarī ("Córdoba según al-Ḥimyarī," 24). Regarding the statue, see also Ch. 4 in this volume.

10. For Córdoba la Vieja, see Pedro de Madrazo, *Recuerdos y Bellezas de España*, 420; for the Roman Colonia Patricia, see Morales, *Crónica general de España*, III:114.

11. Ibn Bassām, *Dakhīra*, II/1, 111–13, cited in García Gómez, "Algunas precisiones," 284–86.

12. Ibn Ghālib, *Kitāb farḥat al-anfus*, 302.

13. It is cited by al-Nubāhī, Ibn al-Khaṭīb, Ibn al-Athīr, Ibn Sa'īd, Ibn Khaqān, al-Nuwayrī, Ibn Ghālib, and by al-Maqqarī in both *Nafḥ al-ṭīb* and *Azhār al-riyāḍ*. See Ch. 4 in this volume.

14. Ibn Shuhayd in Ibn al-Khaṭīb, *Histoire de l'Espagne*, 122–23; trans. (Spanish) (and adapted here with little variation by me) in Pérès, *Esplendor*, 128–29.

15. Gayangos, *History*, I:245 n. 13 includes the Arabic original; this is Gayangos's translation.

16. Al-Maqqarī, *Analectes*, I:344; see also García Gómez, "Algunas precisiones," 292.

17. Al-Maqqarī, *Analectes*, I:345; trans. in Nykl, *Hispano-Arabic Poetry*, 106; this is my translation.

18. Ibn Ḥazm, *Lecollier*, (Arabic) 242.

19. Abū al-Qāsim Khalaf b. Faraj, or al-Sumaysir, cited in al-Maqqarī, *Analectes*, I:347; trans. variously in Nykl, *Hispano-Arabic Poetry*, 193, and Pérès, *Esplendor*, 132; this is my translation.

20. Al-Maqqarī, *Analectes*, II:768.

21. Wasserstein, *Rise and Fall of the Party-Kings*, 281, especially n. 19; al-Maqqarī, *Analectes*, I:81, 355.

22. Al-Maqqarī, *Analectes*, II:672; trans. in Nykl, *Hispano-Arabic Poetry*, 213; this is my translation.

23. Ibn Khafāja (450/1058–533/1139) in al-Maqqarī, *Analectes*, II:162; this trans. by Nykl, *Hispano-Arabic Poetry*, 231.

24. Gayangos, *History*, I:32.

25. According to Ibn Athīr, Abū al-Ḥazm Ibn Jahwar refused all administrative and honorific titles except that of vizier (Ibn Athīr, *Al-Kāmil fī al-ta'rīkh*, IX:200). For a discussion of the end or continuation of the caliphal institution in al-Andalus, see Wasserstein, *The Caliphate in the West*.

26. Hernández Giménez, *Madīnat al-Zahrā'*, 184.

27. J. Bosch Vilá, *Historia de Sevilla: La Sevilla islámica, 712–1248* (Seville, 1984), 107; Wasserstein, *Rise and Fall of the Party-Kings*, 111–15.

28. The palaces outside of the Bāb al-Jahwar were

in the place popularly known as the Bocados de Faraón (Luqam Firʿaūn), where there were orchards (*huertas*) known by the former owner's name, Ibn Maslama [Ibn Ṣāḥib al-Ṣalāt, *Tārīkh al-mann,* (Arabic) 464–65, (trans.) 188; Bosch Vilá, *La Sevilla islámica,* 273–83].

Torres Balbás first suggested that Huerta del Rey might be the site of al-Buḥayra, and his theory was confirmed by excavations carried out there in 1972 by Juan Zozaya and F. Collantes de Terán (Torres Balbás, "Notas sobre Sevilla en la época musulmana," *Al-Andalus* 10 [1945], 89–96; Juan Zozaya, "Excavaciones en el palacio almohade de la Buhayra," *Noticiario Arqueológico Hispanico* 1 [1972]; M. T. Moreno Menayo, "Los jardines y alcázares musulmanes de la Buhayra [Sevilla]," in *Arqueología Medieval Española* [Madrid, 1987], III:43–51).

29. Ibn Khāqān, *Qalāʾid,* reproduced in *Scriptorum arabum loci de Abbadidis,* ed. Dozy, 3 vols. (Leiden, 1846–63), I:61; see also Bosch Vilá, *Historia de Seville,* 273–83. Rocío Lledó Carrascosa, "Risala sobre los palacios abbadies de Sevilla de Abū Ŷaʿfar Ibn Aḥmad de Denia: Traducción y Estudio," *Sharq al-Andalus,* 3 (1986), 191–200.

30. Lledó Carrascosa, "Risala," 194, ch. 5 of the *risāla.*

31. Ibn Ẓāfir, *Badāʾiʿ al-badāʾih* (Bulaq, 1278 A.H.), 212; al-Maqqarī, *Analectes,* II:162.

32. Rafael Valencia, "Islamic Seville: Its Political, Social and Cultural History," in *The Legacy of Muslim Spain* (Leiden, 1992), 143; Ibn Ḥayyān, *Muqtabis* (III), ed. M. M. Antuña, 78.

33. Rafael Manzano had promised a paper on the subject for the ICOMOS Colloquium on the Islamic Garden in November 1973, but his paper was absent from the published proceedings (ICOMOS, *Les Jardins de l'Islam* [Paris, 1975]).

34. R. Lledó Carrascosa, "Risala," 193. Guerrero Lovillo has suggested that Palace al-Mukarram was located at the zone where today are the Calles Amparo, Viniato, Aposentadores, Regina, and Jerónimo Hernández ("Al-Qaṣr al-Mubārak, el alcázar de la Benedición," *Boletín de Bellas Artes de Sevilla* [1970], 96).

35. Ibn Bassām, *Al-Dakhīra,* and Ibn ʿIdharī, *Al-Bayān,* cited in Guerrero Lovillo, "Al-Qaṣr al-Mubārak," 93; Lledó Carrascosa, "Risala," 193.

36. Ibn ʿIdhārī, quoted in L. Torres Balbas, "Aznalfarache = Ḥiṣn al-Faraŷ," *Al-Andalus,* 25 (1960), 225.

37. Pérès, *Esplendor,* 144.

38. For riverbank see al-Shaqundī, *Elogio,* 95; for sugarcane see al-Ḥimyarī, *La péninsule ibérique,* (Arabic) 21, (French trans.) 24–27.

39. Ibn Ṣāḥib al-Ṣalāt, *Tārīkh al-mann,* (Arabic) 468–69, and Spanish trans. A. Huici Miranda, 190–91; Bosch Vilá, *La Sevilla islámica,* 227–30.

40. For pears, etc., see Torres Balbás, "Notas sobre Sevilla en la época musulmana," 191; for planting see Ibn Ṣāḥib al-Ṣalāt, *Tārīkh al-mann,* (Arabic) 464–66; Spanish trans. Rubiera Mata, *Arquitectura en la literatura,* 139–40.

41. For Ibn Bāṣu, see Jerrilynn Dodds, "Aḥmad Ibn Bāso," in the *Macmillan Encyclopedia of Architects* (New York, 1982), I:38; for Abū al-Qāsim and Abū Bakr, see Rubiera Mata, *Arquitectura en la literatura,* 139–40.

42. A mansion was built in the Buḥayra by Juan de Monsalve in the fifteenth century and it survived until the third quarter of the nineteenth century; Torres Balbás, "Notas sobre Sevilla en la época musulmana," 195.

43. Because Rafael Manzano's excavation report remains unpublished, the best discussion of the gardens is found in James Dickie, "The Islamic Garden in Spain," 97–98.

44. Rodrigo Caro, *Antigüedades y principiado de la ilustrísima ciudad de Sevilla* (Seville, 1634), 57, trans. in Dickie, "The Islamic Garden in Spain," 97–98.

45. Guerrero Lovillo, "Qaṣr al-Mubārak, el Alcázar de la Bendición," 105.

46. Wasserstein, *Rise and Fall of the Party-Kings,* 155–60; *The Caliphate in the West,* 104 and passim.

47. Al-Maqqarī, *Analectes,* I:347.

48. Al-Maqqarī, *Analectes,* II:673, citing Ibn Budrūn.

49. Al-Maqqarī, *Analectes,* I:346.

50. Torres Balbás, *Ciudades,* 143–44.

51. Al-Maqqarī, *Analectes,* I:426.

52. Christian Ewert, "Tradiciones omeyas en la arquitectura palatina de la época de los taifas: La Aljafería de Zaragoza" (Granada, 1977), 62–75, and *Spanisch-Islamische Systeme sich Kreuzender Bögen, III, Die Aljafería in Zaragoza* (*Deutsches Archäologisches Institut, Abteilung Madrid, Madrider Forschungen,* 12), (Berlin, 1978–80). There are capitals at the site inscribed with this patron's name, as well as ceiling inscriptions with the names of Isabel and Ferdinand; Pedro IV reformed the site in the fourteenth century, and it was altered again in the sixteenth and eighteenth centuries (Francisco Íñiguez Almech, "La Aljafería de Zaragoza: Presentación de

los nuevos hallazgos," in *Actas, I Congreso de Estudios Árabes e Islámicos (Cordoba, 1962)* (Madrid, 1964), 357–70). Regarding the courtyard "restorations," see E. Ariño Gil and J. A. Souto Lasala, "Sondeos estratigráficos en la Aljafería de Zaragoza (oct.-dic., 1983)," *Sharq al-Andalus* 2 (1985), 121–24.

53. Creswell believed that the fortified exteriors of the Umayyad estates of Syria and Jordan were more of a display than a reality; nonetheless, the vocabulary of defense was there and available to the later Muslim rulers in Spain (Creswell, "Fortifications in Islam before A.D. 1250," *Proceedings of the British Academy* 38 [1952], 89–125).

54. Cynthia Robinson has developed the theme of literature at the Hudid court in a recent doctoral dissertation, University of Pennsylvania, 1995.

55. Al-Maqqarī, *Analectes,* II:148; Gayangos, *History,* I:49.

56. Although seventeenth-century authors mention a mosque, none survives (Torres Balbás, *La Alcazaba y la Catedral de Málaga* [Madrid, 1960], 61–63).

57. The Alcazaba was excavated by Fernando Guerrero Strachan, who was director of the site from 1936 until his death in 1941.

58. Torres Balbás, *La Alcazaba,* 38–39.

59. Al-Maqqarī, *Analectes,* II:147.

60. Torres Balbás, *La Alcazaba,* 38–39.

61. A similar plan is also evident in a house in the Chanca quarter of Almeria, a wealthy commercial quarter in the Almoravid period, known as "al-Ḥawḍ" (Torres Balbás, *Artes almorávide y almohade* (Madrid, 1955), 18; "Patios de Crucero," *Al-Andalus* 23 [1958], 171–92).

62. Gayangos, *History,* II:355.

63. Al-Maqqarī, *Analectes,* II:67; see also ʿAbdel ʿAziz Salem, "Algunos aspects del florecimiento económico de Almería Islamíca durante el período de los Taifas y de los Almorávides," *Revista del Instituto Egipcio de Estudios Islámicos en Madrid* 20 (1979–80), 11–14.

64. In the 1950s, Torres Balbás used the meticulous description of Ibn Khātima's *Taḥsīl* to trace the boundaries of the medina, Alcazaba, and adjacent suburbs of Almeria, but his picture of the city was fourteenth-century (Ibn Khātima, ms. Escorial # 1875, ed. and trans. Müller, *Bericht über die Pest* [1863]; cited in Luis Seco de Lucena, "Palacios del taifa almeriense," 15–16; Torres Balbás, "Almería islámica," *Al-Andalus* 22 [1957], 411–57; and Torres Balbás et al., *Resumen Histórico del Urbanismo en España* [Madrid, 1954]). For al-ʿUdhrī, see Aḥmad al-ʿUdhrī, *Fragmentos geográfico-históricos de "al-Masālik ilā Ŷāmīʿ al-mamālik,"* ed. A. A. al-Ahwānī (Madrid, 1965); Seco de Lucena, "Palacios del taifa almeriense," 17.

65. Al-ʿUdhrī, cited in ʿAbdel ʿAzīz Sālem, "Almería islamíca," 16–18.

66. Seco de Lucena, "Palacios del taifa almeriense," 18.

67. Cara Barrionuevo, *Almería islámica,* 185, 205–22.

68. Seco de Luceno, "Palacios del taifa almeriense," 18.

69. Cara Barrionuevo, *Almería islámica,* 185, 214–18.

70. For Barja and Dalāya see Nykl, *Hispano-Arabic Poetry,* 184. For Ṣumādiḥīya see ʿAbdel ʿAzīz Sālem, "Almería islamíca," 18; Seco de Lucena, "Palacios del taifa almeriense," 20; and al-ʿUdhrī, ed. al-Ahwānī, 85.

71. Nykl, *Hispano-Arabic Poetry,* 184.

72. Seco de Lucena, "Palacios del taifa almeriense," 19–20.

73. Dozy, *Recherches sur l'histoire,* I:245–46; also Gayangos, *History,* I:135–36.

74. Al-Maqqarī, *Analectes,* II:149; Gayangos, *History,* I:69.

75. J. Navarro Palazón and A. García Avilés, "Approximación a la cultura material de Madinat Mursiya," in *Murcia Musulmana,* ed. F. J. Flores Arroyuelo (Murcia, 1989), 296, 301.

76. The Castillo was mentioned in 1078–79 when Ibn ʿAwwām, who was vizier to al-Muʿtamid of Seville, was imprisoned there by the ruler of Murcia (Torres Balbás, "Monteagudo y 'El Castillejo,' en la Vega de Murcia," *Al-Andalus* 2 [1934], 366–72).

77. It was excavated in 1924–25 by Andrés Sobejano but the report was not published (Torres Balbás, "Monteagudo y 'El Castillejo'" 366–72). The source Ibn Ṣāhib al-Ṣala and Abū al-Hasan Hāzim al-Qarṭayannī are cited in Navarro Palazón and García Avilés, "Approximación a la cultura material de Madinat Mursiya," 297. For the Castillejo, see J. Navarro Palazón and P. Jiménez Castillo, "El Castillejo de Monteagudo: Qaṣr Ibn Saʿd," in *Casas y Palacios de Al-Andalus,* ed. Navarro Palazón (Barcelona, 1995), 63–103.

78. Georges Marçais referred to them as pavilions of the Alhambra type, but Torres Balbás, who knew the site better, was not sure if they were pavilions or merely projecting terraces (Marçais, *L'Architecture musulmane d'occident: Tunisie, Algérie, Maroc, Es-*

pagne, et Sicile [Paris, 1954], 214; Torres Balbás, *Artes almorávide y almohade,* 17). See also Navarro Palazón and Jiménez Castillo, "El Castillejo de Monteagudo," 83–84.

79. Torres Balbás, "Monteagudo y 'El Castillejo,'" 366–72, and *Artes almorávide y almohade,* 17.

80. For discussion of the Qalʿa's similarities to Spanish palaces, see Ruggles, "Vision and Power at the Qala Bani Hammad," 28–41.

81. Doris Behrens-Abouseif, "Gardens in Islamic Egypt," *Der Islam* 69 (1992), 302–12.

8. The Alhambra

1. ʿAbd Allāh al-Zīrī, *The Tibyān,* 75 n. 189; *Muqtabas* (III), ed. Antuña, 56.

2. Madīnat Ilbīra was located on a hill near Granada in the Sierra de Elvira, and was the provincial capital until the seat of government was transferred to Granada. It was abandoned then and demolished in 1486, by order of Isabel and Ferdinand (Manuel Gomez-Moreno, *Medina Alvira* [Granada, 1888], 3–4).

3. ʿAbd Allāh b. Zīrī, *El Siglo XI en la 1ª persona: Las "Memorias" de ʿAbd Allāh, último rey Zīrī de Granada, destronado por las almorávides,* Spanish trans. with introduction by E. Lévi-Provençal and E. García Gómez, 2d ed. (Madrid, 1980), 87–88; *Tibyān,* 48 [10]; my translation here is drawn from both the Tibi and the Lévi-Provençal and García Gómez versions, cited above.

4. Ross Brann, *The Compunctious Poet: Cultural Ambiguity and Hebrew Poetry in Muslim Spain* (Baltimore, 1977), 71 n. 53.

5. Bargebuhr, "The Alhambra Palace of the Eleventh Century," 211–12.

6. Ibn Gabirol, *Selomo Ibn Gabirol,* intro. Dan Pagis, ed. and trans. (Hebrew and Spanish) Elena Romero (Madrid, 1978), 174–79; this translation by Bargebuhr, "The Alhambra Palace of the Eleventh Century," 198.

7. Bargebuhr, *The Alhambra,* 99; for the Hebrew text and a simpler translation (in Spanish), see Ibn Gabirol, *Selomo Ibn Gabirol: Poesia secular,* 176–77.

8. Bargebuhr, "The Alhambra Palace," 192; see also Tibi's translation, ʿAbd Allāh, *Tibyān,* 75.

9. ʿAbd Allāh, *Tibyān,* ed. Tibi, 69.

10. Bargebuhr, "The Alhambra Palace," 199.

11. Bargebuhr, *The Alhambra,* 114. In an article criticizing Bargebuhr's translation, Raymond Scheindlin offers his own version of the poem in which he insists on the lions' position above, rather than simply near, the basin's rim:

> . . . and a full sea: It resembles Solomon's sea,
> but it does not stand upon cattle,
> and the lions' standing-place is on its edge,
> as if young lions were roaring for prey.

(Scheindlin, "El poema de Ibn Gabirol y la fuente del Patio de los Leones," *Cuadernos de la Alhambra,* 29–30 (1993–94), 186.

12. Bargebuhr, *The Alhambra,* 30.

13. Bargebuhr, *The Alhambra,* 35–36.

14. Scheindlin, "El poema de Ibn Gabirol," 189.

15. O'Callaghan, "Image and Reality: The King Creates His Kingdom," in *Emperor of Culture: Alfonso X the Learned of Castile,* ed. Robert Burns (Philadelphia, 1990), 14–32.

16. *Mushāhadāt Lisān ad-dīn b. al-Khaṭīb fī bilād al-Maghrib wa al-Andalus,* ed. Aḥmad Mukhtār al-ʿAbbādī (Alexandria, 1958), 90–91, trans. in Dickie, "The Hispano-Arab Garden," 1025–27.

17. Ibn al-Khaṭīb, translated in Rubiera Mata, *La arquitectura en la literatura árabe,* 141–3.

18. *Mushāhadāt Lisān ad-dīn b. al-Khaṭīb,* in Dickie, "The Hispano-Arab Garden," 1026.

19. Rachel Arié, "Une métropole hispano-musulmane au bas moyen âge: Grenade nasride," *Les Cahiers de Tunisie* 34, nos. 137–38 (Tunis) (1986), 57.

20. Darío Cabanelas Rodríguez, "The Alhambra: An Introduction," in *Al-Andalus: The Art of Islamic Spain,* ed. Jerrilynn Dodds (New York, 1992), 127–33.

21. Ibn al-Khaṭīb, *Al-Iḥāṭa fī ta'rīkh Gharnāṭa,* ed. M. ʿA. ʿInān (Cairo, 1973–77) 564; Ibn al-Jayyāb, cited in Rubiera Mata, *El medio literario en la Granada naṣrī en la primer mitad del siglo XIV (Ibn Ŷayyāb y su época),* Ph.D. Madrid, 1972, 251. Both are cited in Pavón Maldonado, *Estudios,* I, 66 n. 1, 2.

22. Torres Balbás, *Ars Hispaniae,* IV:83.

23. Gómez Moreno's plan of the Alhambra shows the outlines of the Abencerrajes Palace in *Guía de Granada* (1892), new edition (Granada, 1982), 24; Juan de Echeverría recorded some of the inscriptions and described decoration (now lost) in *Paseos por Grandada y sus contornos,* vol. II, paseo XVI. For the modern excavations see Pavón Maldonado, *Estudios,* I, 35–50.

24. The following information on the Abencerrajes is from Pavón Maldonado, *Estudios,* I, 35–50.

25. Torres Balbás, "Dār al-ʿArūsa y las ruinas de palacios y albercas granadinos situados por encima

del Generalife," *Al-Andalus* 13 (1948), 185–203; Gómez Moreno, *Guía de Granada,* 175–77.

26. Andres Navagero, *Viaje,* 49.

27. Bermúdez Pareja, "El Generalife después del incendio de 1958," *Cuadernos de la Alhambra* 1 (1965), 9–39.

28. Bermudez Pareja, "Generalife después del incendio," 14–16; Grabar has pointed out that while water was brought easily down the mountain to the Generalife, the ravine separating it from the Alhambra made the introduction of water to the latter difficult (*Alhambra,* 1st ed., 9).

29. Bermúdez Pareja, "Generalife después del incendio," 24.

30. The following is summarized from Bermúdez Pareja, "Generalife después del incendio," 9–39.

31. Navagero, *Viaje,* 47.

32. Navagero, *Viaje,* 48.

33. Navagero, *Viaje,* 48.

34. Bermúdez Parejo, "Generalife después del incendio," 25.

35. Bermúdez Pareja, "Generalife después del incendio," 23; he cites G. Bruin and F. Hogenbergius, *Civitates Orbis Terrarum* (Cologne, 1587) and Francisco Henríquez de Jorquera, in *Anales de Granada,* ed. A. Marín Ocete (Granada, 1934), 262–63.

36. Bermúdez Pareja, "Generalife después del incendio," 16.

37. Dickie, "The Palaces of the Alhambra," 149.

38. Torres Balbás, "El exconvento de San Francisco de la Alhambra," *Boletín de la Sociedad Española de Excursiones* 29 (1931), 212.

39. Torres Balbás, "El exconvento de San Francisco," 126–38, 206–15.

40. Pavón Maldonado, *Estudios, I,* 120.

41. Torres Balbás, *Ars Hispaniae* IV:124.

42. Pavón Maldonado writes that the earlier restoration with brick piers was more accurate than the present columns, *Estudios, I,* 117.

43. Torres Balbás, "El Oratorio y la casa de Astasio de Bracamonte en el Partal de la Alhambra," *Al-Andalus* 10 (1945), 440–49.

44. Torres Balbás claimed that the oratory was built first ("El Oratorio," 440–49); but Carlos Vílchez Vílchez stated that the house was the earlier of the two (*La Alhambra de Leopoldo Torres Balbás* [Granada, 1988], 325).

45. Torres Balbás, "El Oratorio," 440–49.

46. Torres Balbás, "El Oratorio," 445.

47. Torres Balbás, *Ars Hispaniae* IV:124.

48. Marçais, *L'Architecture musulmane d'occident,* 291. In 1860 two Qur'ānic inscriptions in Naskhi script, a foundation inscription, and a verse of poetry were discovered there (Darío Cabanelas Rodríguez, "La Madraza árabe de Granada y su suerte en época cristiana," *Cuadernos de la Alhambra* 24 [1988], 29–54). Regarding the windows, see Dickie, "Granada: A Case Study of Arab Urbanism in Muslim Spain," in *The Legacy of Muslim Spain,* ed. Jayyusi (Leiden, 1992), 100–1.

49. Münzer, *Viaje por España,* 93.

50. Dickie, "The Palaces of the Alhambra," 148–49; Consejería de obras públicas y transportes de la Junta de Andalucía, Consejería de cultura de la Junta de Andalucía, Ayuntamiento de Granada, and Patronato de la Alhambra, *Plan especial de protección y reforma interior de la Alhambra y Alijares* (Granada, 1986), 192–93.

51. Pavón Maldonado, *Estudios, I,* 65–71, citing unpublished excavation notes of Cendoya in the Archivo de Planos de la Alhambra.

52. Dickie, "The Islamic Garden in Spain," 94–95.

53. Navagero, *Viaje,* 46.

54. Dickie, "The Palaces of the Alhambra," 140.

55. Dickie, "The Palaces of the Alhambra," 139.

56. Nykl, "Inscripciones árabes de la Alhambra y del Generalife," *Al-Andalus* 4 (1936), 178–81; Cabanelas Rodríguez, *El techo del Salón de Comares en la Alhambra: Decoración, policromía, simbolismo, y etimología* (Granada, 1988). This Qur'ān translation is from *Al-Qur'ān: A Contemporary Translation,* trans. Ahmed Ali (Princeton, 1984).

57. Nykl, *Inscripciones,* 180–81.

58. Dickie, "The Palaces of the Alhambra," 139.

59. Dickie, "The Palaces of the Alhambra," 137; on the king as object of the view, see Ruggles, "Humayun's Tomb and Garden: Typologies and Visual Order," in *Gardens in the Time of the Great Muslim Empires* (*Muqarnas Supplement* 7), ed. Attilio Petruccioli (Leiden, 1997), 173–86.

60. The double identity of the king as both person and state was studied by Ernst Kantorowicz, *The King's Two Bodies: A Study in Medieval Theology* (Princeton, 1957).

61. Dickie, "The Palaces of the Alhambra," 140; see also Gülru Necipoğlu's discussion of the Tower of Justice at the Topkapı, *Architecture, Ceremonial, and Power: The Topkapı Palace in the Fifteenth and Sixteenth Centuries* (Cambridge, 1991) 84–86.

62. Torres Balbás, *Ars Hispaniae* IV:113; Pavón Maldonado, *Estudios, I,* 76.

63. Pavón Maldonado, *Estudios, I,* 79; Ibn al-

Khaṭīb cited in Francisco Javier Simonet, *Descripción del reino de Granada* (Madrid, 1982), 45.

64. Marçais, *L'Architecture musulmane d'occident* 305.

65. James T. Monroe, *Hispano-Arabic Poetry* (Berkeley and Los Angeles, 1974), 346–65.

66. Gachard, *Collections des voyages*, I:206.

67. Reported in Dickie, "The Islamic Garden in Spain," 100.

68. This method of staking vines is still practiced today in Galicia: instead of the vine supported by a vertical trellis, it climbs freestanding to a horizontal one.

69. There were illustrated works on botany and astronomy but their images were diagrammatic rather than narrative and scenographic (Richard Ettinghausen, *Arab Painting* [New York: Rizzoli, 1977], 125–32).

70. Bargebuhr, *The Alhambra*, 170–72.

71. Grabar, *The Alhambra*, 100.

72. Grabar, *The Alhambra*, 123.

73. Grabar, *The Alhambra*, 121–22.

74. See Ruggles, "The Eye of Sovereignty: Poetry and Vision in the Alhambra's Lindaraja Mirador," *Gesta* 36 (1997), 180–89.

75. Torres Balbás, *Ars Hispaniae*, IV:117.

76. The inscriptions are transcribed and translated in E. Lafuente y Alcántara, *Inscripciones árabes de Granada* (Madrid, 1859); Antonio Almagro Cárdenas, *Estudio sobre las inscripciones árabes de Granada* (Granada, 1879), and Nykl, "Inscripciones," 174–94. More-recent studies rely on the earlier ones, written at a time when the stuccos were in a worse state of preservation but had not yet been restored (in some cases, incorrectly so).

77. Ibn Jayyāb (whose given name was Abū'l Ḥasan ʿAlī b. Muḥammad al-Anṣārī) may also be the author of two other poems on the Alhambra walls, according to García Gómez, *Poemas árabes en los muros y fuentes de la Alhambra* (Madrid, 1985), 31; for Ibn al-Khaṭīb, see Rubiera Mata, "De nuevo sobre los poems epigráficos de la Alhambra," *Al-Andalus* 41 (1976), 207–11, and García Gómez, *Poemas árabes*, 32–36; for Ibn Zamrak (Abū ʿAbd Allāh Muḥammad b. Yūsuf Ṣurayḥī), see García Gómez, *Poemas árabes*, 36–39.

78. The earliest example of a Muslim palace endowed with monumental poetic epigraphy is the palace of Masʿūd III (r. 492–508/1099–1115) in Ghaznavid Afghanistan (Alessio Bombaci, *The Kūfic Inscription in Persian Verses in the Court of the Royal Palace of Masʿūd III at Ghazni* [Rome, 1966]); the Persian verses laud the ruler(s), referring to him or them in the third person.

79. Arabic text and two very different Spanish translations are to be found in García Gómez, *Poemas árabes*, 124–27; and Lafuente y Alcántara, *Inscripciones*, 138–41.

80. García Gómez, *Poemas árabes*, 42.

81. Werner Caskel, *Arabic Inscriptions in the Collection of the Hispanic Society of New York* (New York, 1936), 36.

82. Juan Zozaya, entry no. 50, in Dodds, *Al-Andalus*, 264.

83. Rafael Azuar Ruiz, entry no. 109, in Dodds, *Al-Andalus*, 353.

84. Juan Zozaya, entry no. 52, in Dodds, *Al-Andalus*, 266–67.

85. For objects with personifying inscriptions in the Islamic east, see Eva Baer, "Jeweled Ceramics from Medieval Islam: A Note on the Ambiguity of Islamic Ornament," *Muqarnas* 6 (1989), 83–97. For a more detailed discussion of personification and inscriptions on objects and in the Lindaraja Mirador, see Ruggles, "The Eye of Sovereignty," 180–89.

86. For a discussion of possible eastern precedents see Ruggles, "The Eye of Sovereignty," 185.

87. Lledó Carrascosa, "Risala sobre los palacios," 194.

88. Rubiera Mata, *Ibn Ŷayyāb, el otro poeta de la Alhambra* (Granada, 1982), 90.

89. García Gómez, *Cinco poetas musulmanes; biografías y estudios*, 2d ed. (Madrid, 1959), 216–17.

90. García Gómez, *Poemas árabes*, 35.

91. García Gómez, *Poemas árabes*, 24.

92. García Gómez, *Poemas árabes*, 148–49.

93. García Gómez, *Poemas árabes*, 42.

94. García Gómez, *Poemas árabes*, 98–99, 115–20.

95. Jacques Derrida, *Of Grammatology*, trans. Gayatri C. Spivak (Baltimore, 1977, esp. 6–73).

96. James T. Monroe, *Hispano-Arabic Poetry*, 346–65 for Arabic and translation of the entire poem from which the inscriptions were extracted.

9. Illusion and Paradise

1. *Al-Qur'ān: A Contemporary Translation*, trans. Ahmed Ali (Princeton, 1984), 418.

2. Ibn Faḍl Allāh al-ʿUmarī, *Masālik al-abṣār fī mamālik al-amṣār*, I (*l'Afrique moins Egypte*), trans. (French) de Gaudefroy-Demombynes (Paris, 1927), 226, 288; Ibn Baṭṭūṭa, *Voyages d'Ibn Batoutah*, IV, ed. Defrémery y Sanguinetti (Paris, 1879), 368–69, 371;

al-Malaṭī's comments and others are cited in Torres Balbás, *Ciudades,* 155–57.

3. See Dickie's discussion, "Granada: A Case Study of Arab Urbanism in Muslim Spain," in Salma K. Jayyusi, *The Legacy of Muslim Spain* (Leiden, 1992), 88–111, esp. 104–5.

4. Bargebuhr, *The Alhambra,* 189.

5. Ibn al-Khātima, in Ibn al-Khaṭīb, *Al-Iḥāṭa,* ed. Inan, I:260, cited in Rubiera Mata, *La arquitectura en la literatura,* 90.

6. Abū Marwān al-Jazīrī, cited in Rubiera Mata, *La arquitectura en la literatura,* 92–93.

7. Al-Maqqarī, *Analectes,* I:371, 374.

8. Al-Maqqarī, *Analectes,* I:426 (Toledo) and II:612 (Seville).

9. Nykl, *Hispano-Arabic Poetry,* 255.

10. Al-Maqqarī, *Analectes,* I:321–25; L. Berchem, "Le palais d'El-Mansour á Bougie," *Revue Tunisienne* 29 (1922), 50–56. The animal figures are reproduced and discussed in Marilyn Jenkins, "Al-Andalus: Crucible of the Mediterranean," in *The Art of Medieval Spain,* A.D. *500–1200* (New York, 1993), 73–84.

11. A. F. von Schack, *Poesía y arte de los árabes en España y Sicilia,* trans. (Spanish) J. Valera (Madrid, c. 1988), 243–44.

12. A photograph of the lion spouts is reproduced in *Al-Andalus,* 148.

13. From the *Dīwān,* trans. (Spanish) by Rubiera Mata, *La arquitectura en la literatura,* 96.

14. Bargebuhr, *The Alhambra,* 170–72.

15. Probably by Ibn Zamrak, translated in Lafuenta y Alcántara, *Inscripciones,* 146.

16. García Gómez, *Poemas árabes,* 111.

17. The fountain pavilion is described in Ibn al-Khaṭīb, *Dīwān,* ed. Algiers (1973), 330–31, and Ibn al-Khaṭīb, *Dīwān,* ed. Inan (Cairo, n.d.), I:260; translated in Rubiera Mata, *La arquitectura en la literatura,* 89–90.

18. García Gómez, *Poemas árabes,* 29.

19. Suzanne P. Stetkevych, "The *Qaṣīdah* and the Poetics of Ceremony: Three ʿĪd Panegyrics to the Cordoban Caliphate," in *Languages of Power in Islamic Spain,* ed. Ross Brann (Ithaca, 1998), 1–48.

20. Ruggles, "A Mythology of an Agrarian Ideal," *Environmental Design,* 1986, no. 1:24–27.

21. Al-Khaṭīb al-Baghdādī, *Ta'rīkh Baghdād,* 14 vols. in 7 (Cairo, 1931), I:78–79, trans. in Jacob Lassner, *The Shaping of ʿAbbasid Rule,* 197–98.

22. The water to irrigate these and supply the mosque's ablution fountain was obtained at first from a tank via a camel-driven wheel, partly filled from rainwater that ran off the sanctuary's gabled roofs. This system was replaced or augmented sometime between 961 and 976 by a canal from the mountains, and in 381/991–92 cisterns were dug in the courtyard floor (Gayangos, *History,* I:226; *Una descripción anónima de al-Andalus,* ed. and trans. [Spanish] Luis Molina, 2 vols. [Madrid, 1983], II: 194).

23. Lévi-Provençal, *Hist. Esp. Mus.,* III:386. I am currently preparing an article on this court case.

24. Al-Maqqarī, *Analectes,* I:426.

25. Pavón Maldonado, *Estudios, I,* 87–88.

26. For a discussion of tomb and garden typologies, see Ruggles, "Humayun's Tomb and Garden."

27. Al-Muqaddasī wrote about the city of Jaen, "One could talk about its beauty and pleasantness endlessly because it is the paradise of al-Andalus." (*Description de l'occident musulman au IVe = Xe siècle,* Arabic ed. and trans. Charles Pellat [Algiers, 1950], 37). Praising the healthy climate, salubrious air, broad valleys, numerous rivers, and profitable forests of al-Andalus, al-Rāzī called it "God's paradise" (Lévi-Provençal, "La 'Description,'" 51–108).

28. Al-Idrīsī, *Description,* 188; Ibn al-ʿAbbār, *Takmila,* II:551, no. 1557.

29. Al-Maqqarī, *Analectes,* I:304.

30. The Arabic is cited in Gayangos, *History,* I:52 and 360 n. 123.

31. Dickie, "Mosques, Madrasas, and Tombs," in *Architecture of the Islamic World,* ed. George Michell (London, 1978), 47.

32. W. E. Begley and Z. A. Desai, *Taj Mahal: The Illumined Tomb* (Cambridge and Seattle, 1989), 193–95.

33. James L. Wescoat, Jr. "Gardens of Invention and Exile: The Precarious Context of Mughal Garden Design During the Reign of Humayun (1530–1556)," *Journal of Garden History* 10 (1990), 106–16; "The Islamic Garden: Issues for Landscape Research," *Environmental Design,* 1986, no. 1:10–19; and also his paper "Landscape Transformations of the Mughal Empire: Medieval and Modern Uses of the Narrative Mode" (1987), which Professor Wescoat kindly allowed me to read.

34. *Al-Qur'ān,* trans. A. Ali, 14 and 436.

35. Marçais, "Les jardins de l'Islam," 234; Donald Wilbur, *Persian Gardens and Garden Pavilions,* 2d ed. (Washington, D.C., 1979), 3; John Brookes, *Gardens of Paradise* (New York, 1982), 17–19; Elizabeth B. Moynihan, *Paradise as a Garden in Persia and Mughal India* (New York, 1979), 2–5; Richard Ettinghausen, introduction to *The Islamic Garden,* ed. E. Mac-

Dougall and R. Ettinghausen, 6; and Dickie, "The Islamic Garden in Spain," 90.

36. ʿAbd al-Raḥmān III was severely rebuked once by a *qāḍī* for building an overly ostentatious cupola, and on a second occasion for allowing the construction of his "villas and castles" to keep him from Friday prayer (according to Ibn Ghālib, *Kitāb farḥat al-anfus,* Spanish trans. in *Homenaje a Pedro Sáinz Rodríguez,* III:675–76.

37. Ibn Ḥazm described pleasant ambles and romantic trysts in the gardens (*bustān/basātīn*) of various Cordoba estates (*Le collier du pigeon,* 168–69, 256, and 284). The notoriously libertine Abbasid poet Abū Nuwās wrote that the four most desirable things in life were a garden, water, wine, and a lovely face, and his enjoyment of all four was anything but pious (Abū Nuwās, ed. Ahlwardt, 71.3, cited in G. E. von Grunebaum, "The Response to Nature in Arabic Poetry," in *Themes in Medieval Arabic Literature* [London, 1981], 143).

38. *Al-Qurʾān,* trans. A. Ali, 129.

39. *Al-Qurʾān,* trans. A. Ali, 124.

40. Grabar, "The Islamic Dome, Some Considerations," *Journal of the Society of Architectural Historians* 22 (1963), 191–98; and "From Dome of Heaven to Pleasure Dome," *Journal of the Society of Architectural Historians* 49 (1990), 15–21; Christian Ewert, "Tipología de la mezquita en occidente: De los Omeyas a los Almohades," in *Actas del II Congreso de Arqueología Medieval Española* (Madrid, 1987), I:179–204.

BIBLIOGRAPHY

Abbreviations

al-Rāzī = Ibn Ḥayyān Al-Rāzī wrote a chronicle of the years 360/971–364/975 of al-Ḥakam II's reign, which was copied and reproduced by the annalist Ibn Ḥayyān (377/987-88–409/1076). Here, the reference to al-Rāzī refers to *Anales palatinos del califa de Córdoba al-Hakam II por ʿIsa Ibn Ahmad al-Razi (360–364 H./971–975 J.C.),* translated into Spanish by Emilio García Gómez (Madrid, 1967). The reference to Ibn Ḥayyān refers to the Arabic version of this same text, *Al-Muqtabis fī akhbar bilād al-andalus,* edited by A. A. El-Hajji (Beirut, 1965).

ʿAbd Allāh al-Zīrī. *Mudhakkirāt al-Amīr ʿAbd Allāh, al-musammāt bi-kitāb al-Tibyān,* ed. E. Lévi-Provençal. Cairo: Dar al-Maarif, c. 1955.

———. *El Siglo XI en la 1ª persona: Las "Memorias" de ʿAbd Allāh, último rey Zīrī de Granada, destronado por las Almorávides,* trans. with introduction by E. Lévi-Provençal and E. García Gómez, 2d ed. Madrid: Alianza, 1980.

———. *The Tibyān. Memoirs of ʿAbd Allāh B. Buluggin, Last Zīrīd Amir of Granada,* trans. and annotated by Amin T. Tibi. Leiden: E. J. Brill, 1986.

Abū al-Khayr. *Kitāb al-filāḥa ou le livre de la culture,* extracts French trans. by A. Cherbonneau, ed. Henri Pérès. Algiers: Carbonel, 1946.

Akhbār majmūʿa. In *Colección de obras arábigas de historia y geografía que publica la Real Academia de la Historia,* vol. I, ed. and trans. Emilio Lafuente y Alcántara. Madrid, 1867.

Alemany Bolufer, José. "La geografía de la península Ibérica en los escritores árabes." *Revista del Centro de Estudios Históricos de Granada y su Reino* 9 (1919), 136–42.

Almagro Cárdenas, Antonio. *Estudio sobre las inscripciones árabes de Granada.* Granada: Ventura Sabatel, 1879.

Anon. "Córdoba según al-Himyari." *Al-Mulk* 1 (1959–60), 7–35.

———. *Una crónica anónima de ʿAbd al-Raḥmān III al-Nāṣir,* trans. E. Lévi-Provençal and E. García-Gómez. Madrid and Granada: Consejo Superior de Investigaciones Científicas, 1950.

———. "Los hallazgos de Turruñuelos." *Al-Mulk* 4 (1964–65), 167–68.

———. See also Ibn ʿIdhārī.

Antuña, M. "Ibn Ḥayyān de Córdoba y su historia de la España musulmana." *Cuadernos de Historia de España* 4 (1946), 5–72.

Arié, Rachel. *Historia de España: III, España musulmana (siglos VIII–XV).* Madrid: Labor, 1984.

———. "Une métropole hispano-musulmane au bas moyen âge: Grenade nasride." *Les Cahiers de Tunisie* 34, nos. 137–38 (Tunis) (1986), 47–67.

Ariño Gil, E., and J. A. Souto Lasala. "Sondeos estratigráficos en la Aljafería de Zaragoza (oct.–dic., 1983)." *Sharq al-Andalus* 2 (1985), 121–24.

Asín Palacios, Miguel. *Glosario de voces romances, registradas por un botánico anónimo hispano-musulman (siglos XI–XII).* Madrid and Granada: Consejo Superior de Investigaciones Científicas, 1943.

Attié, Bachir. "La bibliographie de *al-Muqniʿ* de Ibn Ḥağğāğ." *Hespéris-Tamuda* 19 (1980–81), 47–74.

———. "L'ordre chronologique probable des sources directes d'Ibn al-ʿAwwām." *Al-Qanṭara* 3 (1982), 299–332.

Avila, María Luisa. *La sociedad hispanomusulmana al final del califato.* Madrid: Consejo Superior de Investigaciones Científicas, 1985.

Azuar Ruiz, Rafael. Entry no. 109 in *Al-Andalus: The Arts of Islamic Spain,* ed. Jerrilynn Dodds. New York: Metropolitan Museum of Art, 1992, 353.

Baer, Eva. "Jeweled Ceramics from Medieval Islam: A Note on the Ambiguity of Islamic Ornament." *Muqarnas* 6 (1989), 83–97.

Bargebuhr, Frederick P. "The Alhambra Palace of the Eleventh Century." *Journal of the Warburg and Courtauld Institutes* 19 (1956), 192–258.

———. *The Alhambra: A Cycle of Studies on the Eleventh Century in Moorish Spain.* Berlin: de Gruyter, 1968.

Barrell, John. "The Public Prospect and the Private

View: The Politics of Taste in Eighteenth-Century Britain." In *Reading Landscape: Country-City-Capital,* ed. Simon Pugh. Manchester: Manchester University Press, 1990, 19–40.

Beckwith, John. *Caskets from Cordoba.* London: H. M. Stationery Office, 1960.

Begley, W. E., and Z. A. Desai. *Taj Majal: The Illumined Tomb.* Cambridge: Aga Khan Program for Islamic Architecture; Seattle: University of Washington Press, 1989.

Behrens-Abouseif, Doris. "Gardens in Islamic Egypt." *Der Islam* 69 (1992), 302–12.

Berchem, L. "Le palais d'El-Mansour á Bougie." *Revue Tunisienne* 29 (1922), 50–56.

Bergmann, Bettina. Review of Elisabeth B. MacDougall, ed., *Ancient Roman Gardens* (1987). In *Journal of the Society of Architectural Historians* 48 (1989), 387–89.

Bermingham, Ann. *Landscape and Ideology: The English Rustic Tradition 1740–1860.* Berkeley and Los Angeles: University of California Press, 1986.

Bermúdez Pareja, Jesús. "El Generalife después del incendio de 1958." *Cuadernos de la Alhambra* 1 (1965), 9–39.

Beylié, L. de. *La Kalaa des Beni Hammad, une capitale berbère de l'Afrique du Nord au XIe.* Paris, 1909.

Blachère, Régis. "Un pionnier de la culture arabe orientale en Espagne au Xe siècle: Ṣāʿid de Baġdād," *Hespéris* 10 (1930), 15–36.

Blanchet, Paul. "Description des monuments de la Kalaa des Beni-Hammad." *Nouvelles archives des missions scientifiques* 17 (n.d., c. 1897), 1–21.

Bloom, Jonathan M. "The Origins of Fatimid Art." *Muqarnas* 3 (1985), 20–38.

Boardman, J. "The Olive in the Mediterranean; Its Culture and Use." In *The Early History of the Mediterranean,* ed. J. Hutchinson, G. Clark, E. M. Jope, and R. Riley. Oxford: Oxford University Press, 1977, 187–94.

Bolens, Lucie. *Agronomes andalous du moyen-âge.* Geneva and Paris: Librairie Droz, 1981.

———. *La cuisine andalouse, un art de vivre, XIe–XIIIe siècles.* Paris: A. Michel, 1990.

———. *Les méthodes culturales au moyen âge d'après les traités d'agronomie andalous: Traditions et techniques.* Geneva: Ed. Médecine et Hygiène, 1974 (Thèse de doctorat du 3me cycle, l'Université de Paris, I).

Bombaci, Alessio. *The Kūfic Inscription in Persian Verses in the Court of the Royal Palace of Masʿūd III at Ghazni.* Rome: IsMEO, 1966.

Bosch Vilá, J. *Historia de Sevilla: La Sevilla islámica, 712–1248.* Seville: Universidad de Sevilla, 1984.

Boserup, Ester. *The Conditions of Agricultural Growth: The Economics of Agrarian Change Under Population Pressure.* Chicago: Aldine, 1965.

Boswell, John. *The Royal Treasure: Muslim Communities Under the Crown of Aragon in the Fourteenth Century.* New Haven: Yale University Press, 1977.

Brann, Ross. *The Compunctious Poet: Cultural Ambiguity and Hebrew Poetry in Muslim Spain.* Baltimore: Johns Hopkins University Press, 1977.

Brett, Michael. Review of Andrew Watson, *Agricultural Innovation in the Early Islamic World* (Cambridge, 1983). In *Bulletin of the School of Oriental and African Studies* 48 (1985), 126–28.

Brisch, Klaus. "Madīnat al-Zahrāʾ in der modernen archäologischen Literatur Spaniens." *Kunst des Orients* 4 (1963), 3–41.

Brookes, John. *Gardens of Paradise.* New York: New Amsterdam, 1982.

Brunette, Peter, and David Wills. "The Spatial Arts: An Interview with Jacques Derrida." In *Deconstruction and the Visual Arts: Art, Media, Architecture,* ed. P. Brunette and D. Wills. Cambridge: Cambridge University Press, 1994.

Bulliet, Richard. *Conversion to Islam in the Medieval Period: An Essay in Quantitative History.* Cambridge: Harvard University Press, 1979.

Butzer, Karl et al. "Irrigation Agrecosystems in Eastern Spain: Roman or Islamic Origins?" *Annals of the Association of American Geographers* 75 (1985), 479–509.

Cabanelas Rodríguez, Darío. "The Alhambra: An Introduction." In *Al-Andalus: The Art of Islamic Spain,* ed. Jerrilynn Dodds. New York: Metropolitan Museum of Art, 1992, 127–33.

———. "La madraza árabe de Granada y su suerte en época cristiana." *Cuadernos de la Alhambra* 24 (1988), 29–54.

———. *El techo del Salón de Comares en la Alhambra: Decoración, policromía, simbolismo, y etimología.* Granada: Patronato de la Alhambra y Generalife, 1988.

Cahen, Claude. "Notes pour une histoire de l'agriculture dans les pays musulmans médiévaux: Coup d'oeil sur la littérature agronomique musulmane hors d'Espagne." *Journal of the Economic and Social History of the Orient* 14 (1971), 63–68.

Cara Barrionuevo, Lorenzo. *La Almería islámica y su Alcazaba.* Almeria: Editorial Cajal, 1990.

Caro, Rodrigo. *Antigüedades y principiado de la ilustrísima ciudad de Sevilla....* Seville, 1634.

Carruthers, Mary. *The Book of Memory: A Study of Memory in Medieval Culture.* Cambridge: Cambridge University Press, 1990.

Caskel, Werner. *Arabic Inscriptions in the Collection of the Hispanic Society of New York.* New York: Trustees of the Hispanic Society of America, 1936.

Castejón, R. *Excavaciones del plan nacional en Medina Azahra (Córdoba), campaña de 1943.* Madrid: Ministerio de Educación Nacional, 1945.

Castejón, Rafael. "Alamiría." *Boletín de la Real Academia de Córdoba* 25, no. 70 (1954), 150–57.

———. "Córdoba califal." *Boletín de la Real Academia de Córdoba* 8 (1929), 255–339.

———. "Excavaciones en el cortijo El Alcaide. ¿Dar al-Naura?" *Al-Mulk* 1 (1959–60), 163–66.

———. "Las excavaciones de Madinat al-Zahra de 1967 a 1969." *Boletín de la Asociación Española de Orientalistas,* 6 (1970), 205–8.

———. "Las excavaciones de Madinat al-Zahra de 1973 y 74." *Boletín de la Asociación Española de Orientalistas* 11 (1975), 219–21.

———. "Medina Záhira, una Córdoba desparacida y misteriosa." *Boletín de la Real Academia de Córdoba* 3 (1924), 153–74.

———. "La nueva pila de Alamiría y las representaciones zoomorficas califales." *Boletín de la Real Academia de Córdoba* 53 (1945), 197–211.

———. "Nueva pila almanzoreña en Córdoba." *Boletín de la Real Academia de Córdoba* 62 (1949–50), 235–40.

———. "Nuevas excavaciones en Madīnat al-Zahrā': El salón de ʿAbd al-Raḥmān III." *Al-Andalus* 10 (1945), 147–54.

———. "Nuevas identificaciones en la topografía de la Córdoba califal." In *Actas, Primer Congreso de Estudios Arabes e Islámicos (Córdoba, 1962).* Madrid: (s.n.), 1964.

———. "Las piedras rayadas de Medina Azahara." *Boletín de la Real Academia de Córdoba* 17 (1926), 775–78.

———. "Un primer centenario de excavaciones en Medina al-Zahra." *Boletín de la Real Academia de Córdoba* 71 (1954), 308–13.

———. "Las ruinas de Alamiría." In *Anales de la Comisión de Monumentos Históricos y Artísticos de Córdoba.* Cordoba, 1926, 17–21.

———. "Vestigios de alcázares musulmanes en Córdoba." *Boletín de la Real Academia de Córdoba* 20, (1949), 213–22.

———. See also Samuel de los Santos.

Castejón, Rosario. "Madinat al-Zahra en los autores árabes." *Al-Mulk* 1 (1959–60), 63–106; and 2 (1961–62), 119–56.

Chalmeta, Pedro. "Un formulaire notarial hispano-arabe du IV/Xe siècle: Glanes économiques." *Revista del Instituto Egipcio de Estudios Islámicos en Madrid* 23 (1985–86), 181–202.

Colin, G. S. "Filāḥa: Muslim West." *Encyclopaedia of Islam,* new ed., II:901–2.

Compton, Linda Fish. *Andalusian Lyrical Poetry and Old Spanish Love Songs: The "Muwashshaḥ" and Its "Kharja."* New York: New York University Press, 1976.

Conde, José Antonio. *Historia de la dominación de los árabes en España.* (First published 1820) Madrid, 1874.

Consejería de obras públicas y transportes de la Junta de Andalucía, Consejería de cultura de la Junta de Andalucía, Ayuntamiento de Granada, and Patronato de la Alhambra. *Plan especial de protección y reforma interior de la Alhambra y Alijares.* Granada: Patronato de la Alhambra, 1986.

Continente, J. M. "Abū Marwān al-Ŷazīrī, poeta ʿāmiri." *Al-Andalus* 34 (1969), pp. 123–41.

Creswell, K. A. C. *Early Muslim Architecture,* 2 vols. Oxford: Clarendon Press, 1932–40.

———. "Fortifications in Islam before A.D. 1250." *Proceedings of the British Academy* 38 (1952), 89–125.

———. *A Short Account of Early Muslim Architecture,* rev. and supplemented by James Allan. Aldershot: Scolar Press, 1989.

———. See also Ernst Herzfeld.

al-Ḍabbī. *Bugyat al-multamis fī taʾrīkh riyāl ahl al-Andalus,* ed. F. Codera and J. Ribera. In *Biblioteca Arábico Hispana,* vol. III. Madrid, 1885.

Derrida, Jacques. "The Double Session." In *Dissemination,* trans. Barbara Johnson. Chicago: University of Chicago Press, 1981, 175–286.

———. *Of Grammatology* (1967), trans. Gayatri C. Spivak. Baltimore: Johns Hopkins University Press, 1977.

———. See also Peter Brunette.

Dickie, James. "The Alhambra: Some Reflections Prompted by a Recent Study by Oleg Grabar." In *Studia Arabica et Islamica: Festschrift for Iḥsān ʿAbbās on His Sixtieth Birthday,* ed. Wadād al-Qāḍī. Beirut: American University Press, 1981, 127–49.

———. "Granada: A Case Study of Arab Urbanism in Muslim Spain." In *The Legacy of Muslim*

Spain, ed. Salma K. Jayyusi. Leiden: E. J. Brill, 1992, 88–111.

———. "The Hispano-Arab Garden: Notes Toward a Typology." In *The Legacy of Muslim Spain,* ed. Salma K. Jayyusi. Leiden: E. J. Brill, 1992, 1016–35.

———. "Ibn Shuhayd." *Al-Andalus* 28 (1963), 243–310.

———. "The Islamic Garden in Spain." In *The Islamic Garden,* ed. E. B. MacDougall and R. Ettinghausen. Washington, D.C.: Dumbarton Oaks, 1976, 89–105.

———. "Mosques, Madrasas, and Tombs." In *Architecture of the Islamic World,* ed. George Michell. London: Thames and Hudson, 1978, 15–47.

———. "The Palaces of the Alhambra." In *Al-Andalus: The Art of Islamic Spain,* ed. Jerrilynn Dodds. New York: Metropolitan Museum of Art, 1992, 135–51.

———. See also Ibn Shuhayd.

al-Dimishqī. *Nukhbat al-dahr fī ʿajāʾib al-barr wa-al-baḥr . . . Cosmographie de. . . .* (Arabic), ed. M. A. F. Mehren. Leipzig, 1923.

Dodds, Jerrilynn D. "Aḥmād Ibn Bāso." In the *Macmillan Encyclopedia of Architects,* ed. A. K. Placzek. New York, 1982, I:38.

———. *Architecture and Ideology in Early Medieval Spain.* University Park: Pennsylvania State University Press, 1990.

———. "The Great Mosque of Cordoba." In *Al-Andalus: The Art of Islamic Spain,* ed. J. D. Dodds. New York: Metropolitan Museum of Art, 1992, 11–25.

———, ed. *Al-Andalus: The Art of Islamic Spain.* New York: Metropolitan Museum of Art, 1992.

Donner, Fred M. *The Early Islamic Conquests.* Princeton: Princeton University Press, 1981.

Downing, T., and M. Gibson, eds. *Irrigation's Impact on Society.* Tucson: University of Arizona Press, 1974.

Dozy, R. *Recherches sur l'histoire et la littérature de l'Espagne pendant le moyen âge,* 2 vols. Leiden, 1881.

Dozy, R. *Supplément aux dictionnaires arabes,* 2 vols. Leiden: E. J. Brill, 1881; 3d ed. 1967.

———, ed. *Le Calendrier de Cordoue,* new ed. in Arabic and Latin with French trans. by Charles Pellat. Leiden: E. J. Brill, 1961.

Dubler, C. E. "Fuentes árabes." *Al-Andalus* 6 (1941), 135–56.

———. *La "materia médica" de Dioscórides,* 6 vols. Barcelona: Tipografía Emporium, 1953.

Duby, Georges. *Rural Economy and Country Life in the Medieval West,* trans. C. Poston. Columbia: University of South Carolina Press, 1968.

Echeverría, Juan de. *Paseos por Granada y sus contornos . . . por los años de 1764 y ahora.* Granada: Valenzuela, 1814.

Eguaras Ibáñez, Joaquina. (See Ibn Luyūn.)

Enkvist, Nils E. *The Seasons of the Year,* (*Commentationes humanarum litterarum,* 22, no. 4). Helsingfors, 1957.

Escobar Camacho, José M. *Córdoba en la baja edad media.* Cordoba: Caja Provincial de Ahorros de Córdoba, 1989.

Ettinghausen, Richard. *Arab Painting.* New York: Rizzoli, 1977.

Ettinghausen, Richard, and Oleg Grabar. *The Art and Architecture of Islam, 650–1250.* Harmondsworth: Penguin, 1987.

Ewert, Christian. "Elementos decorativos en los tableros parietales del Salón Rico de Madīnat al-Zahrāʾ." *Cuadernos de Madīnat al-Zahrāʾ* 1 (1987), 27–60.

———. *Spanisch-Islamische Systeme sich kreuzender Bögen, III, Die Aljafería in Zaragoza* (*Deutsches Archäologisches Institut, Abteilung Madrid, Madrider Forschungen,* 12). Berlin: de Gruyter, 1978.

———. "Tipología de la mezquita en occidente: De los omeyas a los almohades." In *Actas del II Congreso de Arqueología Medieval Española* (*Madrid, 1987*), 3 vols. Madrid: Comunidad de Madrid, Consejería de Cultura y Deportes, 1987, I:179–204.

———. "Tradiciones omeyas en la arquitectura palatina de la época de los taifas: La Aljafería de Zaragoza." In *España entre el Mediterraneo y el Atlántico* (*XXIII Congreso Internacional de Historia del Arte [Granada, 1973]*). Granada: Universidad de Granada, 1977, II:62–75.

Fernández González, R. "Aportaciones a la localización de al-Madīnat al-Zāhira." *Al-Mulk* 4 (1964–65), 44–46.

Forqada, Miguel. "Ṣāʿid al-Bagdādī y los antecedentes de la agronomía andalusí." *Al-Qanṭara* 16 (1995), 163–71.

———. See also Ibn ʿĀṣim.

Gabrieli, Francisco. "Omayyades d'Espagne et Abbasides." *Studia Islamica* 31 (1970), 93–100.

Gachard, Louis P., ed. *Collection des voyages des souverains des Pays-Bas,* 4 vols. Brussels, 1874–82.

Ganshof, F. L., and A. Verhulst. "Medieval Agrarian Society in Its Prime." In *The Cambridge Economic History of Europe,* vol. I: *Agrarian Life of the Middle*

Ages, ed. M. M. Postan and H. J. Habakkuk, 2d ed. Cambridge: Cambridge University Press, 1966, 290–339.

García de Cortazar, J. A. *La época medieval* (*Historia de España,* vol. II), 7th ed. Madrid: Alianza Editorial, 1980.

García Gómez, Emilio. "Algunas precisiones sobre la ruina de la Córdoba omeya." *Al-Andalus* 12 (1947), 267–93.

———. *Cinco poetas musulmanes; biografías y estudios,* 2d ed. Madrid: Espasa-Calpe, 1959.

———. *Ibn Zamrak, el poeta de la Alhambra.* Madrid: E. Maestre, 1943; reprinted Granada: Patronato de la Alhambra, 1975.

———. "Notas sobre topografía cordobesa en los 'Anales de al-Ḥakam II' por ʿĪsā Rāzī." *Al-Andalus* 30 (1965), 319–79.

———. *Poemas árabes en los muros y fuentes de la Alhambra.* Madrid: Instituto Egipcio de Estudios Islámicos en Madrid, 1985.

———. *Qasidas de Andalucía.* Madrid: Plutarco, 1940.

———. Summary of Ibn Bassām, *Al-Dhakhīra fī maḥāsin ahl al-Jazīra,* III (Publicaciones de la Facultad de Letras de la Universidad Egipcia, no. 26). In *Al-Andalus* 5 (1940), 494–96; 11 (1946), 252–57; and 12 (1947), 232–36.

———. See also al-Shaqundī.

———. "Sobre agricultura arábigoandaluza: Cuestiones biobibliográficas." *Al-Andalus* 10 (1945), 127–46.

———. "Traducciones Alfonsies de agricultura árabe." *Boletín de la Real Academia de Historia* 181 (1984), 387–97.

García Maceira, Antonio. *Apuntes y noticias sobre la agricultura de los árabes españoles.* Zamora, 1876.

García Sánchez, Expiración. "Agriculture in Muslim Spain." In *The Legacy of Muslim Spain,* ed. S. K. Jayyusi. Leiden: E. J. Brill, 1992, 987–99.

———, ed. *Ciencias de la naturaleza en al-Andalus: Textos y estudios,* 2 vols. Granada: Consejo Superior de Investigaciones Científicas, 1990.

Garijo, Ildefonso. "El tratado de Ibn Ŷulŷul sobre los medicamentos que no mencionó Dioscórides." In *Ciencias de la naturaleza en al-Andalus: Textos y estudios,* ed. E. García Sánchez, 2 vols. Granada: Consejo Superior de Investigaciones Científicas, 1990, I:57–70.

Gayangos, Pascual de. *The History of the Mohammedan Dynasties in Spain.* 2 vols. London: Oriental Translation Fund, 1840–43. (a free translation of al-Maqqarī's *Nafḥ al-ṭīb*)

Glick, Thomas F. "Comment on Paper by Watson." *Journal of Economic History* 34 (1974), 74–78.

———. *From Muslim Fortress to Christian Castle.* Manchester: Manchester University Press, 1995.

———. "Hydraulic technology in al-Andalus." In *The Legacy of Muslim Spain,* ed. S. K. Jayyusi. Leiden: E. J. Brill, 1992, 974–86.

———. *Islamic and Christian Spain in the Early Middle Ages.* Princeton: Princeton University Press, 1979.

Golvin, Lucien. *Le Maghreb central à l'époque des zirides.* Paris: Arts et Métiers Graphiques, 1957.

———. *Recherches archéologiques à la Qal'a des Banū Hammād.* Paris: Maisonneuve, 1965.

Gómez-Moreno, Manuel. *Ars Hispaniae,* vol III, *El arte árabe español hasta los almohades, arte mozárabe.* Madrid: Editorial Plus-Ultra, 1951.

———. *Guía de Granada.* 1892; new ed., 2 vols. Granada: Universidad de Granada, 1982.

———. *Medina Alvira.* Granada, 1888.

Gorges, Jean-Gérard. *Les villas hispano-romaines: Inventaire et problématique archéologiques.* Paris and Talence: Université de Bordeaux, III, 1979.

Government of Iraq, Department of Antiquities. *Excavations at Samarra 1936–1939.* Baghdad, 1940.

Grabar, Oleg. *The Alhambra.* Cambridge, Mass., 1978; 2d ed., Sebastapol, Calif.: Solipsist Press, 1992.

———. *The Formation of Islamic Art.* New Haven, 1973; rev. ed., New Haven: Yale University Press, 1987.

———. "From Dome of Heaven to Pleasure Dome." *Journal of the Society of Architectural Historians* 49 (1990), 15–21.

———. "The Islamic Dome, Some Considerations." *Journal of the Society of Architectural Historians* 22 (1963), 191–98.

Grabar, Oleg, Renata Holod, James Knustad, and William Trousdale. *City in the Desert: Qasr al-Hayr East* (Harvard Middle Eastern Monographs, vols. XXIII/XXIV), 2 vols. Cambridge, Harvard University Press, 1978.

Green, Nicholas. *The Spectacle of Nature: Landscape and Bourgeois Culture in Nineteenth-Century France.* Manchester: Manchester Universty Press, 1990.

Green, Nicholas, and Frank Mort. "Visual Representation and Cultural Politics." *Block* 7 (1982), 59–68.

Grimal, Pierre. *Les jardins romains,* 2d rev. ed. Paris: Presses Universitaires de France, 1969.

Grunebaum, G. E. von. "The Response to Nature in Arabic Poetry." In *Themes in Medieval Arabic Literature.* London: Variorum Reprints, 1981; re-

printed from *Journal of Near Eastern Studies* 4 (1945), 137–51.

Guerrero Lovillo. "Al-Qaṣr al-Mubārak, el alcázar de la Benedición." *Boletín de Bellas Artes de Seville* 2ª época, no. 2 (1974), 83–109.

Hadj-Sadok, M. "Ibn Khurradādhbih." In *Encyclopaedia of Islam,* new ed. (1971), III:839–40.

Halm, Heinz. "Al-Andalus und Gothica Sors." *Der Islam* 66 (1989), 252–63.

———. "L'Origine du nom *Al-Andalus.*" In *Proceedings of the Fourteenth Congress of the Union Européenne des Arabisants et Islamisants,* part II, ed. A. Fodor (Budapest Studies in Arabic, vols. XV–XVI). Budapest, 1988, 49–55.

Hamarneh, Sami Khalaf, and Glenn Sonnedecker. *A Pharmaceutical View of Abulcasis al-Zahrāwī in Moorish Spain.* Leiden: E. J. Brill, 1963.

Harley, Jack R. "Crops That Extend the Range of Agricultural Settlement." In *Man, Settlement, and Urbanism,* ed. P. J. Ucko, R. Tringham, and G. W. Dimbleby. London: Schenkman, 1972, 239–43.

Hernández Giménez, Félix. *Madīnat al-Zahrā': Arquitectura y decoración.* Granada: Patronato de la Alhambra, 1985.

Herzfeld, Ernst. "Mitteilungen über die Arbeiten der zweiten Kampagne von Samarra," *Der Islam* 5 (1915), 196–204, excerpted and trans. in K. A. C. Creswell (with Herzfeld's review and approval), *Early Muslim Architecture,* 2 vols. Oxford, 1932–40, II:232–42, 265–70.

———. "Reisebericht." *Zeitschrift der Deutschen Morganländischen Gesellschaft* 80 (1926), 227–28.

Herzfeld, Ernst, and F. Sarre. *Erster vorläufiger Bericht über die Ausgrabungen von Samarra.* Berlin, 1912; excerpted and trans. in K. A. C. Creswell, *Early Muslim Architecture,* 2 vols. Oxford, 1932–40, II: 232–42, 265–70.

———. See also K. A. C. Creswell.

Hill, Arthur W. "History and Function of Botanical Gardens." *Annals of the Missouri Botanical Garden* 2 (1915), 185–240.

al-Ḥimyarī. *La péninsule ibérique au moyen-âge d'après le "Kitāb al-Rawḍ al-mi'ṭār fī ḥabar al-akṭar,"* ed. (Arabic) and French trans. E. Lévi-Provençal. Leiden: E. J. Brill, 1938.

———. *Kitāb ar-Rawḍ al-mi'ṭār* (Textos medievales, 10), Spanish trans. M. Pilar Maestro González. Valencia: Gráf Bautista, 1963.

———. See also Anon.

Hodgson, Marshall. *The Venture of Islam,* 3 vols. Chicago: University of Chicago Press, 1974.

Holod, Renata. "Luxury Arts of the Caliphal Period." In *Al-Andalus: The Art of Islamic Spain,* ed. Jerrilynn Dodds. New York: Metropolitan Museum of Art, 1992, 41–47, and entry nos. 1–4, 190–201.

Honigman, E. "Al-Ruṣāfa." *Encyclopaedia of Islam.* Leiden, 1913–38, III:1279 ff.

Horn, Walter, and Ernest Born. *The Plan of St. Gall,* 3 vols. Berkeley and Los Angeles: University of California Press, 1979.

Ibn al-'Abbār. *Kitāb al-takmila li-kitāb al-ṣila,* ed. F. Codera, 2 vols. Madrid, 1889.

Ibn 'Abdūn. See Lévi-Provençal.

Ibn Abī Uṣaybi'a. *'Uyūn al-Anbā' fī ṭabaqāt al-aṭibbā',* 2 vols. Cairo, 1882.

———. See also Sylvestre de Sacy.

Ibn 'Āṣim. *Kitāb al-anwā' wa-l-azmina al-qawl fī-l-suhūr,* ed. and trans. M. Forqada, in *Fuentes Arábico-Hispanas* 15, Barcelona, 1993.

Ibn al-Athīr. *Al-Kāmil fī al-ta'rīkh,* 13 vols. Beirut, 1965–67.

———. *Annales du Maghreb y de l'Espagne,* French trans. and annotated by E. Fagnan. Algiers, 1898.

Ibn al-'Awwām. *Le livre de l'agriculture d'Ibn al-Awam (Kitāb al-Filāḥa),* French trans. J.-J. Clément-Mullet, 2 vols. in 3. Paris, 1864–67; reprinted Tunis: Éditions Bouslama, 1977.

Ibn Bashkuwāl. *Kitāb al-ṣila fī ta'rīkh a'immat al-andalus,* ed. F. Codera, *Biblioteca Arabico-Hispana,* vols. I and II. Madrid, 1883.

Ibn Baṣṣāl. *Kitāb al-Filāḥa, Libro de agricultura,* ed. and Spanish trans. José María Millás Vallicrosa and Muhammad 'Aziman. Tetouan: Instituto Muley El-Hasan, 1955.

Ibn Bassām. *Al-Dhakhīra fī maḥāsin,* vol. III. Beirut: Dār al-Thaqāfah, 1979.

Ibn Baṭṭūṭa. *Voyages d'Ibn Batoutah,* vol. IV, ed. Defrémery y Sanguinetti. Paris, 1879.

Ibn al-Bayṭār. *Al-Jāmi' li-mufradā al-adwīya wa-l-aghdhīya.* Bulak, 1291 A.H.; French trans. L. Leclerc, "Traité de Simples," in *Notices et extraits de la Bibliothèque Nationale,* xxiii, xxv, xxvi, xxx (1877–93).

Ibn Faḍl Allāh al'Umarī. See al-'Umarī.

Ibn al-Faqīh al-Hamadhānī. See Ibn Khurdādhbih.

Ibn al-Faraḍī. *Ta'rīkh 'ulamā' al-Andalus,* ed. F. Codera, *Biblioteca Arabico-Hispana,* vols. VII and VIII. Madrid, 1891–92.

Ibn Gabirol. *Selomo Ibn Gabirol: Poesía secular,* with an introduction by Dan Pagis, ed. and Spanish trans. Elena Romero. Madrid: Ediciones Alfaguara, 1978.

Ibn Ghālib. *Kitāb farḥat al-anfus,* extract ed. Luṭfī

ʿAbd al-Badīʿ in *Majallat maʿhad al-makhṭuṭāt al-ʿarabiyya* (Cairo), 1 (1955), fasc. 2, 272–310; Spanish trans. Joaquín Vallvé Bermejo, "La descripción de Córdoba de Ibn Gālib." In *Homenaje a Pedro Sáinz Rodríguez,* vol. III. Madrid: Fundación Universitaria Española, 1986, 669–79.

Ibn Ḥawqal. *Biblioteca Geographorum Arabicorum (Kitāb ṣūrat al-arḍ),* (Arabic) II, 3d ed., ed. J. H. Kramers. Leiden: E. J. Brill, 1967.

———. *Configuration de la terre (Kitāb ṣūrat al-arḍ),* French trans. J. H. Kramers and G. Wiet, 2 vols. Paris: G. P. Maisonneuve and Larose, 1964.

Ibn Ḥayyān. *Crónica del califa ʿAbdarraḥmān III an-Nāṣir entre los años 912 y 942 (Muqtabis* V), Spanish trans. M. J. Viguera and F. Corriente. Saragossa: Anubar, 1981.

———. *Chronique du règne du calife umayyade ʿAbd Allāh à Cordoue (Muqtabis* III), ed. M. M. Antuña. Paris: P. Geuthner, 1937.

———. *Al-Muqtabis,* ed. Maḥmūd ʿAlī Makkī. Beirut: Dār al-Kitāb al-ʿArabi, 1973.

———. *Al-Muqtabis fī akhbar bilād al-andalus,* ed. A. A. El-Hajji. Beirut: Dār al-Taḥqāfah, 1965. (For Spanish translation see al-Rāzī, *Anales palatinos.*) Notes indicating al-Rāzī = Ibn Ḥayyān refer to this text and its translation.

———. *Al-Muqtabas* (V), ed. P. Chalmeta, F. Corriente, and M. Ṣubḥ. Madrid: Instituto Hispano-Arabe de Cultura, 1979.

———. *Muqtabis* (III), Spanish trans. Kh. Ghorayyib in *Cuadernos de historia de España* (Buenos Aires), vol. XIII (1950), vols. XXXI–XXXII (1960).

Ibn Ḥazm. *Le collier du pigeon ou de l'amour et des amants (Ṭawq al-ḥamāma),* ed. and French trans. L. Bercher. Algiers: Carbonel, 1949.

———. *The Ring of the Dove: A Treatise of the Art and Practice of Arab Love,* trans. A. J. Arberry. London: Luzac, 1953.

Ibn ʿIdhārī. *El anónimo de Madrid y Copenhague,* ed. and Spanish trans. Ambrosio Huici Miranda. Valencia: F. Vives Mora, 1917 (abridged version of Ibn ʿIdhārī's fourth volume).

Ibn ʿIdhārī. *Histoire de l'Afrique du Nord et de l'Espagne musulmane intitulée Kitab al-Bayan al-mughrib,* new ed., after R. Dozy's ed. of 1849, ed. Lévi-Provençal and G. S. Colin, vols. I and II (cited in Notes as *Al-Bayān* I and II). Leiden: E. J. Brill, 1948–51.

———. *Histoire de l'Afrique et de l'Espagne intitulée al-Bayano l-Mogrib,* 2 vols., French trans. E. Fagnan (cited in Notes as Fagnan trans.). Algiers, 1901–4.

———. *Al-Bayan al-mughrib, Histoire de l'Espagne musulmane au XIe siècle,* ed. E. Lévi-Provençal (cited in Notes as *Al-Bayān* III). Paris: P. Geuthner, 1930.

Ibn Khaldūn. *Histoire des berbères et des dynasties musulmanes de l'Afrique Septrionale,* ed. and French trans. de Slane, 2 vols. Algiers, 1847–51.

———. *Kitāb al-ʿIbar wa-dīwān al-mubtadaʾ wa-l-khabar,* 7 vols. Bulak, 1867–68.

Ibn Khallikān. *Wafayāt al-aʿyān,* 2 vols. in 1. Bulak, 1882.

———. *Biographical Dictionary,* trans. MacGuckin de Slane, 4 vols. 1842–71; reprint, New York: Johnson Reprint, 1961.

Ibn Khāqān. *Maṭmaḥ al-anfus.* S.l., 1907.

———. *Al-Qalāʾid,* reproduced in *Scriptorum arabum loci de Abbadidis,* ed. Reinhart Dozy, 3 vols. Leiden: 1846–63.

Ibn al-Khāṭib. *(Aʿmāl al-aʿlām),* vol. III, *Taʾrīkh al-maghrib al-ʿarabī fi-l-l-ʿaṣr al-wasīṭ,* ed. A. M. al-ʿAbbādī and I. al-Kattānī. Casablanca: Dār al-Kitāb, 1964.

———. *Histoire de l'Espagne musulmane, d'Ibn al-Haṭīb* extracts of *Aʿmāl al-aʿlām,* ed. E. Lévi-Provençal *(Collection de textes arabes publiée par l'Institut des Hautes Etudes marocaines,* vol. III). Rabat: Félix Moncho, 1934.

———. *Al-Iḥāṭa fī akhbār gharnāṭa,* ed. M. A. ʿInān. Cairo: Maktabat al-Khanji, 1973–77.

Ibn Khurdādhbih, Ibn al-Faqīh al-Hamadhānī, and Ibn Rustih. *Description du Maghreb et de l'Europe au IIIe/IXe siècle,* Arabic ed. and French trans. M. Hadj-Sadok. Algiers: Editions Carbonel, 1949.

Ibn Luyūn. *Ibn Luyūn: Tratado de agricultura,* Spanish trans. Joaquina Eguaras Ibáñez. Granada: Patronato de la Alhambra, 1975.

Ibn Rustih. See Ibn Khurdādhbih.

Ibn Ṣāḥib al-Ṣalāt. *The History of the Moroccan Empire in Maghrib, Andalusia, and Ifriqiya,* vol. III of *Tārīkh al-mann bil-imāma,* (Arabic) ed. Abdul Hadi Attazi. Beirut: Dār al-Andalus, 1964.

———. *Al-Mann bil-imāma* (Textos Medievales, 24), Spanish trans. A. Huici Miranda. Valencia: (s.n.), 1969.

Ibn Saʿīd al-Maghribī (or al-Andalusī). *Kitāb al-mughrib,* ed. Shawqī Ḍayf in series *Dhakhāʾir al-ʿArab,* vols. IX–X. Cairo: Dar al-Maarif, 1953.

Ibn Shuhayd. *El-Dīwān de Ibn Shuhayd al-Andalusī, 382–426 H = 992–1035 C., Texto y Traducción,* ed. and Spanish trans. James Dickie. Cordoba: Real Academia de Córdoba, 1975.

Ibn Zāfir. *Badaʾiʿ al-badāʾih.* Bulaq, 1278/1861–1862.

Ibn Zaydūn. *Dīwān,* ed. Kāmil Kīlānī and ʿAbd al-

Raḥmān Khalīfa. Cairo: Matbaat Mustafa al-Babi al-Halabi, 1351/1932.

ICOMOS. *Les jardins de l'Islam,* 2me Colloque International sur la Protection et la Restauration des Jardins Historiques (November 1973). Paris: Unesco, 1975.

Idris, H. R. *La Berbérie orientale sous les Zīrīdes, X–XIIe siècles,* 2 vols. (Publications de l'Institut d'études orientales, Faculté des lettres et sciences humaines d'Alger, 12). Paris: Adrien-Maisonneuve, 1962.

al-Idrīsī. *Description de l'Afrique et de l-Espagne* (*Nuzhat al-Mushtāq*), ed. and trans. R. Dozy and M. J. de Goeje. Leiden, 1866; reprinted Amsterdam: Oriental Press, 1969.

———. *Opus Geographicum . . .* (*Kitab Nuzhat al-Mushtāq*), fasc. I–V, ed. E. Cerulli et al. Naples: E. J. Brill, 1970–75.

Illawi, Ibrahim Abid. *Les cités musulmanes abbassides, la pensée d'Abu'l-A'la al-Ma'ari et ses prolongements contemporains.* Paris: Thèse de doctorat de 3e cycle, École des hautes études en sciences sociales, 1981.

Imamuddin, S. M. *The Economic History of Spain* (*Under the Umayyads, 711–1031 A.C.*). Dacca: Asiatic Society of Pakistan, 1963.

———. "Al-Filāḥah (Farming) in Muslim Spain." *Islamic Studies* 1 (1962), 51–89.

Íñiguez Almech, Francisco. "La Aljafería de Zaragoza: Presentación de los nuevos hallazgos." In *Actas, I Congreso de Estudios Árabes e Islámicos* (*Córdoba, 1962*). Madrid: (s.n.), 1964, 357–70.

Isaac, Erich. "The Citron in the Mediterranean: A Study in Religious Influences." *Economic Geography* 35 (1959), 71–78,

Jakobi, Jürgen. "Agriculture Between Literary Tradition and Experience." In *Timurid Art and Culture,* ed. Lisa Golombek and M. Subtelny. Leiden: E. J. Brill, 1992, 201–08.

Jayyusi, Salma K., ed. *The Legacy of Muslim Spain.* Leiden: E. J. Brill, 1992.

Jenkins, Marilyn. "Al-Andalus: Crucible of the Mediterranean." In *The Art of Medieval Spain, A.D. 500–1200.* New York: Metropolitan Museum of Art, 1993, 73–84.

Jiménez Martín, Alfonso. "Los jardines de Madīnat al-Zahrā'." *Cuadernos de Madīnat al-Zahrā'* 1 (1987), 81–92.

Jones, Jeremy. "A Green Revolution?" *Journal of African History* 25 (1984), 343–44.

Kantorowicz, Ernst. *The King's Two Bodies: A Study in Medieval Theology.* Princeton: Princeton University Press, 1957.

Al-Khaṭīb al-Baghdādī. *Ta'rīkh Baghdād,* 14 vols. in 7. Cairo: Maktabat al-Khanji, 1931.

al-Khushanī. *Aljoxani, historia de los jueces de Córdoba,* Spanish trans. Julian Ribera. Madrid, 1914; reprinted Madrid: Aguilar, 1965.

Koran. See *al-Qur'ān.*

Labarta, Ana, and Carmen Barceló, "Las fuentes árabes sobre al-Zahrā': Estado de la cuestión." *Cuadernos de Madīnat al-Zahrā'* 1 (1987), 93–106.

Lafuente y Alcántara, Emilio. *Inscripciones árabes de Granada.* Madrid, 1859.

Lalaing, Antoine de. See M. Gachard.

Lassner, J. "The Caliph's Personal Domain: The City Plan of Baghdad Re-examined." In *The Islamic City: A Colloquium,* ed. Albert Hourani and S. H. Stern. Philadelphia and Oxford: University of Pennsylvania Press, 1970, 103–18.

———. *The Shaping of 'Abbāsid Rule.* Princeton: Princeton University Press, 1980.

Leclerc, L. See Ibn al-Bayṭār.

Le Strange, G. *Baghdad During the Abbasid Caliphate.* Oxford: Clarendon Press, 1900.

———. "Description of Mesopotamia and Baghdad, Written About the Year 900 A.D. by Ibn Serapion." *Journal of the Royal Asiatic Society* (1895), 33–76, 255–315.

———. "A Greek Embassy to Baghdad in 917 A.D." *Journal of the Royal Asiatic Society* (1895), 35–45.

Lévi-Provençal, Evariste. "La 'Description de l'Espagne' d'Aḥmad al-Rāzī." *Al-Andalus* 18 (1953), 51–108.

———. "Un échange d'ambassades entre Cordoue et Byzance au IXe siècle," *Byzantion* 12 (1937), 1–24; reprinted in Lévi-Provençal, *Islam d'Occident: Études d'histoire médiévale.* Paris: Maisonneuve, 1948, 79–107.

———. *L'Espagne musulmane au Xéme siècle: Institutions et vie sociale,* 3 vols. Paris: Larose, 1932. This is a revision of R. Dozy, *Histoire des musulmanes d'Espagne,* 1861.

———. *Histoire de l'Espagne musulmane,* 3 vols. Paris: Maisonneuve, 1950–53.

———. *Inscriptions arabes d'Espagne,* 2 vols. Paris and Leiden: E. J. Brill, 1931.

———. *Séville musulmane au début du XIIe siècle: Le traité d'Ibn 'Abdūn.* Paris: Maisonneuve, 1947.

———. *Trois traités hispaniques de ḥisba.* Cairo: Institut Français d'Archéologie Orientale, 1955.

Lévi-Provençal, Evariste, and E. García Gómez, ed. and Spanish trans. *Una crónica anónima de ʿAbd al-Raḥman III al-Nāṣir.* Madrid and Granada: Consejo Superior de Investigaciones Científicas, 1950.

Lewin, B. "Adwīya." In *Encyclopaedia of Islam,* new ed., I:212–14.

Lillo Alemany, Mercedes. "Sobre los patios de Madīnat al-Zahrāʾ." In *1 Actas de las Jornadas de Cultura Arabe e Islámica (Madrid, 1978).* Madrid: Instituto Hispano-Arabe de Cultura, 1981.

Lledó Carrascosa, Rocío. "Risala sobre los palacios abbadies de Sevilla de Abū Ŷaʿfar Ibn Aḥmad de Denia: Traducción y estudio." *Sharq al-Andalus* 3 (1986), 191–200.

Lombard, Maurice. "L'evolution urbaine pendant le haut moyen âge." *Annales: Economies, Sociétés, Civilisations* 12 (1957), 7–28; reprinted in *Espaces et réseaux du haut moyen âge,* Paris and The Hague: Mouton, c. 1972.

López, Angel C. *Kitāb fī tartīb awqāt al-girāsa wa-l-magrūsāt: Un tratado agrícola andalusí anónimo.* Granada: Consejo Superior de Investigaciones Científicas, 1990.

———. "Sobre la cronología del Muqtabis." *Al-Qanṭara* 7 (1986), 475–78.

———. "Vida y obra del famoso polígrafo cordobés del siglo X, ʿArīb Ibn Saʿīd." In *Ciencias de la Naturaleza en al Andalus: Textos y estudios,* ed. E. García Sánchez, 2 vols. Granada: Consejo Superior de Investigaciones Científicas, 1990, I:317–47.

López Cuervo, Serafín. *Medina Az-Zahra: Ingeniería y formas.* Madrid: Ministerio de Obras Públicas y Urbanismo, 1985.

MacDougall, Elisabeth, and Richard Ettinghausen, eds. *The Islamic Garden.* Washington, D.C.: Dumbarton Oaks, 1976.

McKay, Alexander G. *Houses, Villas, and Palaces in the Roman World.* Ithaca: Cornell University Press, 1975.

Mackensen, M., J. Boessneck, K. Munzel, U. Willerding, and T. Ulbert. *Resafa I: Eine befestigte spätantike Anlage vor den Stadtmauern von Resafa.* Mainz: Philipp von Zabern, 1984.

Madrazo, Pedro de. *Recuerdos y bellezas de España: Córdoba.* Madrid: Repullés, 1855; reprinted in abbreviated form with the title *Córdoba.* Barcelona: Ediciones El Albir, 1980.

Malthus, Thomas. *An Essay on the Principle of Population.* 2d ed. London, 1803.

al-Maqqarī. *Analectes sur l'histoire et la littérature des arabes d'Espagne [Nafḥ al-ṭīb],* ed. R. Dozy, G. Dugat, L. Krehl, W. Wright, 2 vols. in 3. Leiden: E. J. Brill, 1855–61; reprinted London: Oriental Press, 1967.

———. *Azhār al-riyāḍ fī akhbār ʿiyāḍ,* 2 vols. Cairo: Bayt al-Maghrib, 1940.

———. See also Pascual de Gayangos.

Marçais, Georges. *L'architecture musulmane d'occident; Tunisie, Algérie, Maroc, Espagne, et Sicile.* Paris: Arts et métiers graphiques, 1954 (revised version of *Manual de l'art musulman,* 2 vols. Paris, 1927).

———. *La berbérie musulmane et l'orient au moyen âge.* Paris: Editions Montaigne, 1946.

———. "Les jardins de l'Islam." In G. Marçais, *Mélanges d'histoire et d'archéologie de l'Occident musulman.* 2 vols. Algiers: Imprimerie Officielle, 1957, I:233–44.

Marin, Louis. *Portrait of the King.* Minneapolis: University of Minnesota Press, 1988.

Marín, Manuela. "Al-Ruṣāfa, 4. In Muslim Spain." In *Encyclopaedia of Islam,* new ed. (1994), VIII:631–33.

al-Marrākushī, ʿAbd al-Wāḥid ibn ʿAlī al-Tamīmī. *Kitāb al-Muʿjib fī talkhīṣ akhbār al-maghrib,* (vol. IV of *Colección de crónicas árabes de la Reconquista*), ed. and trans. A. Huici Miranda. Tetouan: Editora Marroquí, 1955.

Martínez-Gros, Gabriel. *L'Idéologie Omeyyade.* Madrid: Casa de Velázquez, 1992.

Meadows, Donella H., ed. *Limits to Growth,* 2d ed. New York: Universe Books, 1974.

Menéndez Pidal, Ramón, ed. *Historia de España,* 4 vols. Madrid: Espasa-Calpe, 1940.

Meunié, Jacques, Henri Terrasse, and Gaston Deverdun. *Nouvelles recherches archéologiques à Marrakech.* Paris: Arts et métiers graphiques, 1957.

———. *Recherches archéologiques à Marrakech.* Paris: Institut des Hautes Etudes Marocaines, 1952.

Meyerhof, Max. "Esquisse d'histoire de la pharmacologie et botanique chez les musulmans d'Espagne." *Al-Andalus* 3 (1935), 1–41.

Meyerhof, Max, and G. F. Sobhy, eds. and trans. *The Abridged Version of "The Book of Simple Drugs" of al-Ghâfiqî, Ahmad ibn Muhammad by Gregorious Abu'l Farag.* Cairo: Government Press, 1932–40, fasc. 1–4 in one volume. (Egyptian University, Faculty of Medicine, no. 4).

Millás Vallicrosa, J. M. "Aportaciones para el estudio de la obra agronómica de Ibn Ḥajjāj y de Abū-

l-Jayr." *Al-Andalus* 20 (1955), 87–105; reprinted in *Estudios sobre historia de la ciencia española,* 2 vols. Madrid: Consejo Superior de Investigaciones Científicas, 1987, II:153–81.

———. "Carácteres de la ciencia hispanoárabe." In *Estudios sobre historia de la ciencia española,* 2 vols. Madrid: Consejo Superior de Investigaciones Científicas, 1987 (article originally published in 1949), I:23–41.

———. "Un manuscrito árabe de la obra de agricultura de Ibn Wāfid." *Tamuda* 2 (1954), 87–96.

———. "Un nuevo manuscrito de la obra agronómica de al-Ṭignarī." *Tamuda* 1 (1953), 85–86.

———. "Nuevos textos manuscritos de las obras geopónicas de Ibn Wāfid e Ibn Baṣṣāl." *Tamuda* 2 (1954), 339–44.

———. "Sobre bibliografía agronómica hispanoárabe," *Al-Andalus* 19 (1954), 129–42.

———. "La traducción castellana del *Tratado de Agricultura* de Ibn Wāfid." *Al-Andalus* 8 (1943), 281–332; reprinted as "El *Libro de Agricultura* de Ibn Wāfid y su influencia en la agricultura del Renacimiento." In *Estudios sobre la historia de la ciencia española,* 2 vols. Madrid: Consejo Superior de Investigaciones Científicas, 1987.

———. "La tradición de la ciencia geopónica hispanoárabe." *Archives Internacionales d'Histoire des Sciences* 34 (1955), 117–29; reprinted in *Estudios sobre la historia de la ciencia española,* 2 vols. Madrid: Consejo Superior de Investigaciones Científicas, 1987.

Miquel, André. *La géographie humaine du monde musulmane jusqu'au milieu de XIe siècle,* 5 vols. Paris, 1967–88.

Mitchell, Timothy. *Colonising Egypt.* Berkeley and Los Angeles: University of California Press, 1991.

Monroe, James T. *Hispano-Arabic Poetry.* Berkeley and Los Angeles: University of California Press, 1974.

———. "Hispano-Arabic Poetry During the Caliphate of Cordoba: Theory and Practice." *Estudios Orientales* 6 (1971); reprinted in *Arabic Poetry,* ed. G. von Grunebaum. Wiesbaden: Otto Harrasowitz, 1973, 125–54.

Moore, Charles W., William J. Mitchell, and William Turnbull, Jr. *The Poetics of Gardens.* Cambridge: MIT Press, 1988.

Morales, Ambrosio de. *La crónica general de España,* vols. II and III (of 3). Alcala de Henares, 1574.

Moreno Menayo, M. T. "Los jardines y alcázares musulmanes de la Buhayra (Sevilla)." In *II Congreso, Arqueología Medieval Española.* Madrid: Communidad de Madrid, Consejería de cultura y deportes, 1987, III:43–51.

Morony, Michael. *Iraq After the Muslim Conquest.* Princeton: Princeton University Press, 1984.

Mort, Frank. See Nicholas Green.

Moynihan, Elizabeth B. *Paradise as a Garden in Persia and Mughal India.* New York: Braziller, 1979.

Mulvey, Laura. *Visual and Other Pleasures.* Bloomington: Indiana University Press, 1989.

Münzer, Jerónimo. *Viaje por España y Portugal: 1494–1495.* Madrid: Ediciones Polifemo, 1991.

al-Muqaddasī. *Description de l'occident musulman au IVe=Xe siècle,* ed. and French trans. Charles Pellat (Bibliotheque arabe-française, 9). Algiers: Carbonel, 1950.

Navagero, Andres [Navaggiero, Andrea]. *Viaje por España (1524–1526)* (originally *Viaggio fatto in Spagna, 1524–1526*), Spanish trans. Antonio M. Fabie. Madrid: Turner, 1983.

Navarro Palazón, J., and A. García Avilés. "Approximación a la cultura material de Madinat Mursiya." In *Murcia Musulmana,* ed. Francisco J. Flores Arroyuelo. Murcia: Ediciones Almudi, 1989, 292–301.

Navarro Palazón, J., and P. Jiménez Castillo. "El Castillejo de Monteagudo: Qaṣr Ibn Saʿd." In *Casas y Palacios de Al-Andalus,* ed. J. Navarro Palazón. Barcelona: Lunwerg Editores, 1995, 63–103.

Necipoğlu, Gülru. *Architecture, Ceremonial, and Power: The Topkapı Palace in the Fifteenth and Sixteenth Centuries.* Cambridge: MIT Press, 1991.

Nicholson, Reynold A. *A Literary History of the Arabs.* Cambridge, 1907; reprinted Cambridge: Cambridge University Press, 1966.

Northedge, Alastair. "An Interpretation of the Palace of the Caliph at Samarra." *Ars Orientalis* 23 (1993), 143–70.

———. "Planning Sāmarrā: A Report for 1983–4." *Iraq* 47 (1985), 109–28.

Northedge, Alastair, and R. Falkner. "The 1986 Survey Season at Sāmarrā." *Iraq* 49 (1987), 143–73.

al-Nubāhī, Ibn al-Ḥasan. *Histoire des Juges d'Andalousie, intitulée Kitab al-markaba al-ʿulya,* ed. E. Lévi-Provençal. Cairo: Scribe Egyptien, 1948.

al-Nuwayrī. (*Nihāyat al-ʿarab fī funūn al-adab*), *Historia de los musulmanes de España y Africa,* ed. and Spanish trans. M. Gaspar Remiro, 2 vols. Granada: Centro de Estudios Históricos, 1917.

Nykl, Alois R. *Hispano-Arabic Poetry and Its Relations with the Old Provençal Troubadours.* Baltimore: J. H. Furst, 1946.

———. *Historia de los amores de Bayāḍ y Riyāḍ.* New York: Hispanic Society, 1941.

———. "Inscripciones árabes de la Alhambra y del Generalife." *Al-Andalus* 4 (1936), 178–81.

O'Callaghan, Joseph F. *A History of Medieval Spain.* Ithaca: Cornell University Press, 1975.

———. "Image and Reality: The King Creates His Kingdom." In *Emperor of Culture: Alfonso X the Learned of Castile,* ed. Robert J. Burns. Philadelphia: University of Pennsylvania Press, 1990, 14–32.

Ocaña Jiménez, Manuel. "Architectos y mano de obra en la construcción de la gran mezquita de occidente." *Boletín de la Real Academia de Córdoba* 51 (1981), 97–137.

———. "Capiteles de la residencia califal de Medina Az-Zahra: Estudios de sus inscripciones." *Boletín de la Real Academia de Córdoba* 32 (1931), 215–26.

———. "Capiteles epigrafiados de Madīnat al-Zahrā'." *Al-Andalus* 4 (1936), 158–66.

———. "Datos sobre al-Zāhira." *Al-Mulk* 4 (1964–65), 41–43.

———. "Inscripciones árabes descubiertas en Madīnat al-Zahrā' en 1944." *Al-Andalus* 10 (1945), 174–94.

———. "Notas sobre la Córdoba de Ibn Ḥazm." *Al-Mulk* 3 (1963), 53–62.

———. "Las puertas de la madina de Córdoba." *Al-Andalus* 3 (1935).

———. "Las ruinas de 'Alamiría,' un yacimiento arqueológico erróneamente denominado." *Al-Qanṭara* 5 (1984), 365–81.

Orlandis, José. *Historia del reino visigodo Español.* Madrid: Rialp, 1988.

Otto-Dorn, Katharina. "Grabung im ummayadischen Ruṣāfah." *Ars Orientalis* 2 (1957), 119–33.

Parrain, Charles. "The Evolution of Agricultural Technique." In *The Cambridge Economic History of Europe,* vol. I: *Agrarian Life of the Middle Ages,* 2d ed., ed. M. M. Postan. Cambridge: Cambridge University Press, 1966, 125–79.

Pavlovskis, Zoja. *Man in an Artificial Landscape: The Marvels of Civilization in Imperial Roman Literature.* Leiden: E. J. Brill, 1973.

Pavón Maldonado, Basilio. *Estudios sobre la Alhambra. I: La Alcazaba, El Palacio de los Abencerrajes, Los accesos a la Casa Real Vieja, El Palacio de Comares, El Partal* (supplement to *Cuadernos de la Alhambra*). Granada: Patronato de la Alhambra y Generalife, 1975.

———. "Influjos occidentales en el arte del califato de Córdoba." *Al-Andalus* 33 (1968), 205–20.

———. *Memoria de la excavación de la mezquita de Medinat al-Zahra.* Madrid: Ministerio de Educación Nacional, Dirección General de Bellas Artes, 1966.

Pedersen, Johannes. *The Arabic Book,* trans. G. French. (*Den arabiske bok,* Copenhagen, 1946). Princeton: Princeton University Press, 1984.

Pellat, Charles. *Cinq calendriers egyptiens.* Cairo: Institut Français d'Archéologie Orientale du Caire, 1986.

———. "Ibn Ḥazm, bibliographe et apologiste de l'Espagne musulmane." *Al-Andalus* 19 (1954), 53–102.

———. See also Dozy, *Calendrier de Cordoue.*

Pérès, Henri. *Esplendor de al-Andalus,* Spanish trans. Mercedes García-Arenal from *La poésie andalouse* (2d ed. rev., Paris, 1953). Madrid: Hiperión, 1983.

Pinder-Wilson, Ralph. "The Persian Garden: *Bagh* and *Chahar Bagh.*" In *The Islamic Garden,* ed. Elisabeth MacDougall and Richard Ettinghausen. Washington, D.C.: Dumbarton Oaks, 1976.

Qazwīnī, Zakarīyā ibn Muḥammad. *Āthār al-bilād.* Beirut: Dār Ṣādir, 1960.

Al-Qur'ān: A Contemporary Translation, rev. ed., trans. Ahmed Ali. Princeton: Princeton University Press, 1984.

al-Rāzī. *Anales palatinos del califa de Córdoba al-Hakam II por 'Isa Ibn Ahmad al-Razi (360–364 H./971–975 J.C.),* Spanish trans. E. García Gómez. Madrid: Sociedad de estudios y publicaciones, 1967. Notes indicating al-Rāzī = Ibn Ḥayyān refer to this translation and its Arabic text (see Ibn Ḥayyān, *Al-Muqtabis fī akhbar bilād al-andalus,* ed. A. A. El-Hajji).

Reifenberg, A. *The Struggle Between the Desert and the Sown: The Rise and Fall of Agriculture in the Levant.* Jerusalem: Jewish Agency, 1955.

Renaud, Henri P. J. *Calendrier d'Ibn al-Bannā' de Marrakech (1256–1321 J.C.).* Paris: Larose, 1948.

Rogers, J. M. "Samarra: A Study in Medieval Town-Planning." In *The Islamic City: A Colloquium,* ed. Albert H. Hourani and S. M. Stern. Philadelphia: University of Pennsylvania Press, 1970, 119–55.

Romero, Elena. See Ibn Gabirol.

Rubiera Mata, María Jesús. *La arquitectura en la literatura árabe.* Madrid: Editora Nacional, 1981.

———. "De nuevo sobre los poemas epigráficos de la Alhambra." *Al-Andalus* 41 (1976), 207–11.

———. *Ibn Ŷayyāb, el otro poeta de la Alhambra.* Granada: Patronato de la Alhambra, 1982.

———. *El medio literario en la Granada naṣrī en la primer mitad del siglo XIV (Ibn Ŷayyāb y su época).* Ph.D., Madrid, Universidad Complutense, 1972.

Ruffner, James, and Frank Bair, eds. *The Weather Almanac,* 4th ed. Detroit: Gale Research, 1984.

Ruggles, D. Fairchild. "Arabic Poetry and Architectural Memory in al-Andalus." *Ars Orientalis* 23 (1993), 171–78.

———. "The Eye of Sovereignty: Poetry and Vision in the Alhambra's Lindaraja Mirador." *Gesta* 36 (1997), 180–89.

———. "Fountains and Miradors: Architectural Imitation and Ideology Among the Taifas." In *Künstlerischer Austausch (Akten des XXVIII Internationalen Kongresses für Kunstgeschichte [Berlin, 15–20 Juli 1992]),* ed. Thomas Gaehtgens, 3 vols. Berlin: Akademie Verlag, 1993, I:391–406.

———. "The Gardens of the Alhambra and the Concept of the Garden in Islamic Spain." In *Al-Andalus: The Arts of Islamic Spain,* ed. Jerrilynn Dodds. New York: Metropolitan Museum of Art, 1992, 162–71.

———. "Il giardini con pianta a croce nel Mediterraneo islamico." In *Il giardino islamico: Architettura, natura, paesaggio,* ed. Attilio Petruccioli. Milan: Electa, 1993, 143–54.

———. "Historiography and the Rediscovery of Madīnat al-Zahrā'." *Islamic Studies* (Islamabad) 30 (1991), 129–40.

———. "Humayun's Tomb and Garden: Typologies and Visual Order." In *Gardens in the Time of the Great Muslim Empires (Muqarnas Supplement* 7), ed. Attilio Petruccioli. Leiden: E. J. Brill, 1997, 173–86.

———. "The Mirador in Abbasid and Hispano-Umayyad Garden Typology." *Muqarnas* 7 (1990), 73–82.

———. "A Mythology of an Agrarian Ideal." *Environmental Design,* no. 1, 1986, 24–27.

———. "A Source of Wood for Madinat al-Zahra'?" *Al-Qanṭara* 12 (1991), 573–76.

———. "Vision and Power at the Qala Bani Hammad in Islamic North Africa." *The Journal of Garden History* 14 (1994), 28–41.

Sacy, Sylvestre de. *Relation de l'Egypte par Abd Allatif* (trans. of Ibn Abī Uṣaybiʿa). Paris, 1810.

Sadek, M. M. *The Arabic Materia Medica of Dioscorides.* Québec: Les Éditions du Sphinx, 1983.

Safar, F. "Archaeological Investigations in the Area of the Main Irrigation Project in Iraq." *Sumer* 16 (1960), 3–12.

Salem, ʿAbdel ʿAziz. "Algunos aspectos del florecimiento económico de Almería islámica durante el período de los taifas y de los almorávides." *Revista del Instituto Egipcio de Estudios Islámicos en Madrid* 20 (1979–80), 7–22.

Samsó, Julio. "Ibn Hiŝām al-Lajmī y el primer jardín botánico en al-Andalus." *Revista del Instituto Egipcio de Estudios Islámicos en Madrid* 21 (1981–82), 135–41.

———. "La tradición clásica en los calendarios agrícolas hispanoárabes y norteafricanos." In *Actas del II Congreso Internacional de Estudios sobre las Culturas del Mediterráneo Occidental (Barcelona, 1975).* Barcelona: Universidad Autonoma de Barcelona, 1978, 177–86.

Sánchez-Albornoz, Claudio. *La España musulmana según los autores islamitas y cristianos medievales,* 2 vols. Buenos Aires: El Ateneo, 1946; 7th ed. Madrid: Espasa-Calpe, 1986.

———. *Investigaciones y documentos sobre las instituciones hispanas.* Santiago: Editorial Jurídica de Chile, 1970.

Santos, Samuel de los, L. M. Cabello Lapiedra, E. Romero de Torres, and R. Castejón. "Las ruinas de Alamiría." In *Anales de la Comisión de Monumentos Históricos y Artísticos de Córdoba.* Cordoba, 1926, 17–21.

Scales, Peter. *The Fall of the Caliphate of Córdoba.* Leiden: E. J. Brill, 1994.

Schack, Adolf Friedrich von. *Poesie und Kunst der Araber in Spanien und Sizilien,* 3 vols. (Berlin, 1865). Trans. J. Valera, *Poesia y arte de los árabes en España y Sicilia.* Madrid: Ediciones Hiperión, c. 1988.

Scheindlin, Raymond. "El poema de Ibn Gabirol y la fuente del Patio de los Leones." *Cuadernos de la Alhambra* 29–30 (1993–94), 185–89.

Seco de Lucena, Luis. "Los palacios del taifa almeriense al-Muʿtasim." *Cuadernos de la Alhambra* 3 (1967), 15–20.

Seguí Pérez, José. See Consejería de obras públicas.

Serjeant, Robert B. "Agriculture and Horticulture: Some Cultural Interchanges of the Medieval Arabs and Europe." In *Oriente e Occidente nel medioevo: Filosofia e scienze (Apr. 1969).* Rome: Accademia Nazionale dei Lincei, 1971, 535–41.

———. "Miḥrāb." *Bulletin of the School of Oriental and African Studies* 22 (1959), 439–53.

Sermet, Jean. "Acclimatation: Les jardins botaniques espagnols au XVIIIe siècle et la tropicalisation de l'Andalouse." In *Histoire économique du monde méditerranéen 1450–1650, Mélanges en l'honneur de Fernand Braudel.* Toulouse: Privat, 1973, 555–82.

Seyrig, Henri. "Les jardins de Kasr el-Heir." *Syria* 12 (1931), 316–18.

al-Shaqundī. *Elogio del Islam Español,* ed. and Spanish trans. E. García Gómez. Madrid: E. Maestre, 1935.

Shaw, Brent D. "Climate, Environment, and History: The Case of Roman North Africa." In *Climate and History,* ed. T. Wigley, M. Ingram, and G. Farmer. Cambridge: Cambridge University Press, 1981, 379–403.

Silverman, Kaja. "Fassbinder and Lacan: A Reconsideration of the Gaze, Look, and Image." *camera obscura,* no. 19 (1989), 55–89.

Simonet, Francisco Javier. *Descripción del reino de Granada* (facsimile after edition of 1860). Madrid: Atlas, 1982.

Smith, Dulci Lawrence. *The Poems of Muʿtamid King of Seville Rendered into English Verse, with an Introduction.* London, 1915.

Smith, R. S. "Medieval Agrarian Society in Its Prime." In *The Cambridge Economic History of Europe,* vol. I: *Agrarian Life of the Middle Ages,* 2d ed., ed. M. M. Postan. Cambridge: Cambridge University Press, 1966, 432–48.

Stern, S. M. "An Embassy of the Byzantine Emperor to the Fatimid Caliph al-Muʿizz." *Byzantion* 20 (1950), 239–58; reprinted in Stern, *History and Culture in the Medieval Muslim World,* London: Variorum Reprints, 1984.

Stetkevych, Suzanne P. "The *Qaṣīdah* and the Poetics of Ceremony: Three ʿĪd Panegyrics to the Cordoban Caliphate." In *Languages of Power in Islamic Spain,* ed. Ross Brann (Occasional Papers of the Department of Near Eastern Studies and the Program of Jewish Studies, Cornell University, 3). Bethesda: CDL Press, 1998, 1–48.

Tabbaa, Yasser. "The Medieval Islamic Garden: Typology and Hydraulics." In *Garden History: Issues, Approaches, Methods,* ed. John D. Hunt. Washington, D.C.: Dumbarton Oaks, 1992, 303–29.

Tagg, John. *The Burden of Representation: Essays on Photographies and Histories.* Amherst: University of Massachusetts Press, 1988.

———. *Grounds of Dispute.* Minneapolis: University of Minnesota Press, 1992.

Tchalenko, Georges. *Villages antiques de la Syrie du nord: le massif du Bélus à l'époque Romaine,* 3 vols. Paris: Paul Geuthner, 1953.

Teall, John L. "The Byzantine Agricultural Tradition." *Dumbarton Oaks Papers* 25 (1971), 33–59.

Terrasse, Henri. *L'Art hispano-mauresque des origines au XIIIe siècle.* Paris: G. van Oest, 1932.

Thünen, Johann H. von. *Der isolirte Staat in Beziehung auf Landwirthschaft und Nationalökonomie* (Hamburg, 1826). 2d ed. French trans. Jules Laverrière, *Recherches sur l'influence que le prix des grains. . . .* Paris, 1851.

Torres Balbás, Leopoldo. *La Alcazaba y la Catedral de Málaga.* Madrid: Plus-Ultra, 1960.

———. "Almería islámica." *Al-Andalus* 22 (1957), 411–57.

———. "Ampliación y tamaño de las mezquitas." *Al-Andalus* 21 (1956), 339–52.

———. *Ars Hispaniae,* vol IV, *Arte almohade. Arte nazarī. Arte mudéjar.* Madrid: Editorial Plus-Ultra, 1949.

———. *Artes almorávide y almohade.* Madrid: Consejo Superior de Investigaciones Científicas, 1955.

———. "Aznalfarache = Ḥisn al-Faraŷ." *Al-Andalus* 25 (1960), 222–28.

———. *Ciudades hispanomusulmanas,* 2d ed. Madrid: Instituto Hispano-Arabe de Cultura, 1985.

———. "Los contornos de las ciudades hispanomusulmanas." *Al-Andalus* 15 (1950), 437–86.

———. "Dār al-ʿArūsa y las ruinas de palacios y albercas granadinos situados por encima del Generalife." *Al-Andalus* 13 (1948), 185–203.

———. "El exconvento de San Francisco de la Alhambra." *Boletín de la Sociedad de Excursiones* 29 (1931), 126–38, 206–15.

———. "Al-Madīnat al-Zāhira, la ciudad de Almanzor." *Al-Andalus* 21 (1956), 353–59.

———. "Monteagudo y 'El Castillejo,' en la Vega de Murcia." *Al-Andalus* 2 (1934), 366–72.

———. "Notas sobre Sevilla en la época musulmana." *Al-Andalus* 10 (1945), 177–96.

———. "El oratorio y la casa de Astasio de Bracamonte en el Partal de la Alhambra." *Al-Andalus* 10 (1945), 440–49.

———. "Patios de crucero." *Al-Andalus* 23 (1958), 171–92.

Torres Balbás, L., L. Cervera, F. Chueca, and P. Bidagor. *Resumen histórico del urbanismo en España.* Madrid: Instituto de Estudios de Administración Local, 1954.

al-ʿUdhrī (Ibn al-Dilāʾī). *Fragmentos geográfico-histó-*

ricos de "al-Masālik ilā ŷamīʿ al-mamālik" (Nuṣūṣ ʿan al-andalus min kitāb tarṣīʿ al-akhbār wa-tanwīʿ al-athār wa-l-bustān fī gharāʾib al-buldān wa-l-masālik ilā jāmiʿ al-mamālik), ed. ʿAbd al-ʿAziz al-Ahwānī. Madrid: Matbaat al-Dirasat al-Islamiyah, 1965.

Ulbert, Thilo. "Ein umaiyadischer Pavillon in Resafa-Ruṣāfat Hiŝām." *Damaszener Mitteilungen* 7 (1993), 213–31.

al-ʿUmarī, Ibn Faḍl Allāh. *Masālik al-abṣār fī mamālik al-amṣār*, I (*l'Afrique moins Egypte*), French trans. de Gaudefroy-Demombynes. Paris, 1927.

Valencia, Rafael. "Islamic Seville: Its Political, Social, and Cultural History." In *The Legacy of Muslim Spain*, ed. S. M. Jayyusi. Leiden: E. J. Brill, 1992, 136–48.

Vallejo Triano, Antonio. "El baño próximo al Salón de ʿAbd al-Raḥmān III." *Cuadernos de Madīnat al-Zahrāʾ* 1 (1987), 141–65.

———. "Crónica años 1985–87." *Cuadernos de Madīnat al-Zahrāʾ* 1 (1987), 169–93.

———. "La infrastructura exterior de Madīnat al-Zahrāʾ." Paper presented at the XXVIII International Congress of the History of Art, Berlin, 1992, unpublished.

———. "Madīnat al-Zahrāʾ: La realidad arqueológica y las fuentes documentales." In *Actas de las I Jornadas de Cultura Islámica (Toledo, 1987)*. Madrid: Editorial Al Fadila, 1989, 125–26.

———. "Madīnat al-Zahrāʾ, pasado, presente, y futuro." In *II Congreso de Arqueología Medieval Española (Madrid, 1987)*, 3 vols. Madrid: Comunidad de Madrid et al., 1987, I:205–18.

Valls I Subirà, Oriol. "El paper al al-ándalus i a la corona d'aragó." In *Actas del II Congreso Internacional de Estudios sobre las Culturas del Mediterráneo Occidental (Barcelona, 1975)*. Barcelona: Universidad Autonoma de Barcelona, 1978, 441–48.

Vallvé, Joaquín. "La agricultura en al-Andalus." *Al-Qanṭara* 3 (1982), 261–97.

———. "Al-Andalus en el siglo X: El gobierno de la nación." In *Homenaje al Prof. Darío Cabanales Rodríguez*. Granada: Universidad de Granada, 1987.

———. *La división territorial de la España musulmana*. Madrid: Consejo Superior de Investigaciones Científicas, 1986.

———. See also Ibn Ghālib.

Varisco, Daniel M. "Medieval agricultural texts from Rasulid Yemen." *Manuscripts of the Middle East* 4 (1989), 150–54.

———. *Medieval Agriculture and Islamic Science*. Seattle: University of Washington Press, 1994.

Vázquez Ruíz, José. "Un calendario anónimo granadino del siglo XV." *Revista del Instituto de Estudios Islámicos en Madrid* 9–10 (1961–62), 23–64.

Velázquez Bosco, Ricardo. *Medina Azzahra y Alamiriya*. Madrid: Junta de Ampliación de Estudios, 1912.

Vernet, Juan. *La cultura hispanoárabe en oriente y occidente*. Barcelona: Editorial Ariel, 1978.

———. "Natural and technical sciences in al-Andalus." In *The Legacy of Muslim Spain*, ed. S. K. Jayyusi. Leiden: E. J. Brill, 1992, 937–51.

Vicens Vives, Jaime, in collaboration with J. Nadal Oller. *An Economic History of Spain*, trans. F. M. López-Morillas, from 3d ed. of 1964. Princeton: Princeton University Press, 1969.

Vílchez Vílchez, Carlos. *La Alhambra de Leopoldo Torres Balbás: Obras de restauración y conservación, 1923–1936*. Granada: Comares, 1988.

Viollet, Henri. "Description du palais de al-Moutasim à Samara" and "Fouilles à Samara." *Memoires de l'Academie des inscriptions et belles-lettres*, ser. I, vol. XII, pt. II, (1909 and 1911), 567–94, 685–717.

Vives, José. *Concilios visigóticos e hispano-romanos*. Barcelona and Madrid: Consejo Superior de Investigaciones Científicas, 1963.

Wasserstein, David. *The Caliphate in the West*. Oxford: Clarendon Press, 1993.

———. *The Rise and Fall of the Party-Kings: Politics and Society in Islamic Spain 1002–1086*. Princeton: Princeton University Press, 1985.

Watson, Andrew. *Agricultural Innovation in the Early Islamic World: The Diffusion of Crops and Farming Techniques, 700–1100*. Cambridge: Cambridge University Press, 1983.

Webster, J. C. *Labors of the Month in Antique and Medieval Art to the End of the Twelfth Century*. Princeton: Princeton University Press, 1938.

Wescoat, James L., Jr. "Gardens of Invention and Exile: The Precarious Context of Mughal Garden Design During the Reign of Humayun (1530–1556)." *Journal of Garden History* 10 (1990), 106–16.

———. "The Islamic Garden: Issues for Landscape Research." *Environmental Design*, no. 1, 1986, 10–19.

———. "Landscape Transformations of the Mughal Empire: Medieval and Modern Uses of the Narrative Mode" (1987), unpublished.

Whelan, Estelle. "The Origins of the *Miḥrāb Mujawwaf*: A Reinterpretation." *International Journal of Middle East Studies* 18 (1986), 205–23.

White, Lynn. *Medieval Technology and Social Change.* Oxford: Clarendon Press, 1962; reprinted 1965.

Wilbur, Donald. *Persian Gardens and Garden Pavilions,* 2d ed. Washington, D.C.: Dumbarton Oaks, 1979.

Williams, John. "Orientations: Christian Spain and the Art of Its Neighbors." In *The Art of Medieval Spain.* New York: Metropolitan Museum of Art, 1993, 12–25.

Wittfogel, Karl. *Oriental Despotism.* New Haven: Yale University Press, 1957.

Wolf, Kenneth B. *Conquerors and Chroniclers of Early Medieval Spain.* Liverpool: Liverpool University Press, 1990.

al-Yaʿqūbī. *Biblioteca geographorum arabicorum, III,* ed. de Goeje. Leiden, 1870–94.

———. *Les Pays,* ed. and French trans. G. Wiet. Cairo: Imprimerie de l'Institut Français d'Archéologie Orientale, 1937.

Zbiss, Slimane Mostafa. "Mahdia et Ṣabra-Manṣoûriya." *Journal Asiatique* 244 (1956), 79–93.

Zozaya, Juan. Entry nos. 50 and 52. In *Al-Andalus: The Art of Islamic Spain,* ed. Jerrilynn D. Dodds. New York: Metropolitan Museum of Art, 1992, 264 and 266–67.

———. "Excavaciones en el palacio almohade de la Buhayra." *Noticiario Arqueológico Hispánico* 1 (1972).

———. "Fortifications in Al-Andalus." In *Al-Andalus: The Art of Islamic Spain,* ed. Jerrilynn D. Dodds. New York: Metropolitan Museum of Art, 1992, pp. 63–73.

Index

Palaces and gardens are listed under the city or place where they are located. There are no surnames in Arabic, and therefore people are listed under the first name or the honorific by which they appear in the text. Parenthetical descriptions and death dates are supplied in cases where it is necessary to differentiate between individuals bearing the same or similar names. When persons are known by both an honorific title and a name or by both an Arabic and a Romanized name, the full name in Arabic is supplied in parentheses. *Page numbers in italics refer to illustrations.*